THE WAR ON TENURE

As academia increasingly comes under attack in the United States, *The War on Tenure* steps in to demystify what professors do and to explain the importance of tenure for their work. Deepa Das Acevedo takes readers on a backstage tour of tenure-stream academia to reveal hidden dynamics and obstacles. She challenges the common belief that tenure is only important for the protection of academic freedom. Instead, she argues that the security and autonomy provided by tenure are also essential to the performance of work that students, administrators, parents, politicians, and taxpayers value. Going further, Das Acevedo shows that tenure exists on a spectrum of comparable employment contracts and she debunks the notion that tenure warps the incentives of professors. Ultimately, *The War on Tenure* demonstrates that the job security tenure provides is not nearly as unusual, undesirable, or unwarranted as critics claim.

Deepa Das Acevedo is a legal anthropologist and employment law scholar. Her previous books include *Beyond the Algorithm: Qualitative Insights for Gig Work Regulation* (2020) and *The Battle for Sabarimala: Religion, Law, and Gender in Contemporary India* (2024).

The War on Tenure

DEEPA DAS ACEVEDO

Shaftesbury Road, Cambridge CB2 8EA, United Kingdom

One Liberty Plaza, 20th Floor, New York, NY 10006, USA

477 Williamstown Road, Port Melbourne, VIC 3207, Australia

314–321, 3rd Floor, Plot 3, Splendor Forum, Jasola District Centre, New Delhi – 110025, India

103 Penang Road, #05–06/07, Visioncrest Commercial, Singapore 238467

Cambridge University Press is part of Cambridge University Press & Assessment, a department of the University of Cambridge.

We share the University's mission to contribute to society through the pursuit of education, learning and research at the highest international levels of excellence.

www.cambridge.org
Information on this title: www.cambridge.org/9781009596824

DOI: 10.1017/9781009596787

When citing this work, please include a reference to the DOI 10.1017/9781009596787

First published 2025

A *catalogue record for this publication is available from the British Library*

A *Cataloging-in-Publication data record for this book is available from the Library of Congress*

ISBN 978-1-009-59682-4 Hardback
ISBN 978-1009-59683-1 Paperback

Dr. T. P. Hari Das (1948–2010)

For acha, *who told me that this was the best job in the world
over and over again
until I believed him.*

Contents

1

Skirmishes

A book with this title could begin in any number of ways.

It could begin, for example, with recent political campaigns to abolish or severely undermine tenure at public universities. Legislative efforts of this type have surfaced in Georgia, Florida, Wisconsin, South Carolina, Iowa, Missouri, and Texas, among others. I know tenured professors who have fled some of these states for what they believe will be more hospitable environments, often sacrificing high institutional rankings and plentiful resources to do so. I know other tenured professors who have lost interest in ever working for a public university again – regardless of regional political climate – because it just feels too difficult to be both a scholar and a state employee right now. And I know many current and aspiring "tenure-stream" professors – that is, professors who are either tenured or on the tenure-track – whose desperation for stable employment or a shared house with their partner has made them willing to go wherever in the country their highly unpredictable job market takes them.

A book like this could also begin with individual stories about tenure – about getting it, losing it, and watching it be disregarded. I could open with the story of Noeleen McIlvenna, a tenured history professor at Wright State University in Ohio. Starting in 2020, "Dr. No" watched and fought as dozens of her pre-tenure, tenured, and nontenure-track colleagues were fired or persuaded to resign by their university-employer. Or I could open with a description of what it's like to be denied the chance to *win* tenure according to Garrett Felber, a former assistant professor at Ole Miss. Felber's contract was not renewed in 2020 because, according to the university, he proved difficult to work with, and because, according to him, his prison-abolition research was unpopular with the university's donors.[1] Or I could open with stories from the growing number of scholars – Steven Salaita and Nikole Hannah-Jones, among others – who've had offers of tenured employment retracted or downgraded after pressure was brought to bear on their intended employers.

Finally, this kind of book could begin with the protests that rocked American university campuses after October 7, 2023. Those protests might seem totally unconnected to tenure, save to the extent that they triggered violations of academic freedom (and one tenured-termination: Maura Finkelstein). But even where professors lost no wages and no campus access – as in the cases of Jodi Dean (Hobart and William Smith) and Abdulkader Sinno (Indiana) – academic freedom wasn't "all" that was hanging in the balance.[2] Being disciplined at work is an *employment* concern, too. Keeping your mouth shut to preserve your job is an *employment* concern, too. Just ask anyone who's ever lost their shift or their bonus or their job because they irritated the boss.

All of these are ways that a book called *The War on Tenure* might reasonably begin. But this book isn't *about* the war on tenure. It's a *response* to the war on tenure. Because of that, and because this book is about academics but not solely for academics, I'm going to start by talking about tenure itself.

Tenure, as Chapter 5 explains in greater detail, refers to a type of contractual relationship. Actually, it's more like a *sub*type of contract, in the same way that dachshunds are a subtype of dog. Tenure is a version of the "just cause" employment contracts that govern millions of American workers across industries ranging from orchestras to fast-food service. This means that tenure both is and isn't special – and explaining how both these statements can be simultaneously true is an important goal of this book.

My broader goal, of course, is to talk about tenure, and ultimately to defend it. But to do this, *The War on Tenure* proceeds along two very different paths.

When it comes to the most common criticisms of tenure, I take a head-on approach. A concrete claim demands a concrete rebuttal – and critics of tenure make some *very* concrete claims indeed when they argue that tenure encourages bad behavior, lazy behavior, or undesirably iconoclastic behavior. They also say that tenure grants the faculty who have it too much latitude to police themselves. But Chapters 12–15 show that these criticisms – even when they're made by other academics – reflect stereotypes about academia and misconceptions about academic life. For the most part, the critics just aren't right.

By contrast, when it comes to explaining why tenure is valuable and necessary, I approach things more indirectly. After all, there's no boogeyman to fight here, just a need to show that tenure matters as an employment protection. It matters for most faculty in most circumstances because it offers job security to workers who face high barriers to entry, long hours, difficult jobs, wage penalties, and poor exit options. Tenure should matter to nonfaculty, too, because the labor that professors perform is wanted by students, needed by university administrators, and beneficial to society. To explain the *whys* and *hows* of all this, Chapters 7–11 take you on a behind-the-scenes tour of American academia as it actually operates today.

For these reasons, as well as a few more I'll explain shortly, this book differs in both scope and audience from many other scholarly writings on tenure. In fact, as far as I can tell, this book is unlike *most* other scholarly writings on tenure. That's not an unmitigated virtue – there is no such thing when it comes to research methods – but it does have its advantages.

First, unlike many well-known books on faculty tenure, this one is not primarily historical in nature. That's partly because there is so much that needs saying about tenure's current realities that a prolonged excursion into the past seems wasteful. At the same time, this book's emphasis on the present also reflects the fact that I have a bone to pick with how histories of tenure are usually told. Most of the time, they come to a halt somewhere around 1940, when tenure was officially "invented" in the United States, instead of continuing on to the post-War era, when tenure became an industry practice in American academia.

That historiographic pattern limits our ability to understand why tenure might matter *today*. It hides the extent to which tenure was popularized by administrators who viewed it as an employment perk, rather than by faculty who viewed it as an expressive safeguard. When I do spend a little time diving into tenure's past, as in Chapters 6 and 16, I do so to show that recruitment and retention – in other words, *employment concerns* – played a much bigger role in making tenure a normative industry practice than is commonly understood. What was valuable about tenure then is still valuable today.

A second way this book differs from standard academic writing on tenure is in its scope – and I mean this in a few senses. As much as possible, I try to talk about *tenure-stream* faculty writ large. These are the university personnel who have or are eligible to earn tenure, and focusing on them effectively excludes most people (around 75%!) who teach or conduct research within a university setting today.[3] Universities have been decreasing the number of people who are hired into tenure-stream positions for decades, to the point where most of the people your child or your friend's child or your constituent's child calls *Professor* isn't considered one by the institution that's paying them. Instead, they are viewed as temporary workers who can be given low wages and usually no benefits and who are hired so incredibly last minute that class schedules merely list them as "(Professor) *Staff*."[4]

But emphasizing tenure-stream faculty also broadens the scope of this book because most studies of tenure are limited to specific subgroups of professors: computer science faculty or law faculty, or professors in a certain geographic area or at a certain type of institution. I rely on all this prior literature because, to be frank, there are surprisingly few empirical studies of tenure at all. Academics may like talking endlessly about themselves at dinner parties and other inopportune moments, but it turns out that we do not particularly relish studying our most famous perk in any sustained and rigorous empirical fashion.

I want to expand the conversation. Consequently, this book talks about faculty tenure across *region*, *discipline*, and *institutional type*, with the caveat that I limit myself to four-year institutions in the United States (which I will mostly refer to as "universities" for ease of reading). Tenure does exist at many community colleges and some special-focus institutions, like art schools, but it is somewhat rarer, and, by many accounts, it is on the wane. Tenure also most definitely exists outside the United States – for instance, in Canada, where I was born, and where my parents spent their careers, and in Germany, where tenure was developed and whose research universities inspired much of the organizational infrastructure behind American higher education. But the significance of tenure as an *employment protection*, as opposed to simply being an indication of professional achievement and prestige, is, to a great degree, unique to the American context.

The exceptionalism of American-style tenure makes sense, as we will see, thanks to the exceptionalism of another American employment practice: the At-Will Rule. Nowhere else in the world – certainly in no peer countries, economically speaking – can the average worker be fired for good reason, bad reason, or no reason at all. In the United States, however, this is entirely possible for the vast majority of workers who are classified as "employees." You can be legally fired here because you support a football team your boss dislikes or because you wore teal to the office or because it's a Thursday. So long as your termination was not because you belong to what lawyers call a "protected category," or for another reason that has been specifically outlawed, if you are an at-will employee – which, again, most employees are – you are very likely out of luck. (Even if you *were* fired for an illegal reason, you are likely out of luck because litigation is costly and punishing, and because legal doctrine is very often stacked against workers… but that's a different story, for a different book.)

My focus on tenure as a type of contractual relationship represents the third way in which this book differs from much of the existing scholarship. Tenure becomes easier to understand when we stop talking about it only within certain disciplines or only as an expressive safeguard and, instead, consider what it means as an employment protection. In the pages that follow, you will see a lot of information about job market statistics, threshold credentials, exit options, and other factors that shape academia as an industry like any other. You will also see less about academic freedom than you might have reasonably expected to find in a book about university professors. It is *not* that I think academic freedom is unimportant – how could I? It's simply that, as someone who teaches employment law, and as someone whose universe is thickly peopled by individuals trying to get and keep one very specific (increasingly rare) type of job, I think tenure matters for reasons that are far more prosaic than pedagogical or intellectual autonomy.

After all, even though tenure is supposed to make someone harder to fire than the At-Will Rule allows, there are still many reasons why a tenured professor might face termination. Tenured faculty do not, despite the favorite slogan of critics inside and outside the academy, have "jobs for life." A professor who has engaged in *academic misconduct* (usually, plagiarizing or falsifying research), *sexual misconduct* (anything from inappropriate relationships to assault), or *unprofessional conduct* (most commonly, nonsexual workplace bullying) can be fired by their university on those grounds. The simple fact that universities must *have* grounds to fire tenured faculty is one of the most important ways in which tenure modifies the At-Will Rule. (That same requirement is also what protects millions of other employees who are similarly exempt from the At-Will Rule on the basis of contractual terms or statutory law.)

But a tenured faculty member can also be fired through no fault of their own. It may happen because their university is restructuring its departments and no longer has an institutional home for them. Or it may happen simply because their university is experiencing financial hardship and can no longer afford their salaries. Very often, these two processes are related. Both are becoming increasingly common. As Chapters 18 and 22 explain, these varied paths to job loss – for individual cause *and* for economic reasons – make academia a lot more like other industries than is commonly appreciated. What makes academia different are the *ramifications* of losing a job, which are surprisingly and unusually severe. Tenure helps to square the circle, but it is not – and is not meant to be – impermeable.

Fourth, this book also differs from earlier scholarship on tenure by not drawing exclusively on the research methods of any single discipline. Sometimes I will zoom out to give you a sky-view perspective, as I do while discussing income statistics in Chapter 10. At other times I will dive deeply into one or two human examples, as I do in Chapter 3 while describing the very real, very material hardships that aspiring professors experience just to have a shot at an excruciatingly tough job market. Often, I will rely on data and narratives that have been produced by other people, whether those people are academics, journalists, government actors, or industry analysts. Many times, I will reach for material that I, with the help of several talented assistants, have created myself.

Finally, my approach to thinking about tenure does more than inform the topics I choose to cover in this book: it also informs the language I use and the tone I strike. For instance, whether I call them *academics*, *faculty*, or *professors*, I make a point of also referring to the people who want, win, or lose tenure as *workers* and as *employees*. This usage is gaining popularity as more and more faculty exist outside the tenure-stream and are finding it both useful and necessary to identify as wage-earning laborers. But I want *all* parties – including tenured and tenure-track faculty, as well as the nonacademics who think about them – to understand that everyone in this book is a worker, that most of them are employees, and that there is neither shame in those facts nor any gains in denying them.

I'll also generally refer to academia as an *industry* even though this description is extremely uncommon among academics themselves, and most of them would consider it to be pejorative. While I understand where they're coming from, I don't think that academia exists outside market forces any more than I think that it *has* to in order to deserve respect. Saying that academia is an industry doesn't mean that the values governing academia should be identical to the values governing any other industry, whether the workers in it produce engines or toothbrushes or salon services.

These kinds of language choices reflect my sense that academic exceptionalism is overblown by both supporters and critics of tenure. Critics of tenure tend to argue that the professors who have it invariably achieve almost superhuman levels of iconoclasm, predatorial behavior, or laziness. Meanwhile, supporters of tenure tend to talk as if academia has a monopoly on noble motives and on contributions to societal well-being, or even to democracy itself. Since I'm a professor, and since one of my goals here is to defend tenure, I won't bother pretending to be neutral. But I also won't bother pretending to find either of these attitudes anything other than a bit silly. Put simply: we're better than you think but not as good as we think.

Taken together, these differences in what I say and how I say it mean that this book will occasionally send mixed messages about tenure itself. It will sometimes sound as if I'm arguing that tenure is a powerful form of protection for any academic who's lucky enough to have it. I am. At other times, it will sound as if I'm arguing the opposite: that tenure isn't anything like the ironclad guarantee of the sun and the moon that it's made out to be. I'm doing this, too. The reason I vacillate between these positions is that tenure gets attacked on *two* sides. It gets attacked by critics who say that it isn't really meaningful (and should therefore be abandoned) and by critics who say it's way too meaningful (and should therefore be abandoned). I think both criticisms are too extreme to be accurate. Tenure is valuable, not impermeable or perfect… but since *no* employment practice is either of these things, I think it's fine to say as much about tenure.

The rest of this book very loosely follows a chronological arc.

The two substantive chapters of Part One are concerned with what it takes to get a tenure-track job. I talk about the material hardships imposed by the credentialization and training processes aspiring academics must go through. I also talk about the long-term consequences of taking on those hardships given the goal that they're meant to be in service of (a tenure-stream job) as well as the odds of reaching that goal. These are considerations that regularly surface in discussions about jobs in other industries without necessarily amounting to fatal indictments of either those jobs or those industries. We need to learn to speak of academia in similar ways.

Parts Two and Three are the core of the book, both conceptually and in length. Some chapters in each part clarify what tenure *is*, legally speaking, and set the record straight on how tenure came to be a normative industry practice, even if it is no longer a dominant one. But most of the chapters here are connected by a shared focus on what tenure *does* – to legal entitlements, to incentives, to personal lives, to exit options, and so on.

The bulk of Part Two explains the costs of pursuing academia. More specifically, it explains the costs of pursuing a tenure-stream job – and, even more specifically, it describes the costs of successfully *winning* tenure. The costs I'm talking about here are both monetary and nonmonetary, and while many of them are well known to academics, they're often hard to see or to fully appreciate if you're on the outside looking in. Tenure-stream academia can be a great way to earn a living, just like many other elite professions, but that doesn't mean it's easy. By remaining silent about the realities of their jobs, tenured and tenure-track faculty have allowed their critics to define what those realities are. We've forced nonacademics to learn about our industry from people who have little first hand – or even *third* hand – knowledge of it. Small wonder, then, that popular perceptions of what it means to be or become a professor are unrecognizable to many of us within the profession.

The bulk of Part Three refutes the most common criticisms of tenure. Both internal critics (other academics) and external critics (politicians, journalists, and other commentators) make these arguments to justify the weakening or abolition of tenure. But, as the chapters in Part Three show, most of these criticisms are based on anecdotal experience or blatant and often incorrect assumptions about how tenure influences professorial behavior. We don't have a wealth of on-point data, but what we do have doesn't support the critics.

The last section of the book, Part Four, considers what happens when tenure is overcome. Some of the chapters here draw on original national-level quantitative data that I've compiled, and they help dispel common assumptions about the circumstances in which individual tenured professors lose their jobs. Another chapter in this section relies on existing scholarship and media coverage to describe the circumstances of professors who did nothing wrong but got fired anyway as part of a "reduction-in-force"; they probably account for an overwhelming percentage of tenured job loss. Chapters 23 and 24 close with some ideas for what all of this means and how to move forward.

Public commentary on tenure is characterized by heated and frequently unsubstantiated rhetoric on both sides. This book lowers the temperature by reframing the debate in terms of employment conditions rather than academic freedom. Scholarly analyses of tenure, for their part, are dominated by history, law, and theoretical critique. This book connects those ideas with empirical information from the field of higher education as well as with media coverage and personal narrative – my own and others' – to provide a more well-rounded understanding of what tenure is, why it matters, and how it could be better. In a way, the chapters that follow represent an expression of faith in one of my home disciplines, anthropology, because they've been written with the idea that greater understanding brings empathy, humility, and maybe even a smile. All of these are valuable aids in navigating the war on tenure.

PART ONE

Getting to Tenure

2

Shepherd

All books are personal because no one sets out to write several thousand words on a topic they don't care about. This book, though, may be more personal than most. I'm writing about the job I have and love, a job that I started training for at the age of twenty-three and first won at the age of thirty-four. I'm also writing about the job that my husband trained for, won, and gave up so that I could pursue the best version of *my* job, wherever and whenever it was offered to me – more on that shortly. And, as it happens, I'm writing about the job that has been held by my parents, uncle, a handful of cousins, and even by my paternal grandfather. Academia is my family's business, although nobody intended it to become that. Because of this, I have a great deal of what is often called "social capital," which in my case means that I grew up understanding the unspoken rules of the academic world.

Social capital is a funny thing, though. My family's education, financial security, and industry experience mean that, on the one hand, I have always felt extremely comfortable in environments that can be intimidating to others. I have a powerfully clear childhood memory of holding a one-on-one conversation with my father's colleague at a faculty dinner party, but in this memory, I am talking to Hermann's knees because that's how tall I was at the time. As a college senior writing her BA thesis, I cold-emailed a professor at another university with a question that, I don't doubt, was silly. But because I had an instinct for how to do that sort of thing, and because the professor was an inherently kind human being, we struck up a friendship that has persisted, loosely but definitely, for some twenty years. Over that period, the professor has written me reference letters, invited me to conferences, and included me in publication efforts – all, I should add, before we ever met in person or spoke over the phone. The dinner party conversation and the cold-email friendship are among the smaller, more benign ways in which my background has helped me over the years, but I share them by way of acknowledgment: when it comes to academia, I am, for better *and* for worse, an insider. This means that I can see some things more easily, but it also means that I miss other things or can only discuss them using someone else's experiences.

At the same time, it's possible to be even more of an insider than I am. Whatever childhood socialization I had in the academic world was dwarfed in importance by my experience of being a hyphenated Canadian. Like so many other second-generation immigrants, my life was defined by a neither-here-nor-there quality that enriched but also overwhelmed every other part of my identity; if you'd asked nine-year-old Deepa who or what she was, she would have promptly replied *Indo-Canadian* instead of *a fourth-grader*, an *only child*, or even just a *girl*. Being the child of two professors wouldn't have even made the top five.

Nor was the academia I knew as a child the elite and well-heeled world I've largely come to occupy as an adult. My parents were employed at small universities in a small Canadian province: there were no informal salons in my home, no future Nobel prize-winners babysat me when they were students, and the movers and shakers in my parents' fields would not have known or cared that I was their child. Growing up in my parents' corner of the academy was emphatically not the same as growing up in my professors' world of elite academia – I know this because I'm friends with many academics who *did* grow up in Ivy+ institutions and who *have* inherited exalted professional mantles. The fact that these folks are, to a person, some of the brightest and loveliest human beings I know in the academy does not diminish the advantage that they began with, just as it would not diminish mine.

Most importantly, my insider status is qualified by the fact that industry knowledge travels surprisingly poorly in academia. It's not easy to apply the lessons learned from being a business professor in Canada to the task of becoming an anthropology or law professor in the United States. In fact, when I applied for the PhD program in anthropology at the University of Chicago, it was largely because a few internet searches had shown me that it was among the very best in the country. It wasn't because I had been carefully guided to the department by familial or professional networks.

(Actually, at the time I was applying to graduate school, I had a hazy belief that Chicago, because it is named after a geographic place and this seemed to be the American convention, was a public institution. I wince a little whenever I remember this because it reminds me just how clueless I was *despite* my privilege when I made one of the most significant professional and financial decisions of my life.)

I say all this for two reasons. First, to introduce myself, because who I am shapes the content of this book. I grew up talking about tenure around the dinner table – who had it, who was denied, how its presence or absence affected everyday behavior – and those conversations continue in my home to this day. As someone who teaches employment law, I've also learned to distinguish between tenure's legal and social implications: I know that what tenure *is* differs from what tenure *does* (and, frankly, I know that professors and public commentators alike often make mistakes on both counts). As an anthropologist who was trained to "make the familiar strange, and the strange familiar," I love re-introducing people to worlds they thought they knew. Sometimes, as for many of the academics featured in this book, that world is their own – and mine.

Second, I want to acknowledge that there are, in fact, *many academies*, even though in the rest of this book I will often refer to the world of institutionalized academia in the singular. Academics, as you probably already know, find it hard to say things simply: we are trained to identify nuance and to point out exceptions, to narrow our statements until we are absolutely confident that they can be defended. We are, essentially, supposed to spot the trees because everyone else tends to see the forest.

For this reason, and particularly when it comes to our own industry and jobs, academics rarely talk about "academia." Instead, we tend to talk about hiring trends in twentieth-century US economic history or best practices at small liberal arts colleges in northeastern Maine. Whenever I have shared this project with my fellow scholars, one of the most common responses I get is the "Yes, but…" *Yes, but… what you say doesn't apply to lab science scholars, who largely fund their own salaries through grants. Yes, but… what you say isn't true about the branch campuses of poor state schools, where tenure offers few advantages.* And so on.

The *Yes, but…* is one of the things that makes me love academia and that keeps me in this game. It signals that nothing is ever as simple as we think it is, and this, in turn, gives me hope because I believe human complexity is both our greatest charm and our saving grace. I also agree with many of the qualifications raised via the *Yes, buts* I've encountered in the process of writing this book. It is undeniably true, for example, that tenure means something very different to lab scientists than to anthropologists. We have been reminded of this repeatedly and painfully ever since the second Trump administration took office. Any statement about tenure that breezily lumps anthropologists and lab scientists together is a little less true than statements that take their different circumstances into account. And the reason I know this is not just because I've conducted research on the topic: it is also because one of my cousins happens to be a tenure-stream immunologist who runs her own lab at Harvard.

Put differently, I see how drastically academic experiences can vary just within the boundaries of my own personal network. There are indeed many academies. Between my family and close friends (most of whom are, unsurprisingly, academics), I have access to disciplines ranging from finance (my uncle) and ethnomusicology (a different cousin's husband) to various types of anthropology, history, and law. My relatives and friends are or have been employed at institutions including Ivies (Harvard and Penn), other wealthy private institutions (Georgetown, Northwestern), flagship state universities (Iowa, Texas, Wisconsin), and small liberal arts colleges (Swarthmore, Wellesley), as well as everywhere geographically from La Verne in California to Wright State in Ohio to Bowdoin in Maine.

My own tenure-track jobs have been at the University of Alabama, where I was first hired, and at Emory University, where I am currently employed. While both universities are well-to-do institutions in the Southeast, and while both of their law schools (where I teach) were recently tied in the national rankings, their organizational cultures and resources differ from one another in many important ways. Learning a new university is like learning a new universe: there are new colleagues with new opinions, habits, and expectations; new buildings with new quirks; new rules about using the corporate credit card (assuming there is a corporate credit card); new customary practices regarding the reply-all function for email, and more. And, while it is certainly true that these kinds of distinctions exist between employers in any industry, academics are socialized to identify themselves with their jobs – and consequently with their employers – to an unusual degree. HMOs aren't supposed to inspire allegiance in their employees. Universities are.

In the face of so much variation, it is indeed hard to maintain that there is just one type of professor or just one set of challenges facing the professoriate. In fact, the American academic landscape is so diverse that, despite the unusual breadth of access I've described, I am still missing out on a large portion of academia because most of my network is based at elite, well-funded, research-oriented universities. They – and I – are fortunate enough to belong to the academic "one percent," and this skews what I see, what I experience, and what I hear about. Consequently, you will probably see me offering a few *Yes, buts* of my own throughout this book.

Nevertheless, it is one thing to occasionally acknowledge differences, and another to avoid painting the bigger picture altogether. I think academics could do a far better job of translating our experiences for other people. When I set out to write this book, I decided to discuss tenure as it applies to many people in many circumstances because my fellow academics do a good job of explaining how it applies to some people under specific circumstances. The chapters that follow are, therefore, not just the story of my individual experiences in academia. They are not even just the stories of my friends and family – although some of them do make appearances. Instead, I also draw on other peoples' narratives, on generally applicable statistics, and on original interviews I've conducted as well as original data I've compiled. I do all this because I believe it is important to talk about tenure and academia *as a whole*.

Tenure, as I said in Chapter 1, matters as an employment protection – and not just for anthropologists or faculty at public universities or for any other subgroup you might think of. It matters for *most* professors, far more than the roughly 25% who currently have tenure or are eligible to earn it. It should matter for students, administrators, and citizens, too, because – despite the public relations beating that higher ed has taken in recent years, not to mention the financial and infrastructural beating it has taken in recent months – we all still depend on professors to do jobs that are difficult to perform *well* without job security. Students and parents count on professors to provide knowledge, mentorship, life skills, and emotional support; administrators count on professors to attract tuition dollars and produce prestigious and lucrative research; the public – including those who are childless – count on professors to produce the knowledge and train the people who will make many aspects of their lives function better (or at all). Without the kind of job security tenure provides, professors are hampered in their ability to meet these needs.

Back in 2020, I didn't fully appreciate any of this. Although I am the child of tenured professors and I was then a tenure-track professor myself, and even though every year I spend weeks discussing the At-Will Rule and its carveouts with my employ-ment law students, I had never seriously thought about how tenure (having it or being able to earn it) factors into your job performance. I had certainly never thought about what happens *after* tenure – much less what happens if, despite being tenured, you lose your job through no fault of your own. All I had ever focused on was get-ting an academic job that made me eligible for tenure and satisfying my colleagues' expectations so that, when the time came, they felt I had earned its protections.

But in the summer of 2020, I was sitting at home with a new baby and a (differ-ent) book project during a world-altering pandemic. As I scrolled through news stories on breaks from my manuscript, it struck me that more and more universities were laying off tenured faculty for financial reasons. Sometimes they were laying off entire programs' or departments' worth. That got me wondering: how often are faculty fired *despite having tenure*?

I started poking around the internet looking for statistics on the terminations of tenured faculty because I wanted to figure out whether tenure's protections were as airtight as I had been socialized to believe. What I found, to my disappointment, was a lot of overblown rhetoric as well as a couple of informed back-of-the-envelope guesses about how many faculty lose their jobs each year. To an eager young profes-sor, this was tantamount to an invitation. Wouldn't it be neat, I thought, if I could offer something more? I figured that I would spend a few of my nonexistent spare hours collecting and collating data, write an article summarizing my findings (that could be included in my own eventual application for tenure) and have a good story to tell at dinner parties, if those still existed after the pandemic. I could not have been more wrong.

It has been immensely difficult to collect any generalizable data on faculty tenure – even on tenured-terminations, which, for reasons I explain in Chapter 18, seemed to me like they would be a comparatively easy foothold. What I offer in this book is the product of over three years' work, the readily shared expertise of people from all over the country who were under no obligation to help me, a small army of research assistants, and my mother, whose statistical skills and shared enthusiasm for the project have kept me going through several mini-crises. But despite all the hard work undertaken by me, my research assistants, my volunteer advisors – and, yes, by my mother – the tenured-terminations data cannot by itself paint a complete picture of academic employment and its most famous feature.

For that, we need more: more numbers, more stories, more excursions into indus-try practices, and more details about labor market realities. We need to understand how academia really operates, rather than how politicians and pundits assume it does. We need to distinguish between what tenure means legally from what it does organizationally (for universities) and materially and psychologically (for faculty). And we need to be open to the idea that there is room for both change and continu-ity in the way that professors are employed. As with any other industry, the academy is its own world, with its own rules, flaws, and charms. Let me take you in.

3

Scrounge

I came to graduate school financially "clear."

The year before, I'd spent several months studying classical dance in India, courtesy of the Canadian and Indian governments. Because my dance fellowship gave me a decent stipend, and because my fellowship plans allowed me to live, free of cost, with an aunt and uncle, I had a debtless gap year in which to recover from college. During that year, my parents paid for half a dozen graduate school applications and my health insurance premium and I, as far as anyone can remember, paid for everything else. The fact that we *can't* remember very precisely says enough.

The bachelor's degree I'd earned just before going to India was also free-to-me. My college paid for around half my tuition and my parents paid the rest, along with all my living expenses. I worked in a cafeteria during my freshman year, and grumbled, and in the rare books section of the library during my sophomore year, where I grumbled less. My junior year I worked as a residential advisor, in which capacity I received a swanky room and made a lifelong friend whose wedding, twenty years later, I am now excited to attend. None of us – college, parents, me – emerged from my undergraduate years owing or being owed any money.

What I've just described is an inordinate level of privilege. I describe it nonetheless because the kind of privilege I've enjoyed is probably what it takes to make doctoral education a reasonable financial choice today. It's still not enough to make doctoral education a financially reasonable *process*.

A research doctorate is, for the most part, what it takes to become eligible for a tenure-stream professorship. There are some fields – mostly professional or fine arts disciplines – where this isn't necessarily true, but even there we have exceptions. A PhD isn't necessary in medicine (where, anyway, tenure isn't as valuable or a normative ideal) or in one of my home disciplines, law (where tenure is both valuable and normative). But you might be surprised to know that a PhD is necessary to become a professor in many subfields of business, despite all the talk about that field's practical orientation. Put simply, getting a doctorate is still a common enough requirement for becoming a professor – across enough disciplines – that we can, for conversation's sake, pretend that it's *always* a requirement. And that requirement can impose some brutal costs and conditions of life.

Again, I'm not referring to myself. I was lucky enough – lucky in my parents, lucky in my graduate school offers (inasmuch as the best school also gave me the best deal), and lucky in my own physical and mental health – that, despite the paltry $19,000 that constituted a *high-end* stipend from my department the year I was admitted, I was actually able to save a few hundred dollars every term. Those savings came in handy when my new boyfriend, now my husband, needed help paying his rent – because even though he started graduate school with a financial slate that was almost as pristine as mine, his advisor left town after a year, and ping-ponging around the country had cost my husband that advisor, a full-ride fellowship, as well as a few thousand dollars in moving debt. Because my husband and I met midway through my second year of graduate school – *and* because we spent our last eighteen months as doctoral students eating ramen, *dal*, and beans with a repetitiveness that I try not to romanticize – I know that *two* privileged people making financially reasonable choices at the start of graduate school can still end up experiencing entirely unreasonable financial hardship.

I suspect a lot of nonacademics don't know this, and consequently that a lot of them imagine graduate school to be a series of afternoons spent on a green quad with an interesting book and some deep thoughts. There *are* many glorious afternoons on quads, and there are even a few deep thoughts. But there are also twenty-one-hour days reading texts in seventeenth-century English while engaging in anxious late-night calculations about the price of gas versus the cost of budget-store beans that are too far away. There is marital discord over an extra 99-cent slider at the drive-thru, and a compulsion to eat as much as you can decorously manage whenever there is free food on offer *whatever* is on offer and even if your advisor is watching. And there's a gnawing awareness that, despite all this, you're still better off than most of your peers.

PhD poverty is enough of an issue that one of the most widely read blogs about American academia, *The Professor Is In*, has an entire category of posts devoted to it. It's enough of an issue that, in 2021, *The Harvard Crimson* published a story featuring a graduate student whose Tuesdays were entirely dedicated to attending the Community Tea events held by her school (where she could eat lunch and collect leftovers) and to visiting the food pantries operated by Harvard's Office of Student Life (where she could expect to find bare shelves by Thursday).[1] And PhD poverty is enough of an issue that campus food pantries have multiplied by ten in as many years, going from 80 to 800 nationwide.[2] What this should tell us is that the graduate student caught stuffing crostini and cheese cubes into her face with unconvincing nonchalance isn't enjoying a rare treat or being gluttonous. She's being hungry. Thanks to inadequate stipends, prohibitions against off-campus employment, and the high cost of living in many university locations, the life of the mind is also often and literally the life of the empty stomach.[3]

This is true even for graduate students from well-resourced families who are experiencing what is hopefully a temporary state of poverty. Their poverty will impose some long-term financial discomfort, per Chapters 4 and 10, but, in its worst excesses, it will hopefully be fleeting. For an aspiring academic who *comes from* poverty, though, the financial challenges of graduate school extend beyond the *important* task of keeping body and mind together. It involves learning a new way to be so that you can get the credential that you were deemed capable of earning for the job you deemed worthy of pursuing – and it involves learning that new culture and adopting its rituals and its insignia when you're trying to find enough to eat.

I want to pause for a minute here to make a point about clothing that is also a point about conditioning. *Dress is particularly fraught for me*, noted a contributor to the collaborative academic blog *Tenure, She Wrote*.[4] *I spent a lot of time developing a style from thrift stores that's a sort of vintage chic to hide my poverty.*

She's not the only one.

Movies and television might make the kind of vintage-bohemian-tweedy-chic she describes seem like it's academia's default sartorial aesthetic. It's certainly common, and I myself find it endearing. My husband and I both lived it for a while, as evidenced by the excessive number of scarves I still own and the elbow-patch blazer deep in his closet. But, coming from a field that pays a lot of attention to representation and being a person who spends idle conference breaks watching the fashion show happening in front of her, let me tell you that the standard academic style appearing on screens of all sizes is a function of necessity as much as it is of preference. Quirkiness, as that blog author noted, is a defense mechanism as much as it is an aesthetic choice or a political statement.

I say this to underscore that cultural acclimation is never *free* in addition to never being easy. When you're trying to develop a new persona while also figuring out your next meal, acclimation is incredibly stressful. When you're forced to do those things while also operating under a set of legal restrictions linked to your immigration status, as many aspiring academics must, it gets even worse.

I pay about 70 percent of my family income for rent, wrote one international graduate student at MIT.[5] *And this is the cheapest option that my family qualifies for. MIT provides no additional subsidy, even for students in its own housing.* US laws, meanwhile, prohibited this student's spouse from working, so after deducting obligatory health insurance costs and student life fees, the family was left with under $60 per week. That's $8.57 per day to cover food, transportation, and everything else for a family of three. Weekends are the worst, noted the student, *[b]ecause – terrible as it sounds – I feel anxious that my child might require medical care, resulting in co-pays that I cannot afford.*

I can believe that $60 figure because, during our *dal*-and-beans time, my husband and I lived on a weekly grocery budget of $35. We still lived very well for a number of reasons: because he had a working car and I had a ferocious determination to avoid debt, because neither of us suffered any major illnesses or chronic conditions beyond easily managed asthma, and because we not only knew that we could *ask* for familial help if we needed to, we also knew that we didn't need to *provide* familial help when we couldn't afford to. We doubled and tripled our birth control because, even in a world where *Roe* still existed and in a state where reproductive care was widely available, I was more terrified of having a child too early than of never having one at all. For five years – two years of graduate school, two years of a post-doctoral fellowship, and through the first full year of my first tenure-track job – I filled old-fashioned account books by hand, logged every expense over 25 cents, and did calculations in a monthly reckoning that always ended in heartache.

And *I* came to graduate school financially "clear."

Unfortunately, what doctoral education begins, post-doctoral fellowships continue. The blog post category that I mentioned earlier, at *The Professor Is In*, was inspired by an article in the *Chronicle of Higher Education* about poverty in the next stage of the academic life cycle. The title of that article declared, quite bluntly, that *The Ph.D. Now Comes With Food Stamps*.[6] Although the title was referencing doctorate holders more broadly, it also applies to the subset of PhDs who become post-docs.

Post-docs are sometimes also known as *fellows, lecturers,* and *visiting assistant professors.* What the holders of all these titles share in common, and what distinguishes them from other nontenure-track faculty, is the dual pedagogical and employment nature of their positions. Post-docs *give* universities valuable cheap labor and, less valuably, they allow universities the chance to stamp their brand onto a potential tenure-stream member of the academy. Post-docs *get* income from an academic job (in the likely scenario that none was forthcoming via the tenure-track market) and an expanded network of possible mentors and references. They may even get further training or practice in research or teaching.

The post-doc is now part of what it takes to become a professor. Over at *Prawfsblawg*, which is run by and for law professors, Sarah Lawsky conducts an annual crowdsourced survey to gauge hiring patterns in legal academia. For the past ten years, the number of entry-level law professors who've completed a fellowship – academic law's equivalent of a post-doc – has *never dipped below 71%*.[7] Law is not an outlier. Post-docs are also almost inescapable in humanities and social sciences disciplines and virtually required for tenure-track jobs in many STEM fields. Unsurprisingly, a 2015 survey found that around 80% of science post-doc were aiming for faculty positions while around 70% of respondents already in tenure-stream science positions described their post-doctoral experience as "required or preferred" for the jobs they eventually won.[8]

There will always be some people who buck the trend by going straight from graduate school to a tenure-track position – my cousin the ethnomusicologist, for instance. But they are increasingly the exception that proves the rule. If you want to be a professor, chances are that you will need to do a post-doc of some type, by some name. Probably many.

The first problem with post-docs is, of course, the low wages they pay. As Chapter 10 explains, academia pays less than many other industries given the credentialing and training that it requires. When I accepted my $60,000 post-doc salary in 2018, I declined a $180,000 law firm salary to do so. Sixty thousand might seem generous – and it was: my new salary was twice what my husband and I had been *jointly* living on for the previous two years, and now he was earning his own money as a tenure-track professor. But remember that, besides being in the higher-industry-paying discipline of law, my $60,000 salary was buying the labor of someone with a *terminal degree* (or in my case, two). For many post-docs, that salary is also supposed to be paying the educational debt of the person holding that terminal degree.

Average doctoral debt is, as Chapter 10 notes, nearly 150% of the average debt held by all student borrowers. At the individual level, the average PhD's total educational debt is almost $88,368 of which nearly $77,410 is from graduate school alone.[9] This is likely a *very* conservative estimate of an individual PhD holder's financial burden because, among other things, the same report notes that "average debt" (not limited to student loan debt) among "PhD holders who attended public institutions" and among "those who earned PhDs at private, nonprofit institutions" was $195,504 and $258,712, respectively. Student loan debt represents just a fraction of the financial burden aspiring academics take on.

Seen from another angle: as of 2019 "households with graduate degrees owed 56 percent of the [nation's] outstanding education debt," even though adults over twenty-five with graduate degrees only account for 14% of the population.[10] That debt concentration becomes even more extreme among those who hold professional degrees and research doctorates, who account for just 3% of the over 25% population but hold 20% of the nation's educational debt.[11] A lot of this debt is coming from MDs, for sure, who rack up big bills but eventually earn bigger salaries. But medical doctors don't explain all these numbers. Graduate school is just *expensive*, even for people who will never earn very much and must still find a way to service their loans during their apprenticeship, or post-doc, phase.

Low salaries might not be such a problem if it weren't for the post-doc queue, which is a fantastic label for a dismal reality.[12] "Postdocs enter the queue," write the creators of this label, "as they start their first postdoctoral appointment, and they leave in one of two ways: (1) obtaining the 'queue service' desired by the majority of postdocs, that is, an assistant professorship or (2) reneging from the queue and seeking other positions."[13] But the post-doc queue, unlike lines at the doctor's office or even at the DMV, "is one of those rare queueing systems where most of the queuers eventually renege rather than receive service."

I have a friend who's a current and queuing post-doc. His PhD is in anthropology, like mine, and his first post-doc was at an elite research university – trust me when I say that it doesn't get much more elite. His three recent campus visits for tenure-track jobs are more than most of his peers will have had, but they still didn't translate into a tenure-track offer. (When I went on the entry-level job market in law almost ten years ago, I was told to expect a campus interview-to-offer "conversion ratio" of 25% to 33%; not only was that expectation set alarmingly high, but this was law, where there are more jobs, and it was almost ten years ago, when there were probably more jobs.)

Still, my friend is lucky. At the time that I'm writing this, he's weighing two new post-doc offers, a potential extension of his current post-doc, and he has at least one full-time job application that's still "live" (if also overseas).

There are five years separating the moments when my friend and I completed our educations, and around the same number of years separate us in age. We're peers in so many of the ways that matter. Our lives, though, could not be further apart. At forty(ish), I have a stable job and a nice house in a good city where my husband is also happily employed, where my son attends an excellent school, and where my mother and mother-in-law are happy to come visit. I am profoundly grateful. My friend, in his mid-thirties, is in a semi-long-distance relationship with his spouse, who commutes for part of each week to another state but who may or may not be able to continue doing so depending on where the next post-doc is. My friend is trying to sort out the next one to three years of his life – the standard duration of most post-docs – so that he has a chance at starting his "real" job afterward. For my friend, like for so many others, queuing means that mid-life and mid-career almost never coincide.

This means that the costs of queuing extend beyond lost wages and heavy debt. The kind of serial apprenticeship that the queue represents forces aspiring academics, as well as their partners, children, and extended families, to endure repeated relocations under suboptimal conditions during prime career-building and child-bearing years.[14] These are not small costs. Social science research has demonstrated that moving frequently can increase feelings of anxiety and social isolation,[15] facilitates "fewer quality social relationships,"[16] has more adverse effects on women than men,[17] spurs behavioral challenges in children,[18] elevates the risk of depression in adulthood,[19] and negatively impacts community life in areas with highly mobile populations. Outside academia, frequent dislocation is widely understood to be hard on the workers who experience it as well as on their nuclear and extended families. Academics and their families are no exception.

As a "non-academic kid" in a university town, Kelly Ritter, the Chair of Georgia Tech's School of Literature, Media, and Communication, writes that she went to school with many children of professors.[20] *[They] came and went from my life without me understanding why.* Looking back now, Ritter recognizes those patterns as part of the academic life. Academic children often leave their friends, schools, hobbies, and familiar surroundings because one or both of their parents are in a profession where even the biggest city likely offers no lateral job opportunities.

[A]ll I knew then, notes Ritter, *was that each August, I would start school with a number of my classmates from the year before missing, seemingly gone without a trace.* And now, she adds, *[d]espite my negative childhood experiences... I have subjected my own family to the same conditions.*

Stability is a gift. Like all gifts, it might not suit every recipient. But choosing to move constantly under conditions of financial duress and extreme professional uncertainty is unlikely to have wide appeal for most people. Choosing to do that after nearly a decade spent working hard while negotiating PhD poverty and deflecting assumptions of lazy afternoons on the quad is even less likely to seem desirable. Aspiring academics nevertheless do all of this. Some of them do it because they don't know any better. Some of them do it because they think they can outsmart the system. (And some of them succeed in doing so, although it's often not because they were smarter.) But, whatever their motivations and outcomes, many aspiring academics take on the hardships I've described in this chapter – and many of them take on the risks that I'll discuss in the next one.

4

Squint

One of the classes I regularly teach focuses on a statute that is dry, even by legal standards. The *Employee Retirement Income Security Act* of 1974 – *ERISA*, for short – is the federal law that regulates most retirement plans and healthcare plans offered by employers. That makes it important, but it doesn't make it fun.

In fact, *ERISA* is a remarkably hard statute to teach. (My own *ERISA* professor affectionately called it the "Every Ridiculous Idea Since Adam" law.) One reason *ERISA* is so challenging is that it can involve a lot of tax law, and nobody goes to law school because they have a penchant for numbers. *ERISA* is also challenging because, at least on the surface, it doesn't raise any of the exciting, big picture questions that are standard fare in constitutional law or criminal law classes. You don't spend class time in *ERISA* discussing hot-button topics like Supreme Court appointments or the prison abolition movement, so it's a lot harder to come away feeling inspired – or, for that matter, to be inspiring. Predictably, only a few law students want to take a class on *ERISA* and even fewer law schools bother offering one.

And yet, *ERISA* is my highest-rated class. I do well enough in the reviews for my other classes, where I'm generally viewed as a capable if not stellar instructor. But I get my best reviews in this course that no student has to take and that few professors want to teach. (I also get more cupcakes.) If my reviews are anything to go by, the reason my "worst" class is also my "best" class is because I make it about the students as much as it is about the law. Everyone gets sick, I remind my students, and everyone gets old. So don't just learn *ERISA* for the sake of your future clients: learn it for your future selves.

Getting twenty-somethings to think about healthcare and retirement at a time when most of them are physically healthy and professionally insecure is no joke – but it's also probably my single greatest contribution to student success. As with so many aspects of life, the United States largely leaves people to fend for themselves in retirement. Most Americans either can't or don't adequately account for their retirement needs. Knowing the ins and outs of *ERISA* can be an empowering life hack, and that, in turn, can be an effective way to pitch a course. But, truthfully, their

ERISA knowledge isn't really what's protecting my law students from the "retirement crisis" awaiting so many Americans. What's protecting them is a grab bag of structural factors far more influential than anything I can do as a teacher.

Because both the schools I've taught at are fairly well-ranked (anywhere from #19 to #42 depending on the year) most of my students will go on to earn starting salaries in the high five-figures to low six-figures. Most of them will end up earning those salaries from employers who offer good 401(k) deferred contribution plans. A lot of those employers will offer "matching contributions" to help boost their employees' retirement savings, while others will offer merit bonuses or other forms of profit sharing. Together, this means my students will likely have extra money to save as well as the infrastructure to easily and effectively save it. Finally, most of my students will be in their late twenties when they graduate from law school. The three years they spend getting their threshold credential will still leave them enough time in the workforce – an average of almost four decades – to accumulate respectable retirement savings. Of course, individual students may have worse outcomes and *all* students will experience anxiety about what their outcomes will be. Statistically speaking, though, my law students will get the jobs they trained for in a timeframe and at salaries that enable them to secure their long-term well-being. They can face the future with eyes wide open, no squinting required.

None of these statements apply to aspiring academics.

Choosing to pursue a career in academia means viewing your future well-being with an eye that is, if not totally blind, at least resolutely blurry. Mostly, this is because the odds of getting the job you spent years training for are heartbreakingly low. As Chapter 8 explains, estimates of success range from 10% to 25% (and this is very likely too high). Those odds, of course, only apply if you have put in the work *and* enjoyed the necessary good fortune to become a viable candidate in the first place. With a 75% to 90% chance of *not* getting the job they train for, people who choose to enter doctoral programs can seem to the outside world like a kind of professional Han Solo – charging forward, all the while muttering "Never tell me the odds."[1]

But aspiring academics must also squint at their futures because the very *process* of pursuing academia imposes its own separate and heavy costs. These "process costs" affect aspiring academics long after they have escaped the graduate school scrounging described in Chapter 3. They are nearly impossible to recover *even if* you are one of the lucky few to land a tenure-track job. And they are hard to spot: neither the would-be professor nor the people who surround her – parents, siblings, friends, neighbors – are likely to see them, or to appreciate their impact. "[N]o one ever spoke to me," writes one BIPOC doctoral graduate, "about retirement, planning for inflation and the rising cost of living, the importance of investing early to maximize compound interest… as a first generation student from generational poverty, I simply lacked financial literacy."[2] To my mind, the pervasive invisibility and delayed consequences of process costs makes them even more pernicious than the scrounging one is often forced to do in graduate school.

What costs am I referring to? Primarily, but not solely, the implicit opportunity costs of pursuing academia instead of a different but comparable profession.

Let's first distinguish between types of costs. An *explicit cost* is when you exchange money for something you would not otherwise have: a new house, a fancy dinner, or knowledge and training. (Many of my colleagues would scold me for the commodification of learning reflected in that sentence, but their displeasure does not change the fact that one must pay out of pocket to learn in this country just as one must pay to acquire food or shelter.) In the higher education context, student loans are the most recognizable explicit cost because they represent money you are spending to get something in return.

An *implicit cost*, on the other hand, is kind of like pantry cooking: it's using what you have on hand instead of spending money to acquire something new. The most obvious implicit costs associated with higher education are how you use your time and your labor: instead of using both to work a paying job, you are using them to study. The income you don't earn and the savings you don't build represent significant implicit costs to pursuing your chosen credential. This is true even if you work part time while studying, and even if someone else in your household can support you financially, because you and your household are still probably earning less or saving less (or both) by virtue of how *you* are spending your time and labor.

Most of the implicit and explicit costs associated with pursuing academia apply to other elite professions, too. Aspiring lawyers and doctors also earn reduced or nonexistent salaries while they are in the credentialing phases of their careers. This, in turn, means that they are saving less for things like retirement and home buying. And of course, both aspiring lawyers and doctors incur significant explicit costs. In fact, the central explicit cost of pursuing these professions – student loan debt – is in many cases the same, on an annual basis, as the comparable cost of pursuing academia, and it can often be greater. In 2023–2024, for instance, Columbia Law School estimated that the total annual cost of attendance, including all university expenses as well as a budget for living in New York City (one that is decidedly optimistic), was around $118,357.[3] During the same year, Columbia's Graduate School of Arts and Sciences estimated that it would cost around $97,233 for a year of full-time residence in doctoral programs like anthropology.[4] That's a difference of over $20,000 for just one year, and taken by itself, it leaves the aspiring anthropologist better off.

If aspiring academics are not the only ones incurring heavy explicit and implicit costs, why can my law students look their futures straight in the eye (hopefully with the added clarity of our *ERISA* conversations) while their peers in doctoral programs cannot? For that matter, why can't doctoral students at universities that are even *better* ranked than the ones I've taught at – for example at Chicago, where I received my PhD, or at the University of Pennsylvania, where I spent two years in a post-doc – why can't *they* look toward the future with a reasonable measure of confidence? The answer has to do with a concept my students and I discuss repeatedly in our *ERISA* class: the time value of money. And that, in turn, is relevant because of how long it takes to become viable for a tenure-track faculty position.

In most disciplines, it takes a long time to prepare for the academic labor market – far longer than the average nonacademic, or even aspiring academic, may realize. (This is why I said new graduate students can *seem* like Han Solo: if they were truly like him, they would be painfully aware of all the obstacles coming their way.) Here, as elsewhere, time is a powerful variable. It may not singlehandedly explain why the process costs of pursuing academia are higher than those of pursuing peer professions, but it does get us most of the way. Time takes costs that were heavy to begin with and transforms them into back-breaking burdens, while the job market realities we'll encounter in Chapters 8 and 10 ensure that there is no therapeutic fix waiting on the other side.

For aspiring academics, the most familiar quantity of time is six years. Six years is the standard estimate of how long it takes to complete a doctorate, counting from the day you begin orientation to the day you walk across the stage. The six-year standard is exceptionally well-entrenched inside and outside academia. Generations of aspiring academics have been told about it, they tell their parents and friends about it, those parents and friends go on to repeat it at social gatherings and in hallway conversations while explaining what the kids are up to these days. This is how someone like my father-in-law – who doesn't hold a PhD himself but who has a son, a daughter-in-law, a niece, and a god son who *do* – can be familiar with the six-year standard even though only one of those four PhD-holding relatives of his actually graduated in six years.

In all probability, the six-year standard is still being relayed to many newly matriculating PhD students. During my own graduate school orientation at Chicago in 2007, I asked faculty in the Department of Anthropology how many years I could expect to spend in the program. They all dutifully answered "Six." During my cohort's first meetings with the department's Director of Graduate Studies, we again heard the six-year standard. There was no reason we couldn't finish in six years, the Director declared, it was just a matter of focus and hard work. She even charted out an *ideal-typical student* who would follow an *ideal-typical path* that would get them out the door and into a job by the end of, you guessed it, six years. (Nevermind that *ideal* and *typical* are antonyms: something that a friend of mine later pointed out.)

Despite its popularity, the six-year standard has two big problems: it isn't accurate, and its inaccuracy is dangerous.

The belief that the average PhD takes six years to complete may, at one time, have had the virtue of being true. But that time ended long before I entered graduate school (or even college) and it was probably over earlier still. Recently collected federal data confirms just how far we are from living out the six-year standard. As of 2021, the average median time-to-completion for PhDs in science and engineering fields was 7.1 years and the subgroup with the longest time-to-completion was health sciences at 8.8 years. Outside "science and engineering" fields, in areas like business, education, humanities, and arts, the median duration of a doctorate is around a decade.[5] And remember: these are *medians*. Fifty percent of doctoral students took longer to get their degrees.

In other words, even in the "quickest" fields, PhDs take almost 20% longer to earn than common wisdom suggests. Because the "science and engineering" category represents an overwhelming majority of all PhDs earned – in 2021, they were 79% of doctorates granted nationwide[6] – this means that most PhDs take longer to complete than academics themselves seem to think. My own doctoral cohort exemplifies this pattern: while three people in our nineteen-person group finished by the six-year mark, three of us took over a decade and nine – 47% of the cohort – took between eight and nine years to graduate. So much for the six-year standard.

But the six-year standard is more than descriptively inaccurate: it is also dangerously misleading. It encourages a belief that the PhD and however long it takes to get it are all that stand between an aspiring academic and job market viability. If you spend six years in school, the standard almost seems to say, and if you get that degree, you will be a viable candidate for full-time academic employment.

In fact, the PhD is now only the first step toward becoming a professor. As Chapter 3 just explained, most aspiring academics must spend at least another one to two years in post-doctoral fellowships or other "apprenticeship" positions if they want to become competitive candidates for faculty positions. Chapter 3 also documented some of the realities of post-doc life, which regularly combine low salary with long hours, high pressure, and frequent relocations to far-off places as part of a process that empties bank accounts and strains relationships. For now, though, what matters is the simple fact that a post-doc is often not much more financially rewarding than graduate school itself and is virtually inescapable if you want to become a professor. I *do* know people who have won tenure-track jobs without completing post-docs. I don't know *many*.

Added together, the not-quite-six-year standard and the mandatory post-doc equal at least a decade. It takes a minimum of around *ten years* to go from freshly minted doctoral student to viable faculty candidate. My law students, by contrast, spend three years getting their JDs and a summer sitting the bar exam of their chosen state. The difference between three years and ten means that aspiring academics spend more time and labor preparing to enter their job market than aspiring lawyers spend preparing for theirs. And, for the most part, the longer you spend crossing the threshold into your chosen profession, the higher its implicit cost.

(Economically minded readers might object that the implicit cost of academic credentialing depends on the value of foregone opportunities – meaning that the cost of your degree also depends on what your time and labor would have earned you if they had been put to another use. This is true, but it's also somewhat beside the point. Most people begin PhDs, JDs, and MDs at around the same age – 22–25 – and with a similar primary credential: their undergraduate degree.)

The longer ramp-up to professional viability is where the time value of money begins to matter. The "time value of money" refers to the idea that $1,000 received today is more valuable than a promise of $1,000 in the future. Today, you might invest the money and earn interest. You know what its purchasing power is and can plan to spend it accordingly. At the very least, you have it in hand. Tomorrow… who knows? You will not have accrued any interest, and you might not be able to buy as much with it, thanks to inflation. At a fundamental level, you can't be sure that you will have that money until you do. For all these reasons, money now is worth more than money later.[7] And that, in turn, is why the six-year standard is misleading: it suggests that all aspiring academics give up is six (or eight, or ten) years of time and, perhaps, some salary. In actuality, they forfeit all the potential – the time value – of that lost money, too.

Again, none of this is unique to academics. But other professions often involve a much shorter credentialing period (law) or an equally lengthy period that's widely *recognized* as such (medicine). They also often come with better employment prospects and higher salaries. (We'll circle back to this in Chapters 8 and 10.) The six-year standard that dominates conversations inside and outside the academy is both descriptively inaccurate and a gross understatement of the risks – the implicit costs – of pursuing a faculty job. By choosing a path that requires them to incur more implicit costs in their twenties and thirties, aspiring academics damage themselves in a way that is hard to understand and nearly impossible to undo, even for very smart people.

Imagine the best-case scenario.

In your senior year of college, from which you will graduate debt-free, you're admitted to a high-ranking doctoral program at an excellent university. You are admitted with both full tuition remission *and* a living stipend. Your stipend provides enough money to rent an acceptable apartment within a reasonable commuting distance of your university. And since your university is in a major metropolitan area – or in a temperate region – you can avoid the expense of bringing your rickety old car to your newfound home by using public transportation or by riding your bike to campus.

Your financial aid package includes subsidized access to a health insurance plan, and since you enjoy good physical and mental health, your out-of-pocket medical costs are low. You have no dependents – or, if you do, you also have another income stream (like a partner's earnings) that covers those dependents' expenses. Your family understands that you cannot afford to come home for the holidays, and your friends understand that their wedding festivities are beyond your budget. Fortunately (since your budget also cannot cover conference attendance) your university allows graduate students to apply for professional development funds, so you manage to avoid incurring debt for necessary work-related travel.

You are accepted onto the research team of a well-respected scholar (if you're in a bench science) or you receive the external grants necessary to conduct fieldwork or archival research at the appropriate moments in your graduate career (if you're in a Social Science or Humanities discipline). Either way, your research produces sufficiently interesting results on the first try to enable the timely completion of your degree. As you research and write, your advisors provide prompt guidance and good references, and they never unnecessarily delay your progress by requiring excessive revisions or reducing your authorship credit. Because of all this, you finish your PhD in eight years – just a little longer than the fastest national median – with zero graduate debt.

In other words, you are in the lucky and exceedingly rare position of having the best possible outcome along every possible metric. Now, let's take matters one step further by imagining that you land a tenure-track job during your first "season" on the market. You even somehow manage to do this without going through a post-doctoral apprenticeship period that would require another move and a few more years of depressed earnings.

Thanks to this fantastic and almost fantastical sequence of events, you will be toasted and envied in not-quite-equal amounts. Friends will congratulate you, junior scholars will whisper about you, and your advisor will walk around with an air of serene if unsurprised satisfaction. And it will all be warranted because you *are* the golden child: you are the exception that proves the rule.

You will also have begun your working life in your early thirties as the financial equivalent of an eighteen-year old: no debt and no savings. In fact, you will be *grateful* to be approaching middle age with no rainy-day funds, no children's college funds, no down payment for a house, and no retirement account. Starting at zero means that you somehow managed to avoid the mountains of graduate educational debt drowning your friends and transforming them into anxiety-ridden shells of their former selves. *You* will not be starting your working life with a negative balance.

True, if you had entered the workforce instead of graduate school, you might have been sitting on a small pile of money. Your friend who was an anthropology major at the same college had a starting salary of over $60,000, while your friend who majored in engineering earned $74,000 right out of college.[8] They each managed to save between $100 and $400/month during the eight years you spent in graduate school and now they have, respectively, over $10,000 and over $45,000 in savings.[9] Mortgage interest rates may be high but at least your friends need to worry about them: you don't, and won't, for decades (if ever). And marriage? Partnership? You knew you'd have no control over where your job took you, assuming that you were fortunate enough to have that problem. Developing a meaningful relationship with someone who probably couldn't follow you seemed unwise. Having a child, as your doctoral advisor regularly warned you, seemed worse. You are learning to make peace with the possibility of not finding a mate and the likelihood of not having a child.

Despite all this, you know how lucky you are. You *got* the job you trained for. You were the only one in your cohort to do so.

How many aspiring academics think about all this before they set out on their chosen path? Few to none, I find. Implicit costs are often overlooked in the decision-making processes that lead to graduate school and, one hopes, to academia. Aspiring academics often view the cost of pursuing academia as simply being the "six" years they spend getting a PhD – and why shouldn't they? Their prospective advisors, their friends and family, and the world around them tell them that the greatest cost of graduate school is the *time they spend* in graduate school. In fact, though, the greatest costs lie ahead.

Besides inaccurate and misleading information, some powerful social norms also prevent aspiring academics from fully seeing the long-term consequences of their choices. The belief that education has both inherent and economic value makes it hard to characterize time spent learning as time wasted. True, this norm is on an increasingly unstable footing in American society. More Americans than ever are skeptical about the value of higher education,[10] almost half of American parents would prefer that their children *not* attend a four-year college (so forget graduate school!),[11] and although undergraduate degrees still produce a *wage* premium they no longer create a meaningful lifetime *wealth* premium.[12] But whether it's because of a contextually reasonable preference, a generalized social norm, or a cognitive bias like "post-purchase rationalization," aspiring academics find it hard to imagine beforehand – or declare afterward – that their decision to pursue graduate school and academia may not be worth the cost. And other norms that also encourage the pursuit of academia, like widespread exhortations to Find Your Passion or Do What Makes You Happy, don't seem to be in danger of going anywhere.

The idea that a particular career path may be financially unjustifiable, if not outright ruinous, is particularly offensive in a country that is captivated by the idea of limitless individual potential. Even advisors who know better will avoid telling would-be-professors that they should not pursue their dream job because they likely cannot afford to do so. This is not necessarily because the advisors in question are malicious, callous, or even lazy. (Some are, no doubt – but there are bad apples everywhere.) It is more often because even academics who study things like culture, politics, and history do not exist outside them.

PART TWO

Tenure's Troubles

5

Cause, Just Cause

A hand tentatively goes up.

"When a contract for employment is indefinite... *(pause)*... either party... *(pause)*... may terminate for good reason, bad reason, or no reason at all... *(lengthy pause)*... any reason except an illegal reason... *(deep breath)*... with no notice and no payment in lieu of notice!"

Applause scatters throughout the room as the student who volunteered exhales triumphantly.

This happened last Thursday in my employment law class, where we are studying the At-Will Rule and its exceptions. At this point in the semester, my students have already been introduced to the four-prong Rule and endured a short history lesson on how the Rule came to be the default assumption for all open-ended employment relationships in the United States. They've heard me say that the At-Will Rule produces both flexibility and insecurity for workers, who may find themselves without a job "for good reason, bad reason, or no reason at all."

Still, I'm not convinced the class understands why any of this matters at a human level. Legalese like *indefinite* and *terminate* and phrases like *in lieu of* have a way of obscuring the everyday consequences of legal rules. I decide to use a classic law school trick to convey a not-so-classic law school point. I ask them to tell me whether each of the following scenarios would constitute wrongful termination under the At-Will Rule. Could the terminated employee sue to get their job back (or, more likely, to get a payout from their former employer)?

"I'm fired because I'm a woman."

Dozens of heads nod vigorously. This one was easy: Title VII of the *Civil Rights Act of 1964* makes it illegal to discriminate against an employee on the basis of their sex.[1] And if a termination is made for an illegal reason, it also – under prong four – violates the At-Will Rule. I would most definitely have a viable lawsuit in this scenario.

"I'm fired because I'm insufficiently feminine. I wear pants, not skirts, no makeup or jewelry, and I swear like there's no tomorrow."

Several heads nod, although a little less vigorously. This termination seems patently wrong to most of my students, and anyway most of them belong to a generation for whom none of these behaviors are exclusively coded as unfeminine. Still, after surviving one or two years of law school, they know that lots of things that feel wrong do not create legal liability. As it happens, though, this termination *would* create legal liability because, in a 1989 opinion called *Price Waterhouse v. Hopkins*,[2] the Supreme Court held that punishing someone for failing to conform to gender stereotypes (however outdated they may be) is a form of sex discrimination that was also made illegal by Title VII.

"I'm fired because I have brown eyes."

No heads nod affirmatively or shake in disagreement, and I see lots of confusion. Was that a sneaky way of firing her because of her race? And isn't race, like sex, a protected category? The awkward truth is that this termination is probably legally acceptable if my eye color really is the reason I was fired. Eye color may be a physical characteristic, but it's not easily connected to race or national origin (both of which are identity markers that, like sex, would be illegal bases for termination). For this reason, firing someone for having a certain eye color, whether it's brown or blue or hazel, is not something the law prohibits. It is undoubtedly a *bad* reason to fire an otherwise satisfactory employee – but that kind of bad reasoning is precisely what the At-Will Rule protects.

I throw out a few more scenarios. "I'm fired because I wore something teal-colored to the office and my boss hates teal." "I'm fired because I support a rival football team" (this example made a lot more sense when I was teaching at Alabama). And, "I'm fired because it's Thursday."

As my students reluctantly acknowledge, none of these last three terminations are illegal – again, providing that they really *are* the reason I was fired in each scenario. Wearing disfavored colors, supporting disfavored sports teams, and simply showing up to work on a Thursday are stupid reasons to deprive a person of their job. But when it comes to employment relationships, the law explicitly protects this kind of stupidity.

There are nonstupid reasons why this may have seemed like a good idea at one point. Until the At-Will Rule gained prominence in the late nineteenth century, the laws regulating labor agreements were inflexible for hiring and hired parties alike. In many situations, employers who had no tasks to assign would still have to pay wages to their employees, at least for some time, or else they could face civil liability. Meanwhile, many workers who wanted to quit their jobs couldn't do so without owing money to their former employers – and, in some cases, they couldn't quit without being vulnerable to criminal prosecution. Imagine that: you try to change your job and you end up risking jail.

These aspects of the pre-At-Will universe are so far removed from us now that they can be hard to relate to. (Not *too* hard, though: *The New York Times* recently reported that employers are increasingly using training repayment agreement provisions, which are sometimes aptly acronymed "T.R.A.Ps," as financial weapons to dissuade employees from quitting their jobs.[3]) Nevertheless, most Americans inhabit a universe where it is rare to be stuck paying someone who can do nothing useful for you, and, equally, it is rare to be stuck working for someone when you want to leave. And the reason they enjoy this flexibility is because of the At-Will Rule.

But how important is the At-Will Rule, *really*? How much does it shape business decisions – and, by extension, how much does it shape the work lives of Americans?

Let's begin with a few caveats … those *Yes, buts* I warned you about in Chapter 2.

The At-Will Rule does not apply to every single worker in the United States. Not all jobs are "employment" relationships, which of course means that not all jobs are subject to the At-Will Rule. (Remember prong one: "When a contract for *employment* is indefinite…") In everyday conversation, we use the word *employment* to loosely signal the exchange of labor for money. To lawyers, however, *employment* is a term of art, and an *employer–employee* relationship creates special rights and obligations for both sides. Most people who exchange labor for money without being considered employees are called "independent contractors." There's a lot of disagreement in the law-and-policy world about the best way to sort individual workers into employee and independent contractor buckets. Generally speaking, however, if your job is more about producing specified outputs than about being told how to do your work, you are probably an independent contractor instead of an employee.

Just as not all jobs are *employment relationships*, not all employment relationships are *indefinite*. Imagine a hiring announcement that reads, "This is a three-year position, with a possibility of renewal." By inserting a definite duration into the terms of the contract, the hiring party has removed it from the sphere of the At-Will Rule. (Again, remember prong one: "When a contract for employment is *indefinite*…") If the hiring party wants to end the relationship at the three-year mark, the worker is out of luck. However, if they want to terminate the relationship *before* the three years are up, they will need to articulate a valid reason for doing so.

Finally, as we'll see shortly, not even all indefinite employment relationships are subject to the At-Will Rule. There are industries, places, circumstances, and contractual arrangements that can alter an indefinite employment relationship so that the Rule no longer applies to it. Tenure is only one of the contractual arrangements that can have this effect. There are many others, and their number as well as the wide range of jobs they impact is something neither critics nor supporters of tenure seem to appreciate. But part of what it means for the Rule to be a "default" is that it is possible to intentionally avoid it or to unintentionally fall outside its scope.

Now that we've got the *Yes, buts* out of the way, here's the punchline: the At-Will Rule probably applies to around 80% of all work relationships in the United States.[4]

Eighty percent. That means that even if the Rule isn't quite universal for all the reasons we've just explored, it is legally powerful and socially influential. Its prevalence means that we are ingrained with the belief that work relationships should be severable "for good reason, bad reason, or no reason at all." That kind of severability is what most of us experience first hand, what we see our spouses and parents and neighbors experiencing, and what our politicians and judges hold up as The Way Things Ought To Be. We also believe that ending those relationships should require "no notice and no payment in lieu of notice" even if, at the dinner party or in the group text thread, we agree that So-and-So's termination was manifestly unfair and they deserved to get some advanced warning from HR after so many years of service.

Because this default Rule is so powerful – because it's now more like a cultural norm – *any* arrangement that deviates from it will seem profoundly suspicious to us. It doesn't help that deviations from the At-Will Rule largely give affected employees more job security than the average worker. *Why should* their *employer have to articulate reasons for firing them? Why should* they *be guaranteed advanced notice of an impending job loss?* That's not what most of us experience and encounter on a daily basis. Particularly in a time of heightened economic anxiety, the special treatment accorded to non-at-will employees can seem profoundly unfair.

It's tempting to dismiss this kind of reaction as simple jealousy, but it's also ungenerous. Job security is a valuable thing. It is valuable to society because it influences employee behavior, and, in many industries, employee behavior has important societal consequences. During the height of the coronavirus pandemic, for instance, studies showed how "at-will employment ... undermine[d] workplace health and safety standards – and public health more generally" because the Rule made it easy for employers to fire workers who reported poor safety standards, requested personal protective equipment, or openly discussed high rates of infection within the workplace. When employees fail to do these good things because they fear losing their jobs, the At-Will Rule is effectively imposing a cost on society at large.[5]

The Rule can also lead employers to treat employees differently in ways that we may not want as a society. Managerial and C-suite employees often have the negotiating power to demand that their employment relationships *not* be at-will. They can demand contracts that oblige employers to articulate valid reasons for firing them, to follow certain procedures before doing so, and to compensate them if they fail to live up to these requirements. Consequently, the Rule, "coupled with employer contracting practices and the law of sexual harassment itself, produces a world in which employers are inclined to tolerate sexual harassment and other misconduct by top-level employees but aggressively police 'inappropriate' behavior by the rank-and-file."[6] This, too, represents the At-Will Rule's imposition of a social cost on society at large.

Of course, job security matters most for the individual, and specifically for the individual who lacks it. It matters for systemic reasons, because of the special rights enjoyed by workers who are labeled *employees*. In the United States, we funnel many elements of the social safety net – minimum wage guarantees, protections against discrimination or harassment at work, easy access to retirement planning and health insurance, and the ability to take family or medical leave, among other things – through employee status. If you lose a job that classified you as an employee and then immediately pick up an otherwise identical job that classifies you as an independent contractor, you will *still* have lost a lot. Wages are not all that matter.

That said, wages *do* matter a great deal and they represent yet another reason why job security is so valuable. Few American families can withstand even the smallest financial shocks. A 2020 survey by the Federal Reserve found that 35% of adults would not have enough cash reserves to pay an unexpected $400 bill, while 12% would probably be unable to pay such a bill by *any* means.[7] Discovering today that you will have no job tomorrow can leave you vulnerable to severe financial hardship, even if you happen to find a new and equally desirable job a week or a month later. All it takes is a broken axle, a hospital visit, or a faulty water heater. (*One week* and *one month* would, incidentally, be impressively short gaps between jobs: in mid 2024, the Department of Labor estimated that the median duration of unemployment was 9.5 weeks while the mean was over twenty-one.[8])

Insecure wages have invisible, long-term effects, too. Think of it this way: if I'm reasonably sure that I will receive income tomorrow, I can confidently – and optimally – allocate the income I have today. I can choose to buy a house (or not), to save aggressively for retirement (or not), to occasionally eat out at a restaurant (or not). In other words, I can use my resources in the way that best suits my needs and the needs of those who depend on me. My ability to make these choices *well* would matter less in a country with a more supportive welfare system, one where individual choices are not overly determinative of individual outcomes. In the United States, though, weak welfare protections and the funneling of many protections through employee status mean that a lot more hinges on the individual decisions made by individual workers. And that kind of decision-making, in turn, requires some knowledge about the financial future.

Most of us recognize that there are industries or occupations where this kind of advanced knowledge is chronically difficult to come by – where an unpredictable cash flow is almost inescapable. The performing arts, freelance work of all kinds (anything ranging from journalism to computer programming), and other feast-or-famine career paths are ones that practitioners enter *knowing* that they can't count on getting a paycheck tomorrow. What remarkably few Americans seem to realize is that the same is true of absolutely anyone who is an at-will employee. If you can be fired for any reason or no reason, you can be out of a job tomorrow even if that job has all the trappings of stability and permanence – biweekly salary, physical office, benefits and bonuses, and a company softball (or pickleball) team. Most workers do not seem to understand this.

There aren't many empirical studies exploring worker misconceptions around the At-Will Rule, but the few studies we do have overwhelmingly suggest that a majority of workers do not know what the Rule means, would not want it applied to them, and wrongly believe that it *does not* apply to them. In 1996, a survey-based study concluded that workers believe "that they have far greater rights against unjust or arbitrary discharges than they in fact have under an at-will contract."[9] Fully 89% of survey respondents believed that an employer could not fire them based solely on "personal dislike" – but according to the Rule, this would be just fine as long as the employer's feelings are actually born of personal dislike rather than from limited types of discriminatory bias.[10]

Another survey-based study published in 2019 compared people's knowledge of what the law *is* along various axes with what they believed the law *should be*.[11] Most people, it turns out, live in states whose default rule for employment relationships conflicts with their preferences. Given that the At-Will Rule is the default in all but one of the states examined in the survey (and, in fact, all but one of the fifty states), the implication is that most people may disagree with the terms of at-will employment. However, the survey also suggested that most people mistakenly believe their preferences and the law are *aligned*.[12] In other words, they say to themselves, "I think it's unfair to fire someone just because she wore teal to the office, and that's what the law says too." But it's not. As the study suggests, this means that most people wrongly assume the At-Will Rule is someone else's problem.

The insecurity imposed by the At-Will Rule and the negative consequences this has for individuals and society alike have not gone unnoticed. Most labor and employment law scholars think that the flexibility created by the Rule is minimally valuable but view the heightened insecurity that the Rule imposes as being quite harmful. Many hours have been spent, and many trees have been sacrificed, as part of scholarly efforts to document the human and societal costs of at-will employment, as well as to propose viable alternatives. Overall, though, scholarship has not much moved the needle on rethinking the At-Will Rule.

Most of the real change in this area has been driven by workers' advocates, by the government – and, to a much smaller extent, by employers. It may seem counterintuitive for employers to tie their own hands by forgoing the flexibility of at-will employment, or for governments to tell parties to an employment contract how to structure their relationship, but it is not. Employers who want to attract the best job candidates or who hope to retain workers with valuable institutional knowledge need to offer those individuals reasons to sign on and, later, to stay. Job security is one of many things that employers can offer. The value of job security (and its overall absence) helps explain big features of the American labor landscape, including why unions are so important: workers employed under a union agreement are, by definition, saved from the At-Will Rule. Collective bargaining agreements establish grounds for termination, procedures that must be followed before a termination happens, and even termination hierarchies like *last-in-first-out* or *first-in-first-out*. The importance of job security probably also helps explain smaller features of our labor landscape, including why professional orchestra musicians often have employment contracts that are not subject to the At-Will Rule: their talents are relatively unique and their ability to play well – literally – with their colleagues is valuable to the orchestra.[13] There's value to the orchestra in not allowing, say, an idiosyncratic conductor to fire the first violin because she wore teal to rehearsal.

Governments have many of the same incentives when they act as employers. In their capacity as legislators, they may *also* want specific types of workers who are not their own employees to enjoy job security greater than what the At-Will Rule allows. Sometimes this is because worker vulnerability and exploitative employer behavior prompt the government to step in. For instance, the National Employment Law Project (NELP), a workers' advocacy and research organization headquartered in New York City, reported that "fast-food workers [here] earn on average $21,700 annually" – around $1,800 per month in one of the world's most expensive cities – and that "[f]orty percent of New York City's fast-food worker-led-families relied on food stamps to supplement their wages."[14] In 2021, New York City introduced the *Fair Workweek Law,* which statutorily exempts fast-food workers from the At-Will Rule if they work for chains with at least thirty stores nationwide.[15]

At other times, government intervention reflects the belief that workers may need to be insulated from the vagaries of the At-Will Rule just to do their jobs effectively. This kind of legal buffer can be tailored to specific circumstances – as when, for instance, employees who act as whistleblowers by reporting employer or coworker wrongdoing are shielded from termination even if they are otherwise designated "at-will." Legal buffers against the At-Will Rule can also be absolute if providing heightened protection is believed to serve societal interests. Probably the largest group of employees who have been absolutely exempted from the Rule is the federal workforce. At least through December 2024, around 800,000 federal employees were governed by the "Merit Systems Principles" (MSP), which is a set of rules laying out the terms of their employment.[16] Covered employees can only be fired for good reason, and, even if they are fired, they can avail themselves of an appeals process that is overseen by the MSP Board. All these process requirements are complicated and time-consuming, to be sure, but as the MSP Board itself declares: "Due process is… a small price to pay to ensure the American people receive a merit based civil service rather than a corrupt spoils system."[17]

The type of contract that is applied to all these workers – orchestra musicians, fast-food workers in New York City, and nearly one million federal employees – is called "Just Cause." Just cause employment responds to the insecurity created by the At-Will Rule in two ways. Most importantly, it requires a nonarbitrary (or "just") rationale for ending the employment relationship. The rationale must concern the employee's failure to provide satisfactory work – and satisfactory work, in turn, is generally interpreted as encompassing (1) regular attendance, (2) obedience to reasonable work rules, (3) a reasonable quantity and quality of work, and (4) avoidance of any conduct that would interfere with the employer's ability to operate the business successfully.[18] The requirement of a just cause responds to prong two of the Rule: the fact that "either party… may terminate for good reason, bad reason, or no reason at all."

Because the grounds for termination must be both articulated and nonarbitrary, just cause contracts can also implicitly impose notice or procedural guarantees before termination that counteract prong four ("with no notice and no payment in lieu of notice"). As an employer, it's hard to be sure that you have valid reasons for firing someone if you haven't taken the time to catalog and consider those reasons – and, practically speaking, it can be both difficult and morale-killing to do all this under conditions of total secrecy. Consequently, even though a guarantee of advance notice is not required for a contract to be considered "just cause" (although many scholars believe that it *should* be[19]) a just cause employee is less likely to be surprised by an impending job loss than someone subject to the At-Will Rule. You'll likely see an exit sign before you're shown the door.

Just cause employment is not nearly as common as the at-will model – remember that around 80% of American employees are subject to the Rule – but it's also not exactly rare. So why does just cause seem *so* unusual and so privileged? One reason is the way at-will employment has become deeply embedded within our culture; it is, as I mentioned, a social norm as much as it is a legal rule. But another reason just cause employment seems so exceptional is that, unlike the Rule, it comes in many different flavors. Who decides when it's met? When and how does the employee need to be notified, and what (if any) appeals mechanisms does she have? By opening up a wide range of issues to consider that can, in turn, lead to significant variations in practice, just cause appears fussier and more idiosyncratic than it really is. The At-Will Rule, by contrast, has an appealing simplicity: no reason, no notice, no cost.

Tenure is a version of just cause employment that answers those logistical questions in a relatively consistent way. To be clear, the exact procedures and protections that come with tenure rarely appear in writing at the moment of hiring because most faculty are hired based on an "offer letter" rather than a formal employment contract. (I signed more paperwork before starting my law firm summer internships than I did before starting my tenure-stream faculty jobs.[20]) Still, there are broad commonalities of practice that we can identify.

As with *all* forms of just cause employment, tenure requires an employer to show adequate cause for termination. As with *many* forms of just cause, tenure creates procedural guarantees that must be followed before termination can happen – and that, if they are not followed, may give a fired professor separate grounds for complaint. These protections are granted after a probationary period that usually lasts between five to seven years after a professor is hired into their first faculty job. (The exact length of the "tenure-track" period depends on the discipline and the institution.) During that probationary period, the professor receives a series of single- or multiyear contracts and the university can easily fire her just by refusing to renew her contract. Once tenure is granted, the cycle of contract renewals ends, and the professor is presumed to remain employed in good standing at the university absent circumstances that might call for either her punishment or her termination.

Because of these requirements, a tenured professor has above-average ability to predict *why* (and therefore *when*) she might lose her job. For instance, at the University of Alabama, where I used to work, acceptable reasons for terminating a tenured professor include but are not limited to:

1. Consistent failure to maintain standards of sound scholarship and/or competent teaching;
2. Willful failure to discharge fundamental obligations as a teacher, colleague, and member of the wider community of scholars;
3. Gross neglect of established University obligations appropriate to the appointment...[21]

... and so on. Adequate cause also includes "financial exigency," which is commonly understood as an "imminent financial crisis which threatens the survival of the institution as a whole."[22] I'll revisit this feature of tenure policies in Chapter 22, when we discuss reductions-in-force, which are mass layoffs of university employees including (but not limited to) tenured and tenure-track faculty.

Whether adequate cause for any specific termination arises from individual bad acts or institutional constraints, advance knowledge regarding the range of *possible* causes is, as I've already said, extremely valuable to individuals for material and psychological reasons. Tenured faculty experience very little of the insecurity that plagues at-will employees because they are given advanced notice of the reasons why they might lose their jobs – also, to be sure, because those reasons are generous (note the qualifying words in my example from Alabama: "*willful* failure," "*gross* neglect").[23] Unlike at-will employees, who only know that they have a job until they don't, tenured faculty know that they have a job until and unless they engage in specific kinds of bad behavior.[24] This is the core of what differentiates tenured faculty (as well as other just cause employees) from most American workers.

If these grounds are ever thought to have been met, tenure ensures that specific procedures must be followed before the faculty member can be fired. At Alabama, the Faculty Handbook states that "the University bears the burden of proof that adequate cause exists" and that this will be satisfied by "a preponderance-of-evidence standard."[25] A university-wide Mediation Committee may engage in a substantive review of severe sanctions, or a procedural review "in matters of retention, tenure or promotion."[26] Other universities' policies vary in their specific terms but tend to follow an approach that is fundamentally similar.[27]

Critics often argue that tenure's procedural safeguards are unusual because of who they designate as acceptable participants in these processes, not just because of the processes themselves. In a way that's true: tenured and tenure-track professors are largely evaluated by other professors, not by human resources departments. The importance of peer evaluation in academia is something we'll return to in Chapter 15, but for now, it's simply worth noting that tenure-stream professors are not the only workers who are mostly judged by their peers – far from it. Doctors and lawyers are also largely held to account by other doctors and lawyers. So are barbers and architects. In this respect, as in so many others, tenure-stream faculty are not unique.

What *is* unique about the way professors are employed in the United States is not tenure itself, but the At-Will Rule it modifies. That's why this entire chapter has been dedicated to explaining the Rule and its origins, effects, and powerful influence. It's impossible to understand tenure as an employment protection without understanding what tenure is protecting you *from.*

No other country in the world has a default rule for indefinite employment relationships that creates as much insecurity as the At-Will Rule or that exposes workers to so much potential harm. This in turn means that no other country could – even *theoretically* – need something like tenure to provide professors with a basic modicum of job security. I have to constantly remind myself of this when I speak with colleagues in Britain or Germany, or even in Canada, whose employment law landscape has, unsurprisingly, more in common with the United States than any other country. Notwithstanding any other similarities between the Canadian and American legal systems, or between the American system and that of any other country, the United States begins from a fundamentally different premise compared to its peers: that a perfectly satisfactory worker who has invested a great deal in their education and developed skills that are valuable to their employer (and to others) can still be fired for *good reason, bad reason, or no reason at all.* Tenure exists to counteract this baseline Rule.

6

Origins

One of the things the Humanities and Social Sciences do best is teach people how to ask Why. Why does the world look the way it does, and why can't it be better? Why do small habits or big wars take shape the way they do? And why, having established a default legal principle like the At-Will Rule, would we want to carve out exceptions for certain workers, like university professors?

In other words, *Why did tenure come to be the normative ideal of faculty employment?*

One answer to this question surfaced in Chapter 5 and could apply just as well to the roughly 80% of American workers who are governed by the Rule: most people want some job security and the At-Will Rule affords them none.

More specific answers, keyed to academia, appear in bits and pieces throughout this book – for example, in Chapters 3 and 4 on the realities of pursuing a tenure-stream job, and Chapters 8–11 on academia as a job and the academic labor market. Collectively, these chapters sketch the risk-reward ratio for university faculty, as well as the range and nature of tasks faculty are expected to perform, to show why heightened job security makes sense in this industry. None of these answers rely on the concept of academic freedom, which is the reason most academics themselves think tenure is necessary.

This chapter begins to describe *how* tenure became a dominant industry practice in American universities as yet another way of explaining *why*. Along the way, the chapter discusses academic freedom a little bit more than the rest of the book... but not by much.[1]

That's because appeals to academic freedom have a way of snuffing out everything else. It's hard, if you're remotely interested in the academy, to argue that freedom in teaching or research *doesn't matter* – so hard that I'm not even trying to make that argument. (I wouldn't want to, anyway!) All I'm suggesting in this book is that tenure also matters for reasons that are far more prosaic than either pedagogical or intellectual autonomy. Here and in Chapter 16, I argue that we might be better positioned to see tenure's value as an employment protection if, among other things, our historical understanding of it wasn't so skewed.

What skews conventional histories of tenure? To begin with, observers tend to not go back far enough. Most thumbnail sketches of tenure's origins focus on the period between 1900 and 1940 because of the landmark events that bookend these years. But focusing on this four-decade period has the effect of prioritizing tenure's function as an expressive safeguard at the cost of its value as an employment protection.

In 1900, Stanford University forced the resignation of an economist on its faculty named Edward A. Ross. Ross was vocal about his support for the "free silver" movement and for one of its primary champions, the Democratic presidential candidate William Jennings Bryan. (He was also a noted eugenicist and opponent of Asian immigration.[2]) Ross' public activism so angered Jane Stanford, the sole trustee of Stanford University, that she demanded and ultimately achieved his termination.[3]

It's hard to overstate just how much the shadow of Ross' forced resignation continues to hang over American academia. To this day, many defenses of tenure and academic freedom open with a recitation of his case study. Several use language that is positively epochal to convey its significance, calling the Ross dispute the "catalyst for tenure as we know it,"[4] or "[a]n event that appears to have triggered the process whereby academic freedom became an established idea in the United States."[5] For its part, the Stanford Historical Society modestly claims that "the American version [of tenure] originated at Stanford in 1900."[6]

The Ross scandal was hardly the first or the last dispute of its kind, even at the turn of the century. Edward Bemis was terminated by the University of Chicago in 1895, William Fisher was terminated by Wesleyan University in 1913, Scott Nearing was denied reappointment by the University of Pennsylvania in 1915, and Charles Beard resigned from Columbia University in 1917 to protest the termination of *other* Columbia faculty.[7] There are dozens of other instances, and depending on whose account you believe, all these terminations implicated something we might comfortably recognize as academic freedom today. But despite all these broadly similar events, the Ross scandal remains "one of the most celebrated academic freedom cases in a period when such cases were, unfortunately, relatively frequent."[8] That's because it prompted one of Ross' colleagues, Arthur Lovejoy, to quit Stanford in protest, and to later on found the American Association of University Professors (AAUP), which is the primary professional association of university faculty in the United States.

The AAUP's creation, in turn, helps explain why 1940 is the other bookend of conventional tenure histories. That's the year in which the Association released its *Statement of Principles on Academic Freedom and Tenure*, the document that remains the definitive guide for university tenure practices. Much like the US Constitution to which it's often (and entirely seriously) analogized, the 1940 Statement is remarkably short: even including a set of Interpretive Comments that was published in 1970, the whole thing is less than ten pages long.[9] At the same time – and again like the Constitution – brevity has in no way diminished the "aura of sacrosanctness" surrounding this ostensibly secular document.[10] When your guidelines are sparse, your interpretive abilities must be great. The task of applying the 1940 Statement to specific and changing circumstances has called forth "an exegetical skill that invites comparison with that of gospel hermeneuts and Talmudic scholars."[11]

For the most part, then, this is the history of tenure as it's told today: starting in 1900 with Edward Ross and ending in 1940 with the AAUP's Statement. There's nothing *inaccurate* about this story – nothing wrong in saying, for example, that the formation of the AAUP was overwhelmingly motivated by assaults on academic freedom, or that concerns for academic freedom found expression in the 1940 Statement. But telling the story this way obscures the extent to which important elements of the modern tenure system were motivated by employment concerns and existed before Edward Ross and Jane Stanford ever began to butt heads.

Consider the prehistory of faculty employment contracts, as told by the most prominent historian of tenure, Walter Metzger.[12] Metzger begins by observing that the founders of the first new colleges in the American colonies hoped to replicate the models they knew from England.[13] In other words, the "aim of the charter of Harvard College" – the first college in what would eventually become the United States – "was to fashion one Cambridge after another," while "[t]he influence of Oxford was supremely evident" in the organization of the colonies' second college, William and Mary.[14]

As they worked to create a kind of Oxbridge-in-America, colonial-era college founders were especially anxious to signal the unique and prestigious status of the learned men who would teach at these new institutions. (And, at this point, they *were* all men.) For instance, like their English forebearers, Harvard's instructors received personal and income tax breaks as well as exemptions from military service. They were also granted significant roles – on paper, at least – in the governance of their institution. And, thanks to a combination of what *was* specified in Harvard's charter (termination processes) and what *wasn't* (contractual duration), these instructors were effectively appointed for indefinite periods subject only to removal for cause.[15] Even in 1650 this represented a special deal: the baseline principle of the time was the "English Rule," which stipulated that any relationship without a definite duration at its outset was presumed to last for a year. Before that year was up, neither party could terminate the relationship without legal consequence – but after twelve months, it was a different matter. Harvard's unofficial practice extended that job security past one year.

Unfortunately, despite all these protections and perks, it turned out that being an instructor *in* Cambridge was not at all like being an instructor *at* Cambridge. The new American colleges were poor – *so poor*, writes Metzger, *that [Harvard] could not pay enough to keep its tutors very long or maintain their complement at full strength*.[16] Those instructors, moreover, were young and inexperienced men, "[d]rawn from the latest crop of college graduates,"[17] for whom teaching was just a stepping stone to some more desirable non-academic profession. Hard as it may be to imagine today, the greatest personnel challenge facing an infant Harvard or Yale wouldn't have been the shedding of underperforming or badly behaving instructors: it would have been the retention of instructors whose best prospects lay elsewhere.

When Harvard's administrators abandoned indefinite employment, in 1734, they were almost certainly *not* responding to an overabundance of deadwood or bad actors.[18] Instructors simply did not stay around long enough to become unwanted. Metzger argues that the real advantage of the new three-year contracts that Harvard adopted lay in the *way* they allowed administrators to end work relationships – quietly, through non-renewal, rather than publicly, via a series of divisive and potentially embarrassing administrative hearings. (The messiness of two faculty dismissals under the old system – both on charges of drunkenness! – no doubt confirmed the desirability of these changes in the eyes of administrators.[19]) The new contracts also allowed administrators to treat instructors more like employees who could be evaluated and rewarded with renewal, to "excite tutors from time to time to greater care and fidelity in their work."[20]

But as it happened, fixed-term contracts started showing to disadvantage almost immediately after they were introduced. Beginning in the 1720s, donor funds began pouring into Harvard for the purpose of creating endowed faculty positions. The holders of these new positions were to be called "professors" (unlike the instructional faculty who had preceded them and were called "tutors") and they would receive fancy titles and better pay as well as valuable personal freedoms like the ability to live off campus.[21] Most importantly, professors were exempt from the three-year contract. Instead, and in keeping with the prestige of their new positions, they would be appointed for indefinite periods on the strength of their prominence, or at least their promise, in specific scholarly disciplines.

By 1820, Metzger writes, professors outnumbered other kinds of instructional staff at Harvard and the mix of permanency and prestige they represented became an important part of the college's institutional brand.[22] Nor was Harvard the only institution whose administrators came to see the recruitment and retention value of indefinite appointments. In 1826, for example, Thomas Jefferson used it (unsuccessfully) to try luring the mathematician Nathaniel Bowditch to the University of Virginia.[23] Toward the end of the nineteenth century, universities like Wisconsin and Cornell quietly adopted policies of indefinite employment subject only to administrative removal.[24] In fact, Metzger argues, the trend between 1860 and 1914 was "clearly" *away* from the harshness of fixed-term contracts with no presumption of renewal.[25]

Put simply, over a span of around 250 years, American institutions transitioned from employing faculty on an indefinite basis to giving them fixed-term contracts before returning, by and large, to indefinite employment. They changed, and then they changed back.

… sort of. Nothing is ever really the *same* after the passage of so much time, which means that the indefinite contracts of the 1860s and beyond could not be identical to the indefinite contracts of the 1660s. Arguably, they were worse. In 1650, remember, Harvard's charter required administrators to show cause for termination, which gave instructors some advanced notice if their job was endangered as well as an appeals process if they wanted to resist. By contrast, the professorships that Harvard established from the 1720s onwards carried no such requirements. Even if they had, it would not have helped very much. At a time when the At-Will Rule was sweeping across the country with its seemingly liberating tenets of no notice, no cost, and no reason, courts were willing to accept virtually any grounds for termination from employers and sometimes to accept no grounds at all. (This part hasn't changed very much.) In 1898, a New York state court all but quoted the At-Will Rule in upholding a faculty termination that took place without any pre-dismissal hearings: "The professor may leave at his pleasure; the board may terminate his professorship at its pleasure."[26]

Because of this deference to university discretion, nineteenth-century faculty enjoyed no more formal job security than other at-will employees of the era. True, Metzger admits, "lengthy terms were common, and outright dismissals rare."[27] Individual faculty might well have felt confident on account of their personal accomplishments or relationships or based on nothing more than a deep-seated and legally unwarranted optimism. But as Metzger goes on to note, "without provision for hearings, indefinite tenure offered very little protection to professors who fell from grace."[28] They were wholly subject to the whims of administrators, donors, and legislators: precisely the set of circumstances that gave rise to the Ross scandal and to the other academic freedom disputes of the early twentieth century.

But it is not correct to say, as most histories of tenure do, that those disputes over academic freedom led to the wholesale invention of tenure. In fact, many key legal elements of tenure – indefinite employment terminable for cause – had existed as far back as the founding of Harvard College in 1650. Even though the security of academic employment underwent transformations (and, let's be honest, down-grades) in the years that followed, seventeenth century ideas about why job security matters and how best to provide it remain strikingly recognizable centuries later. Or, as Walter Metzger himself declared, "[i]n all the ages of academic man… the desire to protect the academic office has run strong."[29] Neither the problem nor the solution was invented whole cloth in 1940.

If a "foreshorten[ing]"[30] of the story is the *first* problem with conventional histories of tenure, another set of problems lies in how they treat the 1940 Statement itself. Three interpretive quirks are worth noting.

First, although academics writing about the 1940 Statement sometimes acknowledge that tenure was meant to promote "economic security," this purpose usually falls by the wayside if it even makes it onto the road. But a secondary goal is a goal nonetheless, and the text of the 1940 Statement makes clear that tenure's value derives from more than the way it allows academics to teach, write, and speak without fear of reprisal. "Tenure is a means to certain ends," declares Paragraph Three of the 1940 Statement, "specifically: (1) freedom of teaching and research and of extramural activities and (2) *a sufficient degree of economic security to make the profession attractive to men and women of ability.*"[31] And immediately again: "Freedom and economic security, hence, tenure, are indispensable to the success of an institution in fulfilling its obligations to its students and to society." The 1940 Statement is, after all, where we find the key outlines of tenure as an employment protection. Practices like indefinite appointment, a seven-year probationary period, and a one-year grace period for any candidate who fails to receive tenure are all outlined within its ten pages. Job security only seems crassly materialistic if you don't think – or don't want others to think – that monthly rent payments pose a challenge.

Second, despite many inspiring analogies to constitutions and scriptures, the 1940 Statement is most like a "no trespassing" sign aimed at *employers* – a point first made by Walter Metzger in his detailed analysis of the Statement and its drafting history.[32] The "dos" and "don'ts" of American academia's foundational document aren't addressed to academics themselves, as they might be in a professional code of ethics, and they're also not a statement of self-actualization in the style of a political constitution. They are not even warnings issued to third parties, "against the external power of the state or church (as they are on the European continent, where [scholars] engaged in a historic battle against the [kings] and [religious authorities])."[33] Instead, the 1940 Statement almost exclusively consists of expectations articulated by employees directed at employers concerning the terms and conditions of work. This deep orientation toward the employer–employee relationship is rarely reflected in conversations about the Statement or about tenure itself.

Third and finally, it seems entirely appropriate for us *today* to be guided by employment concerns (especially job security) when reading the Statement and talking about tenure given the broader historical context in which the Statement was drafted. I won't make too much of this last point because prominent historians of tenure, Metzger included, pay no attention to it themselves. Maybe this means that tenure's historians have found little explicit mention of what I'm about to say in the voluminous archive of conference notes, memoranda, and draft statements that document the AAUP's early years as well as the development of the 1940 Statement. But because I firmly believe that academics are no less members of their society and creatures of their time than anyone else, I think this final point still bears mentioning.

Conversations about what would eventually become the 1940 Statement began in 1934 and drafting meetings started in 1937.[34] As any US labor historian will be able to tell you, 1930s America was in the throes of New Deal reforms. The landmark and still operative *National Labor Relations Act* was passed in 1935 to reduce "inequality of bargaining power between employees… and employers."[35] It had been preceded by other labor law statutes, including the *Railway Labor Act* of 1926, the

Norris-LaGuardia Act of 1932, and the *National Industrial Recovery Act* of 1933. And it was followed by the *Fair Labor Standards Act* of 1938, which established a federal minimum wage and standards for overtime pay.

None of this legislative activity targeted academia or spoke to the principal elements of the tenure system that would be established by the 1940 Statement. Nor was the 1940 Statement drafted for courtroom use, as a kind of "shadow legislation" to govern academic labor. Metzger wryly observes that the scarcity of legal training among the Statement's authors and their interest in eliciting better employer behavior through "moral, not legal, prodding" reveals itself via "the authors' failure to consider the legal implications of their language."[36]

Still, labor reform hung thickly in the air those authors were breathing. It would have taken one heck of an ivory tower to insulate the drafters of the 1940 Statement from the attention being paid, everywhere around them, to the reformation of workplace power dynamics. Nothing about the text of the Statement, which is after all directed at university-employers and is at its most detailed when discussing the terms and conditions of academic labor, suggests that this is in fact what happened.[37]

If the history of faculty tenure in the United States tells us anything, it's that ordinary considerations of job security, recruitment, and retention have played a much larger and longer-lasting role in shaping academic employment than is commonly acknowledged. Faculty employment at the founding of America's first college, in 1650, reflected many core legal features of the tenure system that would be articulated, almost three centuries later, by the AAUP's 1940 Statement. To say that tenure exists for the sole purpose of protecting academic freedom, or even that it exists "because of" the academic freedom scandals of the early twentieth century, is to ignore much of the relevant history. It also requires us to believe that, as both human beings and as workers, professors operate in ways that are totally distinct from the people around them. That, as much of this book shows, is downright silly.

7

Multihyphenate

There are teachers and researchers and grant-writers and publishers and editors and guidance counselors and career coaches and human resources professionals and executives. Each of these is a full-fledged job with its own target audience (often, *many* target audiences). Several demand specialized educational credentials, generate distinct professional communities, and operate according to their own evolving best practices.

Then there are professors, who are all these things at once.

Multihyphenation is everywhere. When Paris Hilton and the Harvard School of Design converge on the desirability of something, you *know* that thing has arrived.[1]

Being a multihyphenate, proclaims the journalist Emma Gannon, who literally wrote the book on it, *is about choosing and strategizing a plan of attack and having the freedom to take on multiple projects… [it's] about taking some power back into our own hands.*[2] Gannon tries hard to distinguish the positive, self-realizing, go-with-the-flow-create-your-own-purpose (see what I did there?) lifestyle she's championing from the kind of "insecurity or project overwhelm" that characterizes *most* people who are multihyphenates because they are gig workers. But speaking as someone who has studied both gig workers and the tenured faculty who are in many ways their opposite *and* as someone who can barely sustain the single hyphen floating unconvincingly between her own two disciplinary identities, I want to state for the record that hyphenation is burdensome even when it's pleasurable. It's also burdensome at both ends of the job security spectrum.

One story that's been told about multihyphenation in the academy is that it's on the wane – that the scholar-teacher of popular and professorial imagination no longer exists. Instead, we have some people to teach students, others to advise them, and still more to track their academic progress. We have some people to write books or lead experiments, other people to help them, and more people to coordinate the mountains of paperwork that go into writing books or leading experiments. No longer do professors teach a class in the morning, fiddle with some writing before lunch, meet with students in the afternoon, and then saunter off to a faculty meeting or a scholarly workshop before heading home. The many kinds of tasks that might have once been done by a single someone titled *Professor* are now done by multiple people, some of whom are blithely called Professor by well-meaning students but only one of whom is probably accorded that status by their employer.

The story I've just told is a story about *de*hyphenation. It's about "disassembling the tacit expertise of highly skilled workers into the simplest components," which are then distilled "down to a mechanical sequence that can be delivered far more cheaply by substituting or supplementing low- to middle-skilled labor."[3] It's a story with a villain, whether their villainy is intentional or not (although, in truth, the story's narrators are usually both convinced and convincing on this point). *[U]nbundling is a crucial arrow in the quiver of Gig Academy managers,*[4] write three of the most recent tellers of the dehyphenation story. *By unbundling traditional faculty roles,* they continue, *administrators can assume a greater degree of control over institutional resource flows and reconfigure them to optimize return on investment.*

I can't argue with this story. It is undoubtedly true that we have more single-focus roles within the contemporary university than we did a few decades ago. It's also true that the expansion of these roles benefits universities far more than it benefits the professors who used to simultaneously perform them. (Maybe *also* more than it benefits the students who now experience them.) But I can't help feeling that this is only one of the stories we might tell about who does what in academia today. There's also a second story – one that contradicts but coexists with the one I've just told – and this is a story about burnout and anxiety caused by rampant, explosive multihyphenation.

Consider the three traditional components of a tenure-stream professor's job: teaching, scholarship, and administrative service. Each of these has become more challenging in ways that affect most faculty and that transforms three tasks into five or eight. Each of these traditional components, on its own, exacerbates the phenomenon of multihyphenation.

Teaching, for starters, has become harder. There are lots of students with more needs and with greater variation in what those needs are.

There are lots of students. You're probably wondering how this can be, since one of the most reliable ways that universities have entered the news cycle in recent years has to do with how they're suffering from a *lack* of students. There's the demographic cliff, which leads to an enrollment cliff, which leads to the demise of the university as we know it. It might seem as if there should be a very small and slightly tarnished silver lining to all this: fewer students should mean fewer lessons, fewer assignments, and fewer exams for the professors who remain, right?

It turns out that the relationship between enrollment and workload is more complicated than that. Fewer students going to university doesn't necessarily mean fewer students at all universities, or even fewer students in the classrooms of universities that have implemented reductions-in-force (RIFs). What it often means, instead, is more students in the classrooms that still exist, more students desperate to get into remaining sections of required courses, more students vying for scarce office hour slots, and more students looking for advisors to oversee their independent projects for graduation. You might think you survived, remarks one assistant dean, if you're still around after a RIF. *But let's consider the reality… All the work that those faculty and staff members did now devolves onto those of you remaining at the institution… Your administration is expecting you to do more work for free.*[5]

At universities that implement RIFs, like at all organizations that implement mass layoffs, the sudden loss of coworkers makes survivors feel doubly bad. They feel guilt because their colleagues aren't around while they still are (although who knows for how long). And they also feel envy. *Fine, I have a job*, they say to themselves. *"But now I've got to do your work and my work too. And I'm not going to be able to do either one as well as I used to."*[6] Cliffs or no cliffs, the professors who are left behind are not twiddling their thumbs in front of sparsely populated classrooms. There are, indeed, a lot of students.

This becomes more significant when we consider who might be sitting in those classrooms.

The diversification of the study body is something we mostly discuss in terms of how it affects society (equity-enhancing), industry (creativity-enhancing), students (education- and earnings-enhancing), and university-administrators (headaches). Classroom diversity can do all these things.[7] That's why, with the exception of those administrative complications, we pursue it. But in terms of how it affects faculty, the diversification of the student body is – *as well as* being inspiring, enjoyable, and validating – also workload-enhancing.[8]

Diverse students, as we acknowledge so readily, bring diverse needs that deserve attention. We seem less ready to acknowledge that responding to those diverse needs demands a lot of additional labor from professors. Implementing inclusive syllabi and student-centered learning is about more than revamping a two-or three- (or ten-) page document so that it *[begins] with an engaging course description and [uses] intriguing questions to guide the narrative.*[9] It's not an hour spent and a paragraph added – not, at least, when it's done in any way that's true to the spirit of inclusive and student-centered learning and stands a chance of being recognized as such. Instead, fostering a sufficiently welcoming classroom environment involves *[o]ffering flexibility around assignment and attendance policies* (Stanford[10]), including *materials written or created by people of different backgrounds and/or perspectives* (Michigan[11]), using *a wide variety of instructional strategies that are highly engaging* (Delaware[12]), and providing *chances to improve a score through revision of work* as well as through *lots of low-stakes assessments* (Elon[13]).

Let me be clear: these are reasonable suggestions driven by good intentions in the service of a worthwhile goal. They are also necessary suggestions driven by ground realities. But they involve massive amounts of labor. They involve turning on the proverbial dime because, as Chapter 12 will argue using the example of my

ERISA class, you don't get do-overs for months at a time. And do-overs *will* be necessary because, if you're a tenured professor, you've already spent the better part of two decades figuring out how to do something – teaching – that nobody ever taught you how to do and that is surprisingly hard to master. Now you need to learn a whole new way of doing the same thing and, again, nobody is going to teach you (although you will now have an internet's worth of documents that you can find, read, distill, and implement into your own materials after the dinner dishes are done). On top of all this, the new way of doing things that you must learn is, by design, more difficult for you to execute. More flexibility and variety for students does not exist without more labor by professors: more readings to curate, more low-stakes assessments to grade, more customized deadlines to track, more alternative assignments to craft, monitor, and evaluate.[14]

Congratulations! You've added a hyphen. In addition to being a teacher, you've become a researcher of teaching methods – an expert in pedagogy. This is probably not what you were trained to do and it's probably also not what you are paid to do, both of which likely have more to do with rhetoric or sociology or organic chemistry than with new advances in instructional strategies. But to teach in any way that is responsible and responsive, you *must* research and revise, and you must create three assignments with supplemental readings and floating deadlines where there were previously none.

Compared to teaching, changes in the "scholarship" prong of professorial responsibilities are simultaneously easier and harder to interpret. On the one hand, there is no question that the sheer number of scholarly outputs you must generate to get, keep, and progress in a tenure-stream job has grown exponentially. I discuss the phenomenon of "credential creep" and the resulting "publication explosion" elsewhere in this book, but the punchline is that you must now simply do more *for* and *in* the same job.

Is that, you might find yourself asking, *really* an example of multihyphenation? Does having to do a lot more of the same thing mean you have to do a new kind of thing altogether?

Sometimes it does. Writing an extra three articles or writing most of a second book absolutely involves doing more of the same work. But because you're working on so many different projects and because some of those projects – particularly in the case of books or experiments – may involve different topics or different teams, you're also doing an additional kind of work in the form of project management. If you bake, you know what it's like to juggle multiple dishes with multiple required temperatures, timings, and optimal placements in your oven. (I don't bake, partly because I get enough of this in my work life.) That type of juggling doesn't get any easier when the oven is *you*.

More required scholarship also adds hyphens because everyone is doing what you're doing. In a universe that's powered by peer evaluation, everyone else's *more research* and *more project management* translate into more freely provided peer review labor *by you*. And if you think all this reviewing doesn't add up to another kind of work altogether, consider the dollar figures at issue – or rather, *not* at issue – in Chapter 10. Peer review is labor that has a great deal of monetary value to the academic publishers who request it, and a great deal of value in terms of job security and professional advancement to the individual scholars who depend on it. For the peers who provide all those reviews, this is simply labor that doesn't fit well into any of the three components of the professorial job.

Finally, more scholarship also means different scholarship because some of the additional work is categorically new. "Public scholarship" has been a thing for long enough now that it's more presumed than provocative. Don't get me wrong: I agree with the view that scholars should translate their knowledge for a general audience and I think the process can be a lot of fun. This book reflects both those beliefs. But writing newspaper columns or op-eds, appearing on or producing podcasts, maintaining blogs or active social media feeds, giving regular television interviews – all the things that fall under the category of "public scholarship" – represent a type of work that, until recently, only a tiny handful of professors expected, or *were* expected, to do.

That is no longer the case. It's no longer politically correct to be uninterested in reaching outside the academy because indifference reads as insularity and draws universal fire. Declarations of public-scholarliness now abound in job application materials, where their presence should be understood as reasonable market-driven behavior as much as principled aspiration. And not only does the requirement to produce for external as well as internal audiences add a whole new type of work to the scholarship part of the job, it also calls for the development of a brand new set of skills. After all, scholarship-for-scholars isn't only considered inaccessible because it's often literally sequestered behind a paywall. It's also considered inaccessible because, as Chapter 11 discusses, it's often hard to understand. Figuring out how to say the same complicated things using less complicated terminology with short paragraphs and catchy titles is like figuring out how to speak a whole new language. That's why more *is* more – but more is *also* different.

The final traditional component of a professor's job, service, deserves a book in its own right and has probably generated a few. It's officially allotted the least amount of a professor's time. According to the "40/40/20" model – a model that's regularly spoken of as if it's long dead, but that seems to enjoy a remarkably active afterlife – according to this model, 40% of one's time should be devoted to research, 40% to teaching, and 20% to administrative or service tasks. In a normative forty-hour work-week, this translates to eight working hours, or around one day per week, spent on service. But what counts as "service"?

At some point, *service* was probably understood to mean that professors would make time for the occasional disciplinary committee hearing or periodic university senate vote. Chapter 15 discusses the ethos of peer evaluation behind these self-governance activities to show how it touches virtually everything professors do, and not necessarily in ways that advantage them. But professors now do far more than serve on the occasional committee or attend the occasional meeting and, as Chapter 15 also notes, these heightened service requirements have been accompanied by decreased functional authority. More talk, less say.

Today, what counts as service has become a complicated question because there are too many possible answers. One junior academic reflected on how their twenty percent service allotment was expected to account for external roles "such as editorships, reviewing, external examining, conference organizing, roles in professional societies," internal roles like "Senate, Court, Academic Committee, etc," and other activities, including "contributing presentations to research seminars, attending research seminars, attending and supporting staff-student social events, interviewing applicants."[15] Another academic who served in an editorial capacity for a scholarly journal spent their entire twenty percent allotment on that task alone – but, perhaps obviously, expected and received no exemptions from other kinds of service work.[16] Two professors who decided to track their time according to the 40/40/20 model realized that they "often went far over the eight-hour mark" and, furthermore, that "the various, interconnected aspects of service made it the hardest category of work to track, plan for, and anticipate." So they created a wholly new category with which to track their time, Administrative Tasks & Email, but found that it ate up 12% to 25% of their workweek *on its own.*[17]

There's heaps of clear evidence that academia requires far more service of far more types than can be accomplished in eight hours per week. Higher ed observers have occasionally responded to this reality by proposing alternatives to the 40/40/20 split – say, 40/25/35 or, conversely, 60/30/10. And yet, the original model stubbornly survives. I recently read about efforts by the education faculty of an Australian university to revise the 40/40/20 model as it applied to them. After a negotiation process with their administrative leaders that generated proposals ranging anywhere from 50/30/20 to 70/15/15 and even to 80/20/0, the faculty found themselves, five years later, right back where they had started: 40/40/20.[18]

The fact that 80/20/0 – *zero* percent time spent on service tasks – could even be a sincere proposal underscores the extent to which all this labor that is wanted and needed by universities and students counts for very little that's positive but a whole lot that's negative. Consider, as just one example, the following excerpts from the faculty handbook that currently applies to me:

Emory Law Faculty Handbook §III(D) (2017)
[Criteria up to and including the award of tenure]

Service is an important consideration for appointment and promotion. However, **service should be viewed as a supplement to, not a substitute for scholarship or teaching.** It is expected that both scholarship and teaching contributions will be weighted significantly and that **service contributions will not be the primary basis for awarding tenure or promotion.**[19]

Emory Law Faculty Handbook §III(G) (2017)
[Criteria for promotion to full professor]

Service should be viewed as a supplement to, not a substitute for, scholarship or teaching. It is expected that both scholarship and teaching contributions will be weighted significantly and that **service contributions will not be the primary basis for awarding promotion.**[20]

You'll never get tenure or be promoted on the strength of your service. You might be *denied* these things on the grounds that your service is lacking. In fact, pre-tenure faculty at many research-oriented universities would be better off – and more rational, in the language of classical economics – if they *saw* 40/40/20 but *read* 80/20/0. No one else would probably be happy. But the professor would almost certainly get tenure.

Part of the problem, then, is that there are too many types of service in need of doing to fit within a twenty percent allotment that won't budge. But *another* problem is in who does the service and who notices. Women do more service measured both as "the number of activities… and in the amount of time spent on such activities" and, furthermore, this "service differential is driven particularly by participation in internal rather than external service."[21] That last observation matters because not all service is equally respected, to the extent that it is respected at all. Internal service is service that amounts to "taking care of the academic family"[22] – it's more daily drudgery than flattering invitation. We should be simultaneously saddened and unsurprised that women do more of it. And much of what is true for female faculty is, moreover, true for other minority and minoritized professors as well.[23]

Faculty who are women, who are Black, who are part of some other minority or minoritized community, are responsible for a disproportionate percentage of student contact hours outside the classroom. In fact, pretty much anyone who's not a cis, straight, white, politically center-left man who grew up with college-educated parents will probably find themselves offering advice and support to students who are not taking their classes or writing their papers, students who have approached them for help because of what they *are* rather than what they *do*.

This is because America's student population is diversifying faster than its professoriate.[24] Most current tenure-stream professors are likely to be cis, straight, white, politically center-left men who grew up with college-educated parents. They're not the ones minority students reach out to. They're not the ones university administrators count on to improve retention rates. And, consequently, they're not the ones who regularly find themselves advising and consoling students who aren't their students at all. The cultural or minority "tax" paid by non-normative professors doesn't even rise to the level of a *regressive* tax because it doesn't extract in a nominally equal way from all potential taxpayers.[25]

The normative white, male professor also doesn't find himself *assigned* extra service work by his employer *because of* his demographic markers. Many of his colleagues do. Sometimes, that extra work is motivated by well-meaning attempts at self-improvement: task forces charged with studying and improving gender equity on campus are, for instance, often staffed by the very female faculty they're supposed to be helping and therefore end up overburdening those faculty even more.[26] Sometimes, though, service assignments are little more than virtue-signaling.[27] I was once told during a job interview that I could expect to be immediately seated on several university-level task forces despite the customary practice of shielding first-year professors from significant administrative service. It's a testament to the privilege I've enjoyed throughout my life that this has only happened to me *once* – and that, when it did happen, I didn't immediately understand why.

Now, I do think administrators are often caught in a difficult position when it comes to committee assignments. It's troubling and risky to have a white professor opine on campus diversity issues that may not affect her. But it's tokenizing and extractive to have a Black professor opine on campus diversity issues that may affect her. And yet, *somebody* has to sit on that committee and opine. The problem is that, more often than not, the Black professor is the one who's likely to end up doing this work, and yet the work she does instead of her white colleague won't help her get tenure, promotion, or anything else that might be valuable to her personally. The problem is also that "[B]lack, Latinx and Asian professors are disproportionately entering academe" – and attending committee meetings and drafting memos – "just as publication standards and expectations to secure tenure-track jobs are rising."[28] So every committee meeting that Black professor must attend is an hour or two less that she has to meet the heightened tenure requirements that she and her white colleagues will both face.

Minority faculty are not the only multihyphenates in academia. True, the *severity* of their hyphenation is likely greater both in breadth (the number of different roles they're asked to inhabit) and in depth (the burden of each individual role). But the underlying problem is not unique to them. And, conversely, tenure-stream faculty – regardless of demographic characteristics – are not the ones who are most negatively affected by multihyphenation. Nontenure-track faculty bear similar burdens in return for even less money, job security, and respect.

Still, hyphenated existence isn't limited to either minority or NTT faculty. Discussing the burdens of multihyphenation overwhelmingly in the context of these marginalized groups, as most current commentary does, has the unfortunate effect of reinforcing inaccurate stereotypes about lazy tenure-stream professors. It doesn't help improve anyone's understanding of what contemporary academic life is like. We need to be able to acknowledge the ways in which *all* faculty are stretched too thin across too many hyphens without dismissing the greater stretch that's experienced by some.

Multihyphenation adds multiple roles to what was once (perhaps) a three-part job. It doesn't only require academics to do more of the same. It also requires them to do more *kinds* of things and often, as in the case of teaching, to do more *harder* kinds of things. Now this, by itself, wouldn't justify faculty tenure. (Let's momentarily set aside the ridiculousness of having to justify job security for anyone; as Chapter 5 explained, the default assumption in the United States, which is that you can quit or be fired for good reason, bad reason, or no reason at all, means that *anything* better than a life spent peering into the abyss does seem to call for explanation.) If it were only that faculty were being asked to do more, that would be one thing. Neoliberalism does bad stuff to almost everyone. If it were even only that faculty were being asked to do more for less, that would be something else, although it would still not be very striking.

What justifies tenure as an employment protection is both the severity of the multihyphenation faculty experience *and* the Catch-22 it creates for them. Without the job security offered by tenure, faculty could either try to simultaneously inhabit all their assigned roles (and lose their jobs because they can't) or try to sequentially inhabit those roles (and lose their jobs because they do). Chapters 12 and 23 further explain how the kind of multihyphenation that is wanted by students and needed by administrators can't and doesn't happen without the security and resources tenure offers. What justifies tenure as an employment protection is, finally, how the multihyphenation I describe here intersects with the *other* phenomena I describe in the next few chapters, all of which are poorly understood outside academia but are widely acknowledged within it.

8

…Choosers

In 2015, the *New York Times* ran an article with the headline, "The Typical American Lives Only 18 Miles From Mom."[1] The authors opened by noting that their analysis upended a commonly held belief that Americans are a "rootless" people, perpetually searching for better opportunities. Earlier that year, *The Atlantic* had also published an article that began by noting that "stories of migration are a big part of the [American] narrative."[2] But *The Atlantic* went on to note that, in reality, Americans value staying put so highly that "only 46 percent… of those who thought that their local area was headed in the wrong direction… said that the possibility of a move was at all likely."

In the years since these articles appeared, more studies have suggested that Americans often choose to live near home – *and* that this preference is one of the rare qualities that exists across generations. In 2023, the online marketplace LendingTree reported that 62% of respondents in its 2,000-person survey of Millennials and Gen Zers live near their parents, while 57% actually live in their hometowns. Americans are homebodies, the research seems to tell us. Americans like living near Mom.[3]

Research also suggests that when Americans *do* move far away, they do so because they can afford to. "Wealthier people can afford to pay for services like child and elder care," noted the original *Times* article, "while low-income families are more likely to rely on nearby relatives."[4] This seemingly benign descriptive statement carries a powerful subtext: even if staying near Mom is a preference – and it apparently is, even for wealthier folks[5] – moving away from her is a privilege.

In a universe where everyone wants you to stay near home and yet assumes that leaving is cause for congratulations, academics lose twice. We almost never stay at home, or even within a reasonable flight or car ride's distance from home. And when we move the first, second, or seventh time, it is not necessarily because we've hit the professional jackpot. Academics usually move because they *have* to: because jobs are rare, are limited to the specific institutional setting of universities, and (as Part Four of this book shows) because those jobs are not nearly as stable as most people, including academics themselves, believe. The vast majority of academics – those who aren't superstars or in select high-demand fields – go where they must, when they must, and whether or not they really want to.

This tends to make our holidays even more tension-filled than average.

> "When are you moving back home?"
> "Why can't you get a job at [Nearby University]? You've got a fancy degree!"
> "But do you *want* to live all the way over there?"

Finding a faculty job in academia is wholly unlike finding a job outside it. The PhD student or post-doc who is aiming for a tenure-track job must prioritize the job they want, wherever it may appear. The aunt, cousin, or high school classmate asking the question probably prioritized the place they wanted to live, then focused on finding the most suitable job available there. I don't think either approach is inherently superior, but one of them is far more common in the general workforce. This is why frustrated academics and their befuddled relatives continue to butt heads during holiday gatherings. When most Americans live near home and even more would *like* to live near home, it's hard to understand people who seemingly choose to stay away yet are disgruntled about that fact.

Behind all this mutual incomprehension is a descriptive truth. American academics live where they do because they are limited to a few, geographically dispersed, institutional employers who seek highly specialized employees.

Let's unpack that.

Start with the bit about "institutional employers." Some of the changes roiling higher education might make it seem like universities are no longer the only places where complex research and advanced instruction take place. Truthfully, they never were: the federal government and private industry have long been powerhouses in all kinds of research – although, to be sure, the federal government appears to be shifting its priorities. Still, it remains the case that learning has always occurred in all kinds of contexts. The rise of open online education providers like Coursera and Udemy means that now even traditional college subjects ("Shakespeare 101") can be learned outside traditional college classrooms. And the proliferation of privately funded research institutes that hire PhDs means that professors no longer have a monopoly on the production of scholarship, even in humanities and social sciences disciplines where governmental and industry opportunities are arguably rarer.

Those were a lot of *Yes, buts…* now here's my claim: it's still hard to be a professor without a university. For the most part, you can only access students (to teach), colleagues (to work with), time, equipment, databases, and money (to conduct research), and entry into the conferences and associations that represent your professional community if you are employed by a university. Academia, in other words, is a heavily institutionalized industry. You can't hang your own shingle or start your own practice. You *could* teach or research via some of the avenues I mentioned earlier, but if you do, society is unlikely to recognize you as a "professor" and you will not have the career path associated with one. You will be a freelance scholar, a writer, a public intellectual, a scientist or some other kind of researcher – or all of these at once – but you will not be a professor.

If you want to be a professor, you must find a specific type of employer – a university – who will hire you to be one. This fact alone differentiates academics from many of their professional peers. A majority of doctors may be "directly employed by hospitals or by integrated delivery systems"[6] but you don't have to be hired by an HMO to be a doctor, and depending on your specialty, you also don't have to be hired by a hospital or even have admitting privileges at one. It's rare, but it's possible. You don't have to work at a large law firm to be a lawyer: you could work at medium or small firms, or start your own practice, or work for the government or for a wide range of companies. You don't have to work at the Big Four (or *any* accounting firm) to be an accountant. You don't have to work at someone else's architecture firm to be an architect. And so on.

...but you do have to work at a university to be a professor.

This becomes a problem, thanks to two other constraints impacting the academic labor market: universities are few in number and geographically dispersed, and academic hiring is subject to extreme but mostly necessary levels of specialization.

I know that it may seem strange for me to say that there aren't many colleges and universities in the United States. India and Indonesia have more, it's true, but the USA isn't exactly hurting for institutions of higher education.[7] According to the National Center for Education Statistics, as of 2021, there were nearly 4,000 two- and four-year colleges around the country; according to *U.S. News*, around 1,400 of them were at least regionally accredited schools offering four-year degrees to more than 200 students.[8]

But "1,400 universities" doesn't make for a dense labor market. Consider this: there are dozens – and very likely hundreds – of law firms in Atlanta, Georgia, where I currently live. In fact, there are enough law firms here that the *Atlanta Business Chronicle* publishes a list of the fifty largest Atlanta firms ranked by number of attorneys.[9] There are also thirty-five law firms in the "100% Club" of the Atlanta Bar Association, meaning that there are at least thirty-five firms with five or more attorneys who are all registered members of the Atlanta Bar.[10] Five law firms based in Atlanta are on the elite "Am Law 100" list, which is a way of saying that five of the country's biggest law firms are headquartered in Atlanta, while thirty-one Am Law 100 firms have offices in this city.[11] And none of this accounts for the innumerable medium and small firms, solo practices, government jobs, or major corporate opportunities to practice law that exist in and around the Atlanta metro. As of 2022, Atlanta is home to nineteen Fortune 500 companies, including Coca-Cola, Home Depot, Delta, and UPS, each of whom will employ at least some in-house lawyers. Altogether this means that there are *tens of thousands* of chances to practice law in Atlanta alone.

There are, by comparison, just five law schools in the entire state of Georgia. If you don't get hired by one of them, you are not going to be a law professor *in this state.* You will need to leave Georgia to have the job you want. You will need to move to another place, uproot any partner, children, or dependent parents you may have, sell your house (if you have one), and haul your family and your belongings to a place where there *is* a law school that wants to hire you. And just like you couldn't choose to stay in Georgia, you can't choose where you will go once you leave. This is what it means to compete in an industry that is both highly institutionalized and geographically dispersed.

With its five American Bar Association-accredited law schools, Georgia is neither the smallest market for legal academia nor the largest. The city of Los Angeles alone has five ABA-accredited law schools (California has eighteen), while New York City has nine ABA-accredited law schools (New York State has fifteen). By contrast, there are fourteen states that have just one ABA-accredited law school each.[12] Despite this relatively middle-of-the-road status, there are only five potential employers for aspiring law professors in Georgia, as compared to Atlanta's hundreds of potential employers for aspiring lawyers.

Between them, Georgia's five law schools have roughly 140 tenure-stream faculty.[13] But that doesn't mean there are 140 chances to be a law professor in Georgia. On the contrary, aspiring law professors can probably count the number of jobs available to them in this state on just one hand. That's because academic hiring is done based on teaching and research specialties that drastically narrow an applicant's odds of success.

Take me, for instance. For the purposes of law school hiring, I am considered a labor and employment law scholar. (I also have an extensive research background in Indian constitutional law, but so far this has rarely figured in decisions to hire me.) In law school, I was advised to cultivate an area of expertise so that prospective employers would know how I would fit in with their existing faculty. I chose labor and employment law because it combined issues that were interesting to me with research questions that might benefit from my anthropological training. I took all the labor and employment law courses that were offered at my school, wrote research papers for those courses whenever possible, published some of those papers as articles when I was a post-graduate fellow, and designed and taught labor and employment law classes before I went on the academic job market. On the curious little "biodata" form used by law school hiring committees, I ranked labor and employment law courses highest among my preferred teaching subjects.[14] In other words, I branded myself because I was (correctly) told that I had to.

Within the ecosystem of Emory Law, I'm now one of two tenure-stream faculty who fill the unofficial "labor and employment" slot. At most law schools, there is just one tenure-stream faculty member teaching labor and employment law courses. *Maybe* two, as at Emory. Many law schools have none at all. Despite its centrality to everyday life, labor and employment law is not a particularly high-demand field of study and it's also not a subject that's tested on the bar examinations that students must pass to become practicing attorneys. As a result, it's a relatively niche scholarly area. Although most law schools will offer at least one of the four traditional classes – Labor Law, Employment Law, Employment Discrimination Law, and Employee Benefits Law – many rely on nontenure-track faculty, some of whom are moonlighting attorneys, to teach that class, whichever one it is, on an ad hoc basis. Having two tenure-stream faculty on staff, as we do at Emory, is considered a mildly impressive commitment to the subject area.

Georgia's overall 140 tenure-stream positions among five law schools thus translate into, at most, ten positions that are unofficially dedicated to labor and employment law. Realistically, the number is less than half that since many schools do not hire any tenure-stream faculty in this area. It is, moreover, impossible to know when any of those five or so slots will open up thanks to retirements, relocations, or deaths. When I first applied for faculty positions in 2017, the number of Georgia law schools interested in hiring a labor and employment law scholar was zero. (I checked.) When I interviewed for my current job in 2022, that number was one and they hired me.

One job in an entire state.

By comparison, Alston & Bird, one of Atlanta's largest law firms, has around seventeen attorneys specializing in labor and employment law.[15] Seventeen is not a huge number, but it reflects the staffing of just one representative (Alston) of one type of employer (large law firms) in one city (Atlanta) within Georgia. A lot of labor and employment law practice is handled by small- and mid-sized firms, some of whom are wholly dedicated to this practice area, so Alston's seventeen-person bench doesn't represent the best odds an aspiring labor and employment attorney has of working in their chosen specialty in a law firm. Besides, there are other ways to practice labor and employment law while living in Georgia, or even in Atlanta, other than working for a law firm. You could practice labor and employment law while working as in-house counsel for a company or as an attorney for the government at municipal, state, or federal levels. But there is only *one* way to be a labor and employment law professor.

This is a good moment to return to that "descriptive truth" I announced a while back: American academics live where they do because they are limited to a few, geographically dispersed, institutional employers who seek highly specialized employees.

Again, all of this is true and it explains why you can't tell your aunt at Diwali or Christmas that, "Yes, I'll move back to Atlanta in a few years to be a law professor." You can't know. In fact, the only thing you *can* know about the job market, if you are an aspiring professor, is that you don't know where it will take you – or, in fact, if it will take you anywhere.

But something that my handy, one-line declaration does *not* convey is any sense of how supply and demand dynamics impact the academic job market. Put simply, where you live and work – and your helplessness in making those choices as an academic – aren't just determined by the kind of employer you're pursuing: they're also determined by the number of people pursuing that same employer alongside you.

I think the problem of oversupply is important but somewhat misunderstood. There are many industries where the supply of aspiring and eligible workers poorly matches demand – more and more such industries, in fact, if we are to believe reports about the availability of primary care physicians, pediatricians, schoolteachers, long-haul truckers, and artificial intelligence experts, among others.[16] Academia is not the only industry experiencing or failing to resolve this problem.

But it's also unquestionably true that universities and senior faculty have little incentive to downsize their production of doctorates and post-docs for the reasons discussed in Chapter 22. Graduate students and post-docs supply cheap labor that lightens the load for tenure-stream faculty; this both helps those tenure-stream faculty (who can be spread a little less thin given the escalating demands of teaching, scholarship, and service discussed in Chapter 7) and it helps administrators (who can phase out costly tenure-stream professors in favor of less expensive nontenure-track faculty). Neither of these groups has any strong motivation to reduce the number of aspiring academics.

If doctoral programs really were as focused on the training of future professors as they claim to be, they would be more responsive to "swings" in the academic labor market. (I've used scare quotes in that sentence because, as many observers of higher ed will tell you, there *are* no swings in the demand for tenure-stream professors: there is only one long slide downwards.) PhD admissions *have* been subjected to some downward adjustments in recent years. But the severity of the downturn in available tenure-stream jobs has not been matched by the downturn in PhD admissions. For that to happen, entire programs would need to shut down. Multiple universities would need to stop producing PhDs altogether. The fact that this hasn't happened – not nearly as much as you'd expect, anyway – shows that larger cohorts are doing something valuable for universities, and that something is independent of producing future professors.

As matters stand, the numbers involved in any supply/demand analysis of academic labor are just… terrifying. The American Historical Association reports, for instance, that 1,799 history doctorates were granted in 2019 and 2020.[17] During those same two years, there were, at most, enough open tenure-track or tenured jobs for around a quarter (479) of those new historians. But, as with labor and employment law specialists on the legal academic market, the story doesn't end there. If we drill down further, during the 2020–2021 history hiring cycle (when many of those 2019 and 2020 graduates would be searching for tenure-stream jobs) just *twelve* positions called for an Africanist, *ten* for a Europeanist, and only *four* positions – nationally – prioritized the "ME/NA" (Middle East/North Africa) region. I don't know how many aspiring historians who received their doctorates in 2019 and 2020 were ME/NA specialists, but I can confidently guarantee you that it was more than four or even several multiples thereof. Once you add in thematic or temporal requirements – "a focus on Indian Ocean trade" or "the Islamic world before 1800" – several 2019 and 2020 graduates may have found themselves ineligible to apply for *any* job.

History, moreover, is no worst-case scenario, even if hiring in History has by some accounts been doing unusually badly of late. Seen from one angle, at least, historians enjoy a kind of security that's available to few other Humanities or Social Science scholars because their discipline is still considered less dispensable than, say, anthropology or comparative literature. The jobs-to-candidates ratio that looks bleak for aspiring ME/NA history professors is probably only now approaching the ratio faced by their anthropology peers. "[I]t feels bad on the ground," said one post-doc in anthropology, before explaining that she (rightly) considered herself fortunate for having landed a tenure-track job within just three years of trying… three years and "120 applications, 25 Zoom interviews, 12 campus interviews, and 3 postdoc interviews" of trying.[18]

This is why observers increasingly compare tenure-track academia to celebrity professions like elite athletics or arts. (The comparison to elite athletics, in particular, is an old one: observers of higher education made the connection between tenure-stream academia and professional sports at least as early as 1988![19]) The odds of making it in academia aren't yet *quite* as bad as the odds in these other industries: any given PhD graduate probably has a 10% to 25% chance of landing a tenure-track job, while high school football players may only have a 6.5% chance of entering collegiate athletics and around 5% of working Hollywood actors attend the Oscars each year.[20] But we're getting there.

You might think these dismal numbers would be enough to scare people off, but human optimism is stubbornly buoyant. After all, the far worse odds of making it in the arts or sports have never been enough to scare off aspiring actors or athletes. And, just like there are self-interested reasons why existing professors and administrators might want to overproduce aspiring academics, there are ways in which this over-production benefits *nonacademics* like students, parents, and the general citizenry.

It would be nearly impossible to generate the "one every few years" kind of supply that is, realistically speaking, all that's required for many academic specialties in many regions – like, for instance, for labor and employment law faculty in Georgia. Professional reproduction isn't quite like biological reproduction: the mechanisms that make it possible won't continue to exist if you only use them at infrequent intervals. Advisors get busy, develop new interests, retire, move, and die; courses needed to learn the subject matter become less frequently offered; conferences and journals that provide valuable professionalization and scholarly feedback wither and close for lack of membership. In academia, to a certain degree, you need to use it or lose it.

Moreover, few people who are interested in higher education are willing to tolerate a state of chronic undersupply. For example, over the last few years, law schools around the country have been desperate to hire environmental law scholars. This is first and foremost a response to growing student demand – which, in turn, is *somewhat* responsive to growing workforce demand. (It's also, if I'm honest, probably driven by law schools' wanting to ensure that they have a seat at the table for prestigious and accelerating policy discussions about climate change.) But because there are currently so few legal scholars who have environmental law expertise, and because the timeline for training new ones – the gestational period, so to speak – is really long, existing environmental law professors have been playing musical chairs between law schools that are trying to outbid one another for the privilege of hiring them. This is good for those professors, assuming they are able to take advantage of their sudden desirability by hopping from school to school as better opportunities arise. It's not so good for students or administrators who must either do without environmental law training or pay a premium to get it. The same phenomenon is now unfolding with respect to artificial intelligence and the law, where the undersupply is even more severe.

This kind of job-hopping is unusual in most corners of academia: law faculty seem to move more than many. That tendency to stay put is not a good thing for academics themselves because leaving your employer is a surprisingly important part of growing your career. (And I'm not just saying this as a member of a generation, Millennials, that's widely believed to engage in excessive job-hopping.) By and large, labor economists view early career job mobility as crucial for increasing lifetime earnings.[21] They also generally hold that changing jobs *later* in your career is likely to harm you.[22] The problem is that both choosing to leave and choosing to stay require a degree of individual agency that usually isn't available in academia.

The dynamics I've discussed in this chapter – high institutionalization, high specialization, geographic spread, and a bleak jobs-to-candidates ratio – are why I've come to think of the academic labor market as quasi-monopsonistic in nature. I say *quasi*-monopsonistic because there is, of course, more than one buyer for professorial labor – there are 1,400 or 4,000, or even more, depending on how you choose to draw the circle. Academia is by no means a true monopsony. Nevertheless, the buyers of academic labor are so few in number relative to the sellers, and they have such gatekeeping power over entrance to the industry, *and* they are so thinly dispersed across regions that they are able to function in monopsonistic ways.

This is not my idea, nor is it a new idea. Thirty years ago, an article published in the *American Economic Review* observed that universities can engage in "monopsonistic salary discrimination" that produces "a negative relationship between seniority and salary" in violation of standard expectations about wage patterns over a working life.[23] Translated, this means that whereas it usually pays to accrue seniority with a specific employer, it does not pay in academia.[24] The *AER* study found that this negative relationship between seniority and salary couldn't be explained by professors' "publication records, education, and experience" – in other words, it wasn't just that only low-performing or less-credentialed professors were staying put.[25] What likely explained the unusual pattern in academia, the article concluded, was the exceptional difficulty of switching university-employers. If leaving your employer is so hard that it probably means leaving your industry, odds are that you will stay put for less and worse.

This monopsonistic quality is the first of several reasons why I think tenure still makes sense for *employment* reasons. For all that universities say about the financial burden of committing to a single professor for two, three, or four decades, that professor is effectively – though perhaps unknowingly – committing to the university, too. Tenure functions as a kind of ballast, evening the risk distribution between professors and the universities that employ them. Chapters 10 and 11 explore other reasons why tenure is warranted on employment grounds. But first, the next chapter takes a short detour to consider how the dynamics of the academic labor market affect one specific subset of professors who have their own peculiarly heightened concerns.

9

Two Bodies

In a deeply personal book, this chapter is the most personal of all. I am the child of a dual academic couple, and I am one-half of one, too. When I was planning this book, I thought I would interview other academic couples to ask them about their experiences negotiating shared careers in our shared industry.[1] But I changed my mind when one of my oldest friends told me that the process of navigating academia with their spouse had proven so traumatizing to them both that they could not relive it. I worried that the same thing might be true of others who had, out of affection, been hesitant to refuse me. Consequently, this part of the story is one that I will tell without any guest stars.

For me, what it means to be part of a dual-academic couple begins with my parents.

My parents worked in cognate disciplines, marketing and management, which meant that they could sometimes collaborate on research and they were often each other's first sounding boards. They had grand debates over the breakfast table that I didn't always understand but loved watching anyway. We often attended conferences together, all three of us, and they would take turns going to panels or disappearing to present their papers while I luxuriated in unrestricted TV time and a little evening sightseeing. And I distinctly remember going through a phase, around age eight or nine, when I loved to answer phone calls asking for "Dr. Das, please?" by chirping back "*Which* Dr. Das?!"

I knew that, more often than not, the caller was asking for my father. He occasionally had administrative roles at his university and he also disliked working in his on-campus office, so the odds of someone trying to get a hold of him at home were always higher. But it felt slyly feminist and very witty (I was eight…) to remind whoever was calling that *both* my parents held doctorates and were professors, and it made me feel a little burst of pride in our family every time I did it.

I still feel that pride in my parents and our family. But now I also know that this aspect of my life – having two tenured-professor parents who were able to share a house for their entire professional lives – is yet another way in which my experience of academia is unusual. Somehow, my parents and I had escaped the two-body problem.

The "two-body problem" is shorthand for the career coordination struggles faced by academics who are romantically involved.[2] Specifically, it refers to the difficulty of getting two secure academic jobs in the same city, county, or even the same state so that you *can* share a house and a life and maybe even some children.

I recognize that coordinating careers is tricky regardless of the industries you and your partner work in. The *Harvard Business Review* dedicated an entire "Spotlight Series" to the topic.[3] I also know that a version of the two-body problem exists in many industries that, like academia, are characterized by high degrees of occupational endogamy. Doctors often marry other doctors, lawyers often marry other lawyers… academics aren't unique in this respect, either.[4] Assortative mating, which is the scholarly term for partnering with someone you share significant similarities with, is a well-studied sociological and biological phenomenon. It's a particularly well-documented phenomenon among elite workers like doctors, lawyers, and professors. And why not? When you spend your young adult life in high-intensity educational and professional environments – environments defined by long hours, odd hours, frequent travel, and maybe frequent relocation, to say nothing of highly technical vocabulary and expertise – it often becomes easier to have a companionate marriage if your companion is also your colleague.

Not everyone feels this way, of course. One of my graduate school friends wanted to keep her professional and personal lives separate, so she was very happy to marry someone with no connection whatsoever to academia. But some people – like myself – *want* to blur those boundaries, while others just find it difficult to do anything else. A recent report on academic coupling found that over one third (36%) of the professors who were surveyed had academic partners.[5] And that's when things get complicated.

Finding two academic jobs in the same place isn't just twice as hard as finding one. It's exponentially harder. In small cities or college towns, it means you are expecting a single employer who hires new employees approximately as often as most people buy cars or houses to simultaneously hire not one but *two* new people. Even in bigger cities, you're hoping that two out of four or five possible employers will want to hire the two very specific types of employees that you and your spouse represent, and that they will want to do this at the exact same moment. And don't get me started on what happens to an academic couple where both parties occupy many of the same research and teaching categories – say, by studying different aspects of post-War German history – because these folks are effectively trying to sell *two of the same* employee to those infrequently hiring potential employers.

The odds are near zero that opportunities for both partners will naturally arise in the same place in the same year. The year I interviewed for my current position at Emory, none of Georgia's five law schools were hiring in my husband's fields of criminal law or legal history. To my knowledge, this has not changed since we moved to Atlanta. If Emory had not hired him, he would have been forced out of academia, dealing a blow to both our finances and our happiness. If Emory had not hired him, we would not have accepted their offer to me. This phenomenon – the "spousal hire" – is a feature of academia that invites particularly strong feelings, including from academics themselves.[6]

"I think about every tiny incremental advantage people can have," said a professor at a private university whose wife wasn't an academic. "Being married is not at all like publishing an extra book or article. I would hate to imagine how many times I've lost a job to a spouse."[7] "[I]f you start a buddy system, it just looks bad," said another professor, "even if there's nothing wrong with the people involved."[8] To a third critic, spousal hires act as internal double agents. Institutions that hire couples risk having them "voting together on tenure cases and other departmental issues, sharing information between programs, and diluting or otherwise altering one another's positions."[9]

I understand their reservations (although, particularly in the last case, I don't agree with them).[10] The academic job market is hard – *brutal, crushing,* and *devastating* are all adjectives that can be used to describe it without the least bit of hyperbole. You might understand, at an intellectual level, that a job created for a spousal hire is a job that likely wouldn't have existed if not for that spousal candidate. But this isn't how you feel when you see two people get hired by a university where there was only one advertised position and where you could have happily imagined yourself working for decades.

(For similar reasons, I'm sympathetic to aspiring academics who rail against retirement-resistant senior faculty on the theory that those faculty are "holding" available tenure-stream jobs. By now, I think that many of us in academia understand that this critique is misguided because the senior scholar's job is likely destined to be disaggregated into several nontenure-track positions after its current occupant retires. A tenure-stream appointment isn't what's being "held" at all. But it's hard to remember this when you're staring at unemployment and an involuntary exit from your chosen profession.)

A dislike of spousal hires is even more understandable because the United States is built on highly individualistic notions of merit and agency that conflict with the idea of employing someone in order to convince their spouse to come to work for you. We can question whether our systems actually work on the basis of individual merit. They often don't. But the idea that they *should* work this way is deeply ingrained in our society and is, for instance, the thinking that fuels both critics of legacy status *and* critics of affirmative action when it comes to college admissions. Spousal hiring doesn't seem to fit within this value system.

I say that it doesn't *seem* to fit because, of course, being labeled a "spousal hire" obscures all the qualifications that a person may have. My husband can teach roughly twice the range of courses I can and his ratings usually exceed mine. He is a seasoned public commentator who translates complex legal concepts and events into everyday language for television and radio programs. He gets invited to present and publish his research, just like I do. We are both good at administrative tasks – organizing people, managing collaborative projects, keeping everyone to schedule – but whereas I am better at working with other faculty, my husband has a way with the range of nonfaculty staff who make up a growing percentage of the university community. Because of his many skills, he has become so indispensable to Emory that, within one year of joining the institution, he was made an Associate Dean. Put simply, Emory may have wanted me, but it needs him.[11] And he is a spousal hire.

So arguments against spousal hiring are partly problematic because they automatically and unjustifiably devalue the spouse in question. But they are also – and I think more importantly – problematic because they make spousal hiring sound like a frivolous practice that gives academics a perk they don't really need and shouldn't get.

There are only a few possible outcomes when one half of a dual academic couple is asked to move without any provision being made for their spouse. Perhaps the spouse stays behind because they already have a satisfying academic job.[12] Something like this happened with one of my graduate school advisors. As a result, he spent several decades shuttling, on a weekly basis, between Illinois (where he worked) and New York (where his wife worked and lived with their children). They somehow managed the logistics and have two fulfilling careers, as well as two lovely children, to show for it. But permanent long distance is not for the faint of heart.

Or, perhaps, the spouse lucks out and finds a suitable academic position in the same city without any help from their partner's institution. This does occasionally happen, but it's rare enough that everyone involved seems awe-struck by their own good fortune. "We very lucky, beyond lucky" exclaimed one relieved academic spouse, before adding "here's hoping that my fairy tale replicates to other people."[13] My parents were also lucky in exactly this sort of way – but good luck is not a life plan.

Finally, of course, perhaps the spouse moves but ends up unemployed or underemployed, or is forced to abandon their academic career altogether. This happens more often than I can say.

It's hard to convey the trauma that career loss stemming from the two-body problem can cause to an individual and to their family. Imagine training for over a decade to become a surgeon, only to be forced out of surgery – and perhaps out of medicine – because your spouse, who is also a surgeon, *got a job*. There is no job for you, and no other job for her. Then imagine being told that your heartbreak is unwarranted because you can always find gainful employment somewhere else in the industry, perhaps as a medical technician (for which you didn't train), or outside of medicine altogether (for which you also didn't train). Never mind the years and dollars you invested or the passion that pulled you to surgery in the first place. Never mind the way this situation pits you against your life partner.

Managing all this is not just psychologically and financially difficult: as my husband and I discovered during our first six months at the University of Alabama, it can become physically debilitating, too. Before I was offered the job, he and I had been living at increasingly long distances from one another for three years. First, we were in Illinois and Florida (while I finished law school and he completed a post-doc), then we were in Pennsylvania and California (while I completed a post-doc and he began a tenure-track job). There were no jobs for me in California, or anywhere west of the Rockies, and the best deal we could manage for him among the offers I did have was the one-year visiting position that Alabama was willing to create.

We took it. We knew it was a relatively good deal: it came with a teaching load, office space, and research support that were equal to what I would receive as a tenure-track professor on the same faculty. But it also came with half the salary and none of the voting privileges I would enjoy, and – most importantly – it had a nine-month expiration date.

From the moment we accepted, my husband was in application mode, frantically searching job boards for announcements, drafting cover letter after cover letter, and flying out to interviews in between classes. We read application materials before bed and discussed CV formatting at dinner. We rented an apartment instead of buying a house despite the economics of the local real estate market making this a worse value-for-money proposition. We socialized minimally because his anxiety and my remorse left us without the emotional bandwidth to make new friends. Everything we did, everything we discussed, was informed by our inability to predict whether he would ever have stable academic employment again.

What, if not academia, would he do in a place like Tuscaloosa? Since my tenure-track job was the only moderately stable income in this scenario, there could be no question of us leaving town to follow his career, whatever and wherever that might be. What, if not academia, would we talk about? This had nothing to do with the love or commitment we felt for each other. By the time we landed in Alabama, we had already been married for nearly a decade. We had survived some circumstances that most couples experience much later in life and other circumstances that most couples, thankfully, never have to experience. But we imagined a future in which I felt perpetually guilty and he felt forever excluded; a future in which the conversations, concepts, people, and projects that made up my daily life would be too painful for him to discuss and the things that made up his daily life would be too boring for us both. We imagined silence.

This lifestyle, these worries, took a powerful and immediate physical toll. During those first six months, in between classes and meetings and interviews, we spent our spare time shuttling him between various doctors on account of a mysterious and almost certainly stress-induced internal bleeding that rendered him periodically anemic. The list of things he could safely eat contracted, expanded, and shifted in ways that I struggled to keep pace with. Thankfully his most acute symptoms began to abate after a few months, but not before doing seemingly lasting damage to his gastrointestinal system that, more than six years later, we have learned to control but not resolve.

Even after the worst of his physical illness disappeared, the effects of living like this for two years (until he received a renewable long-term contract) stayed with us and affected other aspects of our lives. It has taken time, dedication to our relationship, and external changes in his conditions of work for us to once again find joy in sharing a profession that each of us loved before we loved one another. We're still working on it. This is why I immediately understood my old friend's reluctance to share their journey navigating academia as part of a dual academic couple. It is also why I say that dual academic couples who survive these challenging circumstances develop a repertoire of grace and compromise that I find breathtaking.

I want to repeat that none of these circumstances are wholly unique to dual *academic* couples. None are even unique to couples in which just one partner is an academic. But because academia is a quasi-monopsonistic and heavily institutionalized industry in which there are just a few, geographically dispersed employers, its version of the two-body problem is particularly resistant to alternative solutions besides the spousal hire.

Universities know this and are consequently always on the lookout for potential two-body problems. They are helped by the fact that federal legislation in the United States does not prohibit asking job candidates about marital and parental status.[14] My colleagues – despite being law professors – are often incredulous when I say this, and some have fought me on it to considerable lengths. But while many states outlaw this kind of questioning, federal law does not, so long as the questions are asked uniformly of all candidates and are not used as the basis for discriminatory decision-making. (Needless to say, by the time any discrimination *happens*, it's too late. A court may award you money, but it will not award you a job offer.)

Because universities are alive to the two-body problem, aspiring academics are too. Common interview advice ranges from the relatively benign ("Don't mention your spouse or kids unless asked!") to the extreme ("Remove your wedding ring").[15] As an entry-level candidate, I brushed off these stories whenever I heard them. My expectations were, no doubt, skewed by my parents' unusually happy experience and my own personal privilege. But I was also confident that, *surely*, law professors knew well enough to skirt both the illegal and the inadvisable when interviewing potential colleagues – much less a potential colleague who teaches employment law!

Then I found myself sitting next to a hiring committee member who asked me, during my interview dinner, whether the person who appeared repeatedly in the acknowledgments sections of my publications and who shared part of my surname was my husband. When I confirmed that he was, I knew that I was opening the door to an extended conversation about my husband's credentials, specialties, and expectations if I was offered the job. (I wasn't.) Soon after, a law school dean noticed my wedding ring during our interview breakfast, asked about my husband, and spent the rest of the encounter pointedly describing how they and their *first* spouse managed to "make it work" despite living halfway across the country from each other for many years.[16] (I did get that offer.)

From then on, I took my wedding ring off before every interview and my husband and I agreed that we would no longer thank each other in our journal articles even though we, like my parents, are close collaborators.

I've reached a point in my life where it's no longer easy to hide my personal status. It's one thing to fake being single and childless when you're in your mid-thirties and can, on a good day, pass for being in your late twenties.[17] It's another thing to try this when you're forty+ and look it. Fortunately, I've also reached a point in my career where it's no longer as necessary to hide my family status. Any university that interviews me today isn't taking a chance on an untested newcomer: it's seeking to poach an employee with an established record. So, these days, I wear my wedding ring – but I still scrupulously avoid mentioning my family unless I'm extended an offer. One body at a time is enough.

10

To the Dogs

What wages do you think you're worth?

This question – awkward, difficult, and anxiety-inducing for almost everyone – is standard job interview material in many fields. It's not an inherently unreasonable question. Identifying a discrepancy between what's on offer and what's expected can allow both parties to move on to better prospects if needed. And the question is rarely asked in the soul-searching way I've presented it here. Instead, it's usually articulated using the corporatized language of *salary expectations*, which helps lend an objective flavor to the conversation. *Salaries*, like *benefits* and *incentives*, feel like poker chips you can play with, and the word *expectations* implicitly asks you to temper your preferences with standards of reasonableness that exist outside yourself. Asking someone about their salary expectations rather than about the wages they think they're worth creates just enough emotional and psychological distance to transform the topic into something more suitable for the interview table.

But however it's phrased, and however tricky it is for all jobseekers, this question poses an unusual challenge for aspiring academics. That's because academics are trained to think that money doesn't matter – that, in fact, if you *do* care about money, you *don't* care enough about teaching or research to deserve entry into the profession. If you somehow manage to gain entry despite caring about money, your salary expectations are almost guaranteed to go unmet. And if you complain that your wages do not reflect your worth, you will very likely be shamed by peers and public critics alike.

Academic wages, however, hide some eye-popping truths.

Imagine a newly minted PhD or post-doctoral fellow who has just landed her first tenure-track job at the California State University, Los Angeles. This fortunate soul has already beaten significant odds by winning *any* tenure-track position in a universe where there are diminishingly few of them. She's even managed to win this position at a university that is a respectable member of a major academic network: the Cal State system figures among the top twenty largest university systems in the world. Her prospective job promises a great deal of stability (Cal State-LA is not going anywhere any time soon) and an unusual degree of worker leverage (unlike tenure-stream faculty at most private universities and many public ones, Cal State faculty are unionized). Her job, moreover, will take her to a city that is a hub of economic activity and is still, despite the LA fires, largely viewed as a desirable place to live. All of this means that our newbie professor has come as close as it gets to striking gold on the academic job market.

Let me repeat: this outcome is *fantastic*. Sure, our young professor could have been hired by a UCLA or a Stanford – by a university with more prestige and more resources. But getting *any* tenure-track job in today's academic labor market is unusual. As I've already noted, multiple sources across multiple fields estimate that the odds of this happening are, at best, between 10% and 25%.[1] In other words, even if you're admitted to a graduate program, and even if you earn your doctorate, you have – at most – a one in ten to one in four chance of getting the type of job you thought you were working toward. Getting that job at a stable institution in a major coastal city is nothing short of impressive.

Because it is a public university, Cal State salary schedules are widely accessible. According to the 2023–2024 schedule for all Cal State faculty, the standard annual salary of an entry-level professor lies somewhere between $64,860 and $143,928.[2] This sounds like a great deal of money. To the average graduate student or post-doctoral fellow, it *is* a great deal of money. For that matter, it's a great deal of money to the average American household, which lives on a median income of less than $75,000.[3]

But working-age adults in the average American household have not spent eight to twelve years earning little to no money while getting multiple postsecondary degrees. They also do not have the same amount of educational loans to service: the mean graduate debt among PhD holders is nearly $88,000, and the "average student loan balance for research doctorates doubled between 2000–2016."[4] Finally, the average American household does not live in a high-tax, higher-property-value location like Los Angeles. In 2023, when the median home price nationally hit $430,300, it was greeted with hand-wringing and dour commentary across the political spectrum. Meanwhile, the median home price in Los Angeles County was over $1,000,000.[5] California's statistics are not just a one-in-fifty outlier when it comes to academic employment: the state has the most degree-granting institutions of higher education in the country (around 400 of 3,700) and, as elsewhere, a majority of those institutions (215) are located in expensive large cities.[6]

And yet, none of this means that our newbie professor faces exceptional financial hardship when compared to her fellow Angelenos. She will probably take home somewhere between $49,000 and $95,000 per year.[7] That sum must cover her rent or mortgage, buy her food, pay for her medical care, service her loans, allow her to save for retirement, and account for her clothing, transportation, and leisure expenses. It won't be easy. But her overall budget places her squarely within many estimates of what it takes to live as a single, relatively healthy person in California and Los Angeles (around \$53,000 and nearly \$77,000, respectively).[8] To be sure, if she is part of a household, her expenses will increase – but in all likelihood so will her income, because it will probably be augmented by her household's contributions. In absolute dollar terms, then, the financial balancing act awaiting this eager young professor does not make her unique. What *does* set her apart are three discrepancies between the life she will live and the life she's believed to be living.

First among these discrepancies is the gap between what she earns and the kind of financial security she is thought to have. No doubt, many of her relatives and friends will assume that she's waltzed into a high-paying job. They will believe that this job, which she worked so incredibly hard to get, allows her to while away her days reading books and inspiring students instead of worrying about the price of gas or rent. And they will be making a reasonable assumption: highly competitive jobs, and especially highly competitive professional jobs, are often also highly compensated jobs – often, but of course, not always. In truth, our new professor will be earning just enough to manage in the city where she must now live… and earning "just enough" represents, as I've already mentioned, *wild professional success*. Like so many other Americans, our new professor may find herself working a side hustle because her full-time, hard won, tenure-track position does not generate enough income to pay rent.

Meet Sarah Emanuel.

Sarah is an Assistant Professor of Theological Studies at Loyola Marymount University in Los Angeles. She joined LMU in 2020 after receiving her PhD in Biblical Studies from Drew University in New Jersey, and she also has degrees from Wake Forest University in North Carolina and the University of Delaware. At LMU, Sarah teaches classes with names like Prophecy and Apocalypse and the Jewish Jesus, and (in addition to around half a dozen committee roles) she serves as the Associate Chair of her department. She has, by all appearances, at least 2.5 full-time academic jobs.

In early 2022, after just eighteen months in her first faculty position, Sarah wrote an opinion piece for the *Chronicle of Higher Education* titled "The Deflating Reality of Life on the Tenure Track." It was a sensation. The piece garnered her multiple interviews and an email inbox flooded with appreciative messages. *Just… thank you for writing that. Kudos.* And, *Wow! You took a risk.*

Why all this excitement? Why did a one-off op-ed by a relatively unknown author that appeared in an industry publication generate this kind of reaction? It's because, as is often the case, she said the quiet part out loud. In her *Chronicle* piece, Sarah explained how making "it all work" – that is, living on her salary as an Assistant Professor in one of the most expensive cities in the country – led her to moonlight as a dog walker. She was, as she put it, a dog walker by day and night and a professor in between.

"At the height of it," she told me, "I was hiking three days a week, walking five days a week… and then, having at least one [canine] boarder every day."[9]

Sarah is the first to acknowledge that some of her own choices necessitated this side gig. *Of course*, she says early on in her *Chronicle* op-ed, *I could live on the east side and commute an hour to work (as some of my colleagues do). And yes, I could move into a smaller space.*[10] But she also noted that those choices would carry their own consequences, and most of those consequences are bad from the university's perspective. *I get research done because I have a home office. I take part in life on campus because I live close by.*

A professor who doesn't publish fast enough or well enough fails to get tenure. If that happens, her department suffers along with her (although certainly not as much as her): either it must undergo another expensive and time-consuming search process or it loses her spot altogether because the university has refused to authorize a replacement tenure-track hire. Meanwhile, a professor who doesn't participate in campus life – who doesn't advise student clubs, attend workshops or give lectures, and who doesn't take on extensive committee work – that professor contributes to the overall decline of collegiate life. But it's hard to stay for the 5 pm student performance when there's a two-hour drive standing between you and your child's preschool pickup.

Sarah eventually cut down on her dog-walking business because it, too, became unsustainable. "My body was falling apart. My mind was deteriorating. I was just… I couldn't function anymore." Her wife also found a better paying job, which allowed them to absorb a reduction in Sarah's side income. And the two of them received a temporary reprieve in the form of a three year lease on a university-owned house near campus. None of these developments is a permanent financial fix, so the challenge of affording a career in the academy is one that Sarah and her wife will likely navigate for decades. But they do make the present a little less scary.

Few academics are so lucky. The post-docs discussed in Chapter 3 and the nontenure-track faculty mentioned throughout this book are notoriously underpaid and disrespected by their university employers. "We are… the intellectual Kleenex of academia," one NTT professor observed: necessary for keeping up appearances but viewed as low-value and disposable paraphernalia whose most noteworthy quality is being cheap.[11] Because of this approach to university staffing, a majority of people tasked with educating our young adults struggle to buy basic groceries or pay rent. There is an exploding, but still inadequate, conversation about this fact.

What Sarah's *Chronicle* piece highlighted, though, is that financial precarity *also* affects academics who have clambered on to the ostensibly secure perch of tenure-track employment.

It's hard to convey this message without eliciting instant references to tiny violins. Tenure-track and tenured professors are highly credentialed workers with above-average job security. It's reasonable to assume that they also earn above-average wages – and it's difficult to adjust our thinking when confronted with contradictory evidence. "Everyone thinks a PhD pretty much guarantees you a living wage," notes a former president of the Modern Language Association, adding that, in his experience, "most commentators think that college professors make $100,000 and more."[12] There are not many Sarahs out there who can push back on this view without inviting vociferous critique from both inside and outside the academy.

But lower-than-expected wages are not *all* that separate the financial realities of academic employment from the perceptions that exist about it. The second, even less widely appreciated truth about academic finances is that many tenure-line professors could have earned more outside academia than they do inside it. Indeed, they often could have accrued both *more* income *and* less debt because the higher salaries they could have earned in "industry" rarely require the same amount of expensive graduate training. Evidently, George Bernard Shaw was wrong: those who can, teach.[13] Even when they shouldn't.

One of the best measures we have of median salary statistics in any industry is the Occupational Outlook Handbook (OOH) maintained by the Bureau of Labor Statistics. The Bureau is an agency of the federal Department of Labor that describes itself as "the principal fact-finding agency in the broad field of labor economics and statistics."[14] The OOH that the Bureau maintains, like all large-scale datasets, doesn't reflect individual experiences. But, usefully, the OOH provides median outcomes for specific fields both inside *and* outside academia, which allows us to gauge the approximate difference between being a professor and being a practitioner in the same area. In 2022, those median salaries (and the educational credentials usually required to earn those salaries) were as depicted in Table 10.1.

What does this tell us? To begin with, it suggests that earning a doctorate (along with all the associated lost wages and higher educational debt) doesn't necessarily produce a meaningful wage increase at the median. In the examples I've picked out below, professors of anthropology, history, and environmental science (and six others) seem to do better in absolute dollars than their industry counterparts. Everyone else in the table earns less as an academic than they could have earned in industry – sometimes very *little* less (as with chemistry professors, who only experience a salary shortfall of around $1,000) and sometimes a *whole lot* (as with physics and computer science professors, who apparently forego over $50,000 annually). This is no surprise given that academic salaries have not kept pace with inflation: in 2023, the AAUP reported a third straight year of real wage declines for full-time faculty, this time by 2.4%.[15]

One aspiring academic calculated that, based on his "last full year of earnings in the 'civilian' (nonacademic) world and using the very conservative assumption that [he] would never have received a raise or moved into a higher paying position than the one [he] had at age 30, working in the adjunct professoriate has cost [him] roughly $750,000 in foregone earnings to date."[16] *Three-quarters of a million dollars*: that's what he likely paid (not including any student loans) for the privilege of trying to become a tenure-stream professor.

TABLE 10.1 *Credentials and median salaries by discipline (Industry and Academia)*[17]

	Industrial Credential	Median Industry Salary	Academic Credential	Median Academic Salary
Anthropology	Master's Degree	63,940	Doctoral/Professional Degree	85,000
Architecture	Bachelor's Degree	82,840	Doctoral/Professional Degree	93,220
Chemistry	Bachelor's Degree	81,810	Doctoral/Professional Degree	80,720
Communications[18]	Bachelor's Degree	125,620	Doctoral/Professional Degree	76,250
Computer Science	Master's Degree	136,620	Doctoral/Professional Degree	83,040
Economics	Master's Degree	113,940	Doctoral/Professional Degree	103,930
Environmental Sciences	Bachelor's Degree	76,480	Doctoral/Professional Degree	83,040
Foreign Languages[19]	Bachelor's Degree	53,640	Doctoral/Professional Degree	76,030
Forestry	Bachelor's Degree	64,420	Doctoral/Professional Degree	96,500
History	Master's Degree	64,540	Doctoral/Professional Degree	79,400
Law	Doctoral/Professional Degree	135,740	Doctoral/Professional Degree	108,860
Library Science	Master's Degree	61,660	Doctoral/Professional Degree	76,370
Math	Master's Degree	99,620	Doctoral/Professional Degree	77,420
Music[20]	Bachelor's Degree	62,940	Doctoral/Professional Degree	77,280
Nursing[21]	Master's Degree	125,900	Doctoral/Professional Degree	85,900
Physics	Doctoral/Professional Degree	139,220	Doctoral/Professional Degree	86,550
Political Science	Master's Degree	128,020	Doctoral/Professional Degree	83,770
Psychology	Doctoral/Professional Degree	85,330	Doctoral/Professional Degree	78,810
Social Work	Master's Degree	55,350	Doctoral/Professional Degree	66,510
Sociology	Master's Degree	98,590	Doctoral/Professional Degree	78,970

It's important to remember that OOH figures are medians: the highest-paid computer science professors will almost certainly earn many times more than their lowest-paid (or even median-earning) industry counterparts. And it's also worth remembering that this is only a moderately random sample of subject areas: I wanted to represent major academic clusters like STEM, the Humanities, and the Social Sciences, but I also did not want to be biased about the disciplines I chose. (In fact, I chose around half the disciplines and asked a research assistant to choose the others, with the only caveats being that he aim for some representation from each disciplinary cluster and that he *not* cherry-pick examples where industry out-earns academia.) There are surely other fields besides the nine listed here where professors out-earn practitioners – and, even more surely, there are also other fields besides these eleven where practitioners fare better. But even in fields like anthropology where it seemingly pays to be a professor, those higher wages demand years of debt, lost earnings, and foregone financial security.

The single most important caveat regarding the OOH data is about who it includes; however, this *also* doesn't make the data either more or less significant in any obvious way. On the academic side, the OOH counts adjuncts and part-time faculty as "professors" so it includes a lot of the most severely underpaid academics who work outside the tenure-stream. On the industry side, though, the OOH includes many positions that may themselves be part-time or temporary under categories like "Research and development in the social sciences and humanities," which accounts for 31% of practicing anthropologists.[22] In other words, OOH data likely includes both underemployed professors and underemployed practitioners.

We can get even more specific. The Occupational Employment and Wage Statistics survey, or OEWS, is a survey that is sent out by the Bureau of Labor Statistics in collaboration with state workforce agencies; it's distributed on a semi-annual basis to hundreds of employers across the country.[23] The survey is an important source of data for the OOH (so this information is already incorporated into the statistics I described earlier), but it allows us to drill down a bit deeper.

Let's explore OEWS data using the example of anthropology. I've chosen it because it's a field in which a PhD is generally required for tenure-track employment, because it is a minor member of a major academic cluster (the Social Sciences), and because the OOH data provided earlier suggests that it actually contradicts my argument that professors suffer a salary penalty for having chosen academia. (Also, admittedly, because I have a personal curiosity about anthropology.) As we'll see, even seemingly positive statistics about academic wages hide a complicated reality.

Tables 10.2–10.4 show that, for anthropology, it's clear that a career in academia results in higher absolute wages across the board. At every quartile, anthropologists employed as university faculty earn more than their counterparts in industry. At the highest quartiles, academic anthropologists – likely full professors or named chair-holders at elite private institutions – earn over 150% of their industry analogs.

TABLE 10.2 *Percentile wage estimates for Anthropology & Archaeology (Industry)*[24]

Percentile	10%	25%	50% (Median)	75%	90%
Annual Wage	$40,260	$50,020	$63,940	$81,120	$100,560

TABLE 10.3 *Percentile wage estimates for Anthropology & Archaeology (Academia)*[25]

Percentile	10%	25%	50% (Median)	75%	90%
Annual Wage	$50,920	$64,400	$85,000	$119,590	$167,180

TABLE 10.4 *Absolute and percentage differences for Anthropology & Archaeology (Academia relative to Industry)*

Percentile	10%	25%	50% (Median)	75%	90%
Absolute Annual Difference	$10,660	$14,380	$21,060	$38,470	$66,620
Percentage Annual Difference	126.48%	128.75%	132.94%	147.42%	166.25%

These numbers hide some important details.

Higher-earning academic anthropologists have likely incurred far more financial losses than practitioners. As Table 12.1 shows academic anthropology generally requires a doctorate whereas practicing anthropology usually only requires a master's degree. This means that, for the six to eight additional years when they were in graduate school and holding post-docs, academic anthropologists had low or nonexistent wages, could not build retirement savings, and accumulated more educational debt. They probably also paid out of pocket for a few cross-country moves while hopping between post-docs. They may even have funded their own research with debt or side hustles. As Sarah observed during our exchanges (and as she mentions in her *Chronicle* piece), she only landed her tenure-track job after two post-doc positions and some additional consumer debt, and she paid for all three of her moves herself. One of my graduate school friends partly financed his fieldwork using an online business that sold, among other things, pie irons.

Moreover, many academic anthropologists in the bottom fifty percent – those who never won a tenure-track position, or who found one at resource-poor institutions – will have incurred all these losses *without* the accompanying higher wages. As Table 10.5 shows, most people who study anthropology will not work in academia at all. The seemingly higher wages of doctorate-holding academic anthropologists only apply to a very few people because most anthropologists, whatever their highest

TABLE 10.5 *Industries with the highest levels of employment in Anthropologists and Archeologists*[26]

Industry	Employment
Scientific Research and Development Services	2,380
Federal Executive Branch	1,550
Management, Scientific, and Technical Consulting Services	1,410
Architectural, Engineering, and Related Services	690
Colleges, Universities, and Professional Schools	360

credential, work outside academia where they earn less. For these kinds of reasons, we can't simply look at wage statistics and conclude that being a professor of anthropology is more financially rewarding than being a practicing anthropologist. That's not untrue, but it's also kind of besides the point.

Now, there are certainly professors who carry no educational debt because their parents, grant foundations, taxpayers, or some combination of all three made that possible. Some of those lucky folks may receive graduate school stipends that cover all their needs, may have a spouse or a parent who helps with living expenses and who pays for their cross-country moves, and they may even land a tenure-track job at a top 50th percentile-paying university after just one season on the job market. In other words, our imagined golden child from the beginning of this chapter *does* exist.

But optimal experiences are rare and they are certainly not representative of what, in Sarah's language, it takes to make academia "work" financially. Conversely, the professor whose academic job pays less than they could have earned in industry – after incurring less educational debt and losing less earning time – well… they are arguably more representative and unarguably worse off.

Low salaries and salary penalties are two financial harms that many academics will readily acknowledge. But the third discrepancy between perception and reality regarding academic finances is one that invites resistance even from *within* the academy. This third financial harm is the expectation of free labor.

Before I go on, a few *Yes, buts…* are called for. Everyone does work that is not part of their formal job description. This is partly because written job descriptions can't be exhaustive, partly because employers and clients can be extractive, and partly because employees often want – or feel pressured – to do things that are not really their responsibility. For all these reasons, everyone does some work for free. But academia *expects* its flagship employees – tenure-line faculty – to do significant amounts of work for free, punishes them if they don't, and fails to meaningfully reward them if they do.

Sometimes, the expectation of free labor is tied to the time of year. Virtually all research, writing, and class preparation done during summer months is designated as noncompensable because it occurs when regular classes are not in session. It's not that conducting research, writing articles and books, or refining lectures and developing new in-class exercises becomes any less a part of your job because it's June. Your employer still expects you to do these things. It's not even *possible* to stop doing them because it's June. Academic journals and book publishers will ask you to revise your own drafts or review other scholars' submitted scholarship throughout the year.[27] If your research requires travel – to examine archival materials or study novel engineering systems or observe court practices – the summer is likely when you can squeeze that travel in. Even if you don't need to travel you will probably be working because, during the school year, your days are taken up with too many classes, office hours, administrative meetings, student mentorship, and conferences to make meaningful progress on your research agenda or revise your teaching materials.

Opting out of these activities "because it's June" will cause you serious professional harm. Articles and books that don't get written or revised on schedule do not get published – there go tenure, promotion, and grant eligibility. Courses that don't get revised for content or format get bad reviews – there go tenure, promotion, and enrollment levels in a universe where low-enrollment majors are on the chopping block. Like putting on a hard hat or undergoing a security screening as you exit your workplace, these activities are inescapable elements of the job.[28] But (as with the wearing of hard hats and the performance of exit screenings) you won't get paid for engaging in them… *for three months.*

Universities often disguise this fact by paying nine-month salaries over a twelve-month period. They understand that no one who works for a living can forego income for two to three months annually. But their answer, in most cases, has been to designate the nine-month academic year as the time when professors engage in compensable labor and to dole out that money in twelve smaller increments. In certain fields (for instance, law) or for certain faculty (those who succeed in competitive internal processes), there may be what's called a "summer stipend" or "summer grant." These are highly prized because they represent real additional income, unlike prorated nine-month salaries. But they are rare – a highly productive professor at a poor university or in the wrong discipline still won't get a summer stipend – and they can be controversial. Professors *themselves* sometimes criticize the practice of granting summer stipends on the theory that it pays them to do something they were already being paid to do.[29] But that's the thing: without a summer stipend or the rare twelve-month salary they're *weren't* being paid to do it. They were being asked to work without pay because it's June.

Other kinds of free labor occur year-round. I'm not referring to the kind of non-administrative service tasks we encountered in Chapter 7. As time- and energy-consuming as they are, and as much as they are overlooked for evaluation purposes, they can be reasonably understood as part of the job. The problem, as Chapter 7 pointed out, is that they transform one job into four or five and fail to meaningfully recognize performance during internal evaluations.

Instead, the kind of year-round free labor I'm talking about here is the set of wide-ranging activities necessitated by the practice of peer review. Whether it's accepting submissions for conference presentations, journal articles, or book proposals; evaluating candidates for employment, tenure, or promotion; or deciding whether to discipline or terminate a tenure-line faculty member, academia generally runs on the assumption that expert opinion helps produce better decisions. Peer evaluation, as Chapter 15 explains, is the industry's animating ethos. When it comes to written scholarship or applications, the expectation in most fields and for most tasks is that your peers review your work behind a veil of neutrality-enhancing anonymity: either *single-blind* (the submitter is unaware of the reviewer's identity), *double-blind* (both submitter and reviewer are unaware of each other's identities), *triple-blind* (submitter and reviewer are both unaware, and the intermediary – a journal editor or conference organizer – is unaware of at least one of their identities), and so on.

Peer review in publication has passionate critics with justifiable concerns. I've heard of book proposals being scrapped because the hopeful author failed to cite the reviewer's own work in a relevant area, because they failed to cite the reviewer's *friend's* work in a relevant area, and because they failed to cite the reviewer's *favorite article or book* in a relevant area. Plenty of reviewers reject or excessively critique submissions that do not align with their own theoretical, ideological, or methodological preferences. Others ask for so many changes that they are functionally asking the submitter to write a wholly different piece, one that the submitter may not have wanted to write. And the entire process of peer review is slow… often excruciatingly so. It took me less than a year to write my last book and more than a year to get it through the peer review process. As much as this infuriated me, it was considered unremarkable, even speedy, by many of my friends.

Despite all these problems, I am no advocate for the abolition of peer review. As someone who lives between a discipline where all scholarship is peer reviewed (anthropology) and one where most scholarship is *not* peer reviewed (law), I know very well that every model has its shortcomings. Peer review, like tenure, could stand to be improved, and there are many editors, readers, and conference organizers working hard to improve it. Like them, I think the system needs to be better, not discarded.

But what gets largely overlooked in debates over peer review is how much it rests on free labor. It's true that some major publishing houses will pay token honoraria (often $100–300) to scholars who agree to review lengthy book submissions. However, given the number of hours it takes to read book proposals and then properly evaluate them, those token payments often work out to less than the starting base rates that the United Auto Workers negotiated in 2023 on behalf of its members employed at General Motors.[30] Many book publishers don't even pay honoraria: instead, they offer complimentary books from their own catalogs in lieu of payment. Virtually *no* academic journals offer payment (nor, for that matter, do conferences that operate on a peer review basis). By virtue of going unpaid, all this peer review labor saves the scholarly publication industry an estimated $1.5 billion annually in the United States alone.[31]

To be sure, this is not a wholly selfless service: there's some small professional cachet to be had in serving as a reviewer for the most elite journals or publishers in one's field. But, by definition, most journals and publishers are not elite – and having served as a reviewer for the ones that *are* will not get you a job, tenure, promotion, or grant money.

Many academics also view peer review as a service to their discipline, or as an obligation, inasmuch as they themselves have benefited from it in the past… and there is always some value in feeling virtuous. But even if we grant all the arguments in support of uncompensated peer review, there is no gainsaying the fact that its performance translates into unpaid working time for academics and into dollars for a few publication conglomerates. Most worryingly, peer review isn't only performed by *tenure-line* faculty: graduate students, post-docs, and other NTT faculty – all of whom are already financially stressed – are expected to engage in this kind of free labor, too.

Low salaries, salary penalties, and free labor don't, by themselves, make academia unique. Some medical graduates face similar daunting circumstances. Pediatricians, for instance, incur the same debt as doctors who care for adults and they train for the same lengthy period of time (or for even longer), but they earn much less.[32] An op-ed discussing this was written by a pediatrician who noted that he himself had been warned away from the field by his surgeon father, but was committed enough and *privileged* enough to be able to choose his "financially unwise" path. I can relate. I could afford to choose anthropology – and, later, I could afford *not* to practice law. That pediatrician and I are both privileged to have been able to make the choices we made. Still, it took me five years of working in tenure-stream academia at well-resourced schools – seven years after graduating from law school – before I finally started earning the salary I would have been earning as a practitioner the day after I passed the bar exam.

Put simply, academics take on significant educational debt and lose significant financial security, and consequently they face many more financial stresses than they are widely believed to experience. For tenure-line professors, winning the professional lottery does not produce the kind of carefree existence their critics love to hate. For everyone else – all those underemployed faculty stuck in the post-doc queue or in perpetual NTT positions – academia is little more than an ongoing struggle to make rent. Tenure doesn't fix this problem… how could it? But it offers something else that's valuable, job security, to people whose lives are far less financially secure than is widely believed.

11

Butlerian Dialectics

The move from a structuralist account in which capital is understood to structure social relations in relatively homologous ways to a view of hegemony in which power relations are subject to repetition, convergence, and rearticulation brought the question of temporality into the thinking of structure, and marked a shift from a form of Althusserian theory that takes structural totalities as theoretical objects to one in which the insights into the contingent possibility of structure inaugurate a renewed conception of hegemony as bound up with the contingent sites and strategies of the rearticulation of power.[1]

This sentence is famous. Not *Vanity Fair*, meme-worthy, journalistic frenzy famous – but within a certain (pretty sizable) portion of the academy, and even among the literati who exist outside universities, it's famous.

The sentence was written by Judith Butler, a philosopher and gender studies scholar who's taught at Berkeley since 1993. Butler is famous for generating ideas about sex and gender that have proven so influential that they are now, in many circles, common sense. (And even in those circles where they are *not* common sense, people are often arguing against Butler without either meaning to or wanting to.) The notion that sex and gender are distinct? Butler was an important force in championing it. The view that gender identity is something we make real through performance (speech, mannerisms, clothing, etc.) rather than something that inherently, permanently, exists? Butler is largely responsible for it.

In addition to being famous for producing influential ideas, Judith Butler is also famous for producing difficult prose. The sentence quoted earlier won first prize in the 1998 Bad Writing Contest run by the journal *Philosophy and Literature*. It (along with the rest of Butler's writing) went on to be critiqued in the *Wall Street Journal*, the *New Republic*, and more academic articles, books, and blogs than I can name here.[2] And for good reason: even if you understand all the inside-speak of "homologous ways" and "Althusserian theory," I dare you to read that sentence from beginning to end on just one breath of air.

Over the years, supporters have articulated many reasonable defenses of Butler's writing. It's not unclear to its intended audience; it's not unclear at all (otherwise

87

how did Butler's ideas become so influential?); it *needs* to be unclear to be radical because clear writing just replicates existing ways of thinking; it's *no more* unclear than scientific or legal jargon that often gets a pass because those fields, unlike the Humanities and Social Sciences, are viewed as genuinely, technically, complex.[3]

What rarely gets acknowledged, though, is that Butlerian prose is just an extreme example of a larger phenomenon that has devastating employment implications for academics. The phenomenon I'm referring to is the way in which academics are trained to acquire certain skills or are conditioned to behave in certain ways that are not valued in the general labor market or society at large. Even worse, academics are required to abandon, unlearn, and ignore skills and behaviors that could help them in the general labor market. I've been thinking of this phenomenon as a kind of "auto-depreciation" because it involves academics actively reducing the exchange value of their greatest asset – their own skilled labor – in order to succeed in academia.

This argument, as you can imagine, is not popular with academics.

To begin with, the idea of auto-depreciation transforms individuals into commodities for exchange. (The very term "exchange value" comes from Marxist theory and is part of Marx's broader critique of capitalist economics; it carries all kinds of bad baggage in scholarly circles.) At the same time, most academics would agree that we *do* live in an age of rabid capitalism where people *are* thought of as commodities. We build personal brands and develop portable skills, and we are required to explain, if not always explicitly identify, our "value-add" to potential employers. Academics are workers who must do all these things, too. I see little point in pretending otherwise. Our difference lies in the fact that preparing oneself for exchange and advancement in the academic job market requires actively *un*-preparing oneself for almost every other kind of labor market there is.

A second line of objection is substantive in nature. It's not taking issue with the *implications* of what I'm saying ("it feels icky to compare people to things"). It's disagreeing with my conclusion by saying that academia *does* give people generally marketable skills. In other words, if you train to become a professor but ultimately can't or choose not to become one, your education will still have provided you with skills that are valued by nonuniversity employers. Usually, these skills are things like critical thinking, close reading, reasoned argument, project management, and personnel management. (Clear writing does not show up too often on these lists.) If you're thinking to yourself that these are relatively abstract abilities that many nonacademics are also trained to develop, you're right. And, if we take a closer look at the *specific* skills you must acquire to succeed in academia, it becomes hard to agree that scholarly training and professionalization processes translate well outside academia.

Let's start with writing, which is enormously important in academia – even in STEM disciplines where it is often assumed to play a minor role. Almost without exception, scholarly writing is criticized for being unnecessarily jargony, using bad sentence structure, assuming prior knowledge, and having various other qualities that decrease its ability to effectively communicate ideas. There's considerable merit to this critique: a lot of our writing could just be simpler, clearer... better. For the life of me, I don't know why academics can't just say *explain* instead of *explicate* or *elucidate*, and the world needs far fewer sentences that occupy five lines of printed text.

Nevertheless, as many academics (including some of Butler's defenders) have argued, scholarly writing is usually not meant for the general public. It's mostly meant for scholars, and they have different baselines for what constitutes challenging prose. It's also meant to convey complicated information developed over decades or centuries, information that would be unwieldy if it were put into simpler terms. The term *dialectic* may seem obscure, but it's a lot more efficient than *a developmental process of refining ideas through the recognition and resolution of their internal contradictions.*[4] "Scholar speak" is thus often a necessary shorthand for people who understand the code.

As with actual shorthand, learning to use the code takes time and skill. The more effort you put into understanding it, and the more often you're expected to use it, the harder it becomes to function in any other way. Imagine if you had to spend ninety percent of your waking hours writing and speaking (somehow!) in Gregg shorthand. Or if you were suddenly transported to my mother's birthplace of Chennai, India, and had to speak, read, and write exclusively in Tamil. You might still *think* in English after years of living in Tamil or Gregg shorthand, but chances are that your intensive immersion in another language system will change the way you communicate regardless of the language you're asked to use. You become, at least partly, what you are repeatedly asked to be.

Both the shorthand and the foreign language examples are crude proxies for one aspect of the auto-depreciation phenomenon: becoming an academic who is intelligible to other academics means learning to communicate (and especially to *write*) in ways that most nonacademics don't like. It's often reasonable for those other people to not like scholarly writing styles. But it's also often reasonable for scholars to write as they do. If you want to get published, get jobs, get prizes, or get almost anything else that represents success in academia, you need to master communication styles that are complicated and nonintuitive. And mastering those styles eventually makes it harder for you to write in ways that nonacademics – including nonacademic *employers* – value.

Now, consider a second requirement of the academic labor market: the demand for specialization. By now it should be clear that no one is hired to be a "Professor of X" – of law, of history, of anthropology, or of anything else that is similarly broad. That description may be what appears on their letterhead and on the nameplate outside their office door, and it is likely how their mother or spouse describes them in casual conversation with the neighbor. But what they were actually hired to be is a professor of private law with a focus on employment regulation and workplace technology, or a professor of the anthropology of modern South Asia whose research emphasizes themes of religion and spirituality. Specialization is built into the academy in ways that are hard to see from the outside but (as Chapters 8 and 9 show) can be life-determining on the inside.

Chapter 8 observed that specialization impacts job availability within academia, but here I want to focus on how specialization impacts job mobility between academia and the general workforce. I'll begin by noting that heightened specialization – or *hyper*-specialization, as it's often pejoratively called – seems to be one of those rare issues on which academics and nonacademics largely agree. *Everyone* now seems to think that specialization is risky and too much of it is bad. Academics worry that it stifles creativity, while external commentators grumble that it produces useless esoterica. Interdisciplinarity is the "mantra du jour."[5]

We didn't always feel this way. For several decades beginning in the late nineteenth century, Americans and their universities pursued scholarly specialization with a zeal that sometimes perplexed European observers.[6] However, even as enthusiasm for the intrinsic merits of specialization waned, the post-War boom in higher education meant that specialization has always remained inescapable. That's because scholarship in general and doctoral dissertations in particular are expected to make original contributions to human knowledge: with a rapid expansion in the ranks of doctoral students comes a parallel expansion in research outputs – what's often called the "publication explosion." In 2012, there were around 28,000 academic journals being published worldwide (around 789 of which had been founded in the year 2008 *alone*) while by 2023 there were nearly 50,000 journals producing 5 million articles annually.[7] Every one of those articles and the thousands of books that are published alongside them required their author to find something new to say. Interdisciplinarity may be popular, but specialization is inevitable.[8]

Becoming an academic and finding success in academia thus involves transforming yourself into a very big expert on a very small topic. By "small" I don't mean *unvaluable* – far from it. I mean that the patch of intellectual earth on which you've chosen to build your professional home has the dimensions of a New York City studio. It may be tiny, but it's still New York.

What is often overlooked in the debate over specialization is how the drive toward ever-narrowing expertise affects those who train to become professors but ultimately can't or choose not to become them. Once you've spent around a decade learning everything there is to know about a beetle native to southeastern Georgia, a cultural practice observed in northern Kenya, or the lifework of an eighteenth-century American philosopher, how do you apply for a job at Macy's? More often than not, you can't. Your education is too great, while your expertise is too limited. It *had* to be this way for you to stand a chance of getting your degree, winning a faculty job, or achieving tenure and promotion. You had no choice. But all that specialization now means that your knowledge base is both deep and narrow in a way that nonacademic employers will often – reasonably – struggle to make use of.

Writing style and intellectual expertise are both important aspects of the autodepreciation phenomenon, but the third and more general aspect – marketable skills – is where the action really is. Universities and the people they employ regularly argue that graduate education and preparation for the academic job market teach skills that are transferable to the general labor market.

> YOU DO have valuable transferable skills that build upon and extend beyond teaching or research!
>
> – Cornell[9]

> Employers value many skills in addition to the technical knowledge in your discipline that you have honed … You already have developed many of these skills through your academic training, full or part-time jobs, and extra-curricular activities or hobbies.
>
> – Yale[10]

> Your abilities may not seem very special in the high-powered academic world you inhabit, but I can assure you that they are in short supply outside the ivory tower… Look at what employers say they are looking for. The most sought-after skills… include the ability to get things done, common sense, integrity, dependability, initiative, well-developed work habits, interpersonal skills, enthusiasm, motivation to achieve, adaptability, intelligence, oral-communication skills, and problem-solving abilities. Notice that most of these are character attributes that have probably appeared on your list of academic capabilities alone.
>
> – Harvard[11]

Critical thinking, close reading, reasoned argument: these are the kinds of abilities ascribed to aspiring or former academics, even by people who are skeptical about the concept of "transferable skills" or who are not obliged to use them to market graduate education. In a blog post for the academic consulting company The Professor Is In – under a title reading *'Transferable Skills' Are A Lie* – professional coach Adrienne Posner begins by saying that "'transferable skills' are not a real thing" before going on to argue that "[a]cademic work builds competence in areas that are highly valuable to employers."[12] These include *learning and instructional design, leadership and solid communication skills, experience using data to inform critical decisions, skills central to business analytics,* and *skill in drafting business proposals.*

Posner is not wrong: academic training *does* develop these skills and employers *do* want them. But there are cheaper, quicker, and less life-altering ways to acquire them. Aspiring academics may indeed be getting more adept at repackaging themselves for the general labor market after the academic market does not work out. They may, furthermore, be achieving this by pointing to the abstract yet very real skills that academic training provides. But all of this is beside the point. In the words of another academic career coach, "careers outside of academe are not something you do with the Ph.D.; they're what you do after the PhD. The distinction matters."[13] Meanwhile, the specific skills you do pick up through graduate education or while holding a faculty position – precisely because they *are* specific to an industry, and to a specific job within that industry – are not so easy to export.

Take the example of classroom instruction. In one of my disciplines, law, there is a diminishing but still very powerful assumption that professors who practiced law before entering the academy are preferable to those who did not. The idea is that you will be better at explaining something if you have done it yourself. Of course, this assumption misunderstands the work of instruction, which is no more about regurgitating experience than learning is about regurgitating information. Disaggregating, ordering, simplifying, and contextualizing information for people vastly younger and more inexperienced than you, people who may have little interest in the topic but possess a great deal of interest in its (graded) outcome – all of this is a very peculiar and acquired skill. Doing it *well* neither follows from nor translates back into life outside academia in any self-evident way.

Within legal academia, though, it's still the norm to declare that one's practice experience, however brief or topically irrelevant or long ago it may have been, informs one's approach to teaching. Only very occasionally will opposing viewpoints break the surface – as it did, for instance, during one of the more recent iterations of the "practice or no practice?" debate on a major legal academic blog. In the comments thread, one law professor observed that "[a]s someone with a PhD who also practiced for over 10 years… I believe [the practical experience] did little to help me as a teacher, let alone a scholar." The professor went on to explain:

> I find a big part of my job is explaining very simple fundamental concepts, basic logic, in a way that is both clear and engaging, being as attentive as I can to the fact that this is all totally new for [students]. Seldom was I engaged in this sort of thing as a practicing attorney. Indeed, I think most people, my colleagues, opposing counsel, or a judge for instance, would have found me to be somewhat patronizing or slow if I practiced law as I teach law.[14]

What matters here is not whether law practice reliably improves law teaching. (I have a horse in that race, as someone who has never practiced law, but I also have reasonable teaching evaluations.) It's that teaching is a specific skill that calls for ways of engaging with information and people that may not be appropriate in other workplaces. In other words, one of the primary tasks of the university professor – teaching – requires skills that are not, except in a rather abstract sense, transferable.

Other activities that are also part of the bread-and-butter of faculty positions can be similarly unhelpful when job-hunting in the general labor market. Constructing a syllabus that balances established knowledge with new perspectives, while also being mindful of assigned page count and student budgets. Learning to write exams or develop other types of evaluation. Learning to fairly, consistently, and efficiently grade those exams or complete those evaluations. Developing exercises that challenge students without discouraging them, and that can be completed in the allotted classroom time, with the available classroom technology, and within institutional expectations for assessment and accommodations. Identifying a new research question that is complex enough to demand several years' exploration but that can also generate discrete publications along the way for the sake of satisfying hiring, tenure, and promotion committees. Writing grant applications for the same project at various stages of its life cycle and for various funding agencies with distinct application requirements and priorities. Writing articles and books that are longer and denser than most nonacademic forms of writing. Ensuring that those articles and books build on an ever-expanding corpus of earlier publications yet, simultaneously, contribute something original.

The demand for any one of these skills is not wholly unique to academia. Likewise, not all aspiring academics face identical obstacles to making themselves intelligible on the general labor market: it's far easier to move into industry with an engineering or finance PhD than with one in anthropology. (My guess is that there is probably more cross-disciplinary convergence among faculty who want to leave academia after an extended period spent working inside it.) Nevertheless, these are the tasks that aspiring academics learn to perform and become good at performing while their nonacademic peers are learning inventory systems, computer programs, industry trends, administrative practices, and so on. It's no knock on graduate education or faculty life to say that they don't *also* prepare people to be sales managers or product developers. We don't expect MBA programs to turn out nurses, or law schools to produce accountants. But it remains the case that academics have concrete skills that are relatively unhelpful in the wider job market, and abstract skills that many people – who also have relevant job experience – possess, too.

This is why my friend Sid, who is a partner at a major American law firm, says things like "there is this reticence to hire people [like academics] who have experience in the law but not [with] practicing for a significant amount of time."[15] Legal headhunters who recruit for firms like Sid's are more blunt: "Law professors are not marketable... if they think they are they are kidding themselves."[16] And it's true: before I entered the academy, I had full-time job offers at two of the largest, most prestigious law firms in the country, as well as internship offers at around half a dozen others. Today, after nearly a decade of teaching, my best – and likely my *only* – shot at comparable private practice would be Sid. (Assuming he could convince his fellow partners to take me on.) That's because, today, I have skills and habits that Sid's firm can't use, and maybe doesn't want, but few of the skills they need. I *had* to develop these skills to succeed as an academic. But they are, in large part, what make me unemployable outside academia. This is what auto-depreciation looks like in real life.

Auto-depreciation helps explain the rapid growth of a literary genre known as "Quit Lit" and the accompanying proliferation of targeted career coaching services for academics. After the 2008–2009 financial crisis, and later thanks to Covid-19, professors, like almost everyone else in the United States, began reevaluating their professional choices. Is this job worth the hours, the stress, the salary, and the coworkers? Is this *industry* worth it? Should I be doing this to myself and my family? Very often, the answer was "no."

That, by itself, was not remarkable. Academics have been leaving the industry for decades – or, rather, the industry has for decades been showing them the door. This time, moreover, academics were being accompanied by workers in all kinds of other industries who had also tired of extractive labor arrangements. Admittedly, it often felt like the post-Covid departures involved an unusually high percentage of people who had actually *succeeded* in academia, people who were employed in prestigious post-docs, tenure-track jobs, or who were even tenured faculty when they made their exits. But, to my knowledge, we don't have the comparative data needed to know whether "academic winners" were indeed choosing to leave university life at unusually high rates after either 2008 or 2020.

What was unquestionably new were the devastating critiques these folks issued on their way out. The Quit Lit blog posts, op-eds, and tell-all interviews they produced alternated between almost gleeful veil-ripping and unmitigated sadness, pain, and resentment. Rebecca Schuman's 2013 missive, published in *Slate*, was definitely not the first example of Quit Lit, but just as definitely it remains one of the most famous. *Don't misunderstand me,* she writes.[17] *There is unquantifiable intellectual reward from the exploration of scholarly problems and the expansion of every discipline… But there is one sort of reward you will never get: monetary compensation from a stable, nonpenurious position at a decent university.* Two years later, Oliver Bateman wrote about the crisis of conscience and confidence that led him to feel that he was *a priest who had lost his faith,* someone who couldn't explain to a visiting friend why he wasn't *doing something meaningful* with his life.[18] Erin Bartram struck an even more melancholic note in 2018 when she wrote that *This was what I had been trained to do. This was what I wanted to do… And now I know that I won't get to do it for my whole life… I don't know how to come to terms with the fact that I have so much in my head, and so much in my Google Drive, that is basically useless right now.*[19]

There are dozens more. The *Chronicle of Higher Education* created a Quit Lit archive that, even though it contains nearly a hundred entries, is emphatically incomplete. It doesn't contain the departing thoughts of William Pannapacker, formerly an endowed chair in English at Michigan's Hope College and a noted commentator on academic employment.[20] It also doesn't contain the explanatory letter that the bioethicist Alice Dreger sent to the Provost of Northwestern University when she resigned from its medical school.[21] Quit Lit has become commonplace because quitting academia is becoming commonplace. In the face of nearly nonexistent chances at stable employment and escalating demands to do more with less – and *for* less – professors are quitting the only lives they have been trained to know. When they do quit, they encounter the full-blown impact of auto-depreciation.

This is where the coaching services become relevant. Most often, they serve aspiring academics who are emerging, shaken and exhausted, from over a decade of training for a job they'll never have into the search for a job they likely never wanted. Increasingly, however, academic coaches are also advising tenure-stream faculty who emerge disoriented and a bit clueless after years of writing in special ways, performing special tasks, and talking about very highly specialized subjects.

In the industry-speak of academia, what the coaching services do is facilitate all these individuals' transitions into "post-ac" or "alt-ac" lives. The services have clever names like The Versatile PhD, ImaginePhD, Beyond the Professoriate, and The Professor is Out. They also have clever ways of describing themselves, like *career exploration and planning tool*, or *assisting and supporting PhDs as they transition from academia to their career of choice*.[22] But the core work of these services and the reason for their success is the need to reverse years of auto-depreciation brought on by good faith efforts to become, or simply *remain*, an academic.

Does tenure fix this – any more than it fixes the quasi-monopsonistic nature of the academic labor market or the financial stresses associated with it? Of course not. But academia *without* tenure is no better. Universities don't expect fewer credentials, less competent teaching, or – in most cases – a less impressive research agenda for the privilege of working a *non*tenure-track job. And that means that academics are just as vulnerable to auto-depreciation if they function outside the protective circle of tenured employment as they are if they work from within it.

PART THREE

Tenure's Labor

12

Renegade

This chapter tackles the first – and by far the most influential – of three common assumptions regarding tenure's effects on faculty behavior: that tenure encourages faculty to be iconoclastic in their teaching, scholarship, and extracurricular activities. In other words, in the eyes of supporters and critics alike, tenure protects academic freedom.

For a while now, it's occurred to me that nonacademics, as well as many pre-tenure faculty, must imagine that getting tenure is like being handed the keys to a particularly snazzy sports car on the morning of your sixteenth birthday. What a coup! You feel excited and empowered. You're ready to take on the world in a way that simply wasn't possible when you were a lowly pedestrian. If everything unfolds as it should, you and your new car will engage in all kinds of adventures to the consternation and anxious discomfort of your generous, trusting parents. It's a milestone that is simultaneously liberating (to you) and a bit dangerous (to everyone around you).

As many tenure-stream faculty ultimately discover, getting tenure is more like getting the keys to a new house. Of course you want the house. *Of course.* The house provides autonomy and security – not just for you, but for your family, too. You understand all too well that, in today's cutthroat housing market, it took a combination of good luck and great privilege to reach this moment. You are profoundly relieved. You are proud. You did it.

But you're also exhausted by the time closing comes around, and you're frustrated by all the hoops you had to jump through as well as the compromises you found yourself making. You're worried about what lies ahead because, while there were dozens of people eager to help you on your path toward homeownership, there's almost no one standing around now telling you how to *be* a homeowner. Most of all, you thought that getting the keys represented the end of your journey and of your battles. You didn't expect to find a rotting tree next to your new porch or a $5,000 smartphone-controlled oven (seriously?) that goes on the fritz when, a few weeks into your new and unexpectedly sleep-deprived status, you wearily toss in a frozen pizza.

Supporters *and* critics alike thus misunderstand the relationship between tenure and autonomy. There's no question that tenure provides the faculty who receive it with a level of security that's unavailable to the millions of at-will employees across this country, employees who can be subjected to instantaneous or arbitrary dismissal. But both sides of the debate overestimate the degree to which tenured faculty are waiting to zoom off, unsupervised and uninhibited, on adventures that were previously off-limits. They also underestimate the exhaustion, extra labor, and lack of direction waiting on the other side. On both sides of the debate, the rhetoric is overblown.

Before we move on, a few *Yes, buts…* are in order.

First, the kind of autonomy I'll discuss in the rest of this chapter is *individual* academic freedom. According to the German tradition that inspired many of the AAUP's earliest leaders, "academic freedom embraced three interrelated principles: *Lehrfreiheit, Lernfreiheit,* and *Freiheit der Wissenschaft.*"[1] Only one of these concepts – *Lehrfreiheit* – refers to the freedom of an individual instructor. And even though this word literally translates as "teaching freedom," the influential historian of tenure whom we first met in Chapter 5, Walter Metzger, notes that *Lehrfreiheit* encompasses both the scholarly and pedagogical autonomy now widely associated with individual academic freedom. Both the 1940 Statement and an earlier document, the 1915 Declaration of Principles on Academic Freedom and Academic Tenure, define academic freedom in individualistic terms: as the "freedom of inquiry and research; freedom of teaching within the university or college; and freedom of extramural utterance and action."[2]

But there's also *institutional* academic freedom – *Freiheit der Wissenschaft* – and it too elicits strong feelings in the contemporary United States. Metzger argues that this "somewhat cryptic" German phrase, which literally means *freedom of science,* is more properly understood as referring to the freedom of "[a]cademic self-government" and the need for "broad institutional powers."[3] Without these, nineteenth-century German theorists believed that the "university… would be dangerously vulnerable to government or religious censorship."[4] Today, American conversations about institutional academic freedom most often concern curriculum development. That's understandable since politicians and donors are both pushing for universities to teach "good" ideas (for example, via the centers of civic thought being established at various public institutions) and to ban "bad" ones (via the many legislative or executive measures targeting Critical Race Theory and other "divisive concepts").[5]

My focus on individual over institutional academic freedom tracks popular commentary, which tends to emphasize tenure's transformative effects on persons. But that's not to say that institutional freedom gets totally ignored or that commentators overlook the collective consequences of having or lacking individual freedom. Far from it. After all, arguments that academic freedom helps sustain democracy or that academic freedom fuels intellectual indoctrination are, fundamentally, arguments about how tenure affects *society.*[6] These are arguments about how job security for some people affects the lives of many people. Nevertheless, the individual professor and tenure's effects on her incentives remain at the center of the debate. Most people are for or against tenure depending on whether they think it produces renegades or heroes.

A second caveat is that my focus on individual incentives imports with it a theory of human nature according to which people are deeply, almost preternaturally rational. How else do you account for the idea that a person who's played it safe through at least a decade of tertiary education and another five to seven years of pre-tenure probation and regular evaluation will, consciously or unconsciously, let loose upon receipt of a simple piece of paper? But supporters and critics alike implicitly make this claim. In doing so, both sides lean on the idea that human beings – and professors specifically – are "rational actors" who carefully and accurately engage in cost-benefit analysis. It's an idea that's most associated with classical economics, and one that I explain further (as well as partly critique) in the context of Chapter 14's focus on faculty productivity. But it's also central to the assumptions at issue in this chapter and the next one, and it's no less problematic in either case.

Supporters of tenure, as I've already noted, argue that tenure is valuable because it allows faculty to be iconoclastic in their teaching, scholarship, and extracurricular activities. Let's acknowledge the proof problem inherent in this claim: saying that X *is a condition of* Y often means that Y *wouldn't exist without* X. If we didn't have tenure, the argument goes, we wouldn't have academic freedom. By implication, if you like academic freedom, you need to support tenure. (You might also say – and many supporters of tenure do – that X is a *necessary yet insufficient* condition for Y, but this more nuanced argument is less common, maybe because nuance is less rhetorically impactful.)

Why does this claim present a proof problem? Because we have no easy way to examine, in the real world, whether the availability of tenure *has* promoted scholarly or pedagogical freedom.

Imagine the circumstances required to empirically draw this conclusion. If you did a controlled experiment, you'd need two groups of faculty who are equal in every respect – intelligence, social capital, credentials, job security, professional autonomy, professional resources, and disciplinary prestige – except that one group has tenure and the other doesn't. This may be obvious, but: *two such groups almost certainly don't exist.* In most fields, having tenure makes certain things possible (like more scholarly production) that in turn makes other things possible (like research grants or prizes) and so on until the tenured and nontenured groups are meaningfully unlike one another. There just isn't an "all else being equal" way to think about these two types of professors at the same moment in time.

Perhaps, instead, you could think *across* moments in time via the kind of before-and-after demonstration commonly used by advertising campaigns. In this case, you would need a university that once had a policy of granting tenure but then abolished it (or vice versa), a way to eliminate other institutional or environmental variables besides tenure from your consideration (say, federal funding freezes that depress research productivity), and an idea of what professors at that university wanted to research or teach versus what they ultimately did. There *are* institutions that have flip-flopped between tenuring and not tenuring their faculty. Chatham University in Pennsylvania, for example, practiced tenure until 2005, then abolished it for seventeen years, then reinstated tenure in 2022.[7] Similarly, trustees of the State College of Florida at Manatee-Sarasota voted to abolish tenure in 2015, but union-led efforts eventually achieved its reinstatement in 2020.[8] But absent a few such examples accompanied by information about faculty desires *and* a reasonable interpretive framework for comparing those desires with actual behavior, defenses of tenure that rest on its efficacy at protecting individual academic freedom operate at the level of theory.

Saying that tenure's intellectually protective powers are largely unproven amounts to a kind of professional heresy. Apparently, though, I'm not the only heretic. In 2023, on the grounds that "one of the hallmarks of academic life is that our existential purpose is the search for truth… guided by evidence more than intuition," a professor named Mark McNeilly set out to empirically test the claim that tenure protects academic freedom.[9] McNeilly asked two questions – *Does tenure increase the likelihood that a professor is willing to speak up?* and *Is tenure effective at protecting those who have it?* – both of which he ultimately answered in the affirmative.[10]

To measure tenure's effects on faculty freedom – their "willingness to speak up" – McNeilly examined whether tenured professors were targeted for sanctions more often than nontenure-track (NTT) professors. He figured that the rate at which professors were targeted for sanctions might give us a rough proxy for the frequency with which they were willing to butt heads with administrators (essentially: if your hand gets slapped, it must have been stuck out). He found that tenured faculty, who only represented 24% of the US professor population in 2021, faced 58% of sanction attempts, while NTT faculty, who made up 68% of the population, only represented 33% of attempted sanctions.

To measure tenure's protective effects, McNeilly fashioned two sub-questions. First, he considered whether NTT faculty get terminated more often than tenured faculty. We'd *really* have a problem if the answer to this question was "no," because tenure – like all varieties of just cause employment – is meant to impose criteria and processes for termination that don't exist in the at-will world, and that need not even exist in all just cause contexts. Fortunately, McNeilly found that "[t]enured faculty have a 16% termination rate when targeted for sanctions," while the rate for NTT faculty is 53%. This is bad news for NTT faculty, but good news for tenure.

McNeilly's second sub-question smartly acknowledged that losing your job is only one way of being punished by your employer. Even if you keep your job, you could be reprimanded, suspended, demoted, or mandated additional training. He found that tenured faculty who were ultimately sanctioned were more likely to experience something other than termination, but nearly fifty percent of NTT faculty who were ultimately sanctioned were terminated. Again, this is bad news for NTT faculty, but good news for tenure.

McNeilly's findings are reasonable and they help reduce the proof problem for supporters of tenure. But like all work in this area, including my own research on tenured-terminations, there are important limitations to what quantitative data can tell us. For instance, McNeilly's conclusions can't account for the fact that it's often easier to simply fire or fail to renew an NTT professor than to bother sanctioning them for "speaking up." When someone is employed on a per-course or per-term basis, has no contractually established due process rights, and is too financially vulnerable to pursue litigation, it costs less in time and money to dispense with them outright than it does to devise and implement an acceptable punishment. McNeilly's discovery that NTT faculty are punished less but terminated more still suggests that tenure effectively prevents termination. It's just less definitive about tenure's effects on faculty freedom.

Like McNeilly, most defenders of tenure assume that individual academic freedom is self-evidently desirable, so they focus on justifying tenure. Another study about tenure's connection to academic freedom went one step further by testing the justification for academic freedom *itself*. In a survey-based article published by the journal *Behavioral and Brain Sciences* (*BBS*), Stephen Ceci, Wendy Williams, and Katrin Mueller-Johnson asked "whether tenure continues to promote 'honest judgment and independent criticism,'" since these are "key elements of the essence of academic freedom."[11] They did this by surveying what professors *thought other professors would do*, rather than what professors *did* or even what they *said they did*.

This hypothetical approach may seem odd, and it did elicit criticism from scholars who responded to the article in an open peer commentary forum that was also published by *BBS*. But asking some people about other people instead of asking them about themselves – even asking them about other *hypothetical* people – can be a reasonable methodological choice. As the *BBS* authors note (and as one of my own disciplines, anthropology, firmly believes) while you can learn something of value from asking a person direct questions, you can't always learn what they truly think, do, or want. They might not know (but still want to give you an answer) or they might be afraid (to give you an honest answer). Anthropologists often try to mitigate the shortcomings of direct-answer surveys and interviews by also observing their interlocutors and by participating in activities alongside them. The *BBS* survey's use of hypothetical circumstances is another valid approach, even if, like participant-observation, it comes with its own limitations.

The *BBS* study set out to measure "honest judgment and independent criticism" by asking respondents how a typical professor at pre-tenure (assistant) and post-tenure (associate and full) ranks would respond in various situations as described in Table 12.1:

TABLE 12.1 BBS *survey scenarios*[12]

How do you think a *typical* pre-tenure and tenured professor *would act* if...

Situation 1	... they wanted to teach a new course that senior colleagues frown on?
Situation 2	... they had credible evidence that a senior colleague is sexually involved with an undergraduate student?
Situation 3	... they knew that a senior colleague appropriated expensive technology bought with grant funds?
Situation 4	... they wanted to submit for publication an article on a controversial, unpopular, politically charged topic?
Situation 5	... they discovered that a senior colleague had published falsified data?

Overall, the *BBS* study produced five major conclusions, the first of which surprised precisely no one: *all* respondents believed assistant and associate professors were less willing to buck the system than full professors would be.[13] The third conclusion was more intriguing but still not very surprising: "[f]ull professors were not as brazen as junior faculty believed, and lower-ranked professors were more timid than full professors believed."[14] And the fifth conclusion, although the *BBS* authors personally thought it was "the most surprising," barely registered among peer commentators.[15] This was the finding that "[r]esults were consistent across academic fields, types of institutions, and genders," suggesting that rank and tenure status are "associated with a set of values and beliefs" that seems to matter more than anything else.[16]

The second and fourth conclusions contained the *Aha!* moments of the study, and they also generated the most passionate responses from other scholars. The *BBS* authors argued that they found "no support for the 'post-tenure renegade professor' hypothesis" (Conclusion #2) and that, in fact, the "lure of tenure and promotion seems to have muzzled lower-ranked professors, who were more reluctant to report ethical misconduct and relatively more willing to abandon unpopular teaching and research" (Conclusion #4).[17] Put differently, the *BBS* authors claimed that, far from protecting academic freedom by encouraging iconoclastic behavior, tenure seems to *discourage* that sort of behavior – and perhaps to discourage peer-monitoring as well.

Before we get too discouraged by these findings, let's note some of the very powerful critiques that emerged through the forum responses. Most significantly, several readers argued that the *BBS* study measured tenure's connection to *whistleblowing* more than its connection to *academic freedom*, and that whistleblowing is neither an element of academic freedom nor a standard justification for tenure.[18] Sixty percent of the survey questions – situations two, three, and five – tested professors' willingness to report unethical behavior by senior colleagues. Both assistant and associate professors may have scored lower than expected or desired on these questions, and because most associate professors are tenured this may tell us something about tenure. But what it tells us is that tenure doesn't encourage a type of behavior that it was, after all, *never designed to encourage.*

As some commentators to the *BBS* study noted, we struggle to promote whistleblowing in all kinds of workplaces and contexts where tenure is a nonissue.[19] In my employment law class, students learn how we've had to enact laws to encourage workers to share information about unethical or illegal behavior by coworkers or employers. We also learn how, despite these laws, many workers still don't come forward. That ought to tell us that whistleblowing is a complex social and legal issue not reducible to one specific contractual feature.

Going broader, commentators noted that four of the five questions – fully eighty percent of the survey – were "concerned with reactions among one's colleagues."[20] It's true that individual academic freedom is often spoken of in ways that are target-neutral: this kind of academic freedom is supposed to mean that academics teach, speak, and research without fear of reprisal from *anyone.* Coworkers (other faculty) are as much a part of this audience that's not supposed to matter as are employers (university administration) and the nonacademic world (politicians, parents, students, journalists, and so on).

The *BBS* study may show that even if tenure helps professors stand up to everyone else, it does not help them stand up to their own senior colleagues. That would be a fair criticism, but it's a much narrower one. It's also not at all clear that *tenure* is what's responsible for producing those "muzzled lower-ranked professors." One commentator observed that, in the United States, university departments control the substance of major personnel decisions (like granting tenure) much more than they do in other countries where central administration and external reviewers play a greater role in faculty evaluations.[21] This may mean that American professors looking ahead to tenure and promotion have more reason to placate their immediate colleagues by not going against their wishes (situation one) and by not reporting their unethical behavior (situations two, three, and five). Maybe this wouldn't be the case if tenure decisions occurred primarily at the level of main campus. We don't know whether the problem is with tenure or with the primacy given to departments in US academia, but the *BBS* study assumes that we do.

Most strikingly, the *BBS* survey may show that tenure *does* protect individual academic freedom, notwithstanding assertions to the contrary by its own authors. Situation four asked about faculty willingness to pursue publication on a politically controversial topic. The "strongest" answer option, meaning the option reflecting the highest level of independence, was to go ahead and submit the article for publication. The *BBS* authors noted that, to their surprise, this strongest answer option "was chosen relatively more frequently than the strong options for other questions."[22] Even assistant professors (who are generally not yet tenured) chose it most often. But as one commentator observed, this finding means that tenure – and even the *possibility of getting* tenure – "does allow a genuine independence of inquiry from political pressures external to the professoriate," and that this kind of independence "is often regarded as the central point of tenure."[23]

There we have it: *one* finding, based on *one* survey's responses to *one* hypothetical circumstance, suggesting that tenure may, in fact, support academic freedom. It's better than nothing, but not by much.

Does the anti-tenure side fare any better? Do we have any empirical reason to think that tenure encourages professors to be iconoclastic in ways that are *undesirable*? I'll start by pointing out that this side of the debate is more politically diverse than the side defending tenure on academic freedom grounds.[24] That is, there's both a *conservative* argument that tenure promotes undesirable iconoclasm and a *liberal* argument to this effect.

The conservative view is now perhaps most associated with Republican politicians like President Donald Trump, Florida Governor Ron DeSantis, and Dan Patrick, the Lieutenant Governor of Texas who declared in 2022 that he would "not stand by and let looney Marxist UT professors poison the minds of young students with Critical Race Theory."[25] Conservatives worry that tenure allows faculty to indoctrinate students with dangerous liberal ideas. Meanwhile, liberal critics of tenure have their own worries about academic freedom and, in some respects, they're strikingly like the concerns articulated by conservatives. Pointing to scholars like Amy Wax (Penn, law), Bruce Gilley (Portland State, political science), and Andrew Austin (Wisconsin-Green Bay, sociology), they argue that tenure allows faculty to harm students by using hurtful epithets or dangerous ideas. Both sides, in other words, tend to characterize their opponents *and* tenured professors as twisting the truth in service of their ideological agendas at the expense of students and thanks, above all, to the protections of tenure.

I mention this divergence (and convergence) just to show that critics of tenure on academic freedom grounds are not uniformly conservative in their politics. That's worth remembering given that many of the *highest*-profile commentators whose skepticism about academic freedom has fueled their skepticism about tenure *have* been political conservatives: William F. Buckley, David Horowitz, and Stanley Kurtz, for example. I also mention it because, in the end, I don't think the ideological commitments of tenure's critics matter very much. What matters is that critics who object to tenure's protection of academic freedom lack empirical grounds to stand on as much as supporters who assume that tenure *has* this protective power. If the critics' goal is to show that tenuring faculty encourages them to behave in undesirably iconoclastic ways, they must establish what professors *would have done* absent tenure's protections. And this, in turn, means they would have to establish some temporally appropriate metric for what constitutes *undesirable iconoclasm*.

That task may sound difficult inasmuch as it requires coming up with a generally acceptable standard for *un*acceptable iconoclasm by, say, a sociology professor in 1990s Florida. But, believe me, scholars do this sort of thing all the time.

In one of my home disciplines, law, there is a longstanding yet still-passionate debate over the school of constitutional interpretation known as Originalism. In the eternal rat race between schools of interpretation, Originalism has been the rat to beat for nearly forty years. It's well-entrenched in the US Supreme Court, in federal and state courts, and in law school faculties around the country. But that doesn't mean it's conceptually coherent.

Depending on who you ask, Originalism is the idea that constitutional terms should be interpreted today (that is, 2025) according to the original public meaning they had at the time of ratification (in 1788).[26] This requires figuring out what "the public" meant or wanted over two centuries ago. As amply demonstrated, first by historians (in the 1980s and 1990s) and then by linguists (from the 2010s onward), Originalism faces deep and likely insurmountable methodological challenges. *Who* is the relevant "public" whose opinions should guide us today? *How* can we identify their opinions, especially given that many of them didn't leave adequate written records? The challenges of identifying opinions for the sake of guiding constitutional interpretation are not unlike the challenges of weighing unrealized academic pursuits for the sake of evaluating tenure. I doubt tenure's critics will be able to do it any more coherently than Originalism's supporters.

If there's a strong and empirically grounded argument to be made for tenure that primarily rests on its protection of academic freedom, that argument is far more prosaic than either supporters or critics would likely want. It doesn't have to do with intellectual or political iconoclasm. And it begins with something that many academics know (and that one academic actually said in the context of responding to the *BBS* study):

> Most academic disciplines have few extremely controversial or politically or values charged issues. Most scholarship even in the social sciences involves little earth-shaking controversy. It is usually straightforward technocratic parsing of variance.[27]

In other words, most professors aren't interested in pedagogical innovations or research questions that would sufficiently irritate their ideological opponents to make tenure a necessary employment safeguard. And in that case, iconoclasm can't be the sum total of why tenure matters for academic freedom. Tenure may make all the difference in hard cases involving iconoclastic professors – but hard cases, as lawyers often say, make bad law.[28]

If all this is true, what *is* the academic freedom justification for tenure? Inasmuch as it exists, it's that tenure makes scholarly and pedagogical innovation possible when they are *not* iconoclastic. Tenure allows professors the freedom to fail,[29] and that freedom matters greatly for the often-mysterious work of teaching as well as the excruciatingly slow and unpredictable work of conducting research. To fulfill the teaching and research mandates of their jobs, professors need the employment security that comes with tenure. I know this sounds like it's veering into academic exceptionalism, so let me explain...

Teaching requires freedom to fail because optimal pedagogical approaches and course content structures are always changing but faculty have limited opportunities to refine and implement these changes. I'll use myself as an example. I once decided to rearrange the sequence of specific topics in the *ERISA* class I teach. My decision was meant to make the material easier for students to grasp and it was prompted by my sense that the original order had been too confusing for an earlier cohort. I changed my syllabus, revised my notes, and made new PowerPoint slides. In other words, I put considerable effort into making an incremental change for reasons that had everything to do with student success and nothing to do with ideological preferences. I didn't cut or add any material. Pedagogical innovation can't get more benign than this.

As you undoubtedly guessed, the change flopped. Before the end of the first revised session, I knew that this term's students were even more confused than the previous cohort and that my rearrangement was exclusively to blame. But because law is even more path dependent than many other subjects, I couldn't just rewind or redirect: I had to stay the course, unpleasant and unproductive as it was. The cases we discussed in the first revised session *had* to be followed by the cases that were slated for the second revised session, and so on.

This made me nervous. Despite being a junior member of a collegial faculty who had made a minor good faith mistake while trying to improve a course that no one else wanted to teach but everyone wanted to be taught, I was nervous. I couldn't fix my mistake or the perception students now had of me: I could only avoid making the same mistake whenever I next taught the course, twelve to eighteen months later.

Let me repeat: *my next chance to fix this mistake would be at least a year later.* In the meantime, students might grumble through weeks of class sessions, fume in evaluations, complain to my colleagues, and warn off their peers.

It doesn't matter that none of this ultimately happened. The mere prospect was nerve-wracking, despite the fact that I am not naturally prone to nervousness in my teaching life. If I'd had a more anxious personality or was making a major change – if I'd been adding or subtracting controversial material, flipping the classroom, experimenting with student-led pedagogy, or doing any of the other things that are now, in equal measure, demanded and derided – I would have been terrified. Without even the prospect of tenure, I would have probably never tried. I would be teaching material in a way that didn't suit my students because that's how the textbook presented it and I was too afraid to deviate.

(I did, incidentally, finally figure this one out. But it took three-and-a-half years, or three tries, which is what many experienced classroom instructors feel is necessary before you understand how best to teach a subject given your personality, your students' interests and aptitudes, and the course content itself.)

Like teaching, research also requires the freedom to fail. This is probably easier to understand in the context of the experimental sciences whose practitioners spend months, if not years, conducting experiments that might be disrupted (technical malfunction? mouse shortage?) – or, worst of all, that might confirm the dreaded null hypothesis.[30] Imagine spending years of effort, hundreds of thousands of dollars, and betting your own career as well as the careers of the students and post-docs working in your lab only to discover that there is no significant relationship between the things you're studying. The prospect of not finding exciting results is already scary and a little bit dangerous under a system with tenure, but it would be downright terrifying under a system where you could be fired "for good reason, bad reason, or no reason at all."

Research failures are hardly limited to the lab sciences: scholars in the Social Sciences and Humanities can have projects collapse, too. They can be denied visas or necessary institutional access. They can arrive at a moment when their key interlocutor is facing a personal crisis and is therefore unable to help them. They can find out, quite simply, that what they thought was a puzzle worth unraveling was not (a different version of the null hypothesis problem). A good historian, my husband frequently tells me, rarely knows what their argument will be until the archives tell them. A good anthropologist, I reply, feels the same way. Whether you're parsing texts or people, it can take years to develop questions worth asking, years to successfully complete the research, and years more to discover if the answers are worth sharing.

The uncertain and long-term nature of teaching and research helps explain why tenure may, after all, support academic freedom. It *also* helps put to rest the idea that, by supporting academic freedom, tenure produces renegades. Indeed, studies focusing on the post-tenure phase of academic careers refute the "'post-tenure renegade professor' hypothesis" in two ways.

First, these studies show that professors do not secretly harbor risky scholarly or pedagogical interests that tenure, and tenure alone, allows them to unleash. Most likely this is because anyone who gets tenure has spent decades mastering themselves in order to jump through hoops: they've earned all the As, written all the grants, revised all the papers, adjusted all the plans, and so on. By the time they win tenure, the autonomy it represents is something these individuals have operated without for most of their professional lives. (And yes, I include myself among these individuals: the only person I know who enjoys following rules more than me is my mother.)

To be clear, people who don't get tenure, or who don't get tenure-track jobs, have experienced this molding too. My point is simply that independence is a learned quality whether or not you're ultimately granted the opportunity to learn it. As one academic career coach observed, many "newly tenured faculty members show up in the fall with no agenda of their own."[31]

It turns out that after working feverishly for almost two decades to get tenure, academics who reach this milestone are as likely to stall as to zoom off. They don't defiantly clutch their tenure letters while assigning controversial new readings or hitting submit on controversial new articles. Instead, they run into the Second Book Problem,[32] experience Midcareer Malaise,[33] and (my favorite term) they encounter Post Tenure Depression Syndrome.[34] They become "terminal associates" stuck in "academic limbo"[35] instead of climbing the ladder up to full professor. If they do ascend, they likely fall prey to the phenomenon of "slow promotion."[36] Should they decide that they do, in fact, want to overcome these obstacles and reach for the highest rung they may need to hire outside coaches who can advise them on what to do with all that academic freedom they've suddenly got. That's because, aside from a perfunctory light snacks reception or sparsely attended Zoom meeting, their university-employers will assume, just like outside observers, that tenure eviscerates both the need *and* the desire for guidance.[37]

Second, research on mid-career academics reminds us that expertise and innovation, whether they're shared via the classroom or the journal article, take time and money. You don't just wake up one day and decide to write books or teach classes on topics you've never studied using methods you've never learned. Whether it's new training, new materials, new professional dues, or new networking expenses, metamorphosis *costs*.

That's why philanthropists Tom and Cathy Tinsley developed the Haynesville Project, which ran on a trial run at Colby College between 2021 and 2024.[38] During those years, Haynesville gave each newly tenured professor at Colby College a grant of $100,000 that came with only one condition: recipients could "only" spend forty percent of it for personal expenses – the rest had to go toward professional experimentation and self-improvement. (Most professors I know would be over the moon to have $60,000 to spend on their scholarly activities.) The Tinsleys, whom I spoke with briefly, understood tenure's economic value and transformative potential thanks to the experiences of Tom's father, James, who was a longtime member of the history faculty at the University of Houston.[39] But they also understood that that tenure provides only *one* of the conditions – job security – required to boost the kind of risk-taking that's both revered and feared.

Absent extraordinary circumstances like the Haynesville Project (whose motto, incidentally, is *Supporting professors at a pivotal moment*), the job security created by tenure comes with no extra time and, at many universities, with no extra money. In fact, it comes with *less* of one and therefore, on an hourly basis, less of the other. "I have people from the administration contact me," says one associate professor, to ask "'Are you tenured yet? We would love [for] you to do this.'"[40] "[N]ow," declared a department chair to their newly tenured colleague, "now you can start rolling your sleeves up and begin working for us."[41] A study exploring the post-tenure phase of academic careers observed that this "ramping up of service demands is so normalized that some faculty feel that offers to chair their departments are almost 'stapled' to their tenure letters."[42]

Becoming chair, contrary to Netflix and Sandra Oh, is not a sign that you've arrived. Becoming chair doesn't involve a corner office with a large desk and gifts of fancy wooden name plates. It involves budgets and complaints and building maintenance and enrollment targets; endless, interminable meetings; and the pleasure of governing your peers while knowing that you will soon, once your term ends, be right back among them, at their mercy. Chairing a department – like chairing a committee, conducting an investigation, organizing a workshop, and doing any of the other forms of service that more frequently land on your desk after tenure – requires you to take one for the team. It does not unburden you to fly solo. So the question isn't whether tenure really supports the kind of iconoclastic behavior associated with academic freedom: it's how anyone, let alone anyone remotely familiar with the workplace dynamics of tenure-stream academia, could think that it does.

13

Predator

Academic freedom may still dominate debates over tenure, but a second issue is rapidly catching up. This is the worry that tenure protects – maybe even *incentivizes* – bad acts by making wrongdoers difficult to fire.

The acts I have in mind here are ones that resemble or occasionally constitute legal wrongdoing: acts like sexual misconduct, fraud, bullying, and discrimination. As a genre of potential consequences, they're simultaneously less idiosyncratic than the subject of Chapter 12 (academic freedom) yet less universal than the subject of Chapter 14 (low productivity) because they often manifest in ways that are specific to the university environment.

For instance, in the nonacademic world, "employee fraud" often refers to financial theft. In the university context, by contrast, it almost always refers to research-related wrongdoing like the use of falsified data or plagiarized ideas and prose. That difference may make academic fraud seem less worrisome than its nonacademic counterpart: unless you're the President of Harvard or Stanford, who really cares if you engaged in some unattributed pilfering or let a few shoddy numbers slide by? Is it even *possible* to plagiarize in disciplines where all new thinking is "a series of footnotes to Plato"[1] or to falsify scholarship in disciplines where "progress is marked less by a perfection of consensus than by a refinement of debate"?[2]

Of course it is. And, notwithstanding a few high-profile incidents out of the thousands of articles and books written annually by thousands of scholars, most professors are like most people in that they think fraud is wrong and should be avoided as well as punished. Most professors, furthermore, will go on to say that the *reason* academic fraud is so wrong is because it violates the spirit of the scholarly enterprise. Whatever's in your personal mission statement – the search for truth, the expansion of human knowledge, or the modeling of integrity for young people we're supposed to be educating and guiding – most professors will agree that fraud won't get you there.

So academic fraud is wrong for all these reasons – but, as always, I'd like to avoid explanations that paint tenure-stream professors as being categorically different from other workers in favor of explanations that rely on them being the same. Instead of

112

expanding on these reasons to take academic fraud seriously, I'll note that this type of fraud is *also* serious business because it *is* business for the professors, universities, and third parties who may be involved in it. For the professors who engage in academic fraud, there are often prestigious awards, well-cited publications, endlessly watched TED talks, and hefty lecture fees.[3] For the universities and publishers who lend their reputational capital to fraudulent research, there are valuable grants and best-selling books, as well as better donors and advertisers. For the third parties – companies, governments, and individual people – there can be high profits, changed regulations… and crushing, not solely monetary, costs.[4]

We need to take the academic manifestations of various bad acts seriously without portraying them as sillier, pettier, or less materially consequential than they would be if they occurred in another industry. At the same time, we need to avoid making these bad acts out to be more than they are just because they occur in the academy. Like any other industry, academia has plenty of bad actors. Nothing composed of human beings or composed by human beings can be free of human defects. Big Tech has been inching toward this realization with respect to the discriminatory outcomes produced by algorithms and artificial intelligence. When it comes to academia, though, neither insiders nor outsiders seem to understand that having a doctorate or having tenure cannot, by itself, make you a saint. The only question is whether it can make you a sinner.

In the rest of this chapter, I'll focus on one specific type of bad act: sexual misconduct. It's the type of bad behavior that gets the most popular and scholarly attention, and my own data suggest that it's also the type of behavior that gets the most tenured professors terminated. Moreover, there's some support for drawing a correlative, maybe even a causative, link between being in academia and engaging in this particular bad act. That might simply be because sexual misconduct is probably the most well-researched type of academic misbehavior (although academic fraud is rapidly catching up). We can't say. But the mere possibility that there is something unusual going on means there's enough reason to pay extra attention – as I do both here and in Chapter 20 – to the relationship between academia and sexual misconduct.

A 2003 meta-analysis of sexual misconduct prevalence studies grouped workplaces into four categories: academia, military, private sector, and government.[5] The rate at which female employees in academia reported incidents defined as potentially harassing (0.58) was second only to the rate reported by women employed by the military (0.69).[6] Think about that. The academy, where the first female president of a major institution was appointed in 1975 (Lorene Rogers, University of Texas) and where roughly one third of these top positions were held by women as of 2022, was second in terms of harassing behavior *only to the military*, where women were not even allowed to command *units with men* until 1972.[7]

Now this study, like any other, is not without its problems.[8] Most strikingly, its authors say that they expected the lowest incidence of harassing behavior to occur in academia because, according to them, "academic organizations can be viewed as professional organizations with *small power differentials.*"[9] This is news to most of us who work in academia. In fact, this one sentence made me double-check that I wasn't reading the latest social science research published by *The Onion.*[10] Academia is profoundly hierarchical. I say this as someone who never really suffered from academic hierarchy when I was most vulnerable to it and who is now, for the most part, safely on the other side of it. And (as the authors of this study note themselves) entrenched hierarchy and large power disparities are widely associated with inequitable workplace dynamics and, specifically, with increased sexual misconduct.[11]

Perplexing priors aside, we can't dismiss the finding that academic women experience higher than average rates of harassing behavior. We shouldn't dismiss it. And, if recent reporting is any indication, we're increasingly unlikely to do so. The waves of allegations involving just *two* ultra-elite universities – Berkeley (Sujit Choudhry, Blake Wentworth, Nezar AlSayyad, Geoff Marcy, John Searle) and Harvard (Gary Urton, Jorge Domínguez, John Comaroff, Roland Fryer) – could take up a few volumes of printed text by themselves. In addition to all this media coverage, there are now massive, crowdsourced efforts to acknowledge and document sexual misconduct in the academy. A survey launched by Karen Kelsky in 2017 and publicized using the hashtag #MeTooPhD received over 2,500 entries in around one month.[12] The resulting narratives, Kelsky rightly notes, make for "sickening reading." Meanwhile, the Academic Sexual Misconduct Database started by Julie Libarkin in 2016 continues to collect valuable information about perpetrators and resolutions, and to provide publicly accessible proof.[13] I incorporate ASMD data into the *TTS* with gratitude.

Here's the catch: even though sexual misconduct is unacceptably and maybe unexpectedly high in academia, and even if tenure-stream academics' harassing behavior is being inadequately punished, we still can't conclude that *tenure* is what's behind either the prevalence or the obstruction. We also can't say that punishment rates in academia (which are undoubtedly inadequate) are *more* inadequate than the punishment rates in other industries. There's both a comparison problem (between academia and nonacademic workplaces) and an attribution problem (with respect to tenure versus any other feature of academia) – and the two are interrelated.

Take the first proposition: sexual misconduct is less reliably punished in tenure-stream academia than in other corners of the workforce. It may seem commonsensical to say that a protective employment practice like tenure is what's causing the problem by preventing the needed response. But then we would need to explain why so many female workers in other highly protective employment contexts, like government jobs, seem to report markedly lower rates – in fact, the *lowest* rate in the meta-analysis above – of harassment.[14] That study was completed well before 2025, when the second Trump administration began purging the federal workforce, so the lower rates of harassment reported by government workers was probably *not* because those government workers were so much more afraid for their jobs than tenured professors. Indeed, notwithstanding recent federal transformations, the Merit Systems Principles discussed in Chapter 5 created a very secure form of just cause employment, is applicable to most types of federal employees, and is primarily distinguishable from tenure by its uniform structure and lack of peer evaluation – neither of which disadvantage federal workers compared to tenured faculty in any way that's obvious or has been measured.[15]

We would also need to explain why misconduct is committed at high rates by both students and faculty in countries that don't practice faculty tenure (which, remember, is most countries). Studies conducted at the national level (e.g., Greece[16] France[17]) and cross-national level (e.g., a fifteen-country multilevel analysis[18]) all confirm that misconduct ranging from innuendo to rape is common in European universities. Studies from the Global South are far less common, but there are a few and they have similar findings.[19] A *second* meta-analysis study, this time across country contexts and with a special focus on higher education, concluded that "exposure to sexual harassment in higher education [worldwide] varies between 11 and 73 per cent for heterosexual women" with a median of 49%.[20]

Tenure exists in almost none of the countries examined in these studies. (I say "almost" because tenure does exist in Germany, but under drastically different conditions that minimize its legal importance, and it exists in Canada, where it is also in many ways less legally valuable.[21]) When it comes to sexual misconduct, academia is certainly problematic. Tenure, just as certainly, is not the root cause.

Now consider the second proposition: tenure obstructs adequate punishment of harassers – and maybe, as a result, it encourages the people who have it to engage in harassing behavior. We've already established that sexual harassment is highly, perhaps even unusually prevalent in university settings. But this by itself doesn't tell us whether *tenured* harassers are less frequently punished than pre-tenure and nontenure-track professors (which is an effect we should be able to see if tenure is really to blame).

According to the *TTS* data that I discuss later on, universities claimed that an overwhelming majority of terminations were linked to sexual misconduct allegations: 220 terminations, or 75.9% of the total dataset, in fact.[22] No doubt this number of misconduct terminations seems tiny given the study's two-decade window – and, therefore, like *ipso facto* confirmation that tenure protects harassers. But the rate at which sexual misconduct triggers employment actions in the *general* workforce is probably also mind-bogglingly, disappointingly low. The truth is that we just don't know. We don't know how many workers outside academia are disciplined or fired because they engaged in sexual misconduct, and we don't know how many of them trigger legal action under the relevant federal statute, Title VII, or under applicable state statutes. We don't even know how many workers are *eligible to file* claims under Title VII or related state laws. (As a colleague pointed out to me, we really know very little about the breadth and reach of work law!) When we don't even know how many workers are protected against certain bad acts or how many are held accountable for engaging in them, how can we be so sure that a very specific and small subset of workers – tenured faculty – are treated differently? We can't.

What all this shows is just how difficult it would be to make comparative assessments about tenure's effects. There's a heavy empirical burden awaiting anyone who wants to argue that tenured faculty, because they're *tenured* faculty, engage in sexual misconduct at a higher rate and with fewer consequences than other workers. I'm not sure critics can meet that burden and I'm more sure that they haven't done so yet. This, in turn, means that whether they're pursuing an academy that is gender-just or simply one that is tenure-free, critics of tenure are trading in simplistic assumptions about human nature.

Those assumptions form a connecting thread between the worry at the heart of this chapter and the concerns at issue in the two chapters on either side of it. All three types of critics – those who focus on iconoclastic behavior, those who emphasize predatorial behavior, and those who just worry about rampant laziness – are suggesting that, consciously or unconsciously, professors respond in rational but undesirable ways to the job security that tenure provides. At the same time, there's another assumption at play in the worry about predatorial behavior that isn't particularly relevant to concerns about unbridled iconoclasm and is far less troubling in the context of presumed sloth. This is the belief – omnipresent among opponents of tenure, but less central to advocates of gender justice on campus – that the problem lies with tenure-stream *faculty* alone. To fix academia's sexual misconduct problem, remove the shield of tenure.

Don't get me wrong: faculty harassers are to blame for their wrongdoing. But if they escape deserved punishment, it's not because tenure stood in their employer's way. It's because their employer didn't feel like using the tools that were clearly and already at their disposal.

Tenure and other varieties of just cause employment allow terminations for cause. *It's in the name.* A professor who engages in sexual misconduct, bullying, fraud, or discrimination can certainly be terminated under most definitions of tenured and just cause employment. At the margins, adequate cause might indeed be hard to establish, but most of the predatorial behaviors we're talking about here are far, far from the margins.

When tenure's critics argue that the practice insulates faculty who do terrible things, they're really saying that university-employers *prefer to retain bad actors* rather than engage in processes of review, discipline, and termination that are wholly open to them under their own policies and under governing employment law principles. The critics are also saying that universities *should be able to indulge this preference*. And, finally, the critics are saying that universities bear *no moral responsibility* for behaving this way: that the fault lies with tenure and the people who have it, rather than with the people who offer and enforce it. But employer incentives are every bit as relevant to this conversation as employee incentives.

It's true that the fact-finding and analysis involved in terminating for cause can be difficult as well as time and labor intensive. Employers who set out to prove the existence of adequate cause may fail to build a strong case even when there is one. I don't want to minimize either the effort involved or the risk that it won't pan out. But employees trying to disprove unfair or fabricated allegations may similarly fail despite being in the right of things and – given disparities of knowledge and money – this is a far more likely outcome. More importantly, not only are the challenges faced by university-employers typical of *all* just cause environments and *most* types of workplace litigation regardless of contractual universe, they're also morally unconvincing. An employer who can't be bothered to do the work is an employer who's chosen a rational but deeply undesirable course of action, not unlike the rational but undesirable course of action that critics ascribe to tenured faculty wrongdoers.

Given the prevalence of sexual misconduct and other workplace harms outside academia, we have little reason to think that dispensing with the principles and processes associated with tenure will make universities better stewards of their communities. Chapter 5 noted how, during the height of the coronavirus pandemic, the At-Will Rule enabled employers to fire workers for reasons inimical to public health. Even more relevantly, legal scholarship has shown how the At-Will Rule, "coupled with employer contracting practices and the law of sexual harassment itself, produces a world in which employers are inclined to tolerate sexual harassment and other misconduct by top-level employees but aggressively police 'inappropriate' behavior by the rank-and file."[23] All of this is to say that employer incentives under an at-will regime *also* generate socially undesirable outcomes. Tenure may be part of the problem – we don't know – but the At-Will Rule is not part of the solution.

What we already know (and what Chapters 19 and 20 offer further support for) is that academia writ large has a serious problem with hierarchy. I don't mean that it's a problem for academia to *have* hierarchies. Hierarchy isn't always nonsensical. Notwithstanding both sincere statements about professors learning from students and opportunistic statements about the university as family/community/collective, I think it matters that faculty have generally read more, written more, and thought more about their areas of expertise than the students they teach. I think the hierarchical relationship between students and faculty makes sense.

I also think it matters that American universities are about as amenable to Athenian-style direct democracy as America itself. Faculty governance simply cannot mean today what it meant in the seventeenth or eighteenth century. Even our mid-sized universities now offer a range of services and field a range of demands that make them more like municipal governments than like the colleges of the colonial era. The University of Chicago, where I received both my JD and PhD, has an active police force of around *100 officers*; the University of Southern California, where my husband received his JD, employs a police corps of *over* 100 officers.[24] UChicago and USC may be unusually elite, rich, and militarized campuses, but their campus security numbers alone speak to the fact that modern American universities are – for better *and* for worse – not the tiny, tight-knit, improvised entities run by professors in their spare time outside of teaching and research. This makes a different kind of hierarchy, one where even tenured professors like me are near the bottom, inescapable.

Of course, I don't like this very much. I believe that faculty-led governance is self-evidently essential to effective teaching and learning, and I sometimes find myself dazed by the number, variety, and authority of academic administrators (of whom my husband is now one). I also think that, while hierarchy may itself be inescapable, and may not always be bad, the massive and carelessly navigated disparities of power that characterize university life transform these institutions that could do so much good into ones that, too often, do so much harm. Hierarchy may be inevitable but the cruelty of abuse is not.

I don't know why academic hierarchy has proven so toxic, but it hurts me to see that it has. I was raised, intellectually and professionally, by tenured professors whose scholarly accomplishments were only matched by their warmth and conscientious guidance, so I know we can do better. I am friends, personally and professionally, with tenured professors who try to make their corners of the academy hospitable – not *despite* their high positions in various institutional and industrial hierarchies, but *through* them. As escalating public attention to faculty wrongdoing suggests, academia in general and tenured professors in particular need to do a better job of using power responsibly. But, as later chapters in this book suggest, we have no reason to think that getting rid of tenure will help.

14

Slacker

I don't have weekends.

Many nonacademics who hear this assume it means that my life inverts the normative workweek: perform paid labor two or three days a week and enjoy leisure time during the rest. They probably thought that this was always my reality, but now that I'm tenured they're quite sure that it is. And they're not alone.

"[O]nce you're tenured," declared Florida's Governor DeSantis, "your productivity really declines."[1] In February 2023, Mike Lefor, North Dakota's House Majority leader, introduced a bill to revamp tenure at his state's public institutions out of a desire to make "tenured professors accountable, just like anyone else."[2] Journalists like Christopher Beam (in *Slate*[3]) and Susan Adams (in *Forbes*[4]) point to academia – and specifically to *tenured* academia – when compiling lists like the "Least Stressful Jobs" because, as Beam puts it, "[i]f you can't be fired, what's to stop you from refusing to teach an extra course?" All this polemic grows out of the idea that job security disincentivizes work – or, put differently, that tenured faculty, *because* they're tenured faculty, have no reason to work as hard as everyone else. To get professors back to work, get rid of tenure.

I wish I expected better from either politicians or journalists, but I don't. In my more charitable moments, I chalk their views up to reasonable ignorance. After all, and despite being related to multiples of each, what do I know about the daily lives of accountants or musicians or doctors? These people would probably find my assumptions about their lifestyles to be comically inaccurate, too. Fortunately, I don't really need to make any. But politicians and journalists don't have that luxury: they are, in a sense, professionally obliged to generate opinions on a range of issues with a speed that I find disorienting. At least some of those opinions are bound to be misguided.

So while legislative attempts to gut tenure trouble me, the rhetoric that accompanies or encourages them does not. What troubles, disappoints, and frustrates me to the point of midday angry-dances is that *professors themselves* often claim that tenure disincentivizes productivity.[5]

119

"What does tenure do?" asks the University of Chicago economist Stephen Levitt.[6] "It distorts people's effort so that they face strong incentives early in their career (and presumably work very hard early on as a consequence) and very weak incentives forever after (and presumably work much less hard on average as a consequence)." Margit Livingston, a law professor at DePaul, states that "faculty members sometimes abuse tenure, knowing that they cannot be fired or even disciplined" before going on to sketch three personas – the Checked Out Classroom Teacher, the Indifferent (institutional) Citizen, and the Non-Publisher – who may be hypothetical caricatures or anonymized real-life colleagues or both.[7] Mark Taylor, the former chair of the Department of Religion at Columbia University, demands why tenured professors should "enjoy lifetime employment and the economic security it brings no matter how well or poorly they perform or how productive they are?"[8]

All these people ought to know better. Some, like Levitt, *really* ought to know better because they're experts in fields that claim to make accurate and generalizable statements about human behavior based on empirical data. As it happens, though, there isn't much empirical data about tenure's effects on faculty productivity. What little data does exist only ambiguously supports – or often outright disproves – the idea that tenure disincentivizes work.

Fittingly, the gap between what people think (inside and outside the academy) about what people do (before and after they get tenure) is best explained by a division in Levitt's own discipline of economics.[9] Even more remarkably, many of the most prominent figures on either side of this division are also faculty at Levitt's own institution, the University of Chicago. The divide I'm talking about – and slightly exaggerating just by calling it a "divide" – is the one between classical and behavioral economists.

Classical economists, to put matters entirely too simply, view human beings as "rational maximizers." Rationality here means "choosing the best means to the chooser's ends,"[10] while maximization suggests that the chooser will select the outcome that *most* benefits them. The person responsible for this particular definition of rationality is Richard Posner, one of the most famous American judges (and *the* most-cited legal scholar) of the twentieth and twenty-first centuries.[11] Despite those considerable achievements, Posner is just one of several renowned and classically inclined economic thinkers associated with Chicago, the university whose law school he taught at for many years and whose department of economics boasts more Nobel prizewinners than any other.[12]

Behavioral economists, by contrast, view human beings as having "bounded rationality."[13] They argue that people don't often choose the best means to their own best ends even if doing so would be relatively easy or free – in other words, they don't behave as classical economists would expect them to. Like Posner, some of the most famous behaviorally inclined scholars also work at the intersection of law and economics and, like both Posner and Levitt, they also have associations with Chicago. Richard Thaler won the 2017 Nobel in economics while teaching at Chicago's Booth School of Business, while Cass Sunstein taught at Chicago's law school for twenty-seven years before decamping to Harvard. In 2008, Thaler and Sunstein co-authored a book called *Nudge: Improving Decisions about Health, Wealth, and Happiness* to explain how small changes in the way we present choices could, by accounting for bounded rationality, encourage people to actually select the best means to achieving their preferred ends.

How does the division between classical and behavioral economics explain popular perceptions about tenure's effects on faculty productivity? And, more importantly, how does it explain why those perceptions are wrong?

Well, for starters, the idea that professors work less once it becomes difficult to fire them assumes that they work hard to get – and *only* to get – job security. It assumes that once tenure grants them this security, professors see no more value to be had from working hard and so they, acting rationally, stop. They stop refining their teaching methods, stop serving on governance committees, and stop participating in institutional life. Above all else, without the fear of unemployment driving them, professors stop conducting new research and authoring new publications.

The problem with these assumptions is that they're assumptions, and they're also not particularly borne out by the empirical information we have. (I should note here that most of the not-very-extensive empirical research on faculty productivity has focused on scholarly publication levels as a proxy for productivity, an approach that's understandable if not watertight, so I'll do the same.)

Sometimes, these empirical studies have resulted in findings that collectively paint a picture that is incoherent. Research among academic sociologists, for instance, has found both that tenure *reduces* productivity[14] and that it changes the *type of things produced* in ways that don't easily tell us whether faculty are more or less productive after tenure.[15] Maybe the tension between these studies conveys that study methods dictate findings (which is a truism), that some study methods are better than others (probably also a truism, as well as irritatingly unhelpful), or that some other factor – changes in environmental constraints, tenure expectations, or demographics – explains the difference in outcomes. Absent some kind of meta-analysis, we don't know.

At other times, empirical findings of reduced post-tenure productivity have been lukewarm. A study of computer science faculty found some evidence for increasing productivity before tenure and declining productivity after, but the decline was mild and leveled off within a few years.[16] In other words, professors engage in the same kind of performance acceleration you'd expect to see before a major promotion in any industry, and they return to more sustainable levels of work once the promotion has been achieved. *Nobody* works at 110 percent for thirty to forty years.

Finally, a third kind of conclusion emerging from these empirical studies has been that productivity before tenure largely predicts productivity after tenure. A study of law professors determined that, measuring both for publication quantity and quality, with the latter being judged by citational impact, tenure was *not* found to negatively affect the productivity of law school faculty.[17] Highly productive faculty were highly productive before and after tenure; less productive faculty stayed less productive.

All these studies concentrate on specific scholarly disciplines: sociology, computer science, and law. But this last point – that individual patterns hold constant regardless of tenure status – is also the overall conclusion of research done by two of the most influential scholars of faculty work patterns *across* disciplines, Robert Blackburn and Janet Lawrence.[18] As they put it, "[t]here are publishers and there are non-publishers."[19] This suggests that academics are no more rational maximizers of their own preferred outcomes than anybody else because, if they *were*, they would respond more predictably and unambiguously to external factors like the prospect of getting tenure or the changed circumstance of having it. (It also suggests that internal critics like Levitt, Levinson, and Taylor are no better at escaping bounded rationality than the rest of us, because they also generalize excessively from what they personally observe, otherwise known as the "availability heuristic."[20])

We can – and, in a moment, I will – explore *why* many professors are prone to working hard even after tenure significantly diminishes the specter of unemployment. But first I want to say a few things about the challenges of measuring faculty productivity as described by Blackburn and Lawrence themselves.

In a 1986 article titled "Aging and the Quality of Faculty Job Performance," they identify several obstacles to intelligently measuring scholarly productivity. Some of these obstacles are well-known inside academia, and first among them is an idea I mentioned above with respect to sociologists: quantitative decline doesn't reliably signal contribution decline.[21] The easiest way to think about this is via a phenomenon that's common in many disciplines – namely, that publication type changes in predictable ways over an individual's career, primarily going from articles to books. Although books take longer to produce and therefore faculty are likely to produce fewer of them, it's not at all clear that books are less worthwhile than articles.

Second, and conversely, Blackburn and Lawrence observe that quantitative highs don't reliably signal contribution highs.[22] Chapter 7 of this book mentions the "publication explosion" in academic writing while discussing all the other roles, besides researcher or teacher, that faculty must now perform. Chapter 11 mentions the same phenomenon in the context of an inescapable compulsion to specialize. Here, my focus is on the *cause* of this publication explosion rather than on its *consequence*. Higher aggregate publication volume is caused, quite simply, by a combination of more individuals and higher individual volume. While higher volume doesn't necessarily mean lower quality – as knowledge progresses, scholarly contributions will naturally become incremental more than revelatory – professors who are stuck reviewing endless article submissions will be the first to tell you that it often does. Put simply: more is *not* always better.

Third, and most generally, Blackburn and Lawrence gesture toward a sentiment that's widespread within academia, which is that scholarly productivity is fundamentally unlike the production of engines or toothbrushes or any other kind of widget that can be readily counted.[23] I like this argument least, but not because it's wrong: for the reasons explained above and below, it *is* much harder to count publications than toothbrushes, much less to determine what makes for a good one. I like this argument least because it relies on a kind of unanswerable academic exceptionalism that achieves little besides implicitly putting down everyone else.

Those objections to measuring faculty productivity may circulate widely within academia, but Blackburn and Lawrence make others that even academics are unlikely to have considered. A lot of these less obvious objections derive from the inherent shortcomings of *cross-sectional* studies, which are studies that examine the characteristics of individuals within a defined group at a specific point in time. For example, a cross-sectional study of productivity among tenure-stream anthropologists might consider the publication outputs, as of 2025, of all relevant members of the American Anthropological Association or of all relevant members of a single anthropology department. Cross-sectional studies contrast with *longitudinal* studies, which examine the characteristics of individuals across time – say, the publication outputs of relevant AAA members across their careers. Blackburn and Lawrence note that "an overwhelming majority of the academic studies on aging and performance were conducted with cross-sectional data" because "following people over a career or even working with their vitae is expensive in time and in money."[24] I'll mention just one of the shortcomings they attribute to cross-sectional studies because, despite all the reading and thinking I've done about faculty tenure, I'd never thought of it myself.[25]

It's possible, Blackburn and Lawrence note, that senior faculty maintain consistent productivity levels but that credential creep makes it appear otherwise.[26] Credential creep is what makes parents of high school children grumble that, today, they wouldn't have been accepted by the college they actually attended. It's also what makes tenured professors sigh that they wouldn't have been able to cut it in today's entry-level market. Credential creep is an unarguable fact of academic life. It affects both the entry-level hiring market and the standards for getting tenure, and it is one cause of the "publication explosion" I've mentioned. In some fields, empirical analysis shows that "new assistant professors in recent years have already published roughly twice as much as their counterparts did in the early 1990s."[27]

Given that academic productivity standards seem to have inflated alongside real property values, the negative impression we get from hearing that, say, full professors in a department have only published half as many articles as their assistant professor colleagues may be just that: an impression. Those full professors may have *always* produced the same number of articles or books because, when they began their careers, that number was within the normal range of expectations. Expectations, not productivity levels, are what changed. And, as workers across industries know all too well, it can be exceptionally hard to shift course in the later stages of your career. In this, as in much else, academics are not unique.

But what might make a tenured professor even *maintain* her pre-tenure productivity levels despite the considerable job security she now enjoys? This question gets us back to the disagreement between classical and behavioral economists about rational maximization. Perhaps all those academic productivity studies support the behavioralist's view of human nature. Work is hard even if the job security it creates is good: you're arguably not being very rational if you *don't* avoid the former once you can safely do so without endangering the latter.

The fact that tenure's critics assume a decline where there is none (or isn't much of one) just seems to further underscore the problem with viewing human beings as rational actors the way that classical economists do. Tenure's critics are essentially saying, "a *rational* professor would work less after tenure, so this must be what *actual* professors do." But, in so many ways, professors aren't rational, much less *unusually* rational, beings.

Then again maybe, as Posner might say, the problem isn't with the classical economist's view of human nature – maybe it's with the behavioral economist's view of human preferences.[28] That is, perhaps academics don't work hard to get a tenure-track job or to get tenure. Instead, perhaps they also and maybe even *mostly* work hard because they love their work.

I need to tread lightly here, because talking about how much academics love their work – the idea that academia is a "vocation" or a "calling" rather than just a bills-paying job – has lately and very rightly come in for a lot of criticism. Appeals to personal fulfillment have enabled exploitation in all kinds of employment contexts, whether they involve the work of caring for your own child or the work of teaching someone else's. These kinds of appeals allow labor that is difficult and time-consuming to go unrecognized and inadequately rewarded. Elsewhere in this book, I myself criticize the consequences of vocation-speak in ways that are both explicit (Chapter 4) and implicit (Chapter 9).

Today, vocation-speak mostly surfaces in critiques of academia or in heartbreaking accounts of having to leave it. I can't overemphasize how justified this is. The rise of "Quit Lit" described in Chapter 11 is just one of the most publicly visible consequences of asking people to train intensively for long periods under difficult conditions in the hopes of getting a challenging job that won't pay well, of socializing them to accept hard work and low pay in return for deep personal fulfillment, and then telling most of them that they can't even have that job after all. The fact that people continue to pursue academia despite growing awareness of this likely outcome may be the best indication of all that faculty are not unusually rational actors. It's certainly why commentators are increasingly calling academia a *cult* – one where "martyrdom… proves your purity."[29]

Nevertheless, I don't think there's any getting away from the idea that people choose to pursue academia either because they love what it allows them to do or because they discover they're good at what it requires them to do, and they enjoy being good at things. Loving what you do, thinking of it as a vocation, has been the dominant explanation for pursuing academia for decades. To be only mildly facetious, no less a figure than Max Weber (1864–1920) – whose Wikipedia page grandly but accurately introduces him as a "central figure" across the fields of sociology, history, jurisprudence, and political economy, and whose most famous argument is the very famous idea that a Protestant ethic spurred the emergence of modern capitalism – even Weber used the term *vocation* to describe academia… so it must be true.[30]

The widely criticized yet firmly entrenched and not entirely unwarranted belief that academia is a vocation offers a different explanation for why productivity does not, in fact, meaningfully decrease with tenure. The professional ends of academia – of getting a tenure-track job (which is what most aspiring academics want) and of earning tenure (which is what most tenure-track faculty want) – are not only defined by employment security. Make no mistake: employment security matters. That's basically what this book is about. But the ends of academia also include things that don't start or stop being relevant at specific points in time due to changes in contractual relationships. Those ends include the joy of expanding intellectual horizons for yourself and for others, the creation of new knowledge, the freedom to work alone or not as you see fit, and the lure of a legacy that will outlive you. If these are your ends, why *would* you stop working hard just because you have tenure? As the academic productivity studies largely suggest, you won't.

This is why I don't have weekends.

I started working seven-day weeks in 2007, the year I began graduate school, and I only stopped in 2020. Throughout graduate school, law school, a post-doc, and the first eighteen months of my first tenure-track job, my husband and I worked some hours every day and most hours on most days. Yes, we watched television and ran errands, cooked dinners, did laundry, and went out to drinks with friends. We tried violin lessons and Spanish lessons and failed pretty spectacularly at both. I became a licensed (but not practicing) bartender, and he maintains a patio herb garden that produces too much thyme but never enough tarragon. In short, we had lives – we still do, and for the most part we enjoy them very much. But whether we are teaching, preparing for class, grading, advising, researching, writing, attending or presenting at conferences, we worked, and continue to work, almost every single day.

A big part of the reason we do this is because we love our work. It's just fun. Acknowledging that vocation-speak can be exploitative doesn't keep us from feeling that academia is our vocation. We also work a lot because we have a lot of work: it takes time to do all the things that are required of us. And, finally, we work a lot because the nonstructured nature of academic life – the chunks of it that aren't predictably spent in classrooms, offices, meetings, and conferences, as well as the deadlines and targets that you largely create for yourself – all of this can make it impossible to ever say "I'm done." Self-policing is a great way to reduce leisure. Just ask Reed Hastings (Netflix), Marissa Mayer (Yahoo!), and dozens of other CEOs who have implemented unlimited paid time off policies in recent years only to learn that it exacerbates the American tendency to leave vacation time on the table.[31]

When my husband and I finally started taking one day off per week, it had nothing to do with earning tenure. In fact, in 2020, neither of us had tenure. The reason we finally downshifted to six-day weeks was the pandemic. As it did for everyone, the pandemic added a layer of existential angst to our lives. It erased the last remaining boundaries we had between "home" and "work" by transforming our house into a collection of virtual classrooms. And, for us, it also added a twist to the challenges of being new (and hardly youthful) first-time parents.

Something had to give. So we forced – yes, *forced* – ourselves to take one day off per week as a way to stave off burnout. We recognized that being able to do so was a privilege, we just thought we ought to finally use it. But old habits die hard, particularly when one of you is pre-tenure, one of you is nontenure-track, and employers like yours are firing ostensibly un-fireable people in clumps. (For more on these RIFs, or reductions-in-force, see Chapter 22.) During the first few months, our new routine was so difficult to observe that we had to silence our phones and shut down our computers just to make it happen. The stress of *not* working almost made us abandon the experiment.

I'm not saying that everyone in academia is like us. I won't even repeat the error of internal critics like Levitt, Levinson, and Taylor, by assuming that most academics are like us just because I personally know many who are. But beyond the fact that I grew up with parents who were like us and have friends, colleagues, and mentors who are like us, I think an intense commitment to work – regardless of tenure – is a more realistic assessment of how academics live because the research tells me so.

15

In Causa Sua

On Friday April 19, 2019, a former staff clerk of the Indian Supreme Court filed a sexual harassment complaint against Ranjan Gogoi, who was Chief Justice of India at the time.[1] The very next day, Gogoi and two other judges he'd selected held a special Saturday hearing to discuss the allegations. Besides the three judges, this hearing included both the Attorney General and the Solicitor General of India – but not the complainant herself. Gogoi denied the charges and claimed that there was "a larger conspiracy to destabilise the judiciary."[2] The hearing lasted around thirty minutes. After it was over, the three-judge bench put out a statement postponing any substantive conclusion. But on that statement were just two names: Arun Mishra and Sanjiv Khanna, the pair of judges Gogoi had chosen to sit alongside him. Gogoi's own name was nowhere to be found.[3]

Why am I talking about sexual harassment at the Indian Supreme Court? Because the outcry that followed that hearing and the release of that statement reflects a criticism that's often levied against the practice of faculty tenure. This criticism isn't as frequently or vehemently articulated as the concerns about iconoclastic behavior, predatorial behavior, or simply lazy behavior that I just explored. But it's nonetheless there, lurking in the confusion and misconceptions that animate public conversations about what tenure does and how tenure works. It's the worry that tenure – in fact, that the entire system of peer evaluation that runs through academia – violates one of our most basic beliefs about fairness: *nemo judex in causa sua*. No one should be a judge in their own cause.

Gogoi, of course, was literally judging his own case. In the academic context, the worry about self-dealing is a bit more abstract. It's the worry that, whether they are awarding good things (tenure, promotion) or imposing bad things (discipline, termination), professors are likely to go easy on one of their own. Tenure, in other words, is not only suspected of incentivizing behaviors we don't want; it is also suspected of shielding any bad behavior it produces from reasonable consequences… and the people holding the shields are other professors.

Peer evaluation is indeed a defining characteristic of academic life. There's no getting away from it. It surfaces early in academic training processes through the written evaluations of research and grant proposals that graduate students must submit so they can pursue their scholarship. It drives the workshops and conferences where graduate students answer questions, in real time, about all that scholarship they've been pursuing. And, as time goes on, peer evaluation only becomes more important. It's how conference papers get selected, how awards get bestowed, how articles and books get approved for publication, and in many universities, it is part of how new faculty receive feedback on their classroom performance. Most importantly, peer evaluation is how faculty are hired, tenured, and promoted – and ideally (although decreasingly) it is part of how faculty are censured, disciplined, and terminated.

Academics are very attached to peer evaluation. We may have mixed feelings about "peer review," which generally refers to the single-, double-, or triple-blind assessment of written things discussed in Chapter 10. But the principle of peer evaluation defines and inspires the academy every bit as much as academic freedom, even if it isn't spoken of in similarly reverential terms. It is part of American academia's Germanic inheritance, transplanted via that cryptic phrase, *Freiheit der Wissenschaft*, that signals scholarly self-regulation. When former Columbia University President Minouche Shafik promised Congress, in April 2024, that she was taking disciplinary action against certain professors, her colleagues were aghast in part because that promise seemed to undermine the primacy of peer-driven governance. "Congress isn't supposed to tell campuses who they must fire, who they can hire," noted one distraught Columbia journalism professor.[4] "[I]t's none of their business, we do this for ourselves."

Peer evaluation, in other words, reflects a core belief – maybe *the* core belief – of academia: expertise produces better outcomes. After all, why would academics need freedom from external coercion and interference? Because they are better at deciding what makes for good teaching or good research than the politicians, donors, parents, and many others who'd also like to have a say. *Don't judge me*, we are effectively saying to these others, *because you'll do it wrong*.

This, quite obviously, is an inescapably hierarchical, elitist premise. I don't mean that pejoratively – I value expertise. But let's call a spade a spade.

It is also, in an equally obvious way, an idea that's under fire across all aspects of American life. Whether we're talking about political representation or scientific knowledge, Americans have grown mistrustful of establishment experts. (In fact, according to the sociologist Gil Eyal, the crises of expertise affecting politics and science likely feed off one another because the "scientization of politics… leads to the politicization of science," and it leaves both types of establishment voices worse off.[5]) This overarching crisis of expertise "is more than a natural skepticism toward experts," adds political scientist Tom Nichols.[6] Nichols fears "we are witnessing the *death of the ideal of expertise* itself, a Google-fueled, Wikipedia-based, blog-sodden collapse of any division between professionals and laypeople, students and teachers, knowers and wonderers."[7]

Unsurprisingly, given these developments, peer evaluation's centrality to academia, and especially to *tenure-stream* academia, adds to the aura of inexplicable and undesirable privilege that envelopes the professoriate. "Tenured professors," says one tenured professor, "are extremely reluctant to deny tenure to a colleague whom they like as a person even though that colleague may be teetering on the edge of noncompliance with tenure standards."[8] The very idea that professors should get to judge their fellow professors, whether it is to hire them or fire them, smacks of the same *nemo judex* worries raised by Ranjan Gogoi's behavior. Why do *they* get to make their own decisions, control their own lives, ignore the incompetence, iconoclasm, and predatorial behavior of their friends? What makes academics so special?

In a word: nothing. But not in the way you might be thinking.

There *are* some aspects of academic life that are pretty unusual, but academia's reliance on peer evaluation isn't one of them. Other industries and other professions rely on peer evaluation, too. In this, as in so much else, an ostensibly unique element of academic life sits on a spectrum with plenty of other industries hanging out nearby.

Much of what we know about occupational self-regulation comes from a body of scholarship called the *sociology of the professions*. This literature has been around for a long time because the idea of elite self-regulating occupations that can be distinguished from other "non-professional" types of work has, itself, been around for a long time. Prominent nineteenth-century sociologists like Herbert Spencer, Émile Durkheim, and Max Weber all wrote about the professions, whose existence they viewed as a key characteristic of advanced societies.[9] Arthur Lovejoy, who resigned from Stanford in the wake of Edward Ross' termination and who became the driving force behind the AAUP from his new perch at Johns Hopkins, set out four benchmarks that he felt had to be met before academia could itself be considered a profession.[10] And, at least through the first half of the twentieth century, it made a lot of sense to reach for the label of "profession" because, at the time, workers who were thought of as *professionals* were experiencing a kind of golden age: they were well-paid, well-respected, and enjoyed considerable autonomy in their work lives.[11]

The jobs at the heart of all this are ones that we rarely call "jobs" at all. Instead, as I've already noted, we refer to them as *vocations* and we say that people are *called to them* – figuratively, in some cases, and quite literally in others, because the classic professionals are doctors, pastors, lawyers, and teachers.[12] These are occupations characterized by expert knowledge, a service orientation, and high social status and income.[13] Most of all, though, the classic professions are marked by autonomy and power.[14] In any field that's marked as *professional*, "individual practitioners control their own work, and professional groups regulate their members without outside interference."[15] This kind of control over a sphere of action and knowledge, this *jurisdictional claim* over certain kinds of expertise, is what, according to the sociologist Andrew Abbott, defines the essence of professional life.[16]

Sure enough, doctors police doctors, and lawyers police lawyers. In Georgia, where I currently live, complaints about lawyers are largely handled by a state disciplinary board whose lawyer-members outnumber its lay members by more than three to one.[17] In Illinois, where I lived for nearly ten years, this function is fulfilled by a seven-member commission where the ratio is four to three.[18] The country's two biggest legal markets, New York and California, have correspondingly big infrastructures to deal with attorney misconduct and these infrastructures also heavily prioritize lawyers. New York's many attorney grievance committees usually feature a dozen or more lawyers but only around three nonlawyers, while California is the sole state in the union to have an "independent professional Court dedicated to ruling on attorney discipline cases" and staffed by licensed attorneys and judges.[19] For their part, when they are accused of professional misconduct, doctors in all these states (and in most others) encounter entities and processes that are similarly dominated by their peers.

So while critics can gripe about the degree to which professors are in charge of policing and rewarding themselves, they can't do so on the grounds that this arrangement makes professors unique. (Actually, they can't even do so on the grounds that this makes the *classic professions* unique: other professionals, like architects, also operate under licensing and disciplining schemes that are centered on peer evaluation, as do workers, like barbers, who are not traditionally thought of as professionals at all.[20]) Academia *is* a guild, just like many other professions and industries – and irrespective of any positive, negative, or neutral valence we assign to guilds.[21]

Critics who worry about the unfairness and inefficacy of peer evaluation also forget that peers are rarely the *only* ones tasked with evaluation. In fields like law and medicine, the same disciplinary boards that are dominated by practitioners almost universally include laypersons too. In the university, even with respect to the tenure-stream faculty who are believed to be immune from outside oversight, nonacademic actors are a regular, vocal, and increasingly powerful presence.

Sometimes this nonacademic presence makes itself felt at a systemic level. Between September 2020 and April 2024, well before the raft of executive orders issued by President Trump at the start of his second administration, "a total of 246 local, state, and federal government entities across the United States… introduced 805 anti-Critical Race Theory bills, resolutions, executive orders, opinion letters, statements, and other measures."[22] A university professor whose violation of anti-CRT regulations triggers administrative punishment is, not very indirectly, a professor being punished *by her state*. Minouche Shafik's April 2024 congressional testimony was preceded by another hearing in which the presidents of Harvard, the University of Pennsylvania, and MIT were made to defend their universities' handling of pro-Palestine protests and campus antisemitism. Shafik's testimony was also followed by a third hearing involving the presidents of Northwestern, Rutgers, and UCLA. A university leader called to legislative account for their institution's campus policies is, again not too indirectly, a leader who is accountable *to their state*.

Nonacademic intervention can also be individualized. Some professors have essentially been "un-recruited" after the involvement of parties whose role in tenure-stream faculty hiring is traditionally nominal or nonexistent. Kathleen McElroy (university regents, alumni groups[23]), Nikole Hannah-Jones (university trustees[24]), and Steven Salaita (university trustees, donors[25]) are among the most recent and well-known scholars in this category, but they hardly represent its sum total. Likewise, although perhaps more rarely, some tenure-stream professors have been recruited after hiring processes that rendered faculty participation nominal or nonexistent. Joseph Ladapo (tenured full professor at the University of Florida[26]) is among the most high-profile recent figures in this category.

Political involvement in academic self-governance is generally feared and resented by professors, to say nothing about the growing involvement of alumni, donors, parents, and lobbying groups. But despite their qualms about nonacademic influence, a good deal of professorial ire is reserved for the intrusion of *administrative* actors and corporatized values into what is widely considered the properly non-market space of the university.

In its intellectualized form, this displeasure is called Critical University Studies (CUS). CUS is a term that emerged in 2011 for an analytic approach dating to the 1990s, one that studies the university instead of studying something else from within the university. CUS scholars generally view the university not as an "an exemplary public good" but as something "founded on the ongoing violent accumulation regimes of empire, chattel slavery, and settler colonialism."[27] That there is likely very little in the way of *un*critical university studies these days does nothing to diminish the validity of arguments put forward by CUS scholars. Higher education in the United States all-too-often *is* "an instrument of its social structure – reinforcing class, race, and gender discrimination – rather than a tool to alleviate it."[28] But, for me anyway, the greatest takeaway of CUS scholarship isn't that the university is somehow exceptional in its faults: it's that the university is not exceptional at all.

Over a decade ago, the political scientist Benjamin Ginsberg wrote that "institutions of higher education are mainly controlled by administrators and staffers who make the rules and set more and more of the priorities of academic life."[29] It may be true, Ginsberg notes, that most tenure-stream faculty have some input into the classes they teach and the research they do. But it is rarely true that they can determine who they teach (via admissions), who they work alongside (administratively-appointed adjuncts), who leads them (presidents, other administrators), or what their institution offers (majors, degrees, departments, even schools). Professors may still be professionals, but they are, in the language of higher ed scholar Gary Rhoades, increasingly *managed* professionals.[30]

For instance, at one of the institutions I've worked at, a faculty committee was created to help select the new law school dean. Despite email language clearly announcing that the final decision would lie with the university's chief academic officer (its provost) many of my colleagues apparently assumed that their elected committee members *would*, in fact, be largely responsible for selecting the new law school dean. At the other institution I've worked at, where the law school also experienced a decanal transition, no such language was even used. The selection criteria were announced and, a few weeks later, the new dean was announced.

Choosing deans and presidents, even more than appointing mid-level staff and adjunct professors, may seem like business decisions properly or optimally removed from the faculty. Perhaps they are. Perhaps the corporatization of modern universities and their institutional complexity – perhaps the transformation of the university into an "academic capitalist knowledge/learning regime"[31] – means that faculty *can't* meaningfully participate in their own self-governance. If that's the case, then that's also my point. Whether professors have lost some of their governance powers because the practicalities demand it or because the politics demand it, what matters most is the loss of power. *Nemo judex* worries presume power.

The reduction of true governance authority is just one reason why it's wrong to view academia's reliance on peer evaluation as unusual or unusually high. Another reason lies in the ordinary interactions between employer and employee, which are perhaps surprisingly similar inside and outside the walls of the ivory tower. I recently submitted my first annual review report after joining Emory, in which *one* part of a roughly *twenty-eight*-part questionnaire itself had *five* subparts.[32] My chances of being promoted to full professor are influenced, to no small degree, by the exhaustiveness with which I dutifully complete this exercise every year during precisely the same weeks that students want exam grades, conference organizers want participation, and many publishers want finalized manuscripts. This year, one of those twenty-eight-plus parts of the electronic report refused to save… *four times.* You might wonder what the big deal is since everyone experiences irritating supervision and inconveniently timed technology fails – at least, I hope this is what you're wondering because, once again, that's my point. Annoying annual performance evaluation is ordinary fare outside the academic world; as it turns out, it's ordinary fare inside it as well.

Now consider a different window into possible *nemo judex* worries: faculty handbooks. Like all employee manuals, faculty handbooks serve as "an expression of the [employer's] 'philosophy.'"[33] In fact, this expressive function is likely to be even more pronounced in the case of faculty handbooks than with respect to other types of employee manuals because faculty handbooks are virtually guaranteed to be consulted regularly and without any precipitating negative incident. An assistant professor working toward tenure and an associate professor working toward promotion both have reason to read and internalize their handbooks' prescriptions even if they're entirely happy with their jobs. This gives faculty handbooks the qualities of a travel guide or a constitution in addition to being like a fire extinguisher that you reach for when something has already started to burn. It also makes faculty handbooks particularly valuable sources of insight into how university-employers and faculty-employees imagine the role of peer evaluation in institutional life.

As many faculty handbooks make clear, professors aren't the only ones tasked with judging other professors even when it comes to initial hiring or eventual tenuring. These, remember, are two of the personnel decisions where faculty oversight is easiest to defend given the specialized expertise they demand. But look at what faculty handbooks often have to say about professorial involvement in hiring and tenuring decisions:

Initial recommendations concerning **appointments, reappointments, and promotions** normally come from the departments. The Committee on Appointments and Promotions (CAP) considers the recommendations of the departments and transmits its own recommendations to the President, who in turn makes recommendations to the Board of Trustees for final action… **The role of the CAP is an active one**; it does not simply "register" departmental recommendations.

— Williams[34]

The **Provost** is the only official delegated by the President with the authority to **grant tenure, make appointments** of associate professors and professors on the tenure-track, or award special designations and continuing appointments.

— Southern California[35]

Appointments to tenured positions are made only after consultation and approval of the **dean of the college and the SVPP**.

— Iowa State[36]

Upon review of the materials in accordance with University, college/school, and department/unit standards, **the APT Committee** shall vote, and forward its final recommendation regarding **reappointment** of the faculty member to the Department Chair.

— Appalachian State[37]

The **Board of Visitors** has full authority over **faculty personnel matters**, including faculty **appointments**… Faculty recommendations for appointment are forwarded to the Dean of the academic unit in which the appointment is to be made. If concurring with the faculty recommendations, the **Dean** will forward them to the **Provost**.

— George Mason[38]

Tenure is made only with Board of Trustees approval…

— Duke[39]

Now, in all honesty – and despite the protestations of the Williams College handbook – university leaders *do* often just "'register' departmental recommendations" when it comes to these sorts of personnel decisions. Faculty oversight of hiring, tenuring, and promotion decisions is not dead, however much individual circumstances may suggest otherwise. Professors still often have a say in who becomes their colleague, how long they remain a colleague, and whether that colleague can receive the accolades and perks available to similarly situated workers. But professors don't have *as much* of a say as they once had – and they don't exercise that say to the exclusion of other university actors, or even above other university actors. So while critics can take issue with the reality that tenure-stream professors are involved in policing and rewarding themselves, they can't do so on the grounds that professors do this unilaterally or with impunity. They really, really don't.

Besides underestimating academia's similarity to other industries and overestimating tenure-stream professors' control over personnel decisions, the *nemo judex* worry also focuses on one potential consequence to the exclusion of all others. That potential consequence, of course, is that the system of peer evaluation underlying tenure-stream academia allows professors to protect or reward colleagues who are undeserving. But what if the *benefit* of tenure (and of peer evaluation itself) isn't limited, even in an organizational or employment sense, to professors?

Asking *who* benefits from tenure takes us back to that core belief I mentioned earlier on in this chapter, namely, that expertise produces better outcomes. If we believe that scholarly knowledge is required to evaluate scholarly production and potential, then universities need the expertise of existing faculty (whether their own or that of external reviewers) to make good personnel decisions.[40] In turn, as the economist Lorne Carmichael has long argued, incumbents need the protection of tenure if they are going to "identify candidates who might turn out to be better than them, and if they are going to help these young scholars by passing on their accumulated knowledge."[41]

Why? Why would incumbent professors need the security of tenure before they use their expertise to find their employers the best new hires?

Consider what the incumbent has done to get where she is. She's undergone a decade or more of intensive and expensive education followed by a highly competitive job search, as described in Part One. She managed to get the job, despite very bad odds, and her reward has been a position characterized by the phenomena described in Part Two – low pay, no pay, multihyphenation, and auto-depreciation. Why *would* she choose the most promising entry-level candidate to be her new colleague if she lacked the security of tenure? That most promising candidate might divert university resources away from her. That most promising candidate's publication record and future accomplishments will almost definitely make her look bad simply because, as Chapter 14 noted, the candidate was likely trained to satisfy inflated productivity standards. Why would incumbents inflict all this on themselves? Why would they choose the *most promising* candidate instead of choosing someone who's merely *promising* or *adequate* or even someone who's slightly deficient? How many people could, realistically, act against their own best interests in not-insignificant ways repeatedly over the course of a multidecade career?

Some people could and would do this, of course, for precisely the same reason that so many professors work hard even after earning tenure. We're not perfectly rational beings. But the fact that many people – not just academics – *can't* do it is what gives rise to a phenomenon called the Salieri Effect, named for the composer, Antonio Salieri, who reportedly tried to sabotage the career of his younger and more accomplished rival, Mozart.[42] The prospect of losing something you already have exercises a powerful and predictable effect on human decision-making. This is true even if the thing at risk is only a ceramic coffee mug.[43] For the incumbent professor, though, the thing at risk is a job, a career, a vocation (forgive me) for which she has sacrificed so much.

Carmichael's argument is admirable for its acknowledgment that academics aren't superhuman, that they're imperfect and occasionally self-interested just like anyone else. Most professors, I find, are not willing to acknowledge this kind of human frailty among their. Carmichael's logic also doesn't presume an *inverse* type of superhuman ability to do wrong that would be just as unrealistic as the positive kind. He's not saying that, without tenure, hiring committee members could or would deliberately, maliciously, and consistently prioritize their own interests above those of their university (although, since he's an economist, it can sometimes sound like this is precisely what he's saying). Nevertheless, if you've ever worked in an environment with other people – or if you've ever just been around other people – you can imagine how subconsciously held feelings of inadequacy and shame often produce bad thoughts and bad choices. Those undesirable outcomes only become more likely if your own career is hanging in the balance. Tenure, Carmichael argues, ensures that it isn't.

The *nemo judex* worry at the core of this chapter assumes that tenure promotes faculty interests at the expense of other parties. One response, implied by Carmichael's argument, is that even if tenure benefits faculty, it *also* benefits other parties. University-employers want the most impressive employees they can get, while society wants the best minds teaching its students and advancing its collective understanding. Both rely on academic expertise to achieve those goals, but the academics whose expertise is needed by universities and society *themselves* need job security to freely wield that expertise for the common good. Another response, which we saw via faculty handbooks, is that tenure doesn't significantly shield its holders from everyone else because university administrators also have an important say or a final one (or both). And a third response, which was actually my first, is that the importance given to peer evaluation in tenure-stream academia – the heart of the *nemo judex* worry – isn't unique to academia at all. It's a core feature of all professions, and even of some jobs in fields that are not commonly considered "professional."

There's one last response to be made. The *nemo judex* instinct that was so blatantly violated by Ranjan Gogoi assumes that the judge and the adjudged, or at least their *interests*, are identical. *In causa sua*, after all. But faculty do not always benefit from being judged by other faculty. I'm not talking about the dreaded Reviewer #2 of peer review publication woes – the person who criticizes unproductively or who rejects wholly via comments that are equal part ego-stroke and searing self-indulgence.

What I'm referring to are the undesirable consequences *for tenure-stream faculty* of having to please their colleagues inside and outside the building if they want to win that next promotion or next prize.

Take, as one small example, the phenomenon of named-chairs. A named-chair is a title that's appended to a professor's standard designation, along the lines of "Professor of Law, and the Jane Smith Chair of Academic Esoterica." That short add-on represents academia's own system of nobility or VVIP status. You almost always have to be a full professor before you can become a named-chair, so you've already received tenure and climbed the standard promotion ladder to its peak. Your chairship shows, in theory, that you've *exceeded* those standard standards.

Named-chairs are all about prestige. The title might bring you some extra money, it's true, but the amount isn't at all consistent across chairs, and in most cases there's no way for anyone outside your unit to know whether you're receiving a few extra conference dollars, several multiples of your former salary, something in between, or nothing at all. (If there is money, by the way, it likely came from Jane Smith, who may or may not have set the selection criteria for the title she was endowing.)

Since a named-chair is frequently only a symbolic recognition of professional accomplishment, it seems like exactly the sort of thing that academics should be wholly in charge of dispensing. My informal straw poll of law professors suggests that many law schools *do* give faculty the sole power to elect named-chairs and that this power is exclusively exercised by professors who already hold such titles. This is standard operating practice within academia and it has a kind of instinctive appeal: faculty with tenure vote on applications for tenure, full professors vote on promotions to full, and so on, the idea being that only existing club members are qualified to let you in because they've already met the entrance requirements.

But the named-chair system reveals that peer evaluation can also have unpleasant consequences for faculty themselves. In one of the institutions we've worked at, my husband and I walked into the building only to immediately start wondering about the genuflections figuratively happening all around us. People were smiling and nodding at everything a handful of senior faculty said even if they later (or, via text message, simultaneously) complained about it. Twenty-minute verbal excursions during ninety-minute faculty meetings were met with deferential, if seething, silence. Opinions were sought regardless of expertise while formal votes of thanks were issued regardless of performance.

Why? You know why. The silence, deference, and obeisance *weren't* most notably coming from pre-tenure colleagues who still had everything to lose. (In all honesty, it's hard to notice when pre-tenure faculty display such behaviors because so many of them – including myself, before tenure – do. Needs must.) No: these displays of obsequiousness were being put on by *tenured* professors who needed the votes to enter academia's aristocracy. They were playing the long game because the system of peer-appointed named-chairs requires them to.

It's hard to say this sort of thing at a time when tenure seems especially at risk. But the truth is that tenure has *always* been at risk and professors do themselves no favors by protecting an image that's rendered almost inhuman by its virtues. Saying that peer evaluation and tenure aren't perfect is not the same thing as saying that some other approach would be unambiguously better. There's no such thing as a perfect approach to human resources management. (If there were, my father, who taught HR for decades and who co-authored one of the leading Canadian textbooks in the field, would have been out of a job before he got one.[44]) All it means is that while critics can take issue with the ethos of peer evaluation that underwrites tenure, they can't do so on the grounds that tenure's recipients – and those recipients alone – invariably benefit.

16

"This Important Service"

James Bryant Conant became the twenty-third President of Harvard University in 1933 at the age of forty. He isn't the youngest person to have assumed this office – that distinction belongs to C.W. Eliot, who took on the role more than half a century earlier at the dauntingly low age of thirty-five. Conant also wouldn't go on to become Harvard's longest-serving president (that's Eliot, too). But Conant presided over Harvard at a time when important changes were afoot in the way higher education operated, and, while he was the head of the country's most storied university, Conant led many of those changes himself.

One of these changes lay in the way Harvard employed its faculty. Until Conant's administration, there had been no clear script for circumstances in which an assistant professor did not win tenure: sometimes the professor might have been allowed to try again, sometimes they left or were shown the door, sometimes they hung around indefinitely. Early on in his administration, Conant decided to standardize the response. He implemented a strict "up or out" policy whereby professors who didn't win tenure *had* to leave Harvard – and, apparently, he did this as a way to motivate scholarly excellence during the probationary period leading up to tenure.[1]

At the time Conant implemented this change at Harvard, *up or out* wouldn't have seemed like an unusually harsh approach to personnel management in the world of professional workers. Just a few decades earlier, the New York attorney Paul Cravath had made *up or out* the default rule for law firms, many of which still operate according to his Cravath System and consequently require that senior associates who don't make partner find new employment. The precursors to today's Big Four accounting firms – Deloitte, PwC, Ernst & Young, and KPMG – also followed a strict *up or out* policy for decades, although (and, again, like their counterparts in the legal field) these firms are becoming increasingly flexible about how strictly they apply the rule. In fact, the consistency with which universities still adhere to the practice of *up or out* when it comes to their tenure-stream faculty makes them more of an outlier today than Harvard would have been in the 1930s when President Conant first adopted the practice.

Conant, in fact, was no critic of tenure. He supported the idea of powerful job security after a probationary period and a rigorous evaluation process. In a 1935 letter to President Edgar Lovett of Rice University, Conant wrote that "our only hope of recruiting men for this important service is to guarantee the permanency of their tenure when they have reached a certain age and attained to a certain eminence."[2] A strict *up or out* policy combined with a strong policy of tenure for those who remained was, according to Conant, the way to attract excellence as well as the way to retain it.

Conant's views on tenure underscore two aspects of tenure's history that are widely unappreciated even – or especially – by its most dedicated supporters.

First, as Chapter 6 suggested, tenure did not emerge whole cloth from the AAUP's 1940 Statement. Important elements of the practice we now call tenure – indefinite employment that is unusually secure and that follows a probationary period and a quality check – existed many years before. So too did the assumption that anyone who failed the check was "out." Three surveys conducted between 1910 and 1919 each found that, at the time, a majority of institutions already granted indefinite employment to either full professors or associate professors (a grant that was grandiosely and inaccurately called appointment "for life").[3] And in 1935, President Lovett of Rice reached out to dozens of his fellow university leaders for information about how their institutions approached the issue of faculty tenure; among the seventy-eight responses Lovett received, 48% had instituted formal tenure policies and another 37% "described a custom of tenure," albeit one that was "unsupported by written regulations."[4]

What keeps these examples from truly amounting to tenure as we understand that practice today is the almost universal absence of any academic due process. The requirement that university-employers must follow certain processes before disciplining or terminating tenured professors – *this* is what gives the promise of tenure real heft. A failure to follow these processes itself constitutes a violation of tenure. Without academic due process, even the most powerful professor serves at the pleasure of a president or a board of trustees whose promise of job security amounts to little more than "we promise to not fire you so long as we don't *want* to fire you."

So tenure existed before the 1940 Statement – just not fully. What also existed, and what gets hidden by the narrative that tenure was "invented" in 1940, was a widespread sense that job security was desirable enough to professors that it should be desirable to university administrators, too. This segues into the *second* frequently overlooked aspect of tenure's history, a feature that's also visible through the Conant reforms at Harvard: when tenure finally was adopted by universities, it was often at the behest of administrators (not faculty) for reasons that sounded in recruitment and retention (not academic freedom). In other words, tenure became an industry practice because it was a valuable employment protection.

The protagonist of this story is probably its most striking feature. *Administrators wanting tenure?* That's nearly impossible to imagine in today's climate. Ongoing political attacks on tenure make it difficult to think of tenure as anything except the valuable spoils of a primordial war between professors and everyone else.

But even though the formal and far superior articulation of tenure that's contained in the 1940 Statement *was* spearheaded by a group of professors, it would not have become an industry practice without administrators. At one point, the AAUP itself seemed to recognize this. When the Association set out to write its landmark statement, it searched for a co-author among comparable associations representing university leaders and administrators. The co-author it eventually landed turned out to be the Association of American Colleges (AAC), a collection of small, denominational, or teaching-focused institutions whose leaders were not initially receptive to the AAUP's ideas about tenure and who many early AAUP leaders secretly considered to be insufficiently cosmopolitan to be worthy partners.[5] But leadership changes at the AAC meant that it soon became a more suitable partner than the members of either organization might have expected. By 1923, a key AAC leader like Dean Charles Cole of Oberlin College was declaring, at his association's annual meeting, that tenure was "a policy by which teachers of tested competence, character and loyalty are lifted above the plane of annual, biennial or quinquennial appointments and put into the position of trusted partner appointed without term."[6] Although the partnership that followed between the AAC and AAUP wasn't always as amicable as Dean Cole's words might suggest, the two associations agreed more often than they fought. Most importantly, their fights did not always unfold as we might expect given the triumphal tone in which tenure's origin story is usually told.[7]

For one thing, the AAC did not object to the specter – unavoidable if the association agreed to any sort of academic due process – of presidents and other high-level administrators being called to account by a panel of faculty-employees. The historian Walter Metzger, whom we first met in Chapter 6, observes that "[c]alling on the president to… play the part of a humble adversary before a faculty clad in judicial robes… was asking a great deal at a time when the academic executive ego was not exactly of the shrinking kind."[8] But the AAC agreed to evaluation by a faculty tribunal, even if it did adjust the language so that this process was described as *desirable* rather than *necessary*.[9]

More significantly, the AAC *never* called the concept or necessity of tenure into question. Metzger says it best:

> One would hunt in vain through the transcripts of these meetings for a reference to tenured professors as "deadwood"… for a presidential comment to the effect that universal short-term contracts… were needed… [for] a single attempt to lay the distortions of the academic labor market or the low rate of academic productivity at the door of tenure. This was not the silence of persons too filled with loathing to enter into argument or too resigned to an evil to try to fight it; by every indication the presidents regarded tenure as beneficial and the arguments in favor of it as beyond debate… The importance of this concurrence with the AAUP over

fundamentals cannot be overestimated. It is safe to say that tenure would never have taken root in this country if the presidents had not been able to see the good of it, and that it would be moribund today… if they did not have strong self-interested and disinterested reasons for keeping it alive.[10]

Self-interested reasons aren't always heartwarming. As Metzger says, and as the example of Harvard's James Conant suggests, university presidents probably saw the formalization of a strict tenure system as a good way to motivate and retain quality workers, as well as a good cover for an *up or out* system that they had never before implemented.[11] But relentless self-abnegation is the standard for good employer behavior in *no* industry. Early twentieth century universities pursued an articulation and defense of tenure because they saw it as beneficial to their interests. Doing this made them neither much better – nor worse – than the faculty they employed.

If the unexpected protagonist behind tenure's development is both a wily president *and* a heroic professor, it should be no surprise that the core of tenure's appeal is also more complicated than the standard narrative suggests. Put simply: it is and it isn't *all* about academic freedom.

Chapter 6 noted that the AAUP's existence and its 1940 Statement are often attributed to the Ross scandal at Stanford as well as to other academic freedom violations that occurred at the turn of the twentieth century. Remarkably, though, the AAUP *itself* – at least, the current AAUP in the person of one of its senior employees – does not see it this way. "[T]he AAUP was not founded specifically as the primary defender of academic freedom that it subsequently became," writes Hans-Joerg Tiede, a Senior Program Officer at the Association.[12] Instead, it was primarily meant to effectuate changes to university governance, to serve as "a national body" for the professoriate, and to "standardize American higher education."[13] The AAUP, in short, was founded to set the boundaries of the academic profession – to stake a *jurisdictional claim*, as we'll see in the next chapter – so that academia could be a profession like any other.

In 1936, the AAUP appointed Ralph E. Himstead as its first full-time general secretary.[14] Himstead seems to have cut a strong and polarizing figure. On the one hand, Walter Metzger described him as a "thin-skinned law professor from Syracuse University,"[15] George Pope Shannon, who served under Himstead at the AAUP, remembered being greeted with the implicit insult that "no one could be of much help in the Central Office until he had been there a year."[16] Edward C. Kirkland, who went on to become an AAUP President, was sure that university "presidents and deans often thought Himstead quite opinionated and inflexible."[17]

But the same commentators also recall Himstead's devotion to the scholarly community he'd been appointed to serve. Kirkland remembered how, during a dismissal investigation, Himstead lay awake in their shared hotel room after a long day of hearings, "puzzling as to how to save the [professor's] job, his reputation, and also his usefulness to higher education."[18] Shannon described Himstead as so committed to the AAUP that, for several years, he delayed any acceptance of funds earmarked for his own retirement because "he was unwilling to reduce by that amount the savings which he feared that the Association might need for other purposes."[19] And Metzger, who had described Himstead as "thin-skinned," *also* described him as arguing with "an inimitable doggedness" for the welfare and dignity of professors.[20]

During the negotiations leading up to the 1940 Statement, Himstead was seemingly less concerned with expressive safeguards than with employment security even though he would later become known as "Mr. Academic Freedom."[21] He acquiesced to the AAC demand that professors' extramural utterances – statements made outside the protected contexts of the pedagogical or scholarly exchange – could provide a legitimate basis for administrative discipline.[22] But he was totally unwilling to compromise on the matter of a fixed probationary period, after which a professor would *have* to be considered for tenure.[23] Nor was he willing to trust that universities wouldn't engage in bad-faith evaluations at the end of that probationary period, habitually denying juniors tenure and forcing them to wander "like so many Ishmaels from one academic institution to another" only to restart the tenure clock.[24] Consequently, the AAUP negotiated for a transfer of credit that counted "time served" at one institution toward the tenure clock of a second. *The fixed star in Himstead's constellation of beliefs*, writes Metzger, *was that the welfare of the academic profession as well as the peace of mind of the persons in it required against the evil of permanent transience.*[25]

The "evil of permanent transience" and the appeal of a strong tenure policy to mitigate it was apparently very evident to university leaders by the time negotiations over the 1940 Statement had started. Back in 1935, when President Lovett of Rice asked his peers for their insight, most of the seventy-eight leaders who responded to his inquiry justified tenure on economic, not academic, grounds.[26] Lovett himself was ultimately unsuccessful at getting his trustees on board, but fifteen years later, a new president of Rice, Kenneth Pitzer, renewed the push for a formal tenure policy. Pitzer also framed tenure's virtues entirely in employment terms – and, this time, the trustees listened.

Existing faculty might not care very much about job security, Pitzer argued, since they'd already had jobs for several years. But new faculty would. Why should they come to Rice when other institutions offered them the prospect of earning job security a few years down the road?[27] In fact, by the time Pitzer was trying to convince his trustees in 1961, Rice had fallen somewhat behind the industry curve: a 1959 survey of 170 universities in California, Illinois, and Pennsylvania found that 86% of them had articulated tenure policies with explicit trustee approval.[28]

Pitzer seemed right on both counts: existing professors *were* indifferent and aspiring professors were anything *but*. Several longstanding members of Rice's faculty seemed either unaware or unconcerned (or both) that the job security they'd enjoyed for years lacked any formal parameters or guarantees. In fact, only one professor even bothered to comment on Pitzer's proposal – but he was the chair of a department that was getting ready to hire eight new members in the coming academic year. Not only was tenure necessary to recruit and retain accomplished faculty, this department chair wrote, it was even well worth the risk of being saddled with the few "bad guesses" who could, in the ordinary course of things, be expected to slip through the hiring process.[29]

Looking back, the AAUP's 1940 Statement seems to have exactly captured contemporary administrative attitudes toward tenure: it provides *a sufficient degree of economic security to make the profession attractive to men and women of ability.*[30] Those administrators' views were shaped by decades of institutionalization and professionalization that, by 1940, had transformed American higher education. Characteristics of our current academic landscape that I've discussed in this book – phenomena like auto-depreciation, multihyphenation, high barriers to entry, and monopsonistic market tendencies – had already started to surface by the early decades of the twentieth century in ways that made tenure an especially valuable employment protection. I'm not saying that the academic labor market was then what it is now (it wasn't!). But it also wasn't categorically different, and that's why tenure mattered then… as well as why it matters now.

Chapter 6 described how higher education in the United States began with a "borrowed instrument": the English-style college epitomized by the colleges of Oxford and Cambridge.[31] For most of the seventeenth and eighteenth centuries, and even for much of the nineteenth century, American higher education stuck to this model and tried to create a kind of Oxbridge overseas. Institutions like Harvard provided a collegiate life for small groups of white men who took their lessons in the liberal arts together via recitations and lectures.[32] These institutions were "more deeply concerned with the forming of character than the fostering of research" and their tutors, as Chapter 6 notes, were better understood as aspirants to other paths rather than as intentional, professionalized, experts.[33]

For around 200 years, this model didn't budge.[34] American higher education successfully resisted most efforts to change its substance, methods, style, and purpose. It wasn't until 1876, according to many histories of American education, that the bubble of conservatism represented by the collegiate model was triumphantly burst by the arrival of the Johns Hopkins University.

Whereas colonial-era institutions like Harvard and William and Mary were founded on the English college model, Hopkins was built – literally and figuratively – in the style of the German research institutions that its founding president, Daniel C. Gilman, found so inspiring.[35] Gilman's new creation became emblematic of a new genre of educational institution that was defined by rigorous instructional techniques and prolific scholarship. To be sure, Hopkins wasn't the only example of its kind: the German approach was behind the founding or transformation of universities all across the United States, including Harvard, Michigan, Cornell, the University of Chicago, and Columbia.[36] (Even Yale – longtime defender of the collegiate model – was partly swept up by the new wave.[37])

But it was Hopkins that drove much of the transformation. It stood out as "a non-sectarian institution dedicated to the unfettered search for truth."[38] It was an institution dedicated to advancing knowledge for the good of the nation and humanity at large rather than to functionally serving as a finishing school for the sons of American aristocracy.[39] And its influence spread rapidly, both through emulation by other universities and through the daily practice of its graduates. Within twenty years of its founding, more than sixty institutions had three or more professors with Hopkins degrees.[40]

Notwithstanding the Hopkins effect, American educators couldn't just switch from the English college to the German research university. American students didn't arrive at university as mature or as prepared as their German counterparts. American education was also driven by a pragmatism and a populism that had no analogs in either the English or German models. Even the most prominent American institutions of this period found themselves trying to emulate both European styles by combining generalized instruction and character-building with advanced research in specialized subjects. On opening day in 1876, Johns Hopkins may have had fifty four graduate students, but it also had thirty-five undergraduates.[41]

When it worked, this adjusted Hopkins model "made it possible for the first time for the scholar's life in America to be unified… [to] combine teaching and creative research."[42] This one sentence conveys two remarkable truths about academic life and higher education at the close of the nineteenth century. First, by this point in time, there *were* distinct aspects to scholarly life – teaching and research, for the most part, instead of today's idealized tripartite obligations, but they were distinct aspects nonetheless. Second, there were now dedicated scholars who might want to integrate these two roles into a lifelong career instead of mere tutors who wanted to move on to the real thing. Academic life was already getting complicated.

This was partly because academia was becoming more specialized and more professionalized. By 1908, the United States had 120 national learned societies.[43] By 1945, there were eighty-six scholarly journals in history alone.[44] By 1948, there were thirty-five university presses, up from just three in 1900.[45] It quickly became clear that all this scholarly publication and the maintenance of expertise it both reflected and demanded took dedicated chunks of time. In 1880, Harvard awarded America's first research sabbatical to the Sanskritist Charles Lanman in order to lure him from Johns Hopkins; by 1920, seventy-one institutions were offering some kind of sabbatical leave.[46]

But efforts to promote research created fresh complications because the arrival of the Hopkins model hadn't absolved American universities from their instructional and character-building responsibilities. Before the dust had fully settled on Hopkins' founding in Baltimore, objections were being raised against the new fixation with credentials and publications. By the time a few decades had passed, early twentieth century academics and university administrators were caught up in "an intermittent debate between those who thought the university should place more emphasis on teaching and scholars who demanded a greater accommodation of research."[47]

This tension between teaching and research both reflected and reinforced the growing professionalization of the professoriate. As early as 1903, the credential required to be a professor had become standardized to the point that William James could write bitingly about "the increasing hold of the Ph.D. Octopus upon American life."[48] The number of doctorates awarded *nationally* went from forty-four at the founding of Johns Hopkins in 1876, to 562 awarded in 1918, then almost doubled to 1,064 in 1924 and almost tripled to 3,088 by the year of the 1940 Statement, until it finally reached a point where "more doctorates were granted in the United States during the 1950s than in all the years up to that time."[49]

As this exceptionally brief history suggests, turn of the (previous) century academia already exhibited many of the characteristics that make tenure a valuable protection *today*. Professors were already being torn between multiple tasks that require different skills and perhaps different credentials and that definitely require lots and lots of time. Professors were already being encouraged to engage in the sort of topical specialization and idiosyncratic communication that would serve to limit their appeal to a few, geographically dispersed, potential employers. And professors were already being criticized for engaging in both too much research *and* too much teaching.

Writing six years after the 1940 Statement was issued, President Conant of Harvard observed that "the forces of democracy had taken the European idea of a university and transformed it" – and he was right.[50] The American university *is* an "essentially *sui generis*" creation that has imposed and offered very peculiar conditions of work ever since it came into its contemporary form.[51] Those conditions of work have undoubtedly become harder to bear over time. But they were *never* easy, and they were made worse by having unfolded against a landscape of at-will employment. Small wonder, then, that tenure has always been considered an important employment protection.

17

PMCs Unite?

I considered titling this chapter something like *Proletarian Professor* because the phrase is pleasingly alliterative and it seems to describe how even tenure-stream faculty feel about themselves these days: that they're merely wage earners who live by selling their labor and experience many of the indignities heaped on all people who must live by selling their labor. But notwithstanding the very real reputational and material decline of the professoriate, there are two reasons I think we should avoid using the word "proletariat" to describe the portion of it that consists of tenure-stream faculty. Both reasons give us some insight into the potential *and* the limitations of faculty unionization as an effective response to faculty problems.

To begin with, I decided against using that title because it's just hard to stomach the claim that tenure-stream faculty *are* proletarian. That's not because we have it easy: I stand by my arguments that tenured and tenure-track faculty work much harder, sacrifice much more, and receive much less than is generally believed to be the case (even by themselves). I believe that the image of tenured academia as involving well-paid work that is easily won and easily done is, on the whole, both inaccurate and unfair.

But I also believe that there are people who have it so much worse. Graduate student employees, post-docs, and other nontenure-track professors have it *so much worse*. Over 25% of them earn less than the federal poverty line, almost 75% of them lack job security beyond the current academic term, and nearly 20% are dependent on Medicare or Medicaid.[1] We should be able to acknowledge what's bad without denying what's worse. That means that when we use a word like *proletarian* to indicate something more than a relationship between labor and capital – when we use it as a rhetorical device to describe a sense of well-being – we need to do so carefully.

At a less visceral level, I'm also reluctant to describe tenure-stream faculty as *proletarian* because there are few better ways to ensure their instantaneous dissent. Tenured and tenure-track professors may grumble about the corporatized neoliberal university with its extractive labor practices, but they are, at bottom, still unlikely to think of themselves as "workers." Instead, tenure-stream professors want to think of themselves as autonomous agents who don't have supervisors to be bargained with. They want to think of their purpose as the creation of knowledge and the expansion of minds, not the production of widgets. And they don't want to think of their defining privilege, tenure, as an individually valuable employment protection.

I think some of these things myself. I won't pretend otherwise. But because I *know* I think them, and because I'm not sure I *should* think them, I'm hesitant to use a word like *proletarian* to describe myself or people like me. A better way to describe the class identity of tenure-stream faculty – and maybe also of the NTT professors who would like to join their ranks – is a term that Barbara and John Ehrenreich used to describe academics (and others) back in 1977: the *professional-managerial class*, or PMC.

The PMC, according to the Ehrenreichs, are different from "the 'working class,' from the 'old' middle class of small business owners, as well as from the wealthy class of owners."[2] They gained importance rapidly over the second half of the twentieth century: "[b]y 1972, about 24% of American jobs were in PMC occupations. By 1983 that number had risen to 28% and by 2006, just before the Great Recession, to 35%." The PMC "organized itself into professions" that required specialized credentialing and that enjoyed some degree of autonomy – think of industries, like medicine and law, that I've been using as comparators to academia throughout this book. But thanks to a combination of neoliberal policies, technological changes, and labor outsourcing that began in the 1980s, "the PMC's original dream – of a society ruled by reason and led by public-spirited professionals – has been discredited." In a 2013 retrospective, the Ehrenreichs wrote that "the PMC lies in ruins" and, "[a]t the less fortunate end of the spectrum, journalists and PhDs in sociology or literature spiral down into the retail workforce."

This downfall, the Ehrenreichs argue, is partly the fault of PMCs themselves. High and largely self-imposed barriers to professional entry have made it difficult for PMC kids to emulate their parents. And because they're unwilling to think of themselves as workers, PMCs are unable to coordinate efforts to win concessions from their employers in the way that other workers do. This is the attitude I was referring to earlier when I described my second reason for avoiding the word "proleterian."

The Ehrenreichs attribute this attitude to PMCs at large, and other scholars have also shown that professionalization and unionization have been at odds with one another in other industries besides academia.[3] But critical observers of academia (many of whom are academics themselves) suggest that tenure-stream professors are uniquely averse to thinking of themselves as workers in need of unions. A review of 150 years of academic writing about academic labor – fifteen decades' worth of writing! – led one such critic to exclaim that "[t]here is never a moment in any of these books where a faculty member sees a union as a resource."[4]

Blaming faculty attitudes and self-perception for the relative rarity of academic unionization is thus fairly common. It's not entirely unwarranted. But it's also not entirely fair, for the following two reasons.

First, tenure-stream faculty unionization is not all that unusual – contrary to what many professors seem to think, myself included before I started this research. At first, I operated under a vague and incorrect assumption that very few university faculty, including almost *no* tenure-stream faculty, are unionized. A "rare exception" that I'd been told of was the tenured and tenure-track faculty of Rutgers University in New Jersey, which a law school advisor had held out to me as an unusually desirable public school to work at because they, remarkably, *had* a union and it was powerful.

In truth, Rutgers is just one of many public universities where tenure-stream faculty are unionized. The faculty at public universities in California are all unionized, which means that our imagined newbie professor from Chapter 10 would have also enjoyed the protections that come from collective bargaining. In 2023 and 2024 alone, tenure-stream faculty successfully unionized at the University of Michigan-Flint, the University of Kansas, and Miami University.[5] Fully 34% of the new bargaining units to appear at public universities between 2013 and 2019 were composed of tenure-stream faculty *only*,[6] while over 25% of all faculty (regardless of tenure-eligibility) at public four-year universities are unionized.[7] That's not too shabby given a union density rate that, across all industries, hovered at around ten percent in 2023. There's work to be done, but there's also a lot of work that's *already* been done. Moreover, although tenure-stream faculty have most often unionized at public universities, there are also legacy bargaining units at private institutions, like Hofstra University and Adelphi University, which predate the *Yeshiva* decision described below.

I can chalk up my own ignorance about the true state of faculty unionization to any number of factors: to being a Canadian who still assumes (until shown otherwise) that unionization in *any* sector is dead in the United States, to being an employment law scholar who knows that unionization in most sectors is, if not dead, at least on life support, and to being the product of several elite universities where professorial knowledge of or interest in unionization aspires to zero. But whichever one of these explanations does most of the heavy lifting, it clearly doesn't apply to me alone. Many tenure-stream faculty don't seem to think that tenure-stream faculty unionize. They're only partly right.

The second – but *primary* – reason we shouldn't wholly blame faculty for the state of faculty unionization is that other factors besides their own self-conceptions stand in their way. These are factors beyond the ones that the Ehrenreichs associated with the downfall of PMCs, and they're factors that are not, in any meaningful sense, the fault of faculty themselves.

First, American labor law makes it hard for tenure-stream professors (like many other employees) to engage in collective bargaining. Tenure-stream faculty at private universities are not protected from employer retaliation if they choose to unionize. Tenure-stream faculty at public universities may not be protected, and they may even be *prohibited* from unionizing. The legal reasoning – the source of the problem – is different for each kind of university, but the ultimate outcome is similar.

Since its 1980 decision in *Yeshiva*,[8] the Supreme Court has held that tenure-stream faculty are not protected by §7 of the *National Labor Relations Act*, which guarantees employees "the right to self-organization, to form, join, or assist labor organizations, to bargain collectively through representatives of their own choosing, and to engage in other concerted activities for the purpose of collective bargaining or other mutual aid or protection." Section Seven is what prevents employers from retaliating against employees who choose to engage in "concerted activity" like forming a union. The Court's logic in *Yeshiva*, like the *nemo judex* worries discussed in Chapter 15, draws on the idea that faculty are self-governing – and thus *managerial* – employees, rather than rank-and-file workers who *are managed*.

For Justice Brennan, who wrote the *Yeshiva* dissent on behalf of himself and three other justices, the majority's view of faculty life was comically outdated – "an idealized model of collegial decisionmaking that is a vestige of the great medieval university."[9] Brennan argued that even if the majority *did* accurately understand the ground realities of contemporary academia, it was still mistaken because it misunderstood the purpose of excluding managers from the *NLRA*'s protections.

The real point of disqualifying managers, Justice Brennan declared, was to keep separate interests separate. Managers are *supposed* to identify more with their employers than with the rank-and-file; too much fraternization would be bad for the interests of employers and employees alike. Tenure-stream faculty, Brennan argued, aren't "managers" in the same way. It's true that they make ostensibly managerial decisions about students or about themselves: decisions about admission, promotions, and terminations. But when they make those decisions, they're acting in service to a set of principles – disciplinary or professional standards, most likely – that may or may not align with the interests of their university's leadership. In other words, tenure-stream faculty may be mid-level, but they're not in any legal sense managerial.

A good dissent is, alas, still only a dissent. The upshot of *Yeshiva* has been that tenure-stream faculty at private universities are not protected by the *NLRA* if they try to unionize – and as a result, unsurprisingly, they don't try to unionize very often. We have to keep this legal obstacle in mind even as we acknowledge the class interest problems underscored by the Ehrenreichs and others.

At public universities, tenure-stream faculty may not be able to unionize for a totally different reason. Because they are state employees, their ability to engage in collective bargaining is a "gift" bestowed by their state government – and the state can choose not to bestow that gift. Some states, like Virginia and both Carolinas, explicitly deny all public employees the right to collectively bargain with their employers. Others, like Texas, deny most public employees that right but allow certain exceptions (in the case of Texas: police and firefighters). Still others, like my current home state of Georgia, forbid teachers at public schools from collectively bargaining but leave unaddressed the issue of professors at public universities.[10] As with so much else in the United States, it's a patchwork. Because state laws play such an important role, union density is unevenly spread: more than 50% of unionized faculty are concentrated in California, New York, and New Jersey, with around another 15% in Illinois and Michigan.[11]

Across public and private sectors, the outcome is thus often the same whether the relevant legal framework is federal case law or state legislation. At best, this state of affairs means that many universities aren't obliged to negotiate with any union that tenure-stream faculty might try to form. At worst, it means that many universities are legally allowed to fire tenured professors explicitly and only because they tried to unionize. It doesn't seem as if many universities have taken this route, but I wouldn't put it past courts to agree with a university that decides to try. In a country that's as unfriendly to collective bargaining as the United States, it's possible to view formal legal obstacles like the ones I've described as either final straws or beside the point. The truth is probably somewhere in between: law matters, even if it doesn't matter quite as much as lawyers tend to think.

The second important obstacle to faculty unionization has to do with the nature of faculty life. I don't just mean that academia is a solitary path that self-selects for people who want to be left alone (although it often is and it probably does). I mean that the conditions of *tenure-stream* academia make it hard for professors within it to develop the kind of collective identity that is essential to collective action. Make no mistake: these conditions are positive from the individual professor's perspective. They make regular appearances in grad school application essays and interview conversations and dinner party banter about why someone wants to become a professor. But they don't self-evidently help – and may self-evidently harm – efforts to engage in grass-roots organization.

Let's start with the fact that academics have highly specialized training – in other words, they're experts on something. Most people, by definition, are not experts on anything. Having a rare expertise, whether it is about US patent law or about parasitic transmission, can feel empowering: you know things others don't. Having a rare expertise can also feel isolating: you know things others don't value. Paleontology, Ross, *Friends*; for me and my Millennial peers, these three words should convey the point well enough. Being an expert in something can, furthermore, affect your day in unanticipated ways because you're always, inescapably, *being an expert* in that something. A vacationing biologist sees an interesting specimen on the beach and starts planning a new lecture. (Really.) A business professor out to dinner wonders whether age or gender explains who got the check and starts researching a paper. (Ditto.) It can be alternately entertaining (everything is fascinating!) and frustrating (nothing is *not* work!). Whichever it is, expertise is always *differentiating*. Regardless of how much any one of these dynamics applies to your particular circumstances, what being an expert definitely means is that both you and the people around you are likely to feel that you see things differently. This, in turn, can make it hard to think of yourself as a worker like everyone else.

Now, by itself, this doesn't distinguish tenure-stream faculty from their NTT counterparts, many if not most of whom share the same expertise-building credentials. What *does* distinguish these two types of professors is the extent to which their conditions of work *reaffirm* an "expert" identity. When you are *not* juggling six classes at three institutions each fifty miles apart, when you know that you'll have (or that you're very likely to have) a job six months into the future, and when you are required to find puzzles and then solve them via publications as an integral part of your job – well, then, it becomes a little easier to stay slightly removed from your surroundings and, in fact, slightly hard to do anything else. I get to be an anthropologist and a legal scholar in every moment of my day because *the conditions of my job make that possible*. It's a privilege that I'm grateful to enjoy. But that also means I'm an anthropologist and a legal scholar in every moment of my day – right down to when I'm negotiating with my preschooler or having lunch with my husband. I'm always one step removed and everything is potentially work. This book is the much-delayed outgrowth of what was supposed to be idle distraction from a *different* book I was writing.

At a more logistical level, the everyday patterns of tenure-stream life make it particularly inhospitable to developing and maintaining stable forms of collective, localized identity. Those holidays spent working inside the house or researching abroad, the regular conference travel, the sudden relocations to far-flung places – these are not ingredients for a rooted life. Despite being born in Canada and living in the same house for my entire childhood I spent a total of four, maybe five summers in that house before I was eighteen, and most of my Thanksgivings were in conference hotels. This wasn't because my parents were anthropologists – but, in a sense, they might as well have been. Our long biennial trips to India were the kind of "anthropological field experiences" that helped equip me "with the behavioral, psychological, and linguistic toolbox to… simultaneously be the ultimate insider and the forever outsider."[12] My son, who is not yet six, has already lived in two US states and gone to school in two countries. The fact that I loved my childhood (and he will, hopefully, love his) regularly and does not change the way this different orientation to time and place adds yet more obstacles to the task of living outside your head or, at least, outside your nuclear household.

Again, the patterns and practices I'm describing are often necessary for academic work and they are considered some of the greatest perks of academic life. In fact, one of the criticisms justifiably articulated by NTT faculty is that they lack the material support and job security to engage in this lifestyle. It's a privilege that tenure-stream professors like me should be grateful to enjoy (and I am). But the privileged nature of this lifestyle doesn't erase the fact that it also tends to set its practitioners at a remove. The rhythms, the calendars, and the constraints are all unusual compared to the experiences of most other American workers.

I'm hardly the first person to say that professors find it hard to think of themselves as workers, or even to say that the explanation for this partly rests in how academics have been trained to think about themselves. Everyone from the theorist Thorstein Veblen to the novelist Upton Sinclair and including scholars like Stanley Aronowitz and David Damrosch have made some version of this argument. (For an accounting of their ideas, see the work of historian Frank Donoghue.[13]) It *does* seem less common to acknowledge how the quotidian realities of academic life might inhibit collective identity-building among professors, even or *especially* among those who are privileged by virtue of being in the tenure stream. I've been struck by how readily higher ed observers will admit the importance of everyday life when it comes to shaping and constraining the organizational efforts of NTT faculty or Uber drivers – workers for whom the conditions that inhibit collectivity are conditions that few people want. But the same acknowledgment isn't quite as forthcoming when it comes to tenure-stream faculty, for whom solitude, exceptionalism, and separation aren't necessarily an injustice.

If the law keeps many tenure-stream faculty from unionizing while the nature of tenure-stream life makes it hard for those who *could* unionize to do so… what then? What is there to really say about collective bargaining in a book about faculty tenure?

This, as a matter of fact, was my first reaction to a reviewer who noted their surprise at the absence of any reference to unions in my book proposal. *What is there to say*, I wondered. *Many can't, many won't – now what?* But beyond the way this misrepresents the extent to which tenure-stream faculty *do* unionize despite laws and circumstances that make unionization pretty tough, it also overlooks one of the most significant ways in which tenure, by its absence, ties together universities and unions.

"I doubt," writes Donoghue, the historian of education I mentioned earlier, "I doubt that administrators could have foreseen that, by staffing classes with adjuncts, they were unwittingly fomenting a culture of brilliant labor activists with advanced degrees, but that's what they did."[14] The authors of a national report on collective bargaining in higher education add that "[a]n unintended consequence of the significant increase in contingent faculty over the past four decades has been the diminishing import of the United States Supreme Court decision in *Yeshiva*."[15] Indeed. This, perhaps, is the most powerful observation to be made about the relationship between tenure and unionization. By removing tenure and everything that goes with it from the lives of *most* university faculty – by removing job security, salaried income, employment benefits, career progression, and participation in institutional governance – universities have not only made it *legally* possible for most faculty to unionize, they have also made it *circumstantially* possible for NTT faculty to view themselves as workers in need of unions.

NTT faculty at private universities are, in fact, where some of the most vibrant collective activity is taking place.[16] The authors of *The Gig Academy* note that "[b]etween 2006 and 2012, twenty-two new NTT bargaining units were certified in the private sector" and that the same number of NTT units were certified in 2016 *alone*.[17] A wave of organization efforts has cropped up in the recent and not-so-recent past: Higher Ed Labor United ("a national organization founded in 2021 to unite workers throughout U.S. higher education"), the New Faculty Majority ("dedicated to improving the quality of higher education by advancing professional equity"), the Coalition for Contingent Academic Labor ("working to improve working conditions at colleges and universities for contingent faculty"), and even Tenure for the Common Good ("rally[ing] tenured faculty to use their tenured positions to fight for justice on their own campuses and nationally"). In 2024, a slate called United Faculty for the Common Good swept the AAUP elections with a mission to reorient the Association towards solidarity-building and labor organization.

As many of these groups maintain, tenure is valuable– *not* mystical. It brings benefits and privileges that make working lives better and academic work feasible, things that need not be limited to tenured employment (and are in fact becoming less exclusive to it) but things that are, on the whole, still mostly associated with it. The next few chapters draw on data from the *Tenured-Terminations Study* to understand what happens when, despite those benefits and those protections, tenure is overcome.

PART FOUR

Tenured-Terminations

18

Jobs… for Life?

We've come a long way in our discussion of tenure as an employment protection. We began by noting that tenure is a variety of just cause contract, and that just cause contracts remove workers from the default At-Will Rule. Academics are not the only workers who operate under just cause principles, and much like the contextual variations that exist in just cause contracts, there are variations in the substantive and procedural protections offered by tenure. Generally speaking, though, tenure means that you *can't* fire a professor "for… bad reason, or no reason at all": there must be good (enough) reason and there must also be adequate pre-termination procedures. And yes, this does mean that tenure, like all varieties of just cause, makes those who have it harder to fire than at-will employees. That's the point.

We then went on to consider variations of an argument that tenure makes professors *too* hard to fire. That is, even granting that universities shouldn't be able to fire professors for having brown eyes or then wearing teal to the office, they should be able to fire professors far more easily than tenure allows. Consciously or not, this argument continues, professors understand this – that is, they understand that tenure shields them from deserved consequences. That's why, these critics assert, tenured professors *because they are tenured professors* behave in ways that are undesirably iconoclastic, undesirably predatorial, or simply and undesirably lazy.

I'm not above observing that this way of articulating common criticisms of tenure shows more generosity to critics than those critics show toward tenured professors. But the real problem with standard arguments about tenure's negative incentive effects isn't a lack of generosity: it's that these arguments are founded on questionable assumptions about human nature, and they're barely supported – sometimes outright *contradicted* – by the empirical information we have about professorial behavior. Put simply, there is *no* documented causative link between getting tenure and engaging in heightened levels of iconoclastic or predatorial behavior. There is also no *consistent* documented link between getting tenure and reduced productivity. Anyone saying otherwise is working off assumptions and anecdotes.

None of this means that the tower *is* ivory after all. Bad things happen in academia just like they happen in other workplaces, and there's good reason to think

157

that some bad things, like sexual misconduct, happen in academia rather more often than in other workplaces. But they don't happen, and they don't happen more often, *because of tenure*. They also don't happen because of *faculty* alone. Predatory behavior that goes unchecked is going unchecked by employers with ample means of correcting it. Unproductive behavior, to the extent that it can even be linked to achieving tenure, exists partly because employers stop guiding and supporting their employees and because employers start demanding other forms of work that they themselves deem less "productive."

But all of this speaks to what tenure does or does not do *before* termination. What about during termination and afterward? What are the conditions under which tenured faculty are terminated? What can we learn about tenure as an employment protection from the *who, what, where, when,* and *why* of real-life terminations?

These are the questions that originally got me into studying faculty tenure, and they're the driving force behind the *TTS* data that informs most of the remaining chapters in this book. As Chapter 2 notes, I'd never really considered tenured-terminations before I began this work. My oversight was undoubtedly a reflection of my parents' largely happy experiences with tenure-stream life and, just as undoubtedly, it was a product of the way graduate training and early-career experiences in academia had conditioned me to keep my eyes on the tenure-letter prize. But it's also because of a way of speaking common among both supporters and critics of tenure that paints tenured employment as a "job for life."

This job-for-life rhetoric gives me heartburn. It may be that an expectation of continued employment lends tenure an air of permanency – but if so, the resulting language is inapt, and dangerously so. As Chapter 5 made clear, and as any employment law casebook confirms, the At-Will Rule *itself* comes into play only when there is a contract for indefinite duration – in other words, the Rule only applies to situations in which both parties expect that the employment relationship will continue until and unless it is affirmatively stopped. The bare expectation of waking up each morning to the same job you had the night before is not a creation of tenure, and consequently it's also not one of its distinguishing features.

What makes matters worse is that this type of job-for-life rhetoric is spouted by *supporters* of tenure almost as often as by detractors. More troublingly still, these supporters repeat or tacitly endorse a comparison between tenured faculty and the only other workers who seem to be eligible for "lifetime" employment in the United States: the Article III judge.

"[F]ederal judges," says one of tenure's most prominent defenders, "enjoy life tenure, the justifications for which... are similar to those underpinning academic tenure."[1] Another supporter says that "[t]he most analogous group in society to tenured professors are federal judges, who receive life-time appointments."[2] And a third argues that "[i]f today we seem to lack persuasive justifications for tenure, perhaps that's because we've been looking for them in the wrong places."[3] Contrary to the conventional story, "the founders of the AAUP didn't turn to Kant, Fichte, and Humboldt" – instead, "[t]hey looked to the norms of judicial tenure in the American judiciary."

It's true that neither tenured professors nor Article III judges are removed from their positions at any great rate – but there's job security and then there's *job security*. Since the US Constitution was ratified in 1788 up until the time I am writing this, eight federal judges have been removed from office while three more were impeached and resigned before they could be removed. If we include them all, that's eleven federal judges over more than 230 years.

As the *Tenured-Terminations Study* shows, a much larger – though still very small – number of individual tenured professors have lost their jobs in the roughly twenty-year period that the study covers. But before we get into the *TTS* numbers, I want to clarify a few things about faculty exit studies in general and about the *TTS* in particular. This isn't meant as a replacement for the kind of detailed methodological statement that appears in most empirical social science works and that, in this book, is contained in Appendix A. Rather, what I say below is an explanation of some macro-level design choices that inform the *TTS* data and that distinguish it from similar efforts in ways that matter for the next few chapters.

As with many aspects of academic employment, we know surprisingly little about job loss or change among university professors. That's not because no one's tried: scholars writing in the well-established area of "faculty mobility" *have* explored why professors leave their jobs. But because data on faculty exits is notoriously hard to come by, these studies have often had to make do with available or collectible information in ways that hamper their usefulness.

First, the faculty mobility literature has largely used statements asserting an *intent to leave* as proxies for *actual departures*, but these two things are clearly not equivalent.[4] A critique of this proxy approach observed that such studies often find a huge number of professors declaring their intent to leave their current jobs – sometimes nearly fifty percent. But the same study went on to note (with what I can only describe as commendable understatement) that "[b]ased on the numeric reality of available faculty jobs and the difficulty of finding employment outside one's profession, it is highly unlikely that half of a nationally representative sample of faculty actually left their positions."[5]

The faculty mobility literature also often doesn't distinguish professors who leave their jobs for other institutions from those who leave their industry – academia – altogether.[6] This matters a lot because, as in the general labor market, job exits and industry exits tend to express different underlying realities. Switching academic employers but staying in academia is often a positive development that reflects professional success and improves professional prospects – it may be an even *stronger* signal of good things in academia than in the general labor force because academia's weak and quasi-monopsonistic labor market makes it so hard to switch employers at all.[7] Exiting the industry, on the other hand, is unlikely to be a particularly happy transition, even if it's a voluntarily chosen one and even if it eventually leads to greater mental and financial well-being.

Finally, most faculty mobility research doesn't differentiate between professors who leave under nominally voluntary conditions (whether "push" or "pull" factors in the language of this literature[8]), those who leave under more or less involuntary circumstances (whether through firing or forced resignation), and those who are separated from employment for reasons that have nothing to do with them personally, but rather reflect institutional changes affecting multiple faculty (what Chapter 22 calls a "reduction-in-force").[9]

Given all these gaps in our knowledge, the *TTS* makes an important contribution to the task of understanding faculty exits. In fact, the *TTS* is the largest, most generalized dataset regarding faculty tenure that I'm aware of, and I include a few key findings in Appendix B in the hopes of spurring further analysis by scholars who are more technically adept than I am. It is incredibly exciting to know that, thanks to the *TTS* data, we can know something about this world that I inhabit and love that we simply could not know before. But it's important to remember that this contribution is very specific.

Incidents included in the *TTS* meet the following criteria:

a **triggered termination**
 involving a **tenured** professor
 at **institutions** that are *non-profit, four-year,* primarily *bachelors, masters, and doctoral* degree-granting
 colleges and universities in the **United States**
 occurring or beginning between **2000 and 2021**

I'll explain each of the bolded terms.

Here, I'm using ***termination*** in lieu of the more unwieldy but more accurate phrase "separation from employment." *TTS* terminations include both incidents where faculty were fired and those where faculty retired or resigned (almost certainly to avoid being fired). They thus include both separations that were clearly involuntary and those that were nominally voluntary if circumstantially coerced. They do not include incidents that only culminated in administrative demotions – as, for instance, when a tenured faculty member who is also chair of her department is removed from her chairship but remains in her faculty position.

Admittedly, job loss is not the only adverse employment action that a tenured professor might experience. Involuntary leave, limited campus access and roles, monetary penalties, and mandatory training are just some of the other disciplinary measures universities could impose on faculty. I've focused on termination to the exclusion of these other measures for two reasons. First and most importantly, termination is the most severe outcome that tenure could conceivably prevent and, consequently, it's what both supporters and detractors often focus on.

More pragmatically, terminations were easier to capture via the kind of search methods and sources available to me than other negative consequences would have been.

A *TTS* termination is **triggered** by a negative work-related event or series of events. In the *TTS* data, the employer's interpretation of those events is called the "university narrative," while the employee's perspective is called the "faculty counternarrative." A more common terminology for this type of trigger is one that we've already encountered multiple times in this book and even in this chapter – "cause" – but it's so exclusively associated with employer rationales that I decided to avoid using it. It wouldn't be too far-off to think of relevant triggers as being traumatic because they almost always involve one party to the employment relationship saying that the other party did something wrong or reacted inappropriately to some circumstance. But since "trauma" has additional layers of meaning that may themselves not always be relevant, I refer to *TTS* terminations as being "triggered" – rightly or wrongly, according to the party's perspective – by some discrete set of events.

Unlike many other faculty mobility studies, the *TTS* excludes two types of exits that probably account for many – if not most – *individual* terminations. First, the *TTS* does not include separations from employment that happen for work-related reasons but without a negative triggering event: say, departures to pursue a better-paying job inside or outside academia, departures to work in a different industry, or departures to escape a discriminatory workplace or generalized professional dissatisfaction. (If intent-proxy studies are any indication, generalized dissatisfaction likely drives most individual faculty exits overall.[10]) Second, the *TTS* does not include separations from employment that occur for "personal" reasons – quotation marks here because anything that pushes you to leave your job when you'd rather not do so necessarily speaks to the constraints under which you work. Still, exits motivated by things like the need to follow a partner's career or to care for an ailing relative are not reflected in this data.

This means, for instance, that even if their departures had occurred within the study period the nine faculty who left Hamilton College in 2022 would not have been included in the *TTS*.[11] At least three of the nine left for broadly personal reasons, while at least three left specifically because they were dissatisfied with Hamilton. These departures all give us valuable information about working in academia and about the process of earning or living with tenure. But what the *TTS* measures is tenure's ability to act as a shield against triggered terminations – or, more specifically, the *TTS* measures circumstances in which the shield of tenure was fractured to the point of breaking. The Hamilton departures don't speak to this aspect of tenured employment. Consequently, those departures – again, even if they'd happened before 2021 – would not have been included in the *TTS*.

Only incidents involving **tenured** faculty are included in this study. In most disciplines, tenure is conferred along with promotion to Associate Professor status, so

I've assumed that anyone with the titles of Associate Professor or Full Professor, as well as anyone holding a named-chair position, was tenured at the time of termination. This approach could be slightly overinclusive as well as slightly underinclusive. It could be overinclusive because, in some disciplines – academic law, for instance – entry-level faculty are increasingly hired as associate professors without tenure; they would be included in *TTS* data despite being untenured. The same approach could also be underinclusive because federal data suggests that it's possible, although very rare, for some assistant professors to have tenure; they would be excluded from *TTS* data despite having tenure.[12] To the best of my knowledge, however, no incidents that were considered for inclusion in the *TTS* dataset involved faculty fitting either of these descriptions. That suggests that here, as elsewhere, Associate Professor status is a fairly reliable proxy for tenured status.

My focus on tenured faculty is one of the most common *Yes, buts…* I encounter when I share this data because it means the *TTS* doesn't capture tenure denials. Not getting tenure is a devastating experience for the professor who experiences it, and it's also quite a blow to their department or school. I understand why the exclusion of tenure denials may seem perplexing to some readers. But the terminations – or, to be legally exact, the *nonrenewals* – of tenure-track faculty during or at the end of their probationary periods would be even harder to capture than tenured-terminations. Legally, nonrenewal doesn't provide independent grounds for litigation: you need to be able to argue that something else, like discrimination based on race or sex, also happened. Socially, pre-tenure faculty who want to find another academic position are unlikely to publicize their job loss for fear of incurring reputational harm that permanently shuts them out of the industry. They're less likely to post on social media, give interviews to trade publications, or issue the mic-drop statements that are characteristic of Quit Lit. The combination of these legal and social dynamics means that tenure denials are less likely to leave either a litigation record or a media trail that would have allowed me to track them down, which in turn would have made the dataset less reliable.

Like this entire book, the *TTS* focuses on four-year, nonprofit, degree-granting **institutions** (colleges and universities) that primarily grant bachelors, masters, or doctoral degrees.[13] That means I don't include incidents or dynamics from the world of community colleges, or from what the literature calls "special focus institutions" like art schools or music schools. It also means that *TTS* data includes incidents from a huge range of institutions that are not at all like one another. A selective liberal arts college is not a large state university, a branch campus is not a flagship school, a research-focused institution is not a teaching-focused institution. There are, as Chapter 2 noted, many academies. But as that chapter also observed, many quantitative studies exploring faculty life have prioritized specificity in the subject population by examining a small subset of disciplines or institutions. The *TTS* prioritizes population breadth while focusing on a very narrow subset of incidents.

I've focused on institutions in the **United States** for reasons that do not go without saying. My geographic interest is certainly personal: I began studying tenure because I was interested in how it affected people who were more or less like me. In a sense, and arguably like all instances of workers in higher education studying higher education workers, this book and the *TTS* data are both examples of scholarship that's often derided as academic navel-gazing and slapped with the dreaded label, "me-search." I point this out to underscore that what counts as me-search is variable and nonintuitive enough to make it hard to recognize from the outside, and that this unrecognizability, in turn, makes the stigma associated with studying your own community nonsensical.[14] My last book was about a dispute over women's access to a Hindu temple in the south Indian state of Kerala. I am female, my Hindu family is originally from Kerala, and many of the individuals featured in that book actually share our caste and socio-economic statuses. But, in my eyes, that book wasn't me-search. This one is.

I also focus on the United States for reasons having to do with the argument and orientation of this book. My underlying goal has been to show why tenure matters as an employment protection. This emphasis on job security is, as Chapters 6 and 15 specifically argued, pretty rare among tenure's supporters, most of whom have argued that tenure is valuable because it protects academic freedom. But while arguments supporting tenure for the sake of academic freedom may have widespread, even global, applicability, the argument that tenure matters because it gives professors much-needed job security is peculiarly relevant in the United States.

No other country, as Chapter 5 explained, operates with a default assumption like the At-Will Rule, and few countries (arguably none) filter so many benefits and protections through employment relationships. Moreover, few industries demand training and professionalization processes that are as extensive and expensive as what academia imposes on its aspiring practitioners, and the burdensome nature of this training is heightened in the United States because of our debt-financed approach to education. Even among the industries that do require similarly lengthy and expensive training processes, few reward trainees with such comparatively low salary outcomes, few feature labor markets that are similarly weak and monopsonistic and, finally, still fewer industries necessitate and rely on auto-depreciation to the extent that academia does. I don't mean to say that academics elsewhere don't need strong job security – far from it! – or that a practice like tenure may not be the best way to give it to them. But I do think that tenure is an unusually important employment protection for faculty in the United States.

Finally, the *TTS* data is limited to incidents occurring between **2000 *and* 2021**. These temporal boundaries are both arbitrary – why stop in 2021 instead of 2020? – and intentional. I wanted to cover a period that was long enough to provide meaningful insights. But I needed to limit myself to a period that was short enough to make the labor-intensive process of finding both litigated and nonlitigated disputes feasible. Most workplace disputes, including most terminations, are not litigated, so any dataset built from legal databases alone would have been severely underinclusive. At the same time, very few nonlegal datasets collect incidents that would have been relevant for my purposes. To find tenured-terminations that *didn't* produce litigation, my research assistants and I had to painstakingly scrape blogs, newspapers, industry publications, and campus newsletters that were searchable online. It was slow and difficult work.

All these considerations led me to start my window in 2000, when it seemed more likely that relevant terminations would leave an internet "footprint" for us to follow. I originally meant to end my window on December 31, 2020, but I was lured into extending the end date by the prospect of including various events that took place in 2021. The realization that this would keep happening is why I didn't go any further. Not only would new events keep occurring, but because my source material – the internet – is constantly evolving, both *old* events as well as new information about old events would keep surfacing. I had to draw the line somewhere.

This has been a lot of *Yes, buts…* all of which are true, and all of which should be kept in mind as we move forward. But what you should also keep in mind is that the *TTS* is likely remarkably accurate for a dataset that's exclusively built off publicly available information. Tenured-terminations are very rare. In 2020, the University of California system revealed that only six tenured faculty had been terminated system-wide in the past twenty years. The UC system has ten campuses with, as of 2024, around 25,000 faculty; it's among the top forty largest university networks in the world. The fact that only six tenured faculty have been terminated across the UC system in the same period covered by the *TTS* makes the *TTS*, with its total of just 293 incidents, seem very nearly exhaustive.

Those 293 *TTS* incidents are spread across 197 distinct institutions and all major disciplinary clusters (which I've defined as STEM, Humanities, Social Sciences, Arts, and Professional fields). Of these incidents, 266 (90.8%) involve male faculty. Public and private institutions are both present in the dataset, although public institutions are heavily overrepresented (and Chapter 20 explores the implications of this finding). For readers who are interested, I've fleshed out some of the descriptive statistics referenced in the following chapters via a number of handy pie charts in Appendix B. Note that all the analysis shared in the next two chapters is statistically significant using a Chi-square test ($p \leq 0.05$), although the specific levels of significance vary and can be found, along with other information, in the notes.

Most readers, I suspect, will be struck by the small number of incidents in the *TTS* overall. In this chapter, I've offered several explanations for why the number may be so small: the very specific type of incident I searched for, the difficulty of the search process, and the shifting nature of the source material. But I've also pointed out that the *TTS* is likely quite accurate, which means there's no getting away from the sheer rarity of tenured-terminations.

Tenured-terminations *are* rare. This is by design. The purpose of all just cause contracts – not just the kind we call "tenure" – is to make cause for termination difficult but not impossible to find. Until now, I've focused on showing why this level of job security may be particularly valuable and necessary in academia, and why it doesn't create the problems that critics so often attribute to it. Over the next few chapters, I'll use the *TTS* data to make similar arguments, this time from the vantage point of a post-mortem. What can we learn about faculty tenure from the instances when it's been overcome?

19

They Said, They Said

The phrase referenced by this chapter's title has come in for a lot of criticism lately. Originally, *he-said, she-said* was just a descriptive shorthand for cross-gender dialogue. It literally referred to a conversational pattern in which he said something and then she said something, or vice versa. Later, it became shorthand for cross-gender communicative misfires, in the sense that "he said X, but she – understanding him to mean Y – replied." (Perhaps more often vice versa.) Still later, around the Senate hearings to evaluate Supreme Court nominee Clarence Thomas, the phrase *he-said, she-said* became a statement about factual unknowability. In 1991, for instance, the *Chicago Tribune* wrote that an FBI report about Thomas "could not draw any conclusion because of the 'he said, she said' nature" of the allegations that Anita Allen had made against Thomas.[1] This last usage turned out to be the one that stuck.

Over twenty-five years later, during the height of the #MeToo movement and the Senate hearings for another Supreme Court nominee, Brett Kavanaugh, legal commentators began objecting to the phrase altogether. Writing about the Kavanaugh hearings, a law professor at the University of Virginia declared that "[o]ur usual talents and methods for determining credibility do not simply vanish when we need to assess allegations of sexual activity behind closed doors."[2] A former federal prosecutor criticized the "institutionalized skepticism of female testimony" that "still lingers in the concept of 'he said, she said'" and decried the "myth… [that] there is no way to discern the truth… in sex crimes."[3]

I agree with these criticisms, but fortunately I'm not using the phrase to signal the type of epistemic fatalism they object to. The *TTS* data isn't primarily concerned with establishing the truth of the matter with respect to any specific incident, much less with making a statement about the knowability of such truths. What I'm most interested in capturing is how university-employers and faculty-employees *frame* the disputes that led to tenured-terminations. This is most like the original "cross-gender dialogue" meaning of *he-said, she-said*. What, quite literally, did they say?

Framing is a widely studied phenomenon in the law-and-social-science world I inhabit, where it mostly refers to how people conceptualize particular goals or

166

grievances as *legal* goals or grievances. Not every fight becomes a court case, and not every rule is reflected in law. Not every social movement needs to demand legal change. Studying legal framing is useful because it helps us understand how and why law enters the picture (if indeed it does), and how law "shapes activists' perceptions, tactics, and ability to generate social change."[4]

The *TTS* approach to framing is a bit less law-oriented than this. I'm not trying to understand how universities and tenured faculty frame disputes as *legal* disputes; only 36.2% of *TTS* incidents even involved the formal legal system. I'm more interested in trying to understand how universities and tenured faculty present their disputes *at all*. Contract law scholars have long held that what parties to a dispute believe went wrong can tell us something about the agreement that was broken.[5] Every incident in the *TTS* dataset involves an employment relationship that was ultimately severed, and every former employee was tenured at the time of that severing. The frames used by employers and employees to describe these disputes can tell us something about the (terminated, tenured) relationship itself.

I call employer frames *university narratives* and employee frames *faculty counternarratives*. These labels don't mean that universities always "spoke" first, or that I think universities get to establish a baseline interpretation of events that faculty must then counter or disprove. If anything, my conclusion that university narratives and faculty counternarratives show tenure to be largely functioning as it should – as a form of just cause employment where cause is difficult but hardly impossible to find – supports *faculty* by supporting tenure. The terminology I use is just a nonconvoluted way of indicating the oppositional nature of the frames. I'll also capitalize terms when they're being used as specific codes from the *TTS* dataset (e.g., Sexual Misconduct) but use standard capitalization practices when those terms are used in their everyday sense (e.g., sexual misconduct). And, finally, I want to reiterate that all this analysis is statistically significant using a Chi-square test ($p \leq 0.05$), but more specific information can be found in the notes.

A university narrative coded as Sexual Misconduct may signal any of three mid-level: Inappropriate Relationships, Sexual Harassment, and Sexual Assault.[6] Taken together, Sexual Misconduct disputes formed an overwhelming majority – a whopping 75.9% – of incidents. That's bad enough, but it gets worse. When we go one level deeper into the data, to those three mid-level categories, we see that, in the overwhelming majority of Sexual Misconduct incidents, the university argued that a professor had engaged in Sexual Harassment (74.1%). The *TTS* coding for Sexual Harassment largely tracks both social science analysis and employment discrimination law by defining this behavior as "non-consensual but non-criminal acts of a sexual or intimate nature... [acts] that would not normally result in criminal charges." Not only was this broad category of wrongdoing the most common Sexual Misconduct narrative *and* the most common university narrative overall, the *second* most common type of Sexual Misconduct narrative was the most severe subcategory, Sexual Assault (14.1%). The only subcategory involving consensual sexual behavior with someone above the age of consent, Inappropriate Relationships, was the least common type of Sexual Misconduct narrative (11.8%).

The prevalence of Sexual Harassment and Sexual Assault narratives offers some support for the argument put forward in a 2018 law review article that "that actual accounts and complaints of faculty sexually harassing students may be very different from… general perceptions of workplace sexual harassment as consisting mainly of verbal or visual harassment."[7] The *TTS* coding doesn't break down Sexual Harassment into physical and nonphysical behaviors, and the study population of that law review article was much broader because it included nontenure-stream faculty. But to repeat myself while also grossly understating matters: this is bad.

At the same time, this also means most tenured-terminations are likely happening for reasons that even supporters of tenure should want. That is, at least through 2021, most discoverable terminations involving tenured faculty were, from the university's perspective, triggered by faculty sexual misconduct. Most of them were even triggered by behavior best characterized as Sexual Harassment. Notwithstanding the worries of tenure's supporters – and notwithstanding any new dynamics produced by recent legislative efforts to weaken tenure – university explanations for tenured-terminations hinge on behavior that is deserving of punishment. Tenure was never meant to insulate faculty from the consequences of committing sexual misconduct. If tenured professors are terminated because they engaged in this kind of bad act, well, that is as it should be.

There are a few obvious *Yes, buts…* that might be made here, but they're either unanswerable or otherwise not too damaging to my point that tenure is being overcome for good reasons.

The first possible objection is a spin on Chapter 13's imagined critic who believes that tenure protects predators. Looking at the *TTS* data, that critic might say that even if most tenured-terminations involve situations where relationships were *appropriately* severed (because they generated Sexual Misconduct narratives), tenure may nevertheless prevent many instances of sexual misconduct from being adequately punished. Put differently, this type of critic would be saying, "We don't have the real denominator for Sexual Misconduct narratives – all we have are those instances where it resulted in *discoverable termination* – but if we did, it would show that tenure is blocking terminations that should rightly happen."

Let's set aside the question of whether all instances of faculty sexual misconduct should result in termination as opposed to some type of discipline. I'm willing to assume that they should, and I'm further willing to grant that most of these instances *don't* result in terminations or even in adequate punishment because sexual misconduct is underreported and inadequately punished in *most* industries. If we had the true denominator for Sexual Misconduct narratives, it probably wouldn't improve how we feel about tenure. But as Chapter 13 explains, this objection assumes that *tenure* is what's responsible for creating a bad situation that, in reality, exists almost everywhere regardless of industry or contract type. It also places all the blame for that situation on tenure instead of also on the university-employers who choose to hide behind it.

A second but inverse objection might be that we can't take employer perspectives at face value in all situations where the university articulates a Sexual Misconduct narrative. That is, maybe the *TTS* is *over*inclusive instead of being *under*inclusive when it comes to measuring sexual misconduct. Just as tenure's critics often argue that faculty are disingenuously hiding behind academic freedom (a charge that I'll get to shortly), tenure's supporters sometimes worry that universities are disingenuously or at least inaccurately portraying faculty as engaging in sexually inappropriate behavior, maybe because doing so makes it easier to discipline and fire troublesome employees. A milder form of this worry, one that rests on university mistake as opposed to university maliciousness, is what leads commentators like Northwestern professor Laura Kipnis to worry about "sexual paranoia" on college campuses.[8] Supporters of tenure who feel, like Kipnis, that universities encourage students "to regard themselves as such exquisitely sensitive creatures that an errant classroom remark could impede their education" might also feel that not all Sexual Misconduct terminations truly reflect sexual misconduct, much less misconduct deserving termination.

We can infer something about the potential weaponization of Sexual Misconduct narratives by looking at how the faculty who were confronting this university narrative framed their own experiences. When facing a university narrative of Sexual Misconduct, an overwhelming majority of faculty articulated *no* discoverable counternarrative of any kind (79.1%). This means they said nothing at all that I could find – no admission, no rejection, no explanation. Whether they were fired from their jobs or left them under nominally voluntary circumstances, professors who were accused of Sexual Misconduct generally went, as my mother somewhat bemusedly put it, quietly into the sunset.

(There's actually a specific *legal* reason why Sexual Misconduct narratives generally elicited crickets, and it leads to the same conclusion as the discussion below. But because that legal reason is dependent on the topic of Chapter 20 – the distinction between public and private universities – I'll discuss it there.)

The sort of no-response response that most faculty chose to make when facing Sexual Misconduct narratives is roughly analogous to two types of pleas that are often articulated by individuals facing criminal charges. In one, the *nolo contendere* ("no contest") plea, the defendant neither admits guilt nor denies it but accepts a plea to avoid trial. In the other, the Alford plea, which is a variation on the *nolo contendere*, the defendant continues to maintain their innocence but (usually because the state has a strong case) is unwilling to risk both perjury and trial by pleading not guilty. The motivations and the internal mechanics are slightly distinct, but the outcome is the same: no admission or denial of guilt, and no trial.

As it turns out, *nolo* and Alford pleas are strongly associated with violent offenses and especially with sex offenses.[9] One of the few studies to try breaking down the use of these pleas by type of crime found that sex offenses accounted for 21% of state crimes involving *nolo* pleas and 27% of state crimes involving Alford pleas.[10] Neither plea is guaranteed to save a defendant from specific punishments or even to spare them from being labeled a sex offender – those outcomes depend on the particular deal they've struck with the prosecutor's office. This is why lawyers and legal scholars feel that defendants turn to *nolo* and Alford pleas when they want to avoid "embarrassment and shame before friends and family" or when they "refuse to admit guilt to themselves."[11] They can't deny it, but they don't want to admit it… so they enter a no-response response.

The literature on *nolo* and Alford pleas suggests that faculty silence supports the accuracy of the university's framing when it comes to Sexual Misconduct narratives. At the same time, and following a roughly similar logic, the frequency with which professors facing *other* university narratives *do* articulate counternarratives, as well as some patterns in the counternarratives they articulate, also gives us reason to take *their* framing – and their apparent valuation of tenured employment – seriously. This doesn't mean we should unthinkingly take faculty counternarratives at face value: that's the kind of factual evaluation called for by critics of the phrase *he-said, she-said*. All we need to do is believe that it means something when faculty articulate any counternarrative just like it means something when they don't.

Faculty facing university narratives other than Sexual Misconduct were far more likely to articulate some kind of counternarrative.[12] At the *low* end of this spectrum, university narratives alleging Protected Category Discrimination elicited counternarratives 81.3% of the time. Faculty facing university narratives of Unprofessional Conduct articulated counternarratives 97.3% of the time. Fully 100% of faculty facing three other types of university narratives – Academic Misconduct, Institutional Non-Advancement, and School Financial Difficulties – articulated a counternarrative. In other words, most faculty facing narratives other than Sexual Misconduct did *not* go quietly into the sunset: they articulated contrasting perspectives widely enough and loudly enough that those perspectives were discoverable by my research team, just like the university narratives to which those faculty were responding.

Only one in ten professors in the entire dataset – roughly *a quarter (26.3%) of those who offered some counternarrative* – argued that their university's actions violated their Speech and Academic Freedom ("SAF") rights. Moreover, of the faculty who faced Sexual Misconduct narratives, only 2.2% articulated SAF counternarratives. Quite simply, and contra tenure's critics, faculty don't often make disingenuous appeals to academic freedom because they rarely appeal to it *at all*. The rarity of SAF counternarratives in the dataset is especially noteworthy because every incident in the dataset was serious enough to ultimately result in termination, and 36.2% of them involved litigation of some form. Courts are known to "defer significantly to employers' exercise of business judgment"[13] but they are *especially* reluctant to second-guess the personnel decisions of university-employers.[14] Despite this, and despite academic freedom's relatively strong normative appeal, only 10% of faculty in the total dataset framed their counternarratives in terms of SAF and only 16.4% of faculty involved in litigation relied on it.

It's also possible that the relative rarity of SAF counternarratives means that tenure works as a prophylactic rather than as a post-facto correction. In other words, maybe tenure has been so successful at establishing academic freedom as an industry norm that few tenured faculty experience the ultimate negative employment consequence, termination, in violation of that norm – *even by their own lights*. This should offer some reassurance to tenure's supporters, even if that reassurance comes with significant caveats thanks to the as-yet-unseen effects of recent anti-tenure legislation and the likelihood that academic freedom violations can happen without ending in termination.

If we move beyond Sexual Misconduct, the *TTS* also shows that patterns in narratives and counternarratives are highly gendered. Overall, women were more likely than men to offer *any* kind of counternarrative: 63% of women in the dataset articulated some counternarrative in contrast to only 36.5% of men.[15] This is unsurprising given the prevalence of Sexual Misconduct narratives, the tendency of faculty facing such narratives to offer no counternarrative, and the fact that 96.8% of Sexual Misconduct narratives involved male faculty. (The prevalence of male faculty in the Sexual Misconduct subset may itself be unsurprising since most sexual misconduct is perpetrated by men against women, but it's actually higher than you'd expect *even allowing for* the gender imbalance in the dataset: there were around ten times more men than women, but only 3.2% of Sexual Misconduct incidents involved female faculty.)

It's also unsurprising, as well as more than a little disheartening, to know that women and men faced significantly different types of university narratives.[16] The university narrative most commonly faced by female faculty was Unprofessional Conduct, at 44%. Unprofessional Conduct is, in both the *TTS* and in real life, a catch-all term that can be used to signal a professor's failure to exhibit behaviors that are considered appropriate to her age, race, gender, rank, discipline, pedigree, marital status, parental status, socio-economic status, or any of a hundred other factors that people inside and outside academia regularly use to categorize and stereotype one another. There's an entire anthology dedicated to showing, through personal narrative, how "women of color too frequently find themselves 'presumed incompetent' as scholars, teachers, and participants in academic governance."[17] I wish that the *TTS* didn't offer further evidence of this presumption, but it seems to.

Yet what *TTS* also suggests is that female faculty may have more faith in the processes that tenure establishes, such that tenure is – in at least one sense – especially valuable for this population that is still underrepresented in academia. Men and women differed significantly in the *kind* of counternarratives they offered.[18] Two of the top three counternarratives articulated by female faculty were SAF (35.3%) and Wrongful Retaliation (23.5%), which is interesting in itself but becomes more so given that women were most likely to face narratives of Unprofessional Conduct. Men, on the other hand, relied most on Direct Denial (33%).

Make no mistake: if we assume for argument's sake that their version of events is the right one, it's bad news that such a high percentage of female faculty feel their academic freedom was violated and that their employer wrongfully retaliated against them for doing or saying something. But there's also a more hopeful way to view this information, and (particularly given the suspension of factual judgment we're committed to regarding the veracity of narratives and counternarratives) I think it's worth balancing our disappointment with determination.

Articulating a counternarrative that sounds in academic freedom can reflect, and certainly reinforces, a belief that academic freedom is a worthy norm. Coming from a population that is, as that anthology says, *presumed incompetent*, the fact that SAF is the most common response from female faculty suggests that they haven't completely given up on the norm even though academia hasn't generally lived up to its promise for individuals like them. All this may sound odd coming from me after nearly twenty chapters dedicated to shifting the conversation away from academic freedom. But my goal has never been to suggest that academic freedom isn't valuable, or even that it's unconnected to tenure – just that it's not the only reason that tenure's valuable.

Similarly, a high Wrongful Retaliation rate among female professors may seem like unambiguously bad news. After all, wrongful retaliation claims effectively say: "I did or said something that I *should* have done or said, or at least that was *within my rights* to do or say, but I was nevertheless punished for it." Taken at face value, it's not reassuring to think that 23.5% of tenured female faculty who were ultimately terminated felt they were attacked in this way by their employers. But Wrongful Retaliation, even more than SAF, suggests a kind of faith in the process and its principles. It is entirely possible, as *nolo* and Alford pleas show us in the criminal context, and as Sexual Misconduct incidents show us in the *TTS* context, to simply say nothing and accept what's meted out to you. Articulating any counternarrative (even a disingenuous one) suggests a willingness to fight, while articulating a counternarrative centered on wrongful retaliation suggests some trust – whether in the employer, in the legal system, in the public, or in all three – that the wrongdoing will be recognized and corrected.

It may be that female faculty are wrong to engage the system, that they're foolish to articulate counternarratives centered on holding the system accountable to its own principles and processes. I'm not saying they're being rational – and, by extension, I'm not saying that their choice of counternarratives was intentional. But faith in the systems that govern American academia is one way to read how tenured women responded in instances of severe (as it turns out, terminal) employment distress. Even if that faith is misplaced, and even if *these* women deserved to be terminated, the promises afforded by tenure may be empowering to other women who are still working to reach it.

The narratives and counternarratives from the *TTS* thus tell us many things, some of which we knew, and some of which we might find surprising but should also find reassuring. What we knew already is that sexual misconduct is a problem in the academy. As Chapter 13 points out, we don't know that it's *worse* in the academy than outside of it – but, ethically speaking, that should only matter so much. The next chapter digs a little further into patterns relating to the Sexual Misconduct narrative to show why gutting tenure is unlikely to be the resolution to this problem.

What we might *not* have previously known, but should find reassuring, is that tenure is largely functioning as it should: as a form of just cause employment where cause for termination is difficult but not impossible to find. This cuts two ways.

On the one hand, the *TTS* suggests that when tenure is overcome it is likely to be for good reason – in fact, for potentially criminal reasons. Most discoverable tenured-terminations were triggered by circumstances that the employer framed as Sexual Misconduct. And the literature on *nolo* and Alford pleas combined with the high no-response response rate of faculty facing Sexual Misconduct narratives suggests that this framing was likely reasonable. Even if you don't think all types of behavior that can be characterized as sexual misconduct warrant termination, this is – legally and ethically – the kind of behavior that we mean by "just cause."

(Another positive, in my eyes at least, is how this finding reminds us that universities already have all the tools they need to terminate bad-acting tenured faculty. A university that chooses to retain a professor despite their bad acts is making exactly the kind of rational but socially harmful choice that is usually only attributed to the bad-acting professor herself.)

At the same time, the *TTS* suggests that when faculty claim to have suffered violations of their academic freedom, they are *also* likely to be acting reasonably. Professors simply *don't* cry "academic freedom!" disingenuously. In an overwhelming majority of *TTS* disputes – which, remember, were all serious enough to have ultimately ended in termination – professors did not articulate SAF counternarratives, even though they would have had few arguments at their disposal that are more rhetorically powerful.

Finally, the most surprising insight of all may be that even marginalized faculty may find the principles and processes derived from tenure to be valuable argumentative resources. Women articulated counternarratives of SAF and Wrongful Retaliation at statistically significant rates, suggesting that they believe there are still norms and systems to appeal to. Cynicism is an easy response to this finding – but it's not the only one, and it's certainly not the best one. We should be heartened and galvanized by the idea that tenure still means something to some of the newer entrants to the academy. That's no mean achievement for something that is, after all, just a contractual feature of an employment relationship.

20

Public/Private

I'm going to open this chapter with the punchline because it's one of my most surprising results: tenured-terminations overwhelmingly occurred at public institutions (70.6%) even though public institutions never accounted for more than 33% of all four-year nonprofit universities during the *TTS* study period.[1]

Why is the prevalence of tenured-terminations at public institutions so remarkable? It's remarkable for two reasons. One of these has to do with the special circumstances of faculty who are, by virtue of working at public universities, also public employees. The other reason has to do with political efforts to undermine tenure.

Public-sector employees enjoy more rights at work. This isn't to say that they have a *lot* of rights at work. I'm not sure any American workers have "a lot of rights" relative to comparable workers in peer countries. Still, public sector employees can access many state and federal protections that aren't available to any private-sector workers, even to those classified as employees.

For one thing, public-sector employees (not just professors at public universities) are governed by just cause principles. This means that any of them who survive the probationary periods of their jobs are entitled to "some kind of hearing" before they can be terminated.[2] No at-will employee is entitled to this kind of pre-termination hearing. In fact, an employer who promises such a pre-termination hearing to an at-will employee risks *transforming* an at-will contract into one that's only terminable for just cause.[3] Within the academy, nontenure-track faculty and pre-tenure faculty can both easily lose their jobs without pre-termination hearings if their employers simply decide not to renew their contracts.[4] And pre-termination hearings, much like trials, are valuable because they afford people a chance to hear – and rebut – the arguments and evidence against them.[5] What this leaves us with is a situation in which procedural guarantees that are only meaningfully available to tenured professors in academia are available to *all* post-probationary public employees.

Second, public employees have constitutional speech protections at work. For a while, public employees could not be punished for what they said so long as their speech was on a matter of "public concern" and their interest in being able to speak freely surpassed their employer's interest in efficiency (by being able to control workers). Today, though, the circle of protected speech for public employees is smaller.[6] In 2006, the Supreme Court's decision in *Garcetti v. Ceballos* added a kind of threshold analysis (or what I tell my employment law students to think of as a "short cut") to the earlier rule.[7] *Garcetti* held that any speech that an employee engages in "pursuant to their official duties" was outside the zone of protection *regardless* of its subject matter and *regardless* of any balancing of interests.[8] Put differently: if you're speaking pursuant to your duties, you're out of luck.

A law review article stating that "the reaction to *Garcetti* has generally been negative" put matters, I think, quite diplomatically: the decision has taken hits from free speech advocates, workers' rights advocates, and even from academic freedom advocates because Justice Souter's dissent specifically worried about how *Garcetti* would affect faculty at public institutions.[9] But here's the important part: as much as *Garcetti* and nearly two decades of subsequent case law have narrowed the degree to which public employees may speak freely at work, private employees have *no* workplace First Amendment protections *at all*. None.

Third, public employees who might otherwise incriminate themselves with respect to criminal wrongdoing during a workplace investigation can be protected by "Garrity Rights."[10] If your employer compels you to answer some questions or else face termination, you might answer even if you don't want to and even if answering requires you to admit to things that leave you open to criminal prosecution. But if you work for a public entity, Garrity Rights can prevent your employer from turning over any such compelled incriminating statements to law enforcement. This protection stems from the Fifth and the Fourteenth Amendments: if you're a public employee, then your employer is the state, and the state is not supposed to make you testify against yourself in a criminal case – even if the statement was originally made during a workplace investigation.

Garrity Rights are the "specific legal reason" for silence in the face of Sexual Misconduct narratives that I mentioned in Chapter 19. Since some types of sexual misconduct are criminal offenses, it stands to reason that faculty accused of this behavior might stay silent – not just to their employers (who would be prevented from turning over the information to law enforcement) but to friends, neighbors, journalists… anyone who might create the kind of internet footprint I relied on for the *TTS*. For our purposes in this chapter, the point isn't whether Garrity Rights are as ironclad as they might sound or as we might want them to be. It's simply that this is another protection that's unique to public employees: if you work in the private sector and admit to wrongdoing while answering questions that your employer said you *had* to answer, your employer is still free to pass your confession along to the authorities.

Fourth and finally, some courts have held that "[t]enured faculty in public institutions have a 'property interest' in continued employment… but faculty in private institutions may only have a contractual interest in continued employment."[11]

Property interests provide a comparatively powerful basis for legal claims. That's true whether your claims are centered on real property, intellectual property, or (as with public university faculty) what's maybe best called a kind of positional property. When you can make a property claim against the government, that's generally better for you than a simple contract claim against a private actor.

So much for the first reason why the prevalence of tenured-terminations at public institutions is remarkable: faculty at public universities have many rights that their counterparts at private universities lack. Despite this, they still accounted for an overwhelming majority of tenured-terminations.

The second reason why this particular finding is so remarkable is connected, as I said, to the actions being taken with increasing frequency by political opponents of tenure. When state governments enact legislation to ban or weaken tenure – when they enact the kind of laws that were passed in Wisconsin, Texas, and Georgia, for instance – that legislation only affects professors at public universities. But the *TTS* data tell us that public universities aren't uniquely hamstrung in their ability to terminate bad acting faculty – just the opposite, in fact! So it seems that legislative campaigns against tenure have their greatest impact where that impact is least needed.

Now let's move on to another pattern that also falls along the public/private divide but that tells us more about workplace dynamics than about either institutional type or about tenure itself. I'm discussing it here precisely to show how phenomena that aren't really about tenure are made to *seem* as if they're about tenure – and, specifically, how they're made to seem as if they tell us something about the negative consequences that tenure supposedly has.

TTS data showed that Sexual Misconduct narratives were higher at public universities. To be clear, Sexual Misconduct was the most commonly articulated university narrative at *both* public and private institutions. Nevertheless, it was articulated at levels that showed a statistically significant difference between institutional types: 80.9% (public) versus 64% (private). (For what it's worth, the second most common university narrative was also the same at both types of institutions – Unprofessional Conduct – but it also occurred at levels that showed a statistically significant difference: 10.8% for public versus 17.4% for private.[12])

Considered in isolation, this pattern may seem puzzling. The two most powerful anti-discrimination laws in the United States apply to both public and private universities. Most universities are subject to Title IX of the *Education Amendments Act of 1972*, which prohibits many of the behaviors I've coded as Sexual Misconduct when those behaviors are directed toward students.[13] And most universities are also subject to Title VII of the *Civil Rights Act of 1964*, which prohibits many Sexual Misconduct behaviors when those behaviors are directed toward faculty, staff, and other university employees.[14] Why, then, are Sexual Misconduct terminations so much more prevalent at public universities? And why, given immense diversity within the category "public university," do these institutions contribute to a pattern? The University of Georgia is neither Georgia Southern nor Middle Georgia State: why, for this purpose at least, are they more like one another than like comparable private universities?

One plausible explanation emerges from the *TTS* itself. Public universities in the dataset were significantly more likely to be *doctoral* institutions (77.3%), rather than institutions that primarily grant bachelor's (2.9%) or master's (19.8%) degrees.[15] A doctoral institution is more internally diversified than bachelors and masters institutions, and it's likely more internally hierarchical too. Doctoral institutions have some professional schools that their counterparts simply lack (law, medicine), and they're likely to have larger and more powerful versions of other professional schools (business). These fields account for an overwhelming majority of the highest-paid faculty and they're also among the worst offenders when it comes to faculty gender parity.[16]

Similarly, doctoral institutions, by definition, have doctoral students in addition to master's students and undergraduates; because of the greater emphasis they place on research it's fair to assume that they have more post-doctoral fellows, too. Those doctoral students and postdoctoral fellows are among the most vulnerable populations in the academic galaxy since they often not only earn subsistence wages (or worse) but are also beholden to individual professors for money, mentorship, and professional opportunities. To be sure, disparities of power exist at all types of universities, just as they exist at all types of nonacademic workplaces. But they likely exist at a different order of magnitude among the research-oriented institutions that grant doctorates.

Now, saying this doesn't singlehandedly put tenure in a better light – it just shows, once again, that tenure is probably not what's driving many key dynamics in academia, including many dynamics that we rightly object to. It suggests that, rather than *tenure*, a greater source of harm may be the status and material hierarchies that exist in all universities (and all workplaces) but that, within academia, are likely more extreme at universities where some of the greatest harms occur.

This chapter began with one insight into the public/private distinction that flew in the face of some reasonable expectations and much unreasonable politicking: despite the additional legal protections they have, and despite the argument put forward by many politicians that tenure somehow stands in the way of terminating them for cause, tenured faculty at public universities lose their jobs through individual terminations at a rate that far outpaces their private sector peers. Since many anti-tenure laws are new and many other bills are still working their way into becoming law, in the next few years we are like to see a great deal more legal firepower being thrown at a problem that just doesn't seem to exist.

The chapter then moved on to a second insight that was made visible by the public/private divide but wasn't really about it – or about tenure – at all. As Chapter 13 concedes, sexual misconduct is undoubtedly a problem in academia, as it is in so many other industries. But as that same chapter argued, and as this chapter shows, disparities of power, *not* tenure, are likely at the root of this problem. Sexual Misconduct rates were significantly different at public versus private universities, and this can hardly be because public universities are subject to less stringent rules or more tenure. (If anything, they are subject to more rules and, thanks to various political campaigns, they sometimes offer a *weakened* form of tenure.) Instead, the difference in Sexual Misconduct rates is likely because public universities in the *TTS* dataset are more likely to be *doctoral* universities: institutions that are marked by severe hierarchies and power differentials. Addressing this will be hard, but it doesn't begin with gutting tenure.

21

If I Stay It Will Be Double

Critics who believe that tenure incentivizes laziness (Chapter 14) which it then protects through self-dealing (Chapter 15) probably also think that tenured employment is most valuable to people who can't cut it in any other context. And indeed: "the value of tenure," writes our economist friend Stephen Levitt, "is inversely related to how good you are."[1]

Now, Levitt – along with many other economists, STEM faculty, and faculty in professional disciplines (including in my own field of law) – might grudgingly acknowledge that who *is* and who *isn't* considered "good" won't solely be a function of intelligence and work ethic. These folks will hopefully grant that your worth, and therefore your ability to pack up and leave for more hospitable shores, will *also* be determined by the marketability of your expertise. In other words: even if you want assurances that you can stay because you can't easily leave the *reasons* you can't leave might have nothing to do with your intellect or your work ethic. All things being equal, rational actor thinking suggests that we should expect to see professors in disciplines with worse exit options fight more to keep their jobs.

Like many assumptions about what tenure does, this one fares poorly when confronted by anything empirical. We can't really test it using the existing literature on faculty mobility because that literature includes or emphasizes turnover that's at least nominally voluntary: moving to accommodate a spouse, be near family, trade up jobs, or trade in unpleasant working environments. Insights into these sorts of exits (and intentions-to-exit) can tell us about the personal and professional conditions under which university faculty operate. But they can't tell us if faculty fight harder to retain their jobs when they have limited options outside academia.

Here's where *TTS* data can be useful. Incidents in the dataset were sorted into one of three categories – fired, resigned, retired – according to the conditions under which the employment relationship was severed. For most of the analysis that follows, I collapsed these into just two categories to allow for the possibility of statistically significant insights: "Fired" (involuntary terminations) and "Quit" (nominally voluntary terminations). I say *nominally* voluntary because, in most instances, it's clear that faculty resigned or retired to avoid the legal, financial, and reputational consequences of being fired. Still, Quits aren't fully coerced.

Imagine that a tenured professor gets into a serious dispute with her university. At whatever point that termination appears on the table, it appears in one of the three ways depicted in Table 21.1.

TABLE 21.1 *Quits versus Fireds*, Stage 1

Party #1 says…
1. "Quit or be fired!"
2. "You're fired!"
3. "I quit!"

In scenario three, where the professor is Party #1, only one response is likely. Although a university may fight to retain its superstar employees, it (like any other employer) is unlikely to expend energy on an employee who's already the source of some tension. But in each scenario where the *university* is Party #1, the professor has two possible responses. And two of these responses (1b and 2b in Table 21.2) are both instances where Party #2 – the faculty member – fights back in an attempt to keep her job.

TABLE 21.2 *Quits versus Fireds*, Stage 2

Party #1 says…	Party #2 responds…
1. "Quit or be fired!"	a. "I quit."
	b. "I won't quit!"
2. "You're fired!"	a. "OK."
	b. "No!"
3. "I quit!"	"OK."

Of course, since every incident in the *TTS* dataset involves a tenured-termination, we know how this story ends. What matters isn't the ending. What matters isn't even the beginning. What matters here is whether the professor in question *resisted* termination in an effort to keep her job – and that, as Table 21.3 suggests, is what we tried to capture.

TABLE 21.3 *Quits versus Fireds*, Stage 3

Party #1 says…	Party #2 responds…	Coded as…
1. "Quit or be fired!"	a. "I quit."	Quit
	b. "I won't quit!"	Fired
2. "You're fired!"	a. "OK."	Fired
	b. "No!"	Fired
3. "I quit!"	"OK."	Quit

I'll jump to the end: the difference between Quits and Fireds was *not* statistically significant across most study variables, *including across disciplinary affiliation*. This means that faculty whose specializations likely gave them better nonacademic employment prospects were *not* more willing to quit when faced with threats to their tenured jobs. To be even more blunt: professors in STEM and professional fields, who are generally thought of as having more options in the general labor market, did not walk away from their academic jobs at a rate that was any greater than professors in Humanities, Social Sciences, or Arts fields who are often derided as having nowhere better to go. This is despite the fact that, as Chapter 10 suggests, many of those STEM and professional field faculty were likely to have earned below market rate for the credentials they held.

Even though this is a discrete insight, it's a pretty powerful one. Everything derogatory that's said about the Humanities as a cluster is said with a 100-fold more certainty and smugness about Humanities *scholars*. But scholars in the Humanities don't hang on for dear life any more than their presumably empowered colleagues in STEM and the Professional fields. Those empowered folks with exit options *also* stay to fight. If they were truly "rational maximizers," as tenure's critics so often assume, we should expect that faculty with meaningful exit options would leave academia at the first sign of trouble. Why endure intrusive inquiries and disciplinary measures, heartache, and embarrassment, not to mention potential lost income (in the form of penalties or unpaid leaves), when you have viable alternatives elsewhere? If a cushy ride was the only thing that mattered, these folks should have been long gone.

In 2019, Phil Adamo was suspended from his teaching duties at Augsburg University in Minneapolis and fired from an administrative position directing Augsburg's undergraduate honors program.[2] Adamo began teaching history at Augsburg in 2001 and earned tenure there in 2007.[3] In 2018, he was suspended and removed from his director's position, as well as considered for formal dismissal from his tenured faculty position.[4] By all publicly available accounts, this happened because Adamo did three things: first, he read aloud James Baldwin's use of the N-word in an honors seminar class on Baldwin's *The Fire Next Time*, second, he led a classroom discussion about use of the N-word and, third, after that class session, Adamo emailed his students essays by Andre M. Perry and Ta-Nehisi Coates about using the N-word.[5]

The details of Adamo's story are not what matter most for our purposes, much less any determination of who has the moral upper hand. What *does* matter is that Adamo was a longtime and arguably successful professor: someone who the Carnegie Foundation named Minnesota Professor of the Year in 2015, and in whose honor "Dr. Phillip C. Adamo Day" was announced by the Mayor of Minneapolis."[6] What also matters is that Adamo was a professor of medieval history – not, I think it is fair to say, a field with vibrant employment prospects outside academia, especially for someone who has been inside academia for nearly twenty years. And, finally, what matters is that after his suspension was lifted and his university decided *not* to pursue his termination, Adamo walked away.[7]

Just as a tenured professor's decision to stay and fight isn't necessarily reflective of their likely viability in the general labor market, it's also not explainable by other factors that might speak to their individual merit. It's *not* the case, for instance, that faculty in STEM and professional fields were more likely to face Sexual Misconduct narratives, such that the "walk away" response associated with those narratives *also* gets associated with specific disciplines that happen to provide better exit options. In fact, there were no significant patterns in university narratives along disciplinary affiliation: STEM professors weren't more likely to be accused of any given bad act as compared to professors in the Humanities, Social Sciences, Professional fields, or Arts. Taking university narratives into account can help explain some *other* patterns in Quits and Fireds – for instance, it can offer some insight into why Quits are so much higher at doctoral institutions (64.2%), where Sexual Misconduct was more common, than at both bachelor's (50%) and master's (35.6%) institutions.[8] But faculty don't choose to fight (and eventually be Fired) or to walk away (through a nominal Quit) based on the ease with which they'll likely find nonacademic work.

Like so much else in debates over tenure, assumptions about *what* professors do and *why* they do it reflect personal bias more than empirical truth. Faculty in fields that are more likely to provide good exit options don't walk away at the first sign of trouble, and this *isn't* because they get into specific kinds of trouble. They seem to stay and fight for jobs that are neither very high-paying nor unusually low-intensity. Whether or not we would have liked these *particular* professors to win their fights isn't the issue – remember that the *TTS* is concerned with narrative framing more than existential truth. What matters is that faculty want to keep their jobs even when their training gives them options. The value of tenured employment isn't, apparently, inversely related to how "good" you are.

22

Riffed

When I began this research, I wanted to find out how many tenured professors lost their jobs *despite* having tenure. I knew that tenure wasn't a "job for life" – that there is no such thing, especially in the United States, and that even if it exists I wouldn't find it in academia. But I also believed, and I still believe, that tenure offers a great deal of valuable job security for people who need it and whose work is needed by society. I wanted to think about the limits of this thing that I'd spent my childhood hearing about and my adult life chasing.

With physical objects, we identify limits by conducting strength tests. We crash cars into cement walls, we stretch polymers until they snap. When I started data collection for the *TTS*, I was thinking along these lines. *What can we learn about tenure from the instances in which it's been overcome? What can we learn from tenured-terminations?* Individual terminations were only ever part of the answer to my questions. Focusing on individuals in the way *TTS* data does is like focusing on dramatic side-impact crashes when run of the mill rear-end collisions are more common. If we really want to talk about how tenured professors lose their jobs, we ought to be talking about RIFs.

RIFs are reductions-in-force. They're terminations of entire groups of faculty, instead of only individuals. Most RIFs are justified on financial grounds – usually referred to as *financial exigency* – because this is one of the two rationales that, when validly invoked, likely won't bring down AAUP censure on the heads of university leaders. (Plus, the other rationale – *program discontinuance* – often happens for financial reasons even though, according to the AAUP, it's only an acceptable justification for terminating faculty in violation of their contracts if the discontinuance is "based essentially upon educational considerations."[1])

The existence of an escape hatch like financial exigency was the AAUP's way of acknowledging that educational institutions operate under economic constraints just like the individual professors who needed job security via tenure. In 1925, the AAUP and other academic associations co-authored the Conference Statement on Academic Freedom and Tenure. The very last section of the 1925 Statement declared that:

> Termination of permanent or long-term appointments because of financial exi-
> gency should be sought only as a last resort, after every effort has been made to
> meet the need in other ways and to find for the teacher other employment in the
> institution. Situations which make retrenchment of this sort necessary should pre-
> clude expansions of the staff at other points at the same time, except in extraordi-
> nary circumstances.

The 1940 Statement also discussed financial exigency, though as the AAUP itself says, the Statement was "briefer… but more emphatic"[2] than the Declaration had been:

> Termination of a continuous appointment because of financial exigency should be
> demonstrably bona fide.

Then, in the *Recommended Institutional Regulations* – the AAUP's equivalent of a model code or template for university policies on various issues – there is a section, number 4(c), explaining the Association's positions on the mechanics of layoffs due to financial exigency. Section 4(c) of the *RIR* discusses the *whens*, the *hows*, and the *whats* of this type of termination, which is only supposed to happen when "a severe financial crisis that fundamentally compromises the academic integrity of the institution as a whole and that cannot be alleviated by less drastic means."[3]

When it comes to financial exigency, there's a lot of "common sense" thinking that turns out to be nonsensical. It's easy to agree with universities when they claim to be drastically short on money. We keep hearing about educational budgetary gaps from our news media and our politicians. Those of us actively who are embedded in campus life (or paying for someone else to be) keep hearing about budget woes from our institutional leaders. Because we keep hearing about "cash-strapped universi-ties," we've internalized the idea that they are. Repetition is a surprisingly effective way to manufacture truthiness.

The problem is not just that the truth about university finances is far more com-plicated than this messaging suggests. The problem is also that one part of this mes-sage – the part that says matters have become so dire as to leave administrators with no choice but to lay off tenured faculty – very rarely stands up to scrutiny. Remember that "financial exigency" only exists when *a severe financial crisis… fun-damentally compromises… the institution* and *cannot be alleviated by less drastic means*. Between 1974 and 2004, the AAUP investigated twenty-eight institutions that fired faculty (not just tenured faculty) in the name of financial exigency, and found that only four of them actually faced anything that might be reasonably character-ized as exigent circumstances.[4] Most of these instances seemed like exercises in Orwellian doublespeak. To take just one example, Eastern Oregon State College, an institution with a budget of $8 million, claimed that financial exigency forced it to fire a tenured professor with eighteen years of service.[5] What was Eastern Oregon's budget shortfall? Initially, it was projected to be a whopping $58,000.[6] That was later adjusted down to around $12,000. This is somewhat like declaring bankruptcy because you don't *want* to pay your creditors rather than because you can't.

Financial exigency matters, as I said before, because it's the most common justification for RIFs – and RIFs, like any kind of faculty termination, are not limited to *tenured* faculty. In one sense, RIFs might even seem like the great equalizer in a work environment that's rigidly hierarchical because they can affect both the tenured full professor who's been teaching for two decades and the nontenure-track lecturer who's been teaching for two semesters. In practice, though, RIFs affect far more NTT faculty and affect them far worse. Universities usually fire or fail to renew their NTT faculty before moving on to tenure-stream folks because, as Chapter 10 noted, this is legally much easier to do. (By the same token, it's often easier to RIF *pre*-tenure faculty, just like it's also easier to terminate them as individuals.) For every tenured professor among the casualties of a RIF, there are usually several, maybe even several *dozen*, NTT faculty who preceded them. RIFs can also be more financially devastating for NTT faculty because they usually earn much less and receive much less in the way of employer-sponsored benefits. When you've been subsisting on next to nothing – on the scraps of money and resources that characterize the "gig academy"[7] – even losing that little hurts a lot.

For these reasons, I don't mean to suggest that RIFs put tenured, tenure-track, and NTT faculty on an equal footing. They don't. What RIFs *do*, and why they deserve our attention, is they affect tenured professors at a rate that exceeds any type of individual termination that's triggered, justifiably or not, by some kind of discrete cause. A professor who's been riffed has done nothing wrong – *nothing at all*. Even their (former) employer doesn't think so. All that professor has done is have the bad luck to be in the wrong field or at the wrong university.

This is why conversations about the job security created by tenure simply *have* to take account of RIFs. Whether you think that the job security tenure creates is good or bad, real or imagined, needed or not, RIFs account for more of the real-life events you have to grapple with in defending your perspective than the for-cause terminations or academic freedom violations that get most of the attention. I only came to fully appreciate this several months into my research on tenure, and when I did, I immediately started trying to build a second database alongside the TTS so that I could measure RIFs.

At first, I used the same approach I had used with the TTS. My research assistants and I tried collecting publicly available information and simply switched our focus from individual terminations to mass layoffs. This seemed like a workable strategy because, in the early months of the pandemic, publicly available information about RIFs was actually hard to avoid. Universities were firing fistfuls of faculty, either because they were responding to chaos or, depending on your perspective, because they were hiding cleverly behind it. For a while, it seemed like my RAs and I woke up every day to news of more RIFs that had to be entered into our database.

But the media coverage of these pandemic-era RIFs – like media coverage of *all* RIFs, I've since realized – was too inexact for my purposes. It lumped all faculty together regardless of their contractual expectations – tenured, tenure-track, and NTT (indeed, many *types* of NTT). These distinctions may not matter for our sense of fairness, but they do matter for the law. The numbers themselves also kept shifting as negotiations went on and universities, who are rarely eager to be transparent in these situations, kept adjusting their narratives and changing their goals. Ultimately, it proved impossible to nail down exact figures for each type of faculty contract using only online sources. More than once, I found myself emailing faculty whose colleagues had been riffed or who'd been riffed themselves for clarification regarding a particular number. Although I was always sheepish and they were always breathtakingly generous, I found I couldn't stomach the process of imposing on people who had lost so much.

Next, my RAs and I tried to work backward: we started with large changes in the number of faculty employed by each university and then tried using online sources to figure out which of those changes could be attributed to RIFs instead of to natural attrition like retirement, for-cause termination, voluntary resignation, and death. The AAUP helped us out by giving us Excel files of information from the National Center for Education Statistics, which is a federal entity charged with "collecting and analyzing data related to education." But the Excel files only show how many full-time faculty were employed by a university at the end of each year – they're "before" and "after" snapshots of a story whose middle has to be filled in through manual searching. Doing that kind of searching was less ethically troubling than my first strategy, but it was far more impractical. As much as I joked with my RAs about our status as internet sleuths, it was just too hard to reconstruct that kind of story using post-mortem stats. We gave up.

It's tempting, in moments like these, to rationalize away failure. *There are other ways to tell this story*, I told myself. *And this story should be told.* It's particularly easy to convince yourself of this when one part of you is an anthropologist and is consequently predisposed to seeing all types of quantification as dangerously seductive.[8] *Numbers reduce complex realities to simplistic factoids*, I muttered under my breath for several days. *They're not the only things that matter.* They're not, of course. But they do matter. (I've hung out with too many economists to think otherwise.) Consider the numbers in this one sentence: Publicly available data suggests that, since 2020, more tenured faculty have lost their jobs through RIFs at just *thirteen* universities than have lost their jobs through individual for-cause terminations at *all* American universities since the year 2000.[9] Thirteen universities. Five years. More job loss.

To be sure, that sentence comes with a collection of caveats, the most important of which is that RIFs are more likely to leave an internet footprint because they're such spectacular events. It took me, working alone, just 2.5 hours to assemble the RIF stats in that sentence; it took me and half a dozen RAs over 2.5 years to identify the individual terminations that make up the *TTS* dataset. So, yes: it's entirely possible that identical search methods may result in an undercounting of individual terminations. But even if it's likely that I'm undercounting individual terminations, it's *guaranteed* that I'm undercounting terminations due to RIFs. My calculations for that sentence didn't include any tenured jobs that were lost through wholesale institutional closures – that is, I didn't count any instances where tenured faculty were fired because their entire university was permanently shut down. That alone would have massively increased the numbers.

Whatever worries critics may have about tenure as an employment practice need to be weighed against the likelihood that more tenured professors have lost their jobs through no fault of their own in five years at thirteen universities than have lost their jobs through potential wrongdoing in twenty years at all universities. This means that the worries critics have articulated about tenure's bad incentive effects – worries about iconoclastic, predatorial, and lazy behavior – aren't just faulty for the reasons we've already discussed: they're also faulty because they reflect a distinct lack of perspective on the part of those critics. The numbers just aren't comparable.

Now, maybe this comparison of RIFs to individual terminations opens the door to a *different* criticism – namely, to the argument that tenure is what caused all those RIFs and those (again, uncounted) university closures. Instead of blaming tenure for its effects on individual behavior, this type of critique would blame tenure for its effects on university budgets. It would suggest that tenured professors and the tenure-track folks hoping to join their ranks are an expensive, unshakable budgetary line item, and that having them at all, regardless of their individual performance, is what causes RIFs. (Nevermind that, as Chapter 23 will explain, there are strong empirical reasons to doubt anyone who explains decreasing tenure density using budgetary rationales.[10]) In a twist that's ironic enough to be worthy of 1990s alternative rock music, the argument about expensive faculty ends up suggesting that *tenure* is what's responsible for most tenured-terminations.

This argument is popular with university administrators, which shouldn't be surprising under any circumstances but is even less so now that more administrators are coming to their university roles directly from the private sector or from management training programs.[11] Blaming tenure's financial implications instead of blaming its psychological and behavioral effects allows university administrators to speak in calm bureaucratic utterances instead of zany soapbox declarations; it sounds unanswerably adult and it often is factually unanswerable. How is a terminated professor supposed to prove to her own administration that the market *didn't* make them do it?

But beyond the conceptual and evidentiary tangle it creates, as well as the great personal trauma it ignores, the act of blaming RIFs on a combination of tenure and market rationality overlooks the fact that universities are heavily dependent on nonrational, nonmarket thinking being done *by someone else*: professors. I mean this in a few ways.

First, I mean it in the way that Marc Bousquet did nearly twenty years ago, which is to say that "the doctoral degree is the 'waste product of graduate education,'" and its true purpose is simply to produce cheap teaching labor.[12] Large research universities count on multiples more people wanting to become professors than can ever reasonably hope to become professors. While those aspiring academics are getting their degrees and completing their post-docs, they provide cheap teaching labor and cheap research assistance that keeps the university running. Fewer people entering the academic pipeline would mean less of the "waste product" Bousquet refers to, which would be good for those people but bad for the universities that can no longer benefit from the labor they provide while they're in the pipeline.

I also mean that universities count on nonmarket thinking producing too many aspiring academics in a way that's distinct from but related to Bousquet's point. As Chapter 8 suggests, to the extent that universities *are* true consumers of doctorates in the form of tenure-stream hires, they count on always having access to a steady supply of aspiring academics across disciplines and subject areas. This is what ensures that, in a year when they *do* want to hire a medieval historian or a molecular biologist, several such candidates are ready and waiting. The desperate scramble going on right now for professors with expertise in environmental law or in the legal implications of artificial intelligence is, for example, what happens when this need goes unmet, even if the shortfall amounts to just a handful of positions over a handful of years across the country.

Universities, in other words, do not deal well with scarcity – and part of the reason they don't is because students, parents, donors, and legislators don't deal well with it, either. Everyone wants cutting-edge expertise available yesterday. Everyone counts on enough people wanting to become professors in every discipline in every year so that any time a new need arises there are dozens of eager, able candidates waiting to be considered. But, as Chapter 8 notes, expertise takes time to develop. Whether you're an aspiring academic developing your first portfolio of research and teaching strengths or a tenure-stream professor moving on to your second set, you're essentially placing a bet as to what potential employers, society, and the universe (in that order) will want five to ten years in the future. But while you build that portfolio, the world changes and your bet may prove either prescient or very wrong.

Finally, I mean that universities count on nonmarket thinking because they require the people who teach their students, run their labs, and who publish articles and books under their institutional name to do work that makes those same people less marketable outside academia. Teaching five sections of First Year Composition may be necessary. Likewise, there may be a great deal of prestige (and even some legal impact) to be had from publishing a highly regarded historical analysis of the Second Amendment. But both types of work will, in the long run, and despite the sincerely held beliefs of my fellow professors, convey to nonacademic employers that you are not interested in or particularly capable of doing the kinds of work *they* want done.

Now, even if universities depend on a great deal of nonrational, nonmarket thinking being done by someone else, I'm not sure that this is entirely their fault. (It is definitely partly their fault.) Still, besides the *downward demand pressure* that they amplify but don't singlehandedly create, the *specialization of expertise* discussed throughout this book is also something that they amplify but don't singlehandedly create. With every advancement in knowledge and interpretation, it gets genuinely harder to make even the most incremental additional advancement. I think it would probably be tough to make a real contribution in most areas of learning today without having spent years immersed in that area to the exclusion of much else. This is just one more way in which even if there's no blame to be assigned here *whatsoever* – and, again, I'm not sure that's the case – it's nevertheless true that universities depend on individuals ignoring the very types of market rationality that those same universities point to when disposing of those individuals through RIFs.

The problem isn't only that this is unfair (although it is). The problem is that this is unlikely to keep working. *Do as I say* arguments are particularly unconvincing when they come with the rider *not as I do*, something that generations of parents can attest to but that university-employers seem not to realize or remember. Whether academics respond to this mixed messaging by shifting their behavior toward the same kind of market-driven rationality that universities espouse but don't want to see from their employees, or by shifting to a different type of irrationality that no longer benefits universities is almost irrelevant. Eventually, responses to RIFs and to the justifications for RIFs will be something other than what universities want.

A couple of years ago, I spoke with Matt Dickson (not his real name), who used to be a tenured professor of biology at one of the thirteen universities I included in my RIF calculations earlier in this chapter. Matt was not personally affected by the RIF, in the sense that his university did not terminate his employment. And Matt was personally affected by the RIF, in the sense that his university terminated the employment of around one quarter of his colleagues. He decided to walk away.

Matt and I differ along many obvious axes: he's a white guy in a STEM field, he doesn't come from a family of professors, most of his education was completed at public universities, and he spent his entire academic career, around fifteen years, at the same institution. Some of these differences mean that *I* am in the majority, at least among academics. More women earn master's degrees and doctorates today, and Millennials like me will soon become dominant within the professoriate. But one of the most important differences between me and Matt has to do with how and why each of us got into academia. And, in this respect, Matt is likely in the majority.

By his account, Matt stumbled into academia courtesy of an experimental science course he took as a college senior. The course was small, around six students altogether, and it required students to conduct a group experiment whose results they would write up for publication in an academic journal. The experience piqued his interest in both science and academia. After nearly four years spent drifting around college with a vague interest in the lab sciences, Matt finally felt something click. He followed a one-year post-graduation stint as a barista with a master's degree and a PhD. Then he spent a few more years floating around in various adjunct positions that, he was careful to note, paid far better than they would now. When he finally got a tenure-track offer at the university he eventually joined, Matt was happy to settle into academia even though his wife was unenthusiastic about living far away from the more desirable coastal region where her family was based.

Around fifteen years later – after earning tenure and promotion to full, after teaching hundreds of students and publishing over fifty articles, and after serving in a leadership capacity on his faculty senate and in his AAUP chapter – Matt quit. His university had survived the 2008 financial crisis and the first year of the pandemic, and he had survived the RIF. But he still quit. Even if Matt wasn't born into academia, as I was, and even if he didn't stay within academia during almost every conversation he had with his spouse or his parents, as I do, quitting still involved leaving a job that he loved and that he'd succeeded at, as well as an identity that had defined him for more than twenty-five years.

Maybe we should read Matt's decision to leave academia as irrational. His own job was safe, and in some ways it was the same job he'd always had. Seen in this light, quitting just because of disillusionment or hurt feelings might appear short-sighted. True, Matt had been forced to look behind the administrative curtain more than once, thanks to his involvement in faculty governance, and the view was apparently unpleasant. *I [saw] a board of trustees who [was] completely aligned against the university mission*, he recalled. *If they had their own way they would eliminate academics and just have athletics.* Dispiriting, for sure – but a reason to quit?

Maybe, on the other hand, we should read Matt's decision to leave as rationality exemplified. Having just survived a RIF that took many of his colleagues, including several who were tenured, Matt knew that tenure barely meant the one thing he'd most associated with it: job security. His wife was still not thrilled with the region where they lived – it was "a regular conversation and source of conflict in in the relationship" – and, more prosaically, she was stuck with a two-hour commute, thanks to his geographic limitations. Daily life at the university had become defined by what he called a "rachet effect." *We weren't replacing faculty positions, and then office staff [was] getting reduced… lab supplies for student labs [were] being sort of constrained.* The basic parameters of the bargain he had struck might have never been great, but now they weren't even being fulfilled.

Ultimately it doesn't matter which version of Matt we find more convincing, not least because both versions are at least somewhat true. What matters is that Matt's experience represents a path to academia and a set of reasons for inhabiting it that are far more common than my own. Most professors aren't third-generation academics. Most professors didn't spend their childhood sick days in faculty offices or transcribe interview responses to earn spending money in high school, and most professors don't work down the hallway from their spouses or write articles with their mothers. Most professors are probably more like Matt. They are brought to academia by an inspiring course or person, and they pursue academia because, like many other professional occupations, academia promises them stable, respected, and interesting employment at the end of the (perhaps unexpectedly winding) educational road. When academia ceases to be these things for these people – when it becomes unstable, unpleasant, and uninspiring – rational and irrational responses lead to the same outcome. They lead to Matt quitting.[13]

None of this is reflected in the *TTS* because RIFs are not reflected in the *TTS*. Neither are the ancillary effects – the voluntary separations like Matt's – that RIFs often produce. But RIFs account for far more job loss among tenured faculty than individual terminations for cause. They also, and I suspect totally unlike individual terminations, have a tendency to generate *additional* job loss beyond the people, like Matt's colleagues, whose employment is directly affected.[14] That's because RIFs demonstrate that a bargain that had been struck between employers and employees who must both work *and* evangelize – a bargain that is in large part made respectful and rational by tenure – well, that bargain no longer stands.

23

So What?

This question gets asked over and over again in Hyde Park, Illinois, where students and faculty at the University of Chicago – and their guests from elsewhere – are required to clearly articulate the importance of the research they share. My husband often speaks of an entry-level faculty candidate in the History Department whose research was on a European city-state during the Renaissance era. "This is all very fascinating," remarked one Chicago historian, after the candidate had given their interview lecture. "But cross a river or a mountain range and tell me why I care about what you've just said." The historian was inviting the candidate to synthesize their analysis so it could be made relevant to someone without precisely the same interests. The candidate couldn't do it – "But I study *this* city, during *this* period" – and, quite rightly, they didn't get the job.

Accordingly, this is where I tell you the *So What?* for this book. Specifically, it's where I explain what the information in it means for people who aren't current or aspiring tenure-stream professors. Why should people care about tenure if they aren't personally affected by its presence, absence, or dilution? Why should people care about it if neither their jobs (e.g., university administrators) nor their personal circumstances (e.g., students, parents, government officials, taxpayers) seem affected by tenure?

The short answer is that these questions themselves are deeply mistaken. *All* these people are affected by what happens to tenure, and – in varying ways, to varying degrees – *all* their interests would be better served if tenure were stronger and more widespread. Bad things happen when faculty are not employed according to the secure, long-term, autonomy-enhancing system we call tenure – and these bad things happen to students and to society at large. Moreover, each of these bad things is linked to one of the traditional job functions of the professor as a teacher-scholar.

I've saved the *So What?* for the very end because I believe in the power of inductive reasoning. It's hard to view an entire group of people differently just because one of them tells you to do so. It's a little bit easier to *feel* differently when you learn about their constraints and practices and values. But tucked into all the stories and statistics of my behind-the-scenes tour were various reasons why stakeholders *other* than aspiring or existing academics should care about faculty tenure. Let's revisit some of the earlier chapters to see what these are.

First, tenure-stream employment is positively correlated with better student outcomes in the classroom. Chapter 12 recounted my fears about a benign pedagogical experiment gone wrong. What it didn't dwell on were the many ways in which my ability to experiment *itself* reflected the privileges and protections of my tenure-track status. I could find inspiration for how to rearrange the course because I had free access to scholarly articles and multiple casebooks. I could easily revise my PowerPoint slides because I had a functioning laptop and a comfortable home office with the best possible internet connection. I only needed to avoid bad student reviews – not win ones that were gushingly positive – in order to feel confident about having employment the following semester. All of this means that even though my little pedagogical experiment *was* a risk (because I didn't yet have tenure), it wasn't *much* of a risk (because I was at least eligible to earn tenure and had the resources tied to that status). And, eventually, that experimentation led to me learning how to be a more effective instructor.

By contrast, there are many studies documenting the largely negative relationship between student outcomes and short-term nontenure-track contracts. "Contingent faculty tend to use less active learning, less service learning, fewer educational innovations, and fewer culturally sensitive teaching approaches."[1] Likewise, "[d]esign[ing], redesigning, or updating curricula requires time and participation that contingent faculty may not have."[2] NTT faculty employed on a per-course or per-term basis produce students who are less likely to attempt a second course in the same subject area – and, if they do attempt one, those students are less likely to do well.[3] More worryingly, "students who have more adjunct instructors during their first semester [of college] are less likely to persist into their second year."[4] Perhaps *most* worryingly of all for students, parents, and administrators, universities that heavily rely on NTT faculty have lower five- and six-year college graduation rates.[5]

None of this is news – we've known it for years. None of it should be surprising. Teaching responsibly and effectively has always been hard work, and it is becoming harder. Chapter 7 noted that greater student diversity means more labor for faculty (different learning styles, different foundational knowledge) and labor that is often more challenging (more assignments, more flexible deadlines, more feedback). Any institution that purports to care about teaching – or at least about graduation rates – should care about tenure and make more faculty eligible for it. Any student who wants teaching that is more flexible, more customized, more effective, and more innovative should not demand it from faculty who are laboring under precarious working conditions. A professor conducting office hours in a café, finding materials on Google Books, frantically applying for next semester's openings, and driving one hundred miles a day to teach four courses on three campuses – that professor is being set up to fail. That many of them *don't* fail you despite these circumstances reflects their excellence, not yours or your university's.

Second, tenure enables and acknowledges the multiple, draining forms of non-teaching, nonresearch *service* work that's wanted by students and needed by administrators. Professors are not trained to become therapists, counselors, leadership coaches, or ombudspersons – every one of which constitutes a full-fledged job in itself – but, as Chapter 7 noted, they are increasingly expected to serve willingly and effectively in these roles. Many of them *do* serve willingly because they find it fulfilling to mentor the young people in their orbit and they feel an obligation to do this. They know how much faculty–student interactions matter, particularly for "racially minoritized students, low-income students, and first-generation college students" – indeed "[n]o other factor plays as strong a role for racially minoritized students" as connections with faculty.[6]

But knowing all this doesn't make the work itself any less emotionally laborious, or the nonrecognition of this emotional labor by students, administrators, and the public any less insulting. It doesn't make service work any less time-consuming at a moment when expectations for innovative teaching and rapid-fire publications are escalating. Chapters 7, 11, and 14 considered the publication explosion from different angles, but what connected all those discussions is the fact that it takes more articles, more conferences, more peer reviews, and more committee meetings to become or stay employed as a professor today. Finally, the willing performance of invisible service work doesn't erase the fact that the faculty who are most often called on by students and administrators to perform this kind of labor are those who have the least social capital, the least privilege, and the most obstacles to overcome if they want to win either job security or their colleagues' respect.

In a way, academic life has probably always seemed deceptively easy because some of this invisible, taken-for-granted labor has been built into the system since its earliest days. Chapters 6 and 16 described the American university as "more deeply concerned with the forming of character" than either the English or German models it was patterned after. Even today, a significant minority (35%) of Americans believe that the main purpose of college is to "help [students] grow and develop personally and intellectually" while still others (13%) value personal growth and workforce readiness *equally*.[7] A lot of that personal growth is powered by professors sitting in endless office hours, writing "check-in" emails, guiding students through campus bureaucracies, and coaching university clubs and teams. Put simply, American professors have *always* been expected to do much more than be scholar-teachers – but the number, kind, and difficulty of the additional roles they are required to inhabit has increased exponentially.

Tenure won't reduce that work, but it will acknowledge and facilitate it. A tenured professor can, within reason, juggle her multiple responsibilities. She can try to fulfill all of them over a period of time even if she can't fulfill all of them at precisely the same time: she needn't worry, for instance – and provided that her university hasn't adopted a punitive post-tenure review policy – that a semester spent holding extra office hours and attending to student crises instead of writing articles will be her last semester on campus. Even a *tenure-track* professor has some latitude in this respect because, as Chapter 10 observed in connection with Sarah Emanuel's op-ed, that professor's department also stands to lose something if she fails to win tenure because she is trying to do all the things. She has no guarantee, of course, and "too much service" is one of the pitfalls junior faculty are regularly told to avoid. But being tenure-stream gives you some flexibility to inhabit all the roles assigned to you without risking your job in the process. It helps ameliorate the faculty Catch-22.

Third, tenure grants professors the freedom to be independent and to fail in their research endeavors. The first element – *being independent in research* – is the most commonly articulated view of what academic freedom entails (although, as Chapter 12 noted, it is far from being the only one). Parental, political, or even administrative interference in research means that a professor's job rests on the scholarly approval of nonscholars. This kind of interference transforms the dislike of expertise discussed in Chapter 15 into an embrace of the lowest common denominator because it means that students will only learn what nonexperts can understand and accept. Future scientists will only learn what the neighbor thinks is ok, future historians will only learn what their uncles find compelling. Admittedly, all indications are that many Americans would find this state of affairs acceptable. But it's not an outcome without negative consequences for our collective and future well-being.

Chapter 12 also explored the second element – *the freedom to fail* – while explaining how tenure mitigates the risk inherent in all research. In many disciplines, it takes years to conduct research and years more to discover whether your efforts have produced anything of interest. And while tenure won't eliminate that risk, it does mitigate the consequences of a disrupted field trip or a null finding. By contrast, when you're trying to keep your place in the post-doc queue discussed in Chapter 3, or otherwise stay fresh on the academic job market, you have every incentive to pursue low-hanging fruit that allows you to check all the boxes but contributes less to our collective well-being.

Now, I don't want to overstate those consequences. All research is not going to stop or be lost if university-affiliated academics cannot engage in it without outside interference and the freedom to fail. But much that is worthwhile *will* be lost. Academic research adds to our collective well-being in ways that are, regardless of whether you agree with them, highly influential and often underacknowledged. For instance:

Drew Weissman and Katalin Karikó (Penn) won the 2023 Nobel Prize in Physiology or Medicine for their groundbreaking work on mRNA technology, which contributed to the COVID-19 vaccine.[8]

Arun Ghosh (UIUC, then Purdue) developed darunavir, marked as Prezista, which was the first treatment for multidrug-resistant strains of HIV.[9]

Patricia Bath (UCLA) invented a laser probe that revolutionized cataract surgery by making it faster and less invasive; her invention made Bath the first African-American female physician to receive a patent for a medical invention.[10]

Raymond Damadian (SUNY Health Science Center) developed the technology and machine for non-invasive mapping of the human body that we now refer to as MRI (magnetic resonance imaging).[11]

...and in case this suggests that only STEM professors make influential contributions to society:

Cass Sunstein and Richard Thaler (Harvard, Chicago) developed the concept of the *nudge,* a cheap, small intervention that positively impacts behavior without significantly constraining choice; nudges have shaped – among other things – the federal retirement planning legislation known as *Secure 2.0.*[12]

Ibram X. Kendi (American, then BU) developed the concept of *antiracism* as a proactive rejection of unequal outcomes due to skin color and the true antonym of racism; antiracism has been widely incorporated into curricula and institutional practice.[13]

Robert Bork (Yale) developed the concept and Paul Brest (Stanford) coined the term *originalism* to mean an approach to constitutional interpretation that prioritizes past meanings and contexts; this approach now dominates the Supreme Court and is prominent in judicial and scholarly thinking.[14]

Kimberlé Crenshaw (UCLA and Columbia) developed the concept of *intersectionality* to capture how multiple marginalized identities can overlap to produce distinct experiences of discrimination; intersectional theory has been used to analyze everything from employment discrimination to police violence to forestry.[15]

Scholarship affects society. Scholarship benefits society. But scholars are best positioned to contribute to society – and in many cases, they may *only* be able to make major contributions – when they have the security and autonomy (as well as resources and respect) afforded by tenure.

Until now, I've been discussing costs to reduced or weakened tenure that are most directly felt by people other than professors. I led with these consequences because I think they matter most to people who are not academics. "In an institution like ours," observed a friend of mine, after reading a draft of this book, "we are clearly living under a 'tenure as liability' canopy and the institution is projected as primarily for the students and not for anyone else." My friend wanted to know if there was any way I could "address a problem that we have been facing, namely, [that] it has become abundantly clear to us that the university is definitely not interested in the following two components that should matter." And what were those two component factors that *didn't matter but should?* They were *retaining faculty* and *student success* – the latter of which, my friend clarified, "is important only insofar as it matters to the financial bottom-line of the university."

There is only so much you can say to someone who begins from fundamentally different first principles. I don't expect to convince the administrator who views students and professors alike as distractions from the "real work" of running a business known as the *University of* ___. I also don't expect to convince the politician or parent who views professors as human-shaped megaphones, tools that exist only to amplify their own words and ideas and are devoid of any motivations, aspirations, or constraints of their own. If I can persuade either of these individuals to momentarily consider how job security for professors translates into more effectively spent tuition dollars, more resilient and well-rounded graduates, and more widely beneficial ideas and discoveries, I will be grateful for their willingness to listen (and, let's be honest, I'll be pretty pleased with myself). That's why, in this penultimate chapter, I began with the kind of bottom-line costs to inadequate tenure that I think *these* individuals might find compelling.

But not all administrators, politicians, and parents start from such nakedly anti-academic first principles. Despite the dire circumstances currently obtaining in academia and likely awaiting us in the coming years, it's important to not lose sight of that fact. Human complexity is both our greatest charm and our saving grace. I suspect – no, I *know* (because my colleagues and I experience it regularly) – that many of our relatives, neighbors, friends, and casual acquaintances are benignly *and reasonably* unaware of what academia, even tenure-stream academia, is like. This means they are well-positioned targets for the ungenerous and plainly inaccurate characterizations that dominate public and policy conversations about academia. Whether those conversations contain broadsides alleging rampant laziness or iconoclasm, or blithe assumptions about free time and income levels, the lived reality of tenure-stream academia is not what it's made out to be.

So a major goal of this book has also been correcting the record regarding the costs to pursuing, winning, and keeping tenure-stream academic employment. It takes longer than is commonly believed to get the threshold credential needed for tenure-stream academia (Chapter 4) and the process is often very painful (Chapter 3). There are so few available jobs that aspiring professors must be open to moving anywhere in the country (Chapter 8) and they should anticipate serious trouble if, as is quite likely, their spouse is someone they met during their long years of training and apprenticeship and who is also interested pursuing tenure-stream employment (Chapter 9). If, against the odds, an aspiring academic actually wins a tenure-track job, she should expect more kinds of responsibilities demanded at greater levels of difficulty than either her mentors or her neighbors have ever suggested would be true (Chapter 7). She should also expect less money and more assumed free labor (Chapter 10).

As a tenure-stream professor, she will come to learn that her employers, her students, her friends and family, her preferred politicians and her favorite pundits – and even many of her colleagues, tenure-stream or otherwise – assume that she is professionally invincible (Chapters 5 and 18). They will assume that the source of her seeming invincibility, tenure, has always existed and was a gift that professors bestowed on themselves (Chapters 6 and 16). Because they view her as invincible, they will also explicitly accuse her of or implicitly attribute to her levels of laziness, predatorial behavior, or iconoclasm that are almost superhuman (Chapters 12–14). And they will assume that the principle of peer review that informs many aspects of her job is both singular and singularly advantageous (Chapter 15), possibly more so than the union activity that she doesn't engage in and, they assume, probably wouldn't be interested in engaging in even if she could (Chapter 17).

Should the job – or the industry – ever disappoint, this professor must undergo an exceedingly painful transition. The monopsonistic tendencies of the academic labor market make it nearly impossible to switch employers, while the twin demands of hyper-specialization and escalating productivity will have forced her to depreciate her own skill set (Chapter 11). But even if the professor has above-average exit options, she's likely to fight for her job (Chapter 21) – and yet, even if she has above-average legal protections, she's likely to *lose* that job (Chapter 20). We can be reasonably confident that if an individual faculty member like her is terminated from a tenured position, that's likely because they committed an act, like sexual misconduct, that provides just cause (Chapter 19). But it is far *more* likely that any given tenured professor will be terminated from a job that is supposedly "for life" on grounds that are unconnected to their behavior because their termination was part of a reduction-in-force (Chapter 22).

This book, as I began by saying, is not about the war on tenure: it's a response to the war on tenure. It is an effort to explain what tenure-stream academia entails because that information is too rarely shared by anyone with first-hand knowledge. Tenure matters as an employment protection, and it always has. But even though the benefits of tenure may most immediately and profoundly accrue to the individual who has it, there are important benefits to everyone else – students, parents, administrators, taxpayers – when professors work under the protective conditions of tenure-stream employment. The nonacademics who continue to ask more of their faculty should make more of those faculty eligible to earn the security that tenure provides. We are now at a ratio of roughly 1:3 in the division between tenure-stream and NTT faculty. In 1975, we were at almost 1:1. It's time to move the needle back.[16]

This is a big ask contained in a few words – or so we've been conditioned to think. For decades now, academics and nonacademics alike have heard that universities have shifted to NTT employment "to offset drops in instructional revenue, particularly at public institutions that have faced cuts in state support."[17] It's drummed into us that universities have been *forced* to shift from one type of contract to another. But much like the back-and-forth movement between indefinite contracts and fixed-term employment that occurred in the seventeenth, eighteenth, and nineteenth centuries, this most recent change in contractual form is also more complicated than the budgetary rationale allows.

"If the budgetary rationale for contingency is correct," argue Sue Doe and Steve Shulman, then "institutional types with higher contingency rates would show lower instructional spending per student."[18] In other words: you spend less on faculty (by hiring them on NTT contracts) because you can't afford to spend much on students. The problem, Doe and Shulman show, is that "this is generally not the case." Private institutions that spend more per student also tend to hire NTT faculty *more* often than the public institutions that regularly justify NTT hiring by pointing to deep cuts in state spending. In other words, universities that can afford to spend more actually skimp on labor costs even *more* than universities that can (or claim to) afford less.

So money does matter – but not because it's *missing*. "Budget considerations are relevant," argue Doe and Shulman, "because administrators choose to hire contingent instructors in order to maximize the surplus generated by instruction."[19] Generally speaking, instructional labor generates surplus revenue: it earns more than it costs. And, with a very few exceptions, private nonprofit universities generate greater surplus instructional revenues than public universities – a finding that should be unsurprising given that private university tuition levels are usually higher. But Doe and Shulman also point out that "instructional surplus is consistently positive *across higher education*" – meaning that public universities are *also* earning a profit off faculty labor, including off the faculty labor they purchase at a steep discount by contracting for it off the tenure-track.[20] "In 2019," they observe, "the total instructional surplus across all of higher education was more than \$67 billion." That's sixty-seven billion dollars' worth of instructional surplus from institutions protesting that they can't afford tenure-stream employees.

A 2017 pair of studies by the Delta Cost Project also undermine excuses of *The budget made me do it!* variety. These studies demonstrated that when public universities cut *instructional* expenses, they mostly shifted those savings around by spending more in *noninstructional* categories like administration, student services, and maintenance.[21] They also showed that even as universities sacrificed tenure-stream hiring at a higher rate (by switching to a greater percentage of NTT contracts) they didn't seem to be tightening their belts as much with respect to their *other* full-time employees. Essentially, the Delta Cost Project research revealed that universities are squeezing faculty *the most* – not treating them on par with other employees, much less prioritizing them as the core personnel of the institution.

Even if personnel costs – wages and benefits – are the largest category of university expenditures, full-time *faculty* wages and benefits aren't always the largest slice of the largest slice. The National Center for Education Statistics (the subsidiary of the Department of Education I mentioned in Chapter 22) breaks down university expenses by type.[22] During 2020–2021, private four-year nonprofit universities spent *more* on "academic support, student services, and institutional support" than they did on instruction (40% versus 39%). Public four-year universities did spend more on instruction than on these support services, but the gap wasn't nearly as large as you might expect: 34% versus 28%.

Still, *The budget made me do it!* has intuitive resonance for most of us. It's easy to believe that there just isn't enough to go around, and consequently that any movement away from tenure-stream hiring is a bitter pill reluctantly swallowed by cash-strapped university leaders. But, as we are now learning, this budgetary rationale is not the unassailable commonsense it's regularly presented as being. It's simply not self-evident that universities can't hire more of their faculty into tenure-stream positions. The only thing that is self-evident is that universities are *choosing* not to do this. They may have reasonable grounds for doing so. But if universities want to retain their exceptional status in American society – if they want legal, financial, and reputational leeway that's not equally available to profit-driven corporations – then they need to do a better job of demonstrating that they *are not*, in fact, simply profit-driven corporations. And the students, parents, politicians, and taxpayers who are demanding more from faculty need to demand more from universities, too.

I spent most of this book explaining why tenure matters as an employment protection to the workers who have it or are eligible to earn it – and, by implication, why its absence can be so detrimental to workers who are left outside its scope. In this chapter, though, I've focused on why tenure should matter to people whose jobs will never be directly affected by it. Simply put, the security and autonomy that tenure creates are essential to the performance of work that students, administrators, parents, politicians, and taxpayers want from professors.

Can that work get done by overworked, underpaid, insufficiently supported NTT faculty? More or less, depending on the stars and any individual's tolerance for pain. That's why tenure is better. Tenure is better for the same outcome-agnostic reasons that fair labor is always better regardless of the industry in question. And tenure is *also* better for the outcome-dependent reasons sounding in the core professorial responsibilities of teaching, research, and service that I've discussed in this chapter and throughout this book. Regardless of what motivates you – fairness or outcomes – tenure is better.

That doesn't mean tenure *itself* couldn't be better. There's always room for improvement. The next and final chapter offers a few ideas, none of which are being articulated for the first time here, about how to improve the recruitment, evaluation, tenuring, and career progression of tenure-stream faculty. But remember: you can only improve something that still exists.

24

Tenure 2.0

Around ten years ago, the *Chronicle of Higher Education* asked its contributors to peer into the proverbial 8-ball. *What's the future of tenure?*, asked the editors. *What discussions will we be having about tenure in ten years?*

Josh Boldt, who was then a nontenure-track professor at the University of Georgia, replied:

> Where will tenure be in 10 years? No adjunct professor should care...
>
> Sure, tenure's a good idea. I hope it endures. I mean, it seems nice.
>
> But I have a different question that I believe is even more important: not "Where will tenure be in 10 years?", but "Where will professors be in 10 years?" Because as of right now, things are not looking good. While we worry about the erosion of tenure (which affects a very small proportion of academic labor), the entire profession is crumbling. It's like painting your living room while the house burns down.[1]

A lot has happened in the ten years since Boldt published his op-ed. The United States has experienced massive protests over sexual violence, massive protests over racial violence, an attempted coup, a pandemic, a former (now current) president under criminal investigation(s), massive protests over Israel/Palestine... and that's a heavily truncated summary of events that have taken place within our geographic boundaries alone (although, obviously, not limited by them).

Despite all this, we're still talking about tenure. We're still talking about how not enough professors have tenure or are eligible to earn it, about the dangerous behaviors tenure supposedly encourages, and about tenure's connection to academic freedom and therefore to democracy itself. *Plus ça change...*

That we're still talking about tenure – which means we still feel tenure is worth talking about – should be a signal that there's something there. Tenure may be inadequately available and inadequately respected; in fact, it's undoubtedly both. Still, its continued existence and our continued interest in it suggests that observers are right to say that "tenure remains the worst form of university employment save all of the others."[2] Like many concepts or practices that remain "sticky" even when they've been accused, time and again, of being faulty, tenure has the virtue of responding adequately to some needs even though it doesn't respond adequately to them all.[3]

Most of this book has been devoted to explaining what some of those well-met (or well-*enough*-met) needs might be. I've argued that tenure acknowledges and partly compensates for the high barriers to entry, low financial rewards, challenging expectations, heavy personal sacrifices, and auto-depreciation associated with pursuing an academic career. I've also argued that tenure doesn't seem to create a lot of the problems associated with it, most of all iconoclastic, predatorial, and lazy behavior.

However, none of this means that tenure can't stand to be improved, and I'm hardly the only person to say so. For all the incendiary rhetoric floating around out there about tenure, there have been a lot of reasoned, good faith attempts to reform tenure so that it's more meaningful and accessible without becoming even more endangered. The suggestions I'm about to make here have all been made before – maybe not quite in this way or combination or order, but none of them is appearing for the very first time in these pages. I'm nevertheless including them here for two reasons.

First, I want to show, once again, that we *can* improve matters. This isn't me falling prey to the obsession with prescriptive fixes that legal scholars tend to suffer from: tweak this, add that, and everything will be ok. Everything won't be ok – everything is too complicated – but a lot of things can be better. This is me embracing the persistent optimism that lies, usually unrecognized, beneath the law professor's fix-it attitude. *Fatalism helps…* said no one, ever. Anger helps sometimes. A willingness to believe and to try helps always.

Second, I'm reassembling and re-presenting some familiar tenure reforms because I think you can never say too often that many of these reforms are small asks. In the world of higher education studies, and especially in the corner of that world dedicated to improving faculty conditions, university administrators often figure as intentional villains or unintentional opponents or, at best, as confused functionaries. They're believed to say *no* impulsively, compulsively, and to be motivated by money or fear or anything else except the well-being of students, of faculty, and of the scholarly enterprise. But this attitude forgets that when your day is spent far away from students and faculty, and when your interactions with them largely consist of fielding complaints or demands for resources, you get used to assuming that *no* is the most appropriate default answer. It's hard to remember that some smallish changes could have big(ish) effects. Consequently, it's worthwhile for those of us on the other side, whether we are faculty or students, to say that small changes do matter, and to say so regularly, clearly, and calmly.

What are these suggestions? How *do* we start fixing tenure? Below are four *dos* and one *don't*. I thought I had listed them from easiest to hardest, but it occurs to me now that number one could just as easily be number four. Still, seen from some angle, these suggestions exist in an order that reflects how challenging I think they'll be to implement.

24.1 *DO* REFRAME TENURE AS A LABOR PROTECTION

This suggestion is the vaguest, which is why it's both easy and hard. It's also a task for both administrators *and* professors. But, with due respect to many members of the AAUP (and a sincere hope that their collective indignation won't strike me down in my chair), I think it's high time that we reframe tenure as primarily a labor protection rather than as an expressive safeguard.

Once again: I think academic freedom is valuable and I also think it's under siege. I even think tenure may be necessary for its protection (although I certainly think tenure isn't sufficient for that task). But the dismantling of academic freedom is a *desired outcome* of the war on tenure, not a negative consequence to be avoided. If we're hoping to convince tenure's critics that they shouldn't do what they're doing *and* that they shouldn't want what they want – well, that's a principled stance, but it hasn't proven to be a very effective one. We, as professors, need to show some of the same conceptual flexibility we're constantly demanding from our students, our employers, and our society. We need to accept that what's most inspiring about tenure to us may not be what's most important to someone else.

We professors also need to show a little humility by understanding that, first, we *are* workers, and second, that we do not operate under the same conditions as *most* workers – not even the professional ones, like lawyers and doctors, with whom we'd probably like to be lumped. In one sense, this exceptionalism is positive: tenure-stream jobs *can* offer a lot of autonomy and flexibility even if they don't always do this. But in another sense, the kind of exceptionalism I'm referring to here isn't particularly appealing. Our skills aren't easily recognized or transferred, and while that doesn't make those skills less valuable to society it does make them less valuable to *us* because we can't easily take them to another employer when the current one misbehaves. We don't have a lot of options. We also don't have a lot of money – at least, not relative to our debt, or to what similar levels of educational debt can buy in peer professions. We are *not* above needing the labor protection that tenure provides.

We're unlikely to convince university administrators of all this until we accept it ourselves. And, as Chapters 6 and 16 pointed out, administrators *must* be convinced (along with the trustees, donors, and legislators to whom they're beholden). Tenure may have been articulated in its current, strongest form under the leadership of professors, but its ebbs and flows – and even its original articulation – have always been informed and have often been driven by administrative action. University administrators are human resources personnel with concerns centered on the recruitment, retention, and management of human resources. From the faculty perspective, this may not seem like a virtue, but it shouldn't be treated as a flaw, either. We shouldn't only be willing to meet *students* where they're at.

Finally, reframing tenure as a labor protection clarifies that tenure, although it's unusual, is hardly unique. Plenty of Americans, ranging from most federal employees to some fast-food workers, enjoy the benefits of just cause standards. There's no question that just cause standards range widely in terms of the protections they offer, and there's no question that tenure represents an unusually strong variant of just cause employment. But it seems equally clear that portraying tenure as a *sui generis* practice when it isn't one harms more than it helps anyone who would like to defend tenure.

All of this is to say – as Chapter 19 already pointed out – that framing *matters*. Law and society scholars have long known this, have pointed out that framing determines goals, authorizes appropriate speakers, and identifies appropriate audiences.[4] These tasks become especially important when there's no single legal demand to make but there *is* a profound need for long-term, diffuse, agenda-setting.

24.2 DO REVISE THE EVALUATION PROCESSES USED FOR HIRING, TENURING, AND PROMOTING FACULTY

Almost everyone who talks about reforming tenure is troubled by the inequities of prevailing evaluation processes. There's extremely good reason for this – several good reasons, in fact. Administrators, advised by faculty, can and should make some changes. None of these changes involve repudiating the ethos of peer evaluation that I believe is rightly one of academia's animating principles.

The most common criticism of existing evaluation processes is that they undervalue or actively *de*value the work that professors do beyond research and teaching. Some of this work is formally recognized as "service," but a lot of it doesn't even get labeled that way and consequently it goes completely unseen. Moreover, a disproportionate amount of this work is done by the very types of faculty who students are looking for because, on some level, these faculty are *like* those students: women, racial minorities, gender and sexual minorities, first-generation, lower-income, non-citizen, and disabled professors. Students wouldn't thrive and universities wouldn't run without the work these professors do – the meetings, pep talks, late-night emails and texts, advocacy, mediation, and resource-gathering – and, for that reason, this work should be acknowledged and rewarded.

But how?

Weight service more heavily is easy to say, but it's not really a strategy you can ask the beleaguered chair of your tenure and promotion committee to directly implement. Neither is *Favor holistic assessments over quantified assessments*. You need to explain how to weight service more heavily and how much more heavily to weight it. You need to explain how holistic assessments will be produced. And you need to explain how either of these strategies can be implemented in a way that will reliably recognize the labor of professors who are being inaccurately valued by current practices. In other words, to weight service more heavily you need to weigh it first. You need to assign a value to the mentoring, encouraging, and acculturating activities that professors undertake, and while this may seem both ridiculous and impossible, it's neither. If we can weigh *and* weight the production of knowledge – however approximately, however imperfectly – why can't we do the same for the performance of service?

My fellow professors will undoubtedly rail against any further quantification of their profession. As my own earlier grumblings suggest, I don't enjoy filling out twenty-eight-part surveys, either. But arguing against quantified assessments writ large is tilting at windmills: universities are not the intimate, collegial, thickly interwoven – or insular, homogenous, gossipy – communities they once were, and there is much to be grateful for in this fact. Still, if we want universities to include more people who don't share the same norms and priors, we must acknowledge that universities will then consist of more people who don't share the same norms and priors. We must find a different vernacular or value system so all these people can talk to one another to make the decisions they'd rather be able to continue making themselves instead of handing those decisions over to nonacademic administrators. While quantified assessments are hardly a perfect way to do this, perfection should not be our standard. Common languages in a multilingual community are always the lowest common denominators. (Even the metaphor is quantitative!)

So what about, say, creating a system that assigns point values for specific service activities, up to a maximum, subject to a minimum, and with the possibility of limited point transfer between categories? Many universities already have unspoken point systems for research. For instance, a single- or first-author, full-length, research article in a top-ranking peer-review journal will often count as "one unit." By contrast, a co-authored article or less prestigious journal or short essay or conference proceeding might equal a "half-unit." The specific valuations don't matter (and anyway, they will vary by discipline and institution). What matters is that such valuations often exist for research and they could exist for service as well.

For instance, overseeing a BA thesis or other capstone project could count as one unit, but so could advising *two* campus groups, or helping *four* students with their course or college planning. Maybe professors would list the names of the groups or students they advised, maybe they wouldn't. Maybe, if winning tenure required a certain number of points in each of the three categories (teaching, scholarship, and service), a professor could be allowed to rollover one or two points between categories to acknowledge how different people will pull their weight in different ways. Again, the specifics are not particularly important and could be tailored to suit disciplinary and institutional needs. My point is simply that if we want to weight service more heavily in order to accurately acknowledge and reward professorial labor, we need to first find a way to weigh service – *and* that doing this is entirely possible.

At Emory, for example, the law school faculty recently agreed that every full-time professor at the associate level or above will be expected to advise not less than three and not more than five of the independent writing projects that JD students must complete before graduation. If, in a particular year, fewer than three students ask you to advise their papers – and if, in the same year, no other students are lacking advisors – the expectation is that our dean needs to know, but also that our dean should be flexible. In the future (I hope!), we might institute partial point value for serving on the doctoral committees of SJD candidates, who often require less hand-holding than JD students but whose projects are much longer and more complex, and whose committees, right now, do not count toward the three-project minimum at all. It's a brand-new system so it's bound to have bugs. Affected faculty, including me, are bound to grumble. But it's also a good faith effort to weigh, and eventually weight, service activities.

Another common complaint about faculty evaluations concerns the evaluators themselves. Despite student interest and administrative rhetoric, professors are often at a disadvantage if their research focuses on marginalized populations or if it's truly interdisciplinary. That's because the most desirable reviewers – the professors who are the most senior and the most prolific, and who are employed at the most prestigious universities – are sometimes less equipped to evaluate scholarship that, by definition, breaks from their more established style. The mildest version of this problem unfolds when we ask senior scholars to fairly evaluate juniors whose methods or theories or topical interests are deeply unfamiliar. Under less benign circumstances tenure and promotion committees could be asking senior scholars to fairly evaluate juniors who are critical – sometimes deeply so – of how the seniors went about their work.

Now, to some degree, this problem affects all peer evaluation processes, whether they're focused on individual articles or applications for tenure. And, conversely, this problem doesn't affect all evaluators equally: some seniors develop reputations as particularly good (or bad) reviewers even when the work they're being asked to review is outside their expertise or comfort zone. Peer evaluation always demands self-control and critical reflection; not everyone is equally good at this, and not everyone who's good is good at it all the time. Unless we want new knowledge to undergo *no* vetting, or to be vetted in the court of public opinion (where, if it's lucky and particularly attention-grabbing, it will end up anyway), these slight imperfections are a price we should readily pay for peer evaluation.

But because the external reviews done for employment purposes *always* involve hierarchies of age and seniority – unlike scholarly publications, which might be evaluated by someone who's your peer or even your junior – and because, after all, they concern important professional landmarks that exceed any single publication or conference, they present a problem that demands response. Tenure-track faculty whose work is particularly interdisciplinary or nontraditional are often assessed more harshly, while the few senior faculty whose research portfolios and personalities make them desirable reviewers are overburdened by uncompensated labor.

Again, the question is *What do we do?* What do we tell our committee chairs, what do we ask for from our universities, what do we figure out with our professors? Well, for starters, we might consider adjusting the number, timing, selection, or weighting of tenure review letters.

Consider the timing factor: most review letters are solicited the summer before a professor formally applies for tenure. (That is, if I'm planning to submit my application for tenure in Fall 2025, I will probably need to notify the chair of my tenure and promotion committee in Spring 2025 so that the chair can collect letters over the summer break.) This in turn means that, effectively, tenure letters remain viable for six to nine months. That can easily become problematic if there are only one or two scholars nationwide who understand and can fairly evaluate your portfolio – a circumstance that's less rare than you might think. What if those one or two scholars go on sabbatical and become literally or functionally unavailable? What if they or someone in their household becomes critically ill? What if they retire, what if they find themselves in the middle of a divorce or a relocation, what if they're simply so overwhelmed by their existing work obligations (which, given that they're one of very few people in your field or studying your topic, is quite likely) that they cannot commit to reading the entirety of your scholarly oeuvre and writing a suitably thoughtful review in the allotted time frame?

We might mitigate this problem by allowing professors to source a percentage of their tenure letters themselves, and to do this slowly over the five or six years of their probationary period. Many universities already allow pre-tenure faculty to indirectly participate in selecting letter-writers. For instance, the law schools at both Alabama and Emory ask candidates for tenure to name a few potential tenure reviewers, while the tenure and promotion committee also identifies a few potential reviewers. Requests are ultimately made to scholars from both lists. The new system would simply make the candidate's participation in this process *direct* for a percentage of their letters without changing who literally solicits the letters (usually, the committee or department chair) or who has access to them (*not* the candidate). Letters would simply go into the candidate's file until they're ready to be used. By allowing those letters a longer shelf life, and by giving pre-tenure faculty a longer time span to collect letters, this system helps candidates mitigate the problem of bad timing.

It's not a perfect solution because nothing is. Pre-tenure faculty will obviously only refer their institutional committees to letter-writers who are going to write nice things. But this happens under the current system, too, and anyway we think that volunteered references can still provide worthwhile information across many industries and application contexts. You might also object that the first couple of years in a tenure-stream professor's career are likely to be useless as far as the accumulation of letters is concerned, because they haven't published enough, conferenced enough, or otherwise had the time to expand their networks and their portfolios much beyond where they were at the time of their initial hiring. They're not all that different from where they were at the end of graduate school or a post-doc. But an extra three or four years to collect letters is nothing to sneeze at because it would give professors working with interdisciplinary methods or nontraditional topics, theories, and communities, more time to build a portfolio that is fair to them. (It would also give overburdened letter-writers some time to breathe.)

This was just *one* suggestion regarding *one* aspect (timing) of *one* problem with evaluations (getting appropriate letter-writers)… from one person, no less. There are likely hundreds of other possibilities. Evaluations, like other troublesome aspects of tenure, are not resistant to reform.

A final word on evaluations: everything I've just said flies in the face of long-standing AAUP policy, which is that tenure isn't a reward for good performance so much as it is an acknowledgment of time served. (If we're talking in terms of "probationary periods" we might as well also talk in terms of "time served.") This is what's known as the *de facto* theory of tenure.[5] In the words of a former chair of the AAUP's Committee on Academic Freedom and Tenure, *anyone who works for the probationary period stays on with tenure… it's not a badge of honor.*[6]

Tenure isn't *just* a badge of honor, that much is true – it's *also*, to a certain degree, "a prediction about future performance."[7] The degree to which the tenure process is meant to fulfill either of these functions – reward versus forecast – as well as the degree to which tenure differs from similar evaluation processes, like promotion to law firm partnership, are both up for debate. Either way, though, and notwithstanding the dogged insistence of the AAUP, evaluations and the potential to fail them are a part of tenure. We need to focus on making those evaluations better.

24.3 *DO* INSTITUTE "TEACHING TENURE TRACKS"

I'm so far from being the first person to suggest this that I'll try not to spend too much space saying what others have said better. Some of the most well-known proposals have been made by Michael Bérubé and Jennifer Ruth, and by Marc Bousquet acting through the AAUP.[8] There have been criticisms of the idea, too. But since those criticisms often respond to a claim that's not being made – namely, that creating teaching tenure-track appointments could "simply make inequities and long-standing hierarchical structures within the institution magically disappear"[9] – I'll leave the *Why not* and *How not* aside for now.

Chapter 16 told a story that Chapter 23 reiterated: American universities are a *sui generis* blend of English colleges, German research institutions, and local demographic and political dynamics. Thanks to this legacy, American universities and the people they employ have assumed that tenure-worthy faculty are *both* engaged instructors and active researchers. But there's no reason why tenure should remain limited to the teacher-scholar.

In fact, there are plenty of reasons why the teacher and the scholar should each be deemed independently eligible for tenure. Chapter 7 discussed the many types of work that all professors – including tenure-stream professors – perform. It also argued that some of this work is necessitated by changes in the landscape of American higher education that are morally necessary and socially beneficial but that are also inhospitable to the teacher-scholar. Expectations of the student–teacher relationship have increased, in part because first-generation and low-income students may require additional support. (No doubt they have also partly increased because the soaring costs of post-secondary education have raised the stakes as well as the transactional feel of the college experience.) Fulfilling all these expectations requires extensive subject matter knowledge, extensive ongoing and professionally risky work, as well as specialized and minimally transferrable skills. Tenure practices need to reflect the reality that teaching and scholarship are now, *separately*, full-time jobs instead of being one-half (or one-third) of a hyphenated role.

Once again, what would this look like? How would universities evaluate faculty on a teaching tenure-track to determine if they had earned tenure?

It could look like counting syllabi that were developed for department-wide use. Or it could look like counting programs that were developed and executed for campus-wide benefit. And it could look like counting publications and conference presentations on innovative instructional methods. Yes, that's a lot of counting. But it's what we already do. And it *can* be done in a way that simultaneously respects the great work involved in responsibly and responsively teaching today's university students *and* the great security offered by tenure. Faculty who are tenured in teaching positions will have more to give students who need support and mentorship, and they will have more to gain by offering that support and mentorship. Faculty who are tenured in teaching positions can develop the kind of diverse teaching portfolio that makes it less necessary to hire professors on an as-needed, nontenure-track basis. Faculty who are tenured in teaching positions can help relieve the burden on their colleagues who are more skilled at research without shifting the burden to students who deserve better.

Teaching tenure: Professors should ask for it. Students should ask for it. Universities should implement it immediately.

24.4 DO HIRE MORE DIVERSE FACULTY, HOWEVER DEFINED, AND WORK HARDER TO TENURE THEM

This is a big ask because it's hard and it can cost – *and* because it is increasingly politically unpopular (if not impermissible). At the same time, it's also a small ask, because it's now a common one and it is morally easy to support.

I admit that I'm not the most effective advocate for diversity initiatives: I might be a petite, brown, foreign-born, non-Christian woman, but – as I confessed at the outset – my background gives me so much broad socio-economic privilege and specific industry privilege that I haven't really lived my demographic markers. Because of this, I'm going to speak briefly and move on in the hopes of saying something useful and nothing harmful.

If universities are remotely serious about putting students first, about wanting to meet students where they are, and about centering student perspectives, then they must also be serious about responding to students' overwhelming interest in learning from people they can identify with on a personal level. If universities are remotely serious about *not* being viewed as standard corporate actors – and their attachment to tax and antitrust exemptions suggest that they are – then they cannot behave like retail employers by overburdening and undervaluing the workers who are, effectively, their front line. (For that matter, *retail* employers shouldn't behave "like retail employers"… but I'll pick my battles.) Universities also need to treat existing underrepresented faculty better by equalizing (not "lightening"!) their loads. This isn't an argument about what certain kinds of workers deserve: it's an argument about what certain kinds of employers owe. If the professions *are* different from other industries, if universities *are* different from corporations – well, let's see it.

What would this look like in practice?

Most easily, it would involve efforts to reimagine the tenure process – things like changing the timeline and the sourcing of tenure letters – so that it's better at retaining and supporting diverse faculty once they're in the door. Less easily, it involves acknowledgment that *all* faculty need support and guidance even after they survive successive rounds of elimination to win tenure, but that diverse faculty reach that stage with less privilege and less social capital to cushion them against posttenure malaise. Least easily of all, it involves getting more people to the doorstep.

In the spirit of not shirking hard work, I'll focus on this last challenge.

Maybe getting more diverse candidates to the tenure-track doorstep involves targeted outreach to minority-serving institutions and national affinity organizations. In their book on surviving academia while Black, Kerry Ann Rockquemore and Tracey Laszloffy describe the experiences of "Michael," a Black pre-tenure professor who disagreed with a senior colleague on whether qualified diverse candidates would naturally emerge through the same processes that the department had always used to recruit new hires. Michael was right to be skeptical: the same old processes are bound to throw up the same old results.[10] And, in the larger scheme of things, it's hard to justify *not* spending some university dollars – on additional advertising, on get-to-know-you receptions at major conferences, on an active presence in national affinity organizations or disciplinary subcommunities – in order to recruit the faculty who can support your students and see them through to graduation. If universities want to be guided by market rationality, then they should know that it makes sense to attract faculty who can attract and retain and graduate diverse students. If, on the other hand, universities want to be guided by a commitment to noncommercial values – instead of or in addition to the fiscal bottom line – then they need to *live* those values. Both motivations point to the same change in behavior.

Maybe, in addition to the type of outreach described earlier, getting more diverse candidates into the academy involves creating and supporting more spousal hire (ideally *partner* hire[11]) programs. A report on academic coupling that I referenced in Chapter 9 observes that better dual-hiring policies may help improve faculty diversity for several interrelated reasons.[12] First, more women than men are married to academics (40% versus 34%). Second, women seem to value partner hiring more:

"the number-one reason women refused an outside offer was because their academic partners were not offered appropriate employment at the new location." (As Chapter 9 recounts, this factor was certainly important for me.) Because of this higher valuation of partner prospects, "women more often than men perceive a loss in professional mobility as a result of their academic partnerships (54% for women versus 41% for men)." Academic endogamy is especially high for women in the natural sciences (a whopping 83% versus 54% for men) so, to the extent that we really want more women in science, we need to increase partner hiring in those fields. Beyond these contributions to gender diversity, dual-hiring may also help expand racial diversity, because male and female underrepresented minorities are *equally* likely to have academic partners.

I'll close this fourth suggestion out with a *Yes, but…*

The problem is not that the average university currently follows recruitment or retention practices that explicitly discourage diverse candidates. It's that the average university has recruitment or retention practices that are fundamentally the same as what they were forty years ago. Doing the same thing while expecting different results makes no sense. Conversely – as I've been saying throughout this chapter – doing things differently doesn't require the kind of sea-change that's likely to raise academic and administrative hackles in almost equal measure.

24.5 DON'T IMPLEMENT FORMALIZED POST-TENURE REVIEW

…it vitiates tenure.

I was sorely tempted to make those three words the sum total of my comments on this point, if for no other reason than that it's nice to occasionally find myself in total agreement with an organization I admire as much as the AAUP. But I suspect that a little elaboration is called for.

Post-tenure review that carries the possibility of real negative consequences – punishment, whether monetary or otherwise, and termination – means that tenure no longer exists. We can call what remains something else and that something else will still be better than what most employees in the United States enjoy. But it won't be tenure.

Why? Because, to return to our conceptual beginnings, tenure is a variety of just cause employment. The idea behind just cause and the way it works in most industries is that once you've passed your probationary review, you can only be disciplined or terminated for cause. What often goes unarticulated but is nonetheless essential to the system of just cause employment is that these relationships do not come with the rider *And every year your employer shall try to find cause for termination*. But that's what post-tenure review entails.

Now, as even the AAUP has acknowledged, there are ways to review professorial behavior after tenure without vitiating tenure itself. It seems entirely reasonable to me that a tenured professor should be asked to meet with their chair or dean on an annual basis to discuss the year. The faculty at Alabama Law were invited to do so. Tenured professors may even be asked to have these meetings more frequently, if there are persistent concerns about their interactions with students, colleagues, or other members of the university community. It also seems reasonable to me that a tenured professor may be informed of any consistent patterns in the feedback received about them through formal and informal mechanisms (student evaluations, hallway chatter). And I think a tenured professor should participate in reasonable dialogue regarding the substance of that feedback so that they might find ways to improve.

None of this comes with an "or else." None of this is *summative*, to use the AAUP's language, rather than *developmental*. And none of this "place the burden of proof on faculty members to demonstrate that they should be retained."[13] As soon as an institution crosses any of these lines, it no longer practices tenure – it no longer even practices just cause. What it practices is something that's most appropriately called *If I can't find just cause* employment.

Post-tenure reviews are increasingly common, so to some degree any argument against them is also an exercise involving windmills. As of 2022, the AAUP determined that around 58% of institutions had some sort of post-tenure review.[14] But that means that around half of the institutions surveyed by the AAUP had *no* such policy, however benign, and that half is ground well worth protecting.

Post-tenure review is also, in all likelihood, ineffective. A 2003 study found that "90 percent of institutions were not doing cost-benefit analyses of post-tenure review, and that only 14 percent had set up any procedure for periodically evaluating it 'with respect to its effectiveness.'"[15] What this means is that universities using post-tenure review are very likely destroying tenure for no gains at all. If the point of a post-tenure review system is to find fault where fault exists, either there's very little fault to be found or the review systems being adopted are no good at finding it, because post-tenure review "rarely results in negative evaluations and almost never leads to dismissal for cause."[16]

What post-tenure review *unarguably* produces is a lot of paperwork. Even if these reviews aren't as exhaustive as tenure and promotion evaluations, the small forest that dies (or, perhaps, the half-dozen computers that crash) due to the volume of material produced at these similarly career-defining moments should tell us that reviews that achieve nothing still don't *cost* nothing. On the contrary, they cost a whole lot of time for the reviewer and the reviewed party alike. One description of materials often provided as part of a tenure file included:

> a detailed table of contents; a condensed one-page CV; a full CV; a personal statement; statements of teaching, research and service; future goals and plans in those areas; student course evaluations; peer observations and evaluations of teaching; letters from former students; syllabi; assignments; exams; photographs of successful student projects; evidence of collaborative scholarship with students to showcase mentoring; copies of all books, peer-reviewed articles and book chapters; nonreferreed publications; conference presentations; essays; exhibits; works in progress;

consulting work; invited talks; evidence of service on multiple levels including the program, department, university, community, region, discipline and the greater public; annual reviews; internal review letters; external review letters from colleagues previously unknown to the candidate; the department chair's letter; material that is generated and duplicative of what the university has on file, like the person's offer letter, departmental and university criteria for tenure and promotion; and more.[17]

…and the person who put this list together confessed that their application for promotion to full professor "totaled 3,837 pages." But this is what we should expect when we put job security on the line for workers who've invested so much in skills that they can't easily take elsewhere, either to another employer in the same industry or to a different industry altogether.

The truth, as Chapters 19–22 suggest, is that individual tenured professors probably provide cause for termination far less than groups of tenured professors get riffed through no fault of their own. Most professors who *do* provide sufficient cause for termination do so for reasons that wouldn't be better captured through post-tenure review than through the ample institutional policies and state and federal laws that already exist. For most professors, given the value we tend to place on autonomy, the sheer annoyance of periodic meetings may well be a remarkably effective and far less expensive method of deterring or incentivizing specific behaviors. But for those meetings to have any impact – to inspire the sense of security that's needed to justify meaningful change – they need to be suggestions without swords. Otherwise, once again, we have left tenure (and even just cause employment) far behind.

There are plenty of other possible changes we might make to improve tenure-stream academia. But we can't pursue any of those improvements if we stick to unwarranted assumptions about what problems tenure creates – and, equally, we can't pursue any improvements if we insist on static conceptions of why tenure matters and how it should work. There is room for both continuity and change, but it begins with acknowledging that tenure matters as an employment protection.

Conclusion

I've spent twenty-four chapters' worth of words talking about what it takes to get tenure, what it means to have it, and what it's like to lose it. But all of this could probably be summed up using eight words – from a *non*tenure-track professor – that I quoted not too long ago:

[T]enure's a good idea. I hope it endures.[1]

Tenure *is* a good idea. It provides material and psychological security to people whose work is needed, whose credentials are expensive and difficult to earn, whose jobs are both harder and less remunerative than assumed, and whose options for leaving those jobs are low and constantly decreasing through no particular fault of their own.

Tenure *isn't* an unusual idea. It's on a spectrum of employment contracts and industry practices, and while it's absolutely toward the more-protective end of that spectrum, we're talking about differences of degree, not of kind.

Tenure also isn't a perfect idea. Like any employment practice or contractual element – including the At-Will Rule that makes tenure so valuable – tenure is vulnerable to abuse. But that abuse is probably far less severe and widespread than critics, even internal ones, blithely assume, and it's not at all clear that tenured employees behave worse than ones who are employed at-will (or even those who are pursuant to other forms of just cause). And, as also with most human inventions, there's room for improving tenure without destroying it.

Tenure's a good idea. I hope it endures.

Acknowledgments

There is no such thing as a solo-authored monograph, but this book is an extreme case.

Although it's dedicated to my father, whose conviction that pushing something often enough can make it appealing has been somewhat vindicated by my choice of career and love of spinach, this book exists because of my mother, Mallika. Without her, I would have never had the gumption to attempt the quantitative data collection that kick-started my research on tenure. Without her, I would have given up a hundred times over when faced with data troubles, unpleasant discoveries, and analytical tangles. Without her, I would not have a disciplinary catholicism that survived graduate training in anthropology or a disciplinary humility that survived graduate training in law. Thanks, *amma*.

Everything I've done on my way to tenure has been defined by the experience of doing it alongside, in collaboration with, and with the help of my husband, John. He gives my thinking breadth and humor, as well as a combination of idealism and cynicism that I continue to find perplexing. Hiring committees notwithstanding he will always, henceforth, be in my star footnote.

Matt Gallaway, my editor at Cambridge, makes me want to write books. He initially took me on as a first-year professor, which is a decision I've always wondered about but never wondered about too closely. When I later went to him with this project, he trusted my decision to do things differently. I've learned the hard way to not assume that Matt's competence and professionalism are universal.

An army of research assistants helped with the research for this book as well as for the articles that inform it. They spent hours doing literature searches, scraping websites and databases, coding and recoding incidents, writing memos, and indulging my odd requests for anecdotal flavor. In alphabetical order, they are: Paul B. Barringer III (Alabama Law '23), Alana C. Cammack (Alabama Law '21), Jahnavi Chamarthi (Emory University '25), Nicholas Hebebrand (Alabama Law '22), Andrew Hull (Emory Law '25), Emily Latham (Emory Law '27), Allison Powers (Emory Law '25), Courtney Kirbis (Alabama Law '24), Arthur B. Laffer III (University of Alabama '22), Jurong Liu (Emory Law '25), Constanza Mayz (Alabama Law '23), Chloé Saad (Emory Law '27), Diana Snellgrove (Alabama Law '23), Ann Yoon (Emory Law '26).

Thank you, folks: I'm grateful for your help and for the chance to have worked with each one of you.

I'm also grateful to the handful of researchers who helped me despite the strangeness of my questions and the utter lack of obligation to help me answer them: Glenn Colby (American Association of University Professors), Komi Frey (Foundation for Individual Rights and Expression), Lindsey Ice (Bureau of Labor Statistics), Maya Pinto (National Employment Law Project), Leigh Anne Schriever (Occupational and Safety Health Administration), Sean Stevens (Foundation for Individual Rights and Expression). Your willingness to take time from your own busy lives and important work is inspiring. To Karen Kelsky, an academic coach and industry expert whom I've never hired but from whom I have nonetheless learned much, I want to express appreciation for many things including, most relevantly, teaching me that one can view academia as an industry with determination rather than bitterness. Additionally, my mother-in-law, Rosa Lee Acevedo, provided much-needed childcare as I wrote the bulk of this manuscript and thereby made it possible for me to feel good both as a parent and as a scholar.

Finally, friends who have also been colleagues, mentors, and fellow travelers have read drafts, debated concepts, and made introductions. For reading portions of this book or the articles that led to it, or for discussions that have been illuminating, I'm grateful to Siddesh Bale, Leo Coleman, Shahar Dillbary, Sarah Emanuel, Mirit Eyal-Cohen, Matthew W. Finkin, Catherine Fisk, Ilana Gershon, Tom Ginsburg, William Herbert, Neal Hutchens, Anil Kalhan, Adrianna Kezar, Amy Kimpel, Sarah Lawsky, César Rosado Marzán, Noeleen McIlvenna, Benjamin McMichael, Russell Miller, Daiquiri Steele, Charles Sullivan, Adnan Zulfiqar, and participants of the 2021, 2022, and 2024 iterations of the Colloquium on Scholarship in Labor & Employment Law (COSELL). None of them should be blamed for either the style or the content of this book, especially since many of them offered wise counsel that I did not heed. To Arvind Elangovan, a longtime friend and frequent conversational sparring partner, I owe a particular thanks. And to the many professors who spoke with me, most of whom preferred to remain anonymous: this book is yours as well as mine. Thank you for making it possible.

Appendix A

This Appendix explains the methodology behind the *Tenured-Terminations Study*
data presented in Chapters 18–21, as well as in Appendix B. Much of this explanation
appears verbatim in an article, also titled *"The War on Tenure,"* that was published
by the *Tennessee Law Review* in 2023.[1]

The *TTS* dataset was constructed using information located in the public domain.
Between June and November 2021, I created an Original Data Population (ODP)
using key word searches on two legal databases, WestLaw and Lexis Advance, on
Google, as well as through manual searches of campus newspapers and industry
publications including *The Chronicle of Higher Education*, and *InsideHigherEd*.[2]
The latter two were used both to identify relevant incidents and to provide detail and
verification. I also examined scholarly works that might have contained relevant incidents, including a law review article by Nancy C. Cantalupo and William C. Kidder
and a doctoral dissertation by Julee Tate Flood.[3] The ODP also reflected searches
of reports issued by the University of North Carolina Faculty Hearing Committee,
but no entries from those reports were ultimately included in the dataset because
the reports were so heavily redacted as to preclude necessary information gathering
about the individuals involved.[4]

From December 2021 to January 2022, I conducted a second round of data collection by culling incidents from the Academic Sexual Misconduct Database (ASMD)
maintained by Julie Libarkin and from the Foundation for Individual Rights and
Expression (FIRE) database.[5] Both the ASMD and FIRE populations required
further editing and scrubbing, described below, before their information could be
incorporated into the ODP.

When I accessed their database, FIRE allowed users to set initial filtering parameters before downloading the raw dataset, but it did not distinguish between professors, administrators, students, and non-academic faculty. I first excluded incidents
where the institution refused to sanction the faculty in question as well as incidents where the institution actively supported the faculty. I collected information
on how the professor's employment ended (termination, resignation, or retirement)
and whether the professor was still employed at the university at the time of data

collection. Although imperfect, this approach allows me to roughly account for motivated resignations and retirements, including those that occurred well after the underlying incidents.

Next, I filtered out incidents involving non-professors and deans. (Department chairs, who more reliably rotate back into faculty positions after a period of service, were left in.) Although deans and even presidents are often also tenured faculty, they were excluded because terminations involving them commonly result in their removal from their administrative post but not their tenured faculty position. However, whenever I was able to confirm that the administrator was also terminated from their tenured faculty position, they were retained in the dataset. I also filtered out incidents where the faculty member was not ultimately subjected to employment consequences and incidents where students (not university personnel) were responding to faculty behavior. I checked remaining entries for relevancy using Google searches and filtered for redundancy against the ODP.

Unlike the FIRE database, the ASMD database had no pre-download filtering mechanism. I removed non-professors, deans, and nontenured faculty, then checked remaining entries for relevancy using Google and filtered for redundancy against the ODP.

Finally, a third round of Google searches, industry publication searches, and ASMD searches was conducted between March and May 2022 ("Phase 3"). Incidents gathered during Phase 3 were scrubbed, filtered, and checked for relevancy using the same processes as before. Altogether, this left a population of 293 tenured-terminations at four-year institutions between 2000 and 2021.

To check the robustness of coding, I verified a 10% random sample of entries (n = 29) across all nineteen study variables. The reliability percent agreement (PA) scores for all but one variable ("Event Year"[6]) exceeded 80%, which is widely considered to be an acceptable level of congruence.[7] On eight variables the agreement was 100%, on seven variables agreement was over 90%, and on one variable ("Faculty Age"), agreement was over 80%.[8] Overall – that is, for all nineteen variables combined – the PA was a robust 92.63%.

After the data were finalized, I conducted two targeted verifications of thirty-eight entries (=13.7%) that were affected by an alteration in the coding for "Resolution" (that is, how the employment relationship ended). This time, entries were verified across the fourteen variables that had *not* been impacted by the coding change. Overall, PA scores for the two targeted verifications were even higher than the scores obtained earlier: 97.87% and 99.81%.

The dataset collects information regarding, among other things: institution type (public/private and Carnegie classification[9]); date (of the underlying event or, where that is unavailable, of the employment action); faculty disciplinary affiliation; faculty demographics; related litigation and litigation outcomes; and how the employment dispute was ultimately terminated (resignation, retirement, or dismissal). Some of this information was coded at both "mid" and "high" levels of abstraction.

TABLE A.1 *TTS Codes for Sexual Misconduct and Protected Category Discrimination Relative to Title VII*

Sexual Misconduct: Sexual Harassment	roughly analogous to disparate treatment *and* hostile work environment
Protected Category Discrimination: Towards Women Protected Category Discrimination: Towards Transgender Individuals	roughly analogous to disparate treatment, pay inequity, disparate impact

For example, "Faculty Affiliation–High Level" categorized individuals as belonging to Arts, Humanities, Social Sciences, STEM, and Professional Disciplines. "Faculty Affiliation – Mid Level" subdivided STEM into Applied Sciences, Formal Sciences, Life Sciences, and Natural Sciences.

Most significantly, the dataset includes the university's narrative regarding any actions that were taken against the faculty member as well as the faculty member's counternarrative. Because Chapters 19 and 20 pay special attention to sexual misconduct, I want to note that the *TTS'* categorization of sex-related workplace harms differs from federal anti-discrimination legislation. The relevant federal legislation here is Title VII of the Civil Rights Act of 1964. Title VII recognizes three broad types of sex-related harm: *disparate treatment* (roughly, treating someone worse because of their identity), *disparate impact* (harm resulting from an employment practice that is facially neutral but that affects people differently depending on their identities), and *hostile work environment* (creating or tolerating workplace conditions that cause harm based on someone's identity). Subsequent judicial interpretation has held that Title VII prohibits these three types of harm both with respect to gender identity and sexual orientation.[10]

Title VII's categories of sex-related harm are largely coterminous with the *TTS* codes for university narratives listed in Table A.1.

Additionally, the *TTS* coding for *Sexual Misconduct: Sexual Assault* and *Sexual Misconduct: Inappropriate Relationships* captures behavior that is criminal (and therefore beyond the purview of Title VII) or that is not necessarily an offense under either civil or criminal law.

Both university narratives and faculty counternarratives were coded at mid- and high levels and, as with other variables, they were developed using searches on WestLaw, Lexis Advance, Google, and other publicly available sources. The narratives and counternarratives discussed here provide an unprecedented glimpse into why tenured-terminations occur, in addition to the (also unprecedented) insights regarding where terminations happen and who they affect. While it is true that these narratives and counternarratives mostly reflect statements that were made for public consumption or legal action, they still possess explanatory value for two reasons.

First, employers regularly fail to offer legally or culturally benign explanations for their actions. Examples range from the insidious and highly influential to the absurd and non-precedential. In the landmark sex discrimination case *Price Waterhouse v. Hopkins*,[11] mentioned in Chapter 5, a star female employee was denied a promotion and told, among other things, to "take 'a course at a charm school.'" Similarly, in *Kunkle v. Q-Mark, Inc.*,[12] a supervisor informed their subordinates that anyone who voted to re-elect President Obama would be the first to be terminated if Obama was, in fact, re-elected. Put simply, even publicly available information – like the kind that appears in litigation records, judicial opinions, and news articles – can be revealing rather than pretextual because employers often fail to act rationally by saying something other than what they really mean.

Second, even where parties to litigation *do* articulate pretextual positions, their choice of rhetorical or legal frame is itself illuminating. How often do university narratives rest on professional versus personal misconduct? How often do faculty counternarratives appeal to a powerful norm like academic freedom? These kinds of insights can tell us what parties believe will be publicly and/or legally persuasive when tenured employment is at stake.

I want to underscore, once again, that *TTS* data is bound to be underinclusive because of the design choices mentioned in Chapter 18, and also because not all terminations – even in the narrow usage I'm employing here – will leave an internet footprint. Furthermore, *TTS* data does not capture a wide range of incidents that are worthwhile topics of investigation, including the number of tenured professors who voluntarily resign (either as job exits or industry exits) because of inhospitable working conditions, as well as the number of tenure-track professors who resign before winning tenure or are non-renewed (or terminated) before winning tenure. It's both an imperfect picture and a partial picture – but, to my knowledge, it's the best picture we have across discipline, region, and institutional type regarding what tenured-terminations look like. Understanding what happens in cases where tenure is overcome is an important step toward understanding tenure itself.

Appendix B

This Appendix shares descriptive statistics from the *Tenured-Terminations Study* data. B.1–B.6 depict institutional and individual characteristics. All incidents occurred between 2000 and 2021. Total cases numbered 293.

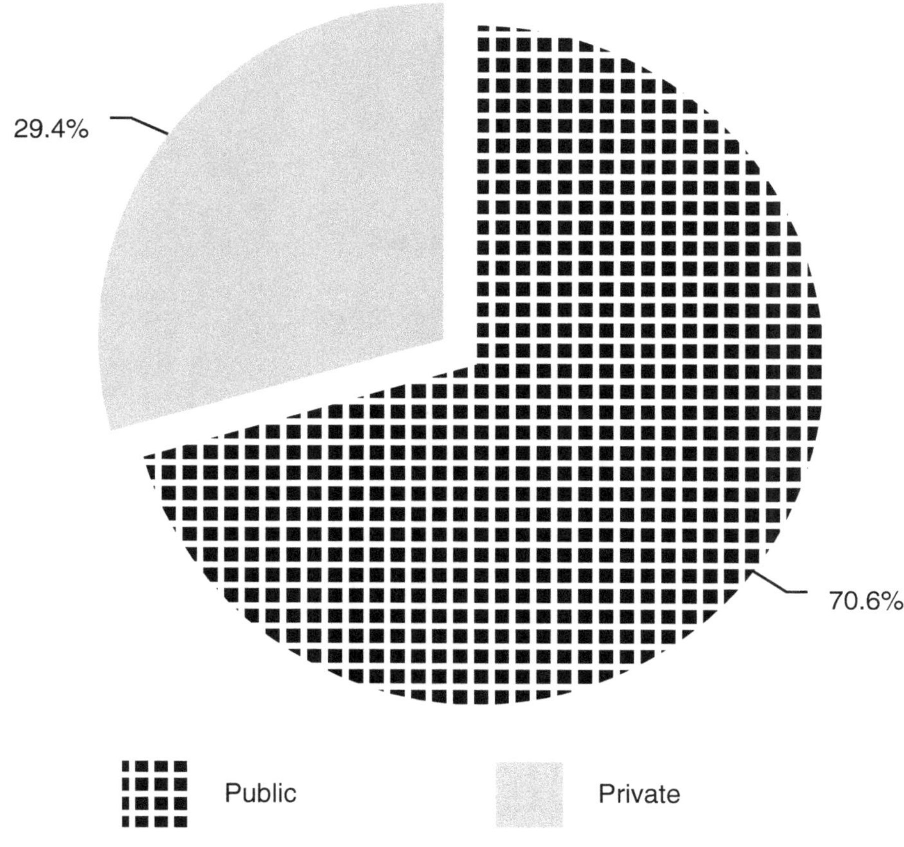

FIGURE B.1 Funding status ($n = 293$)

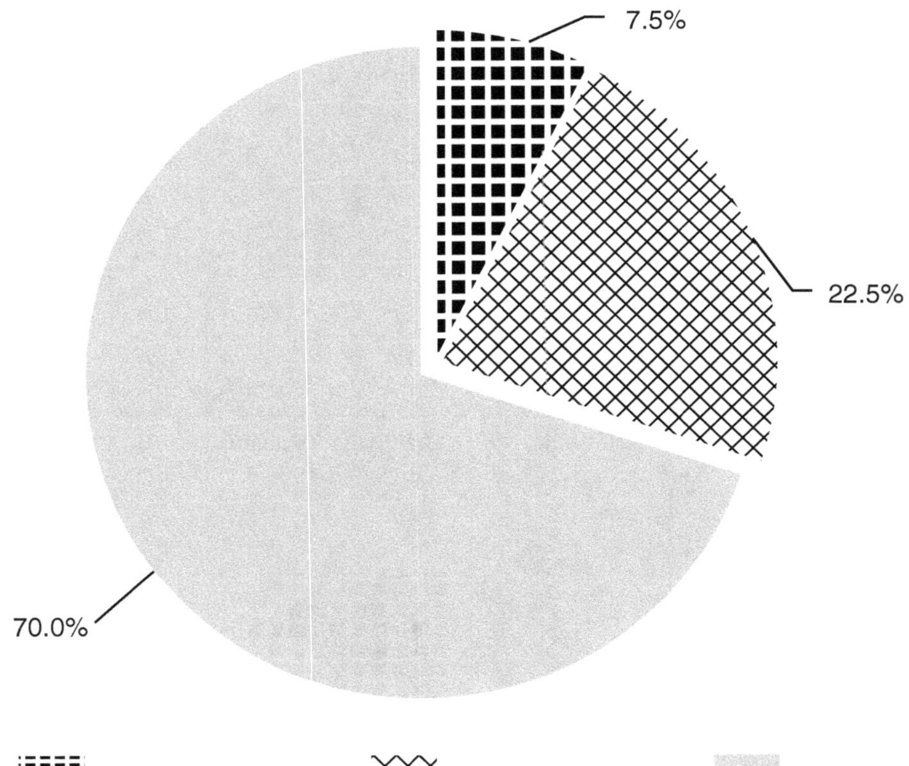

FIGURE B.2 Carnegie ($n = 293$)

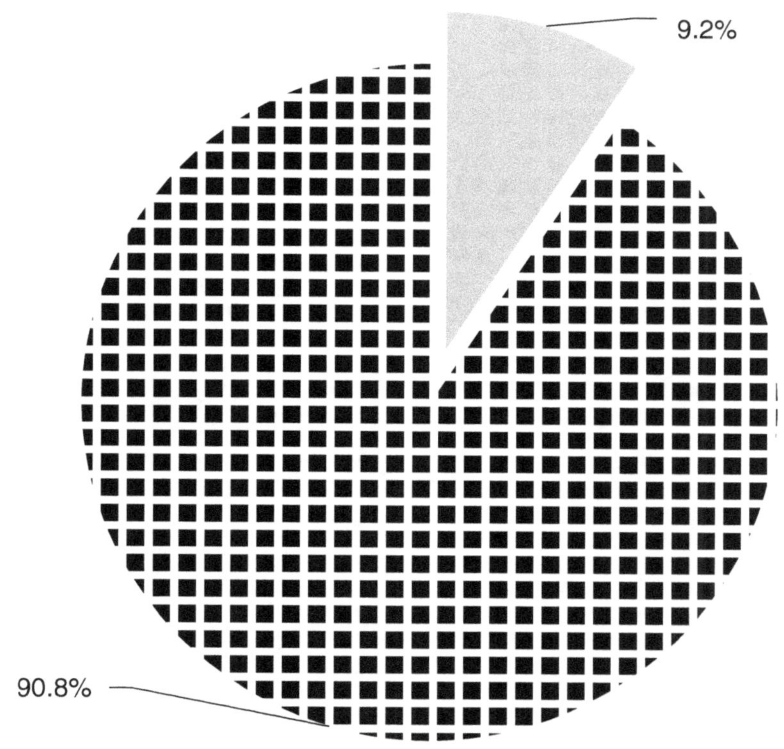

FIGURE B.3 Faculty gender ($n = 293$)

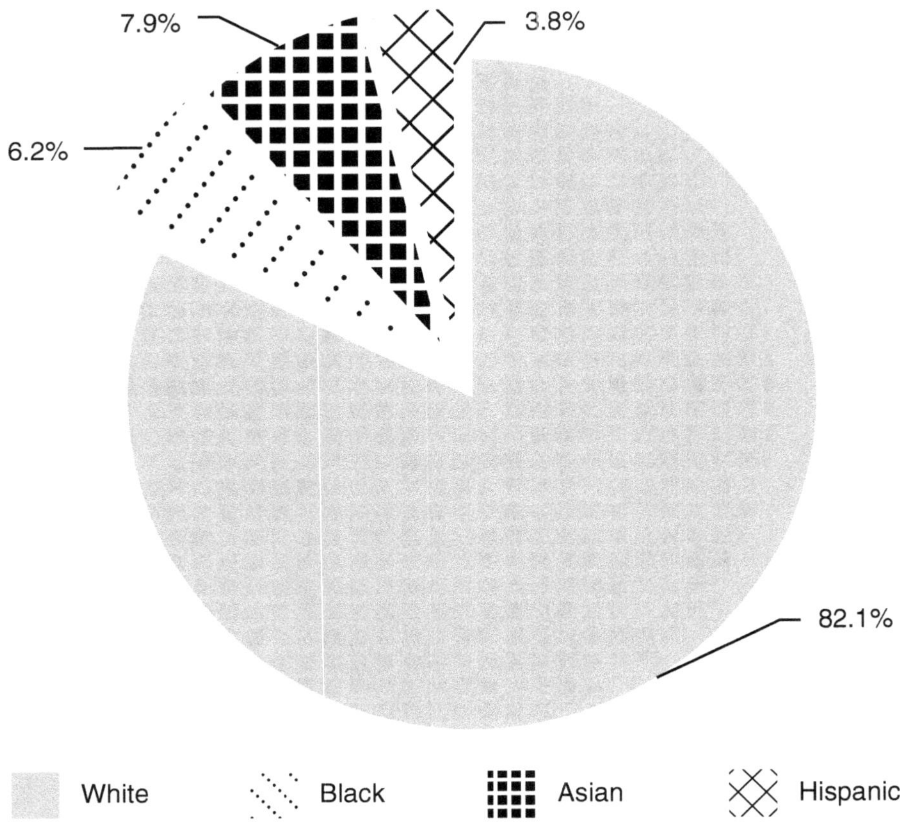

FIGURE B.4 Faculty race ($n = 291$)

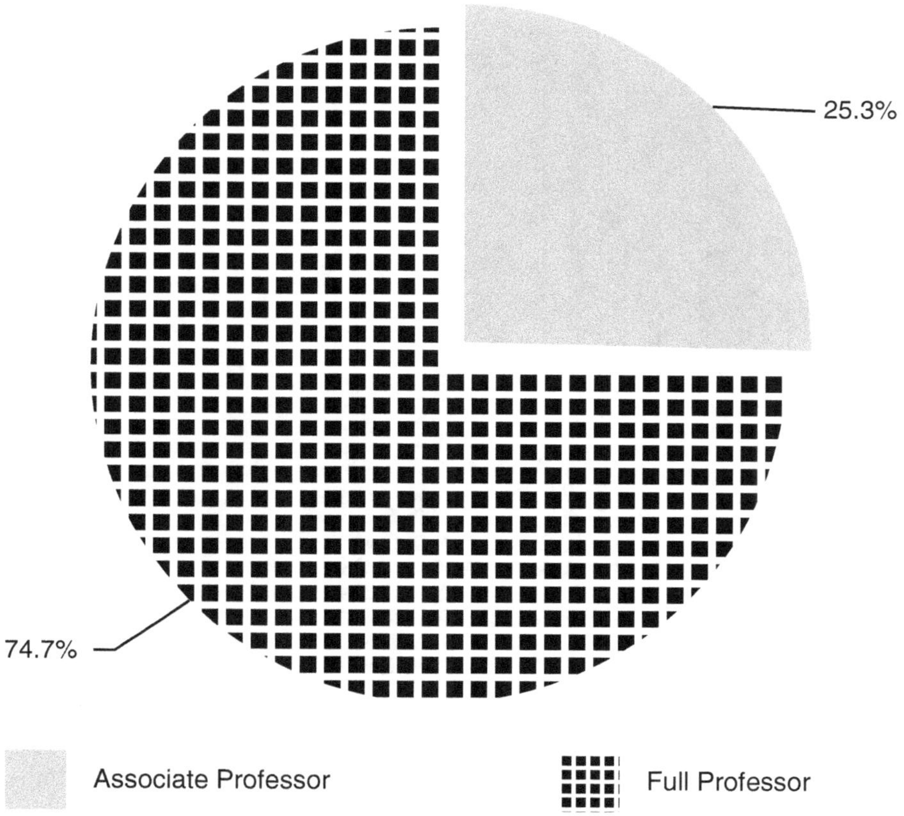

FIGURE B.5 Faculty rank ($n = 293$)

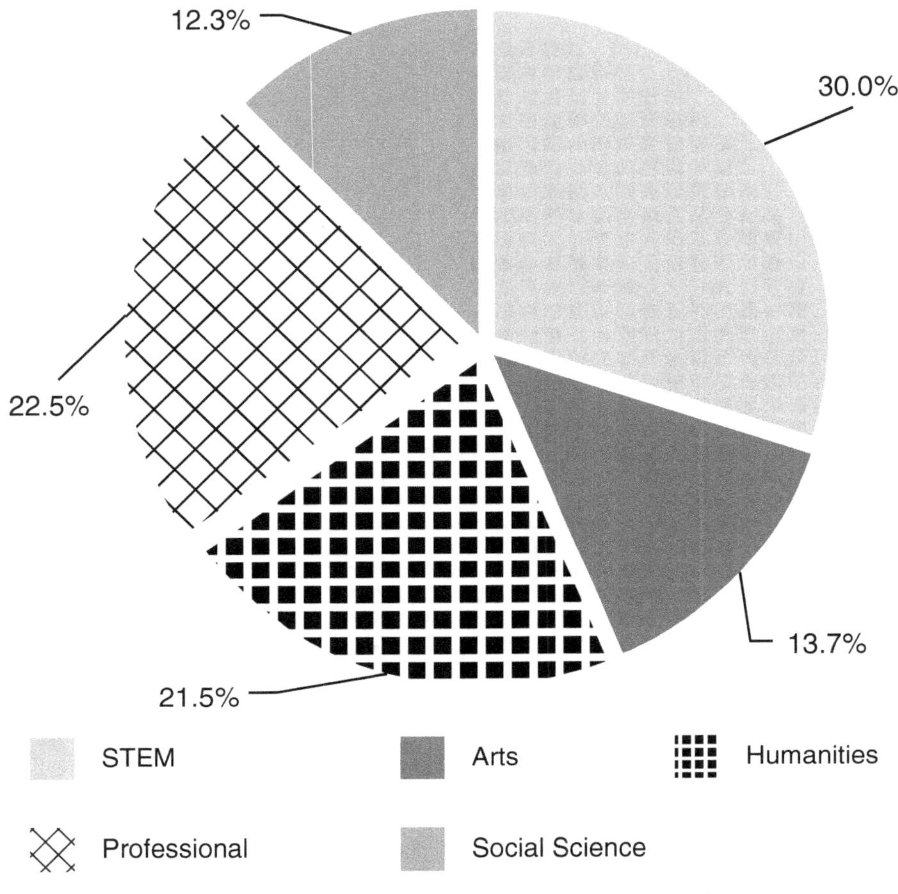

FIGURE B.6 Faculty discipline affiliation ($n = 293$)

B.7–B.10 depict information regarding *TTS* disputes. Note that, unlike B.1–B.6, information for some of the following variables may not equal 100% (denoted with an *). This is either because information was unavailable (University Narratives, Fired/ Quit) or because the variable was irrelevant (not all faculty offered counternarratives). All incidents occurred between 2000 and 2021. Total cases numbered 293.

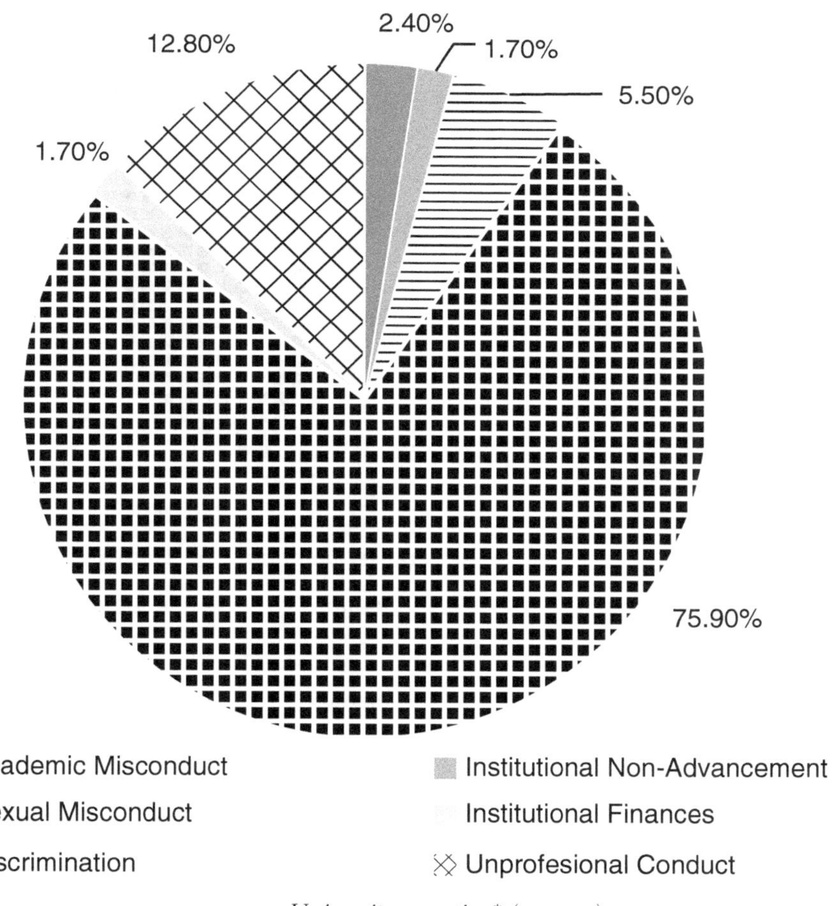

FIGURE B.7 University narrative* (*n* = 290)

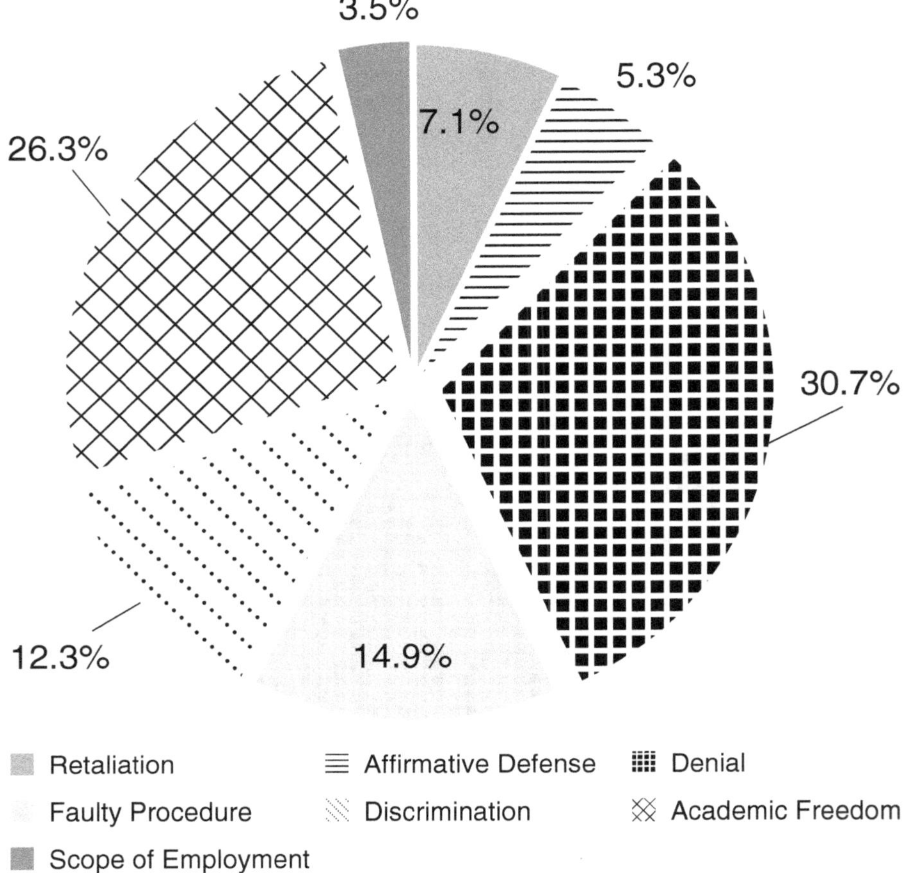

FIGURE B.8 Faculty counternarrative* ($n = 114$)

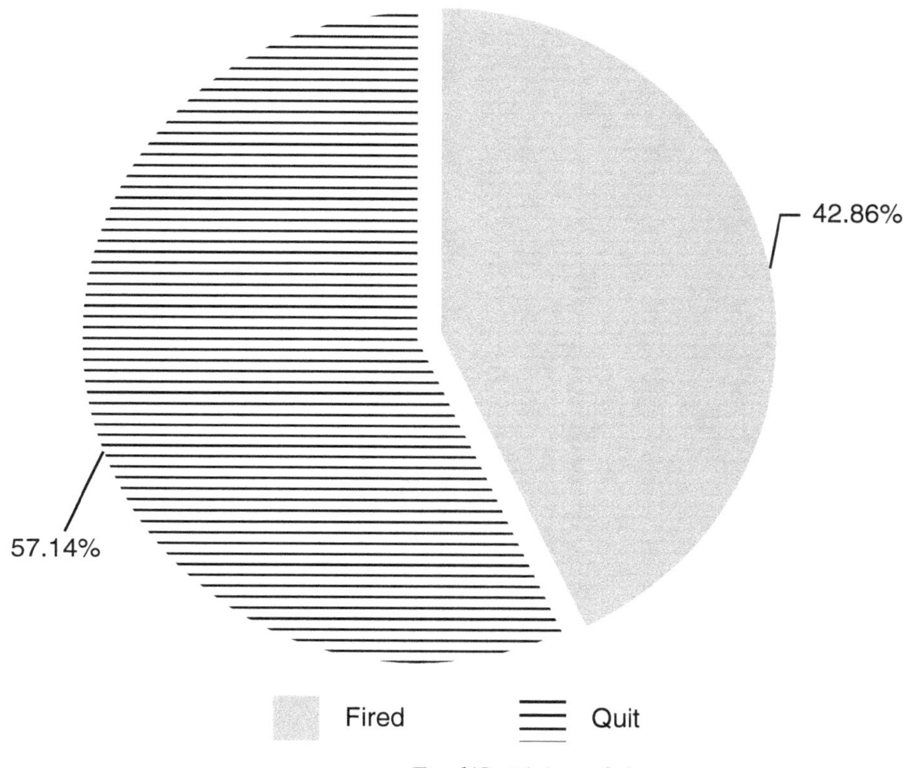

FIGURE B.9 Fired/Quit* ($n = 280$)

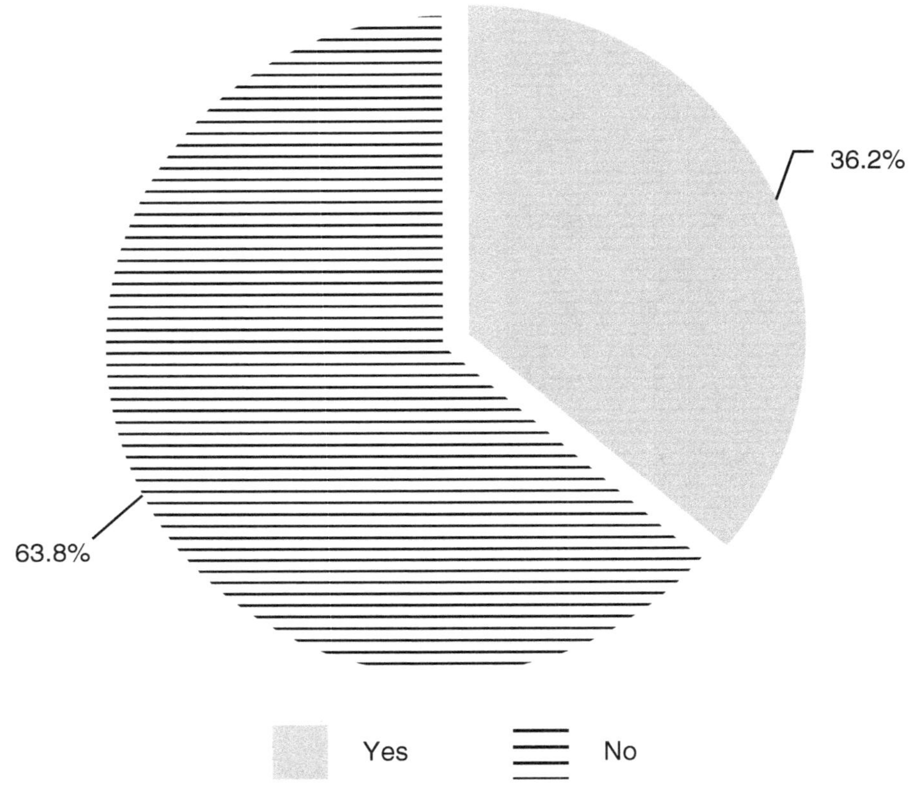

FIGURE B.10 Lawsuit (Yes/No) ($n = 293$)

Notes

1 SKIRMISHES

1. Flaherty (2021b).
2. Bellows (2024); Palmer (2024).
3. Flaherty (2018).
4. Street et al. (2012).

3 SCROUNGE

1. Iqbal and Muthukumar (2021).
2. Preston (2024).
3. Northwestern University (2022) (noting that "[a]ll recipients of University funding must… [r]efrain from remunerative work"); Anonymous (2022).
4. Sarcozona (2014).
5. Mano (2019).
6. Patton (2012).
7. Lawsky (2024).
8. Sinche (2016).
9. Hanson (2024). To arrive at the second figure, I took the "average 2020 PhD graduate's total inflation-adjusted student loan debt" (which was $88,368) and calculated the 87.6% of it that is *not* attributable to undergraduate study.
10. Baum and Looney (2020).
11. Baum and Looney (2020).
12. Andalib et al. (2018).
13. Andalib et al. (2018, 675).
14. Kwok (2019).
15. Oishi et al. (2012).
16. Oishi and Schimmack (2010).
17. Butler et al. (1973) (regarding differential effects on men and women); Magdol (2002) (finding that relocation was more predictive of depression among women than men).
18. Oishi and Schimmack (2010).
19. Barry (2024).
20. Ritter (2023).

4 SQUINT

1. Cuff (2017).
2. Caballero (2022).
3. Columbia Law School (2024).
4. Columbia University (2024).
5. National Center for Science and Engineering Statistics (2022, 26).
6. National Center for Science and Engineering Statistics (2022, 14).
7. Adapted from V.G. Narayanan's online Financial Accounting course for Harvard Business School, in which Narayanan offers three reasons for the time value of money: opportunity cost, inflation, and uncertainty. Narayanan (accessed 2024).
8. The salary estimates are drawn from the National Association of Colleges and Employers (showing a 2023 average salary projection of $60,107 for social science majors and $74,405 for engineering majors). National Association of Colleges and Employers (2023, 5).
9. Actual figures are $10,301 and $45,837. These estimates assume a $100/month investment for eight years at a 2% rate of return and a $400/month investment for eight years at a 5% rate of return.
10. Brenan (2023).
11. Barshay (2021).
12. Emmons et al. (2019).

5 CAUSE, JUST CAUSE

1. Among other things, Title VII forbids employers from failing or refusing "to hire or to discharge any individual, or otherwise to discriminate against any individual with respect to his compensation, terms, conditions, or privileges of employment, because of such individual's race, color, religion, sex, or national origin." 42 U.S.C. §2000e-2.
2. *Price Waterhouse v. Hopkins* (1989).
3. Brown (2023).
4. The exact number may be impossible to determine because of the way employment data is collected and categorized. The human resources firm Betterteam estimates that "About 74% of US workers are considered at-will employees" but does not explain how it arrived at that figure (Coulson 2021). Colleagues of mine at the National Employment Law Project used data from the Bureau of Labor Statistics at the federal Department of Labor to estimate that "the at-will worker population is up to 82.1% (of all workers)" (Pinto and Tung 2023).
5. Andrias and Hertel-Fernandez (2021).
6. Arnow-Richman (2018–2019, 87).
7. Board of Governors (2021).
8. U.S. Bureau of Labor Statistics (2025).
9. Kim (1997, 106).
10. Kim (1997, 110–111).
11. Rowell (2019, 255).
12. Rowell (2019, 255–256).
13. Hernández (2024).
14. National Employment Law Project (2019, 7).
15. Department of Consumer and Worker Protection (2023).
16. My 800,000 estimate reflects the total executive branch workforce (approximately 4 million employees) *not* including those affiliated with the Department of Defense (approximately

3.2 million) as of late 2023 (The White House, accessed 2023). Given recent changes to the federal workforce, it is difficult to assess the MSP's efficacy at the time of writing.

17. U.S. Merit Systems Protection Board (2015, iii).
18. Abrams and Nolan (1985, 597).
19. Arnow-Richman (2010).
20. For what it's worth, I suspect that the absence of contracts riddled with legalese also exacerbates the tendency of tenure-stream faculty to think of their circumstances as exceptional and of themselves as something *other* than workers. A former department chair once told me that, despite working at her university for over two decades, she "had no contract." Of course she had a contract. It may not have been a separate document from the letter she received that offered her the job – and she may have even received her offer by phone (although, given the need to specify things like research funds and teaching packages at the time of hire, this is unlikely). But she nonetheless had a contractual relationship with her university-employer. The fact that this PhD-holding, department-chairing professor of over two decades could not see herself as being subject to a contract is an example of the academic exceptionalism I think is harmful.
21. University of Alabama (2023).
22. University of Alabama (2023).
23. University of Alabama (2023).
24. E.g. University of Alabama (2023).
25. University of Alabama (2023).
26. University of Alabama (2023).
27. Williams College, for instance, also places the burden of proof on the institution but uses a "clear and convincing" standard of evaluation. Williams College (2021). Duke University has a standing Faculty Hearing Committee empowered to hear appeals regarding "an adverse employment or disciplinary action" where University action "is otherwise complete" and the appeal alleges "procedural rather than substantive issues." Duke University (2019, 3–4).

6 ORIGINS

1. This chapter draws significantly from Das Acevedo, Tenure as a Labor Protection (2023).
2. Ross developed the theory of "race suicide" – namely, "the belief that low birth rates and increased immigration would lead to the extinction of the white race." Stanford Eugenics History Project (accessed 2024).
3. The exact basis of Jane Stanford's dislike is a matter of some dispute, even at Stanford. The Stanford Historical Society states that "Ross was a eugenicist and racist, but that's not why he was fired." Stanford Historical Society (2023). Meanwhile, the Stanford Eugenics Project notes that Ross "was particularly concerned with Asian immigration" and that "[b]ecause of his anti-Asian rhetoric and his criticism of the railroad industry, Jane Stanford successfully called for Ross' resignation from the University." Stanford Eugenics History Project (accessed 2024).
4. Fishman (2000, 165).
5. Gersen (2022, 783).
6. Stanford Eugenics History Project (accessed 2024).
7. Bergquist (1972) (discussing Bemis); Metzger (1973, 146) (discussing Fisher); Pollitt and Kurland (1998, 50–51) (discussing Nearing); Barrow (2014) (discussing Beard).
8. Samuels (1991, 183).
9. Brown Jr. and Finkin (1978, 6).
10. Metzger (1990, 6).

11. Metzger (1990, 6).
12. The rest of this history draws heavily on Metzger (1973). Specific claims and quotations are accorded pin cites, but even otherwise, the information as a whole relies on Metzger.
13. Although this book generally uses *university* to describe institutions of higher education, in this chapter I'll largely adopt Metzger's term, *college*, for reasons of historical accuracy. At the same time, whereas Metzger uses institutionally specific language to refer to teaching staff before the development of the modern professorship – *tutor* at Harvard, *master* at William and Mary, and so on – for ease of reading, I'll refer to them all as *instructors*.
14. Metzger (1973, 112–113).
15. Metzger (1973, 116) ("the Harvard charter said nothing about the duration of the corporate fellowship"); (1973, 118) ("under the charter, the corporation… did not have… the power to remove [a tutor] without a show of cause").
16. Metzger (1973, 112).
17. Metzger (1973, 112).
18. Metzger (1973, 117–118). The Harvard Corporation adopted three-year contracts in 1716, but this change was only ratified by the Board of Overseers in 1734.
19. Metzger (1973, 119 and 127–128) (discussing the dismissals of Thomas Prince and Isaac Greenwood, neither of whom were covered by the new system of three-year contracts and both of whom, consequently, could only be dismissed after a showing of adequate cause).
20. Quincy (cited in Metzger 1973, 118).
21. Metzger (1973, 120).
22. Metzger (1973, 121).
23. Metzger (1973, 120).
24. Metzger (1973, 123).
25. Metzger (1973, 123).
26. Metzger (1973, 134).
27. Metzger (1973, 128).
28. Metzger (1973, 128).
29. Metzger (1973, 94).
30. Metzger (1973, 93).
31. Emphasis added.
32. Metzger (1990).
33. Metzger (1990, 11).
34. The revised version of the 1940S states that the document was preceded by "a series of joint conferences begun in 1934," while Metzger states that the two associations behind the Statement, the AAUP and the AAC, "met officially four times between 1937 and 1940" (Metzger 1990, 47).
35. 29 U.S.C. §§ 151–169, at §151.
36. Metzger (1990, 7).
37. Indeed, Hans-Joerg Tiede, now a Senior Program Officer at the AAUP, notes that although "one might surmise that the AAUP was founded first and foremost to defend academic freedom… this was not the main or exclusive aim of the founders." Instead, Tiede argues, "the AAUP was conceived to further the professionalization of the professoriate" and "to make collective action possible" (Tiede 2014, 2).

7 MULTIHYPHENATE

1. Gannon (2021); Harvard University (2023).
2. Gannon (2020).

3. Kezar et al. (2019, 22–23).
4. Kezar et al. (2019, 22).
5. Mueller (2024).
6. Ludema and Johnson (2020).
7. See generally, National Center for Education Statistics, Characteristics of Postsecondary Students (2023).
8. See, e.g., Childress (2019, 92–96).
9. University of Massachusetts, Amherst (accessed 2024).
10. Stanford University (2024).
11. Saunders and Kardia (1997).
12. Richardson and le Blanc (2016).
13. Elon University (accessed 2024).
14. Baucher (2016).
15. Grisard (2023, 15).
16. Grisard (2023, 15).
17. Dixon and Tervanotko (2021).
18. Kenny et al. (2012).
19. Emory University (2017, 14) (emphasis added).
20. Emory University (2017, 19) (emphasis added).
21. Guarino and Borden (2017, 690).
22. Guarino and Borden (2017, 690).
23. Trejo (2020).
24. June (2015); see also National Center for Education Statistics, Characteristics of Postsecondary Faculty (2024).
25. Padilla (1994).
26. Bird et al. (2004, 198).
27. Ghosh and Barber (2021).
28. Rucks-Ahidiana (2019).

8 ...CHOOSERS

1. Bui and Miller (2015).
2. White (2015).
3. Linton et al. (2023).
4. Bui and Miller (2015).
5. The LendingTree survey, for instance, found that "Higher-earning individuals are more likely to say living near family is important – 74% of respondents with household incomes of $100,000 or more annually say they value it, versus 64% of those earning less than $35,000" (Linton et al. 2023).
6. Ehrenreich and Ehrenreich (2013, 7).
7. Statista (accessed 2024).
8. National Center for Education Statistics, Educational Institutions (2022) (reporting 3,931 Title IV-eligible two- and four-year institutions); Moody (2021).
9. Conn (2023).
10. Atlanta Bar Association (accessed 2023). "100% Club denotes firms of five or more lawyers that have registered all of their practicing attorneys as members of the Atlanta Bar."
11. Georgetown Law (accessed 2024).
12. American Bar Association (accessed 2024).

13. This estimate was developed between December 2023 and January 2024 and is likely to have changed by the time of publication. My RA and I arrived at this number by combing the faculty directories of the University of Georgia School of Law, Georgia State University College of Law, Emory University School of Law, Mercer University School of Law, and Atlanta's John Marshall Law School. We included faculty holding the titles of Assistant, Associate, and Full Professor, as well as those full professors holding named chairs. Because most clinical faculty, legal research and writing faculty, and faculty holding the titles of Lecturer or Adjunct Professor are not tenure-stream, we excluded them from this group. The work was done in two rounds; after each round I cross-checked a random sample using institutional website bios.

14. A *biodata*, in the South Asian/South Asian diaspora worlds I inhabited growing up, refers to a one-page document describing a single person who's interested in marriage. It's like a personal resume, and it will likely include traditional resume categories like "education" and "hobbies" as well as marriage-specific types of information like height, religious or caste affiliation, and number of siblings. You can now even hire someone to craft an appealing biodata sheet instead of making one yourself or leaving the task to your friends, relatives, or a professional matchmaker. Bhagyoday (accessed 2024). The first time I saw the Faculty Appointments Register form used by the Association of American Law Schools as part of its hiring process for new law professors, I instantly recognized it as a type of professional biodata because it was simultaneously shorter and more exhaustive than many academic CVs.

15. I filtered by "Labor and Employment" under "Service" filter and "Atlanta" under "Office" filter; excluding two retired partners.

16. Carroll (2024); Howard (2023); Jotkoff (2022); Goodman (2022); Spitz (2022).

17. Das Acevedo (2023).

18. Email from anonymous (April 20, 2024) (on file with author).

19. Carmichael (1988).

20. Cuff (2017). In 2019, Main et al. estimated that 40% of doctorates in humanities and humanistic social sciences were in tenured or tenure-track positions six months after graduation, and 67.5% were in such positions eight to twenty-six years after graduation. Although these numbers are much higher, they're also very particular: All the graduate students in this sample received degrees from selective research institutions, which – by the authors' own admission – gave them above-average metrics in some areas, like time-to-completion, and almost certainly improved their success rates on the tenure-track market as well (Main et al. 2019, 1319–1320). See also Stafforini (2020), which estimated that "Between 10% and 30% of PhD alumni get a permanent position at academia."

21. One of the classic studies in this area is Topel & Ward (1992), which found that "[w]age gains at job changes average about 10 percent, and account for about one third of total wage growth during the first ten years in the market" (Topel and Ward 1992, 442). See also Yankow (2022).

22. Forsythe (2019, 243); Pavan (2010, 123).

23. Ransom (1993, 232).

24. Since Ransom's study was published other studies have qualified or challenged his findings. See, e.g., Hallock (1995). But there are always qualifications to qualifications: Hallock's study focused on one institution, the University of Massachusetts at Amherst (UMass), whereas Ransom's was based on national data. Moreover, as Hallock himself notes, UMass has at least two qualities that may help explain why staying put pays there: there are lots of geographically close alternatives (so that if you choose to stay at UMass it is likely because

you *want* to), and UMass is unionized (which tends to both increase the earnings of long-time faculty and reduce the windfall for recent arrivals) (Hallock 1995, 656).
25. Ransom (1993, 232).

9 TWO BODIES

1. Ferber and Loeb (1997).
2. Wolf-Wendel et al. (2004).
3. Petriglieri (2019).
4. Drawing on census data from 1970 and 1980, Kalmijn (1994, 434) observed that lawyers, doctors, and professors were three of the four groups with the highest rates of occupational endogamy (sometimes also called "occupational homogamy"). Similarly, in 2015–2017, Schwartz et al. (2021, 14) found that lawyers, doctors, and professors were three of the four groups in which occupational endogamy increased since 1970 – although this effect was limited to *men*.
5. Schiebinger et al. (2008, 4).
6. I'm intentionally using the term *spousal* hire instead of the increasingly common *partner* hire. I suspect that more universities that engage in couples hiring offer the same benefits regardless of marital status, but some of these are public universities located in states where "legislation prevents offering benefits to unmarried couples" (Schiebinger et al. 2008, 12). And for universities without official policies – a very large group, incidentally – it's my strong albeit unverified suspicion that accommodations are more likely to be made for couples who are legally married.
7. Wilson (2001).
8. Wilson (2001).
9. Kay (2007).
10. I appreciate this critic's acknowledgment of intra-organizational politics, which too often gets ignored because of a mistaken sense that academics are above all this. But I think the proposal – a severe restriction or elimination of spousal hires – aims to solve a problem that has no permanent solution. Getting rid of spousal hires, or even limiting them within a department, won't eliminate voting blocs, information leaks, or conflicting incentives… not by a long shot. All it will reliably do is make life harder for the couples in question.
11. You may be wondering why Emory wanted *me* in the first place. That's a fair question with many possible answers that I can hypothesize about but not confirm. I publish a lot, and publications remain the single most prestigious activity a professor can engage in. I write about and teach a subject – employment law – in which the law school had a teaching need as well as permission to hire. And I am a petite, cisgender, brown woman whose CV includes names like Princeton, the University of Pennsylvania, and the University of Chicago.
12. Again, this arrangement isn't unique to dual academic couples. I know more than a few families where the higher-earning nonacademic spouse lives in one place with the house, kids, and expected trappings of an upper-middle class life, while the academic spouse travels – sometimes flying across several state lines – on a weekly basis to their university job.
13. mathgirl (2013).
14. U.S. Equal Employment Opportunity Commission (accessed 2024).
15. At least one critic of spousal hires has criticized this advice and the practice it generates, saying that "It is very poor practice, as some candidates have done, to take off a wedding ring or to otherwise mislead the hiring department into thinking that a candidate is single until the moment an offer is made" (Kay 2007).

16. For better and for worse, these experiences aren't universal. I went on ten campus visits and only had two such experiences. My husband, by contrast, had no such experiences, and neither did a very close friend who is also a straight, cisgender, married man.

17. My adjusted approach seems very like the approach described by David Farley (a pseudonym) in his column defending spousal hiring: "I myself took off my wedding ring the last time I went on the market when my wife and I were in positions in different locations. I did that not to 'mislead' interviewing departments… but to protect my privacy. I never lied… [b]ut I made sure to act equally interested when the conversation turned to local nightlife as when it focused on area public schools" (Farley 2007).

10 TO THE DOGS

1. Cuff (2017) (citing multiple other studies that all hover around the 5% to 35% range).
2. The California State University (2023, 62).
3. Guzman & Kollar (2023).
4. Hanson (2024).
5. NerdWallet (accessed 2023) estimated the median price in Los Angeles for a three-bedroom, two-bathroom house, was \$1,037,503, while Payscale.com (accessed 2023) estimated the median home price was \$1,083,995.
6. National Center for Education Statistics, 1949–1950 through 2020–2021 (January 2021) (describing numbers for academic year 2022–2023); National Center for Educational Statistics: Trend Generator (2024).
7. The exact numbers are \$48,651.24 and \$94,695.84. I arrived at a rough estimate by using biweekly and monthly payroll periods, at both the \$64,860 and \$143,928 salary ranges, and assuming a salary spread over twelve months (which is not normal practice). I used the calculator provided by Californiapayroll.com.
8. The California estimate is from the U.S. Bureau of Economic Analysis (2022), while the Los Angeles estimate is from Johnson (2023).
9. Interview with Sarah Emanuel (October 26, 2023) (on file with author).
10. Emanuel (2022).
11. Burkhalter (2016).
12. Patton (2012) (quoting Michael Bérubé).
13. Shaw (1903) ("He who can, does. He who cannot, teaches.").
14. U.S. Bureau of Labor Statistics, About the U.S. Bureau (2024).
15. Quinn (2023b).
16. Burgos (2015).
17. This data was sourced from the *Occupational Outlook Handbook* of the Bureau of Labor Statistics. According to the *OOH*, median wages across all occupations were \$46,310 in May 2022; median wages for all post-secondary instructors were \$80,840.
18. Note that I have used "Communications Manager, Public Relations" as the industry correlate.
19. Note that I have used "Translator, Interpreter" as the industry correlate.
20. Note that I have used "Music Director" and "Composer" as industry correlates, not *practicing musician*; this likely inflates the figure for median industry salary.
21. Note that I have used Advanced Practice Registered Nurses (APRNs) as the industry correlate, not Registered Nurses (RNs); this likely inflates the figure for median industry salary. According to the American Nurses Association, "APRNs include nurse practitioners,

clinical nurse specialists, nurse anesthetists, and nurse midwives." ANA Enterprise (accessed 2024).

22. U.S. Bureau of Labor Statistics, OOH: Anthropologists and Archaeologists (accessed 2024).
23. See generally U.S. Bureau of Labor Statistics, Occupational Employment and Wage Statistics (accessed 2024).
24. U.S. Bureau of Labor Statistics, OEWS: Anthropologists and Archaeologists (accessed 2024).
25. U.S. Bureau of Labor Statistics, OEWS: Anthropology and Archeology Teachers, Postsecondary (accessed 2024).
26. U.S. Bureau of Labor Statistics, OEWS: Anthropologists and Archeologists (accessed 2024).
27. Academics know this instinctively, while nonacademics disbelieve it implicitly. Compare, for instance, these two statements:

> University professors have a lot less stress than most of us. Unless they teach summer school, they are off between May and September and they enjoy long breaks during the school year, including a month over Christmas and New Year's and another chunk of time in the spring (Adams 2013)

Readers should note that Adams added an addendum after receiving numerous critical responses.

> There is absolutely NO WAY to compartmentalize time, e.g., "I'm going to spend Sept.-Dec. only teaching, and then switch back to research and service activities." Everything is happening all of the time, even through summer. I honestly can't even imagine a scenario where a tenure-track faculty member would take time off or reject department service because it was the period when they weren't being paid by the university (Random Asst.Prof. 2014).

28. See, e.g., *Sandifer v. U.S. Steel* (2014), which found that time spent "donning and doffing" protective gear is not compensable under §203(o) of the *Fair Labor Standards Act* of 1938, 29 U.S.C. §201 et seq., and *Integrity Staffing Solutions v. Busk* (2014), which found that time spent waiting to undergo anti-theft security screenings is not compensable under same statute, as amended by the *Portal-to-Portal Act* of 1947, §251 et seq.
29. Merritt (2013).
30. Klayman (2023). The *starting* base rates negotiated by the UAW were $30.60–42.95 per hour. Using a conservative estimate of five to seven hours to read the manuscript *and* write the review – an allowance that few faculty will feel comfortable operating within for fear of doing the manuscript injustice – honoraria of $100–300 would result in an hourly rate of $15–60.
31. Aczel et al. (2021).
32. Carroll (2024).

11 BUTLERIAN DIALECTICS

1. Butler (1997, 13–15).
2. Dutton (1999); Nussbaum (1999, 37–45).
3. Salih (2002) (describing versions of these defenses).
4. This definition was borrowed, but unfortunately I can no longer identify the source. Still, I want to make clear that this is a quotation (and to apologize to its unidentified author). The definition bears some similarity to the Wikipedia entry for "dialectic" but does not, as of June 2024, seem to exactly replicate any portion of it that is longer than two or three words.

5. Jacobs (2013, 2) quoting Julie Thompson Klein.
6. Higham (1980, 13). "By 1920… America had embraced the specialist and sanctified the expert with an enthusiasm unmatched elsewhere" but adding that "While American opinion shifted from one extreme to another – often repudiating specialization in the early nineteenth century and embracing it uncritically in the late nineteenth century – European intellectuals displayed a persistent ambivalence."
7. Ware and Mabe (2012, 5) (2012 figure); Jacobs (2013, 6) (2008 figure); Curcic (2023) (2023 figure).
8. Former Emory professor Mark Bauerlein describes this phenomenon as applied to literary commentary, in which the explosion of scholarship "was a curse for young aspirants, the graduate student in search of a dissertation (like I was in 1985) and the assistant professor in need of a book." Bauerlein and I agree that it gets harder to make a meaningful contribution as knowledge progresses (and that this exacerbates the pressure already felt by junior scholars) – where we differ is in how we feel about this and whether we think it's avoidable (Bauerlein 2009).
9. Cornell University Graduate School (accessed 2024).
10. Yale University Office of Career Strategy (accessed 2020).
11. Newhouse (1998).
12. Posner (2019).
13. Wood (2019).
14. Lawsky (2023).
15. Interview with Siddesh Bale, Partner, Reed Smith LLP (October 23, 2023).
16. raycam (2014) (quoting Larry Latourette).
17. Schuman (2013).
18. Lee (2015).
19. Bartram (2018).
20. Pannapacker (2021).
21. Dreger (2015).
22. ImaginePhD (accessed 2024), Versatile PhD (accessed 2024).

12 RENEGADE

1. Metzger (1988, 1269).
2. Wilson (2016).
3. Metzger (1988, 1270).
4. Metzger (1988, 1270).
5. Storey and Storey (2024) (noting that schools of civic thought have been created at the University of North Carolina at Chapel Hill, the University of Florida, the University of Tennessee, the University of Texas at Austin, and the University of Toledo). UCLA School of Law (accessed 2024) (noting that, beginning in September 2020 and as of 11 April 2024, "a total of 246 local, state, and federal government entities across the United States have introduced 805 anti-Critical Race Theory bills, resolutions, executive orders, opinion letters, statements, and other measures").
6. See, e.g., Tierney (2021, 3) ("Democracy and higher education are inextricably linked… universities have the ability, not only to be key arbiters of how one advances democracy, but also to reflect democratic values in their practices, objectives, and goals.").
7. Flaherty (2022).
8. Flannery (2020).
9. McNeilly (2023).

10. McNeilly also asks a third, more specific, question that I don't discuss here: *Does tenure protect moderate and conservative professors more than liberal professors?*
11. Ceci et al. (2006, 555).
12. Readers should note that I've paraphrased the scenarios but retained their original numbering and some of their terminology.
13. Ceci et al. (2006, 565).
14. Ceci et al. (2006, 565).
15. Ceci et al. (2006, 566).
16. Ceci et al. (2006, 566).
17. Ceci et al. (2006, 565).
18. See the responses to Ceci et al. by Jacobson (2006, 579), Buck (2006, 570), MacLeod (2006, 581), and Wettersten (2006, 585).
19. MacLeod (2006); Wettersten (2006).
20. Jacobson (2006, 579).
21. Fuller (2006, 577).
22. Ceci et al. (2006, 563).
23. Jacobson (2006, 579).
24. That's not to say that supporters of tenure on academic freedom grounds are ideologically uniform. Still, at least within the professoriate, there does seem to be greater homogeneity – or, at least, greater consistency in who vehemently supports tenure. Republican faculty are around twice as likely as their Democratic colleagues to characterize tenure as "essential." This may be because the best predictor of a professor's support for tenure is how endangered they think academic freedom is, and Republican faculty more often rate academic freedom as being secure (Rothman et al. 2011, 169–177).
25. McGee (2022).
26. Das Acevedo (2024). For a description of historical and linguistic criticisms of public meaning Originalism, see sections II(A) and II(B) of the same article.
27. Farley (2006, 574).
28. The phrase "hard cases make bad law" is usually attributed to Justice Holmes. *Northern Securities Co. v. United States*, 193 U.S. 197, 400 (1904) ("Great cases, like hard cases, make bad law.").
29. Beauboeuf-Lafontant et al. (2019, 652).
30. Dean (2017).
31. Rockquemore (2016).
32. Macdonald and Stevens (2024).
33. Beauboeuf et al. (2017).
34. Perlmutter (2015).
35. Dow (2014) (discussing terminal associates); Chung (2018, 10) (discussing academic limbo).
36. Pomeranz (2013).
37. The University of Tulsa (accessed 2024); National Center for Faculty Development and Diversity (2024). See also Matthews (2014, 5), saying "what is often written off as faculty disengagement or more cruelly, "tenure's mistakes," is in fact the observers' inability to consider the institution's culpability for the roadblocks to faculty progression."
38. Flaherty (2021a).
39. The Haynesville Project (accessed 2024).
40. Chung (2018, 69).
41. Viladrich (2018).
42. Beauboeuf-Lafontant et al. (2019, 649).

13 PREDATOR

1. Whitehead (1985, 39).
2. Geertz (1973, 29).
3. See, e.g., Scheiber (2023) (discussing Francesca Gino); Dominus (2017) (discussing Amy Cuddy); Lewis-Kraus (2023) (discussing both Gino and co-author Dan Ariely).
4. Wise (2013) (noting that "many of [Joachim] Boldt's studies were included in the evidence used to form clinical guidelines worldwide").
5. Ilies et al. (2003).
6. Ilies et al. (2003, 624).
7. Bauer-Wolf (2023), the University of Texas at Austin (accessed 2024), DeSimone (2023). Other (noncomparative) studies confirm high levels of sexual misconduct experiences among women in the academy, whether faculty, students, or staff. See, e.g., Richman et al. (1999); Lorenz et al. (2019); Bondestam and Lundqvist (2020).
8. Besides the assumption described in this paragraph, which does not meaningfully bear on the study's results, the study assumes the shortcomings of the studies it aggregates. But those flaws often reflect the difficulty of studying sexual misconduct as much as, or more than, author error. For example, Richman et al. (1999, 359) note the low response rate in their convenience sample – but also note that the "lower than desired response rates are reflective of the fact that the questionnaires were self-administered and contained highly sensitive material and identifiers for subsequent tracking."
9. Ilies et al. (2003, 613–614) (emphasis mine).
10. *The Onion*, as readers of a certain generation will know, is a satirical news magazine.
11. Ilies et al. (2003, 613) (observing that "Highly structured and stratified organizations are more likely settings for harassment") (internal citations omitted).
12. Kelsky (accessed 2024).
13. Libarkin (accessed 2022).
14. Ilies et al. (2003, 622).
15. We might also want to think about why so many of the sexual harassment scandals involving universities *don't* involve professors. High on the list of campus offenders are nonfaculty doctors (Michigan, Ohio State, Southern California), athletic coaches (Penn State, Maryland-Baltimore County); and students (Baylor, Columbia, Princeton, Stanford).
16. Athanasiades et al. (2023).
17. Bullens (accessed 2023).
18. Humbert et al. (2022, 17).
19. Marsh et al. (2009, 318).
20. Bondestam and Lundqvist (2020, 403).
21. Most strikingly, the academic freedom of German scholars is protected by something much more powerful than a type of employment contract that, over time, has become a normative industry practice. Article 5(3) of the German Basic Law enshrines academic freedom *as a constitutional right*. Art. 5, GG. This gives academic freedom in Germany a legal heft that's unimaginable in the United States, and it also makes tenure's function as an expressive safeguard somewhat besides the point in the German context.
22. Readers should note that the *TTS* disaggregates various sex-related workplace harms differently than federal anti-discrimination legislation under Title VII of the *Civil Rights Act of 1964*. I describe these categorization differences in Appendix A.
23. Arnow-Richman (2018–2019, 87).
24. Ross (2021).

14 SLACKER

1. Kumar (2022).
2. Quinn (2023a).
3. Beam (2010).
4. Adams (2013).
5. There are, of course, other internal critics of tenure besides the three professors discussed above the line. See e.g., Farley (2006, 574) ("a negative feature of tenure is the drag on innovation and growth provided by 'dead wood' – tenured professors who do little scholarly work post-tenure and who are nearly impossible to get rid of"); Rubinstein (2011) ("The tenured live in a different world than ordinary mortals, a world in which fears of unemployment are banished, futures can be confidently planned, and retirement is secure"); Wetherbe (2013) ("While not all of academia's problems can be laid at tenure's doorstep, tenure has hamstrung colleges' ability to fulfill their two fundamental missions of advancing knowledge and disseminating it."); Helfand (1995) (describing, in one of the rare examples of an internal critic *not* speaking after decades of tenured employment, "a curious, 18-month period" at the start of his career in which he "struggled, with an uncomprehending and irritable administration, to refuse tenure").
6. Levitt (2007).
7. Livingston (2020).
8. Taylor (2010, 206).
9. By explaining the perception–reality gap this way, I'm choosing to focus on why *some* people *might* think tenure promotes slacking rather than on why *these* people *do* think tenure promotes slacking. But even if I won't speculate about individual motivations, I can observe something about individual characteristics: most of the academic critics of tenure I have encountered, including the three named here, are white, tenured, full professors at large research universities. Not all internal critics fit this typology – but many do.
10. Posner (1997–1998, 1551).
11. Caplan (2016); Shapiro (2021).
12. The Nobel Foundation (as of 2023).
13. Sunstein et al. (1998, 1477) ("Bounded rationality, an idea first introduced by Herbert Simon, refers to the obvious fact that human cognitive abilities are not infinite. We have limited computational skills and seriously flawed memories") (internal citations omitted).
14. Holley (1977, 185–186).
15. Wilder and Walters (2020, 262–263); Phelan (1995).
16. Way et al. (2017, E9218) (finding "rising productivity that peaks after around 5 years, declines slowly for another 5 years, and then remains roughly constant for any remaining years.").
17. Chilton et al. (2021, 6–7).
18. Blackburn and Lawrence (1986, 276) ("the first years are critical ones in predicting future publication rates and career output"). The same finding was reported a few years before by a much smaller-scale study (Orpen 1982).
19. Blackburn and Lawrence (1986, 275).
20. Tversky and Kahneman (1973, 207) (defining the heuristic as "a judgmental heuristic in which a person evaluates the frequency of classes or the probability of events by availability, i.e., by the ease with which relevant instances come to mind... reliance on the availability heuristic leads to systematic biases").
21. Blackburn and Lawrence (1986, 274) ("counting becomes more of an indicator of quantity than quality, many say").

22. Blackburn and Lawrence (1986, 274).
23. Blackburn and Lawrence (1986, 270–71).
24. Blackburn and Lawrence (1986, 281).
25. Another explanation offered by Blackburn and Lawrence is that cross-sectional studies overestimate the productivity of senior scholars because a senior scholar who's productive at the time of the study may later become less productive with age and illness. Conversely, however, Blackburn and Lawrence note that cross-sectional studies may underestimate the productivity of junior scholarship because an unproductive junior (especially *pre-tenure*) scholar who's included in the study may soon be weeded out precisely because of their low productivity (Blackburn and Lawrence 1986, 281).
26. Blackburn and Lawrence (1986, 282).
27. Warren (2019, 172).
28. Posner (1997–1998, 1553–1554) ("A much larger problem is JST's failure to distinguish between impediments to clear instrumental reasoning and preferences that we enlightened observers may think silly… instrumental reasoning cannot be thought pervaded with irrationality merely because a frequent goal of such reasoning is a preference that we would not have if we were not emotional beings.").
29. Kelsky (2021), at 6:36.
30. As many readers will know, Weber's famous lecture on the subject referred to *science* as a vocation. Those same readers will hopefully acknowledge that, for Weber in particular, to talk of "science" was to talk of the scholarly enterprise itself (Weber 1946 [1919]).
31. Lufkin (2022).

15 *IN CAUSA SUA*

1. Das Acevedo (2021).
2. India Today (2019).
3. Krishnan (2019).
4. Quinn (2024) (quoting Helen Benedict).
5. Eyal (2019).
6. Nichols (2017, 3).
7. Nichols (2017, 3).
8. Livingston (2020, 1–15).
9. Kurtz (2022, 266).
10. These were: intentional selection by aspiring practitioners, distinct occupational purpose and values, defined and specialized entry credentials, and readily available training (Tiede 2014, 2–13).
11. Gorman and Sandefur (2011, 277–278).
12. Kurtz (2022, 273).
13. Gorman and Sandefur (2011, 281).
14. Adams (2015, 160) (discussing differences between UK and US scholars of the profession).
15. Gorman and Sandefur (2011, 279).
16. Abbott (2014, 2–3).
17. Georgia Rules of Professional Conduct, Ch.2, Rule 4-201.
18. Attorney Registration and Disciplinary Commission (accessed 2024).
19. New York State Unified Court System (accessed 2024); State Bar of California (accessed 2024).

20. Georgia Secretary of State Brad Raffensperger, Board of Architects (accessed 2024); California Architects Board (accessed 2024); Georgia Secretary of State Brad Raffensperger, Board of Cosmetology (accessed 2024); American Bar Association, Schools by State (accessed 2024).

21. Contrast Metzger's (1973, 97) relatively neutral characterization of academia as a guild ("as the etymology of the word suggests, a university denoted a guild, or rather a congeries of guilds, organized ethnically into 'nations,' by habitat and endowment into 'colleges,' by field and degree-granting power into 'faculties'") with the negative characterizations in Newman (1982, 8) and Macfarlane and Jefferson (2022, 38).

22. UCLA School of Law (accessed 2024).

23. Schermele (2023) (naming individual regents and the alumni groups Sul Ross Group and the Rudder Association).

24. Ellis (2021).

25. Mackey (2014).

26. Sarkissian (2023).

27. Singh and Vora (2023, 42).

28. Johns Hopkins University Press (accessed 2024).

29. Ginsberg (2011, 1).

30. Rhoades (1998).

31. Slaughter and Rhoades (2009, 12).

32. In fact, there were *seven* questions comprising this one sub-part, but because three of them concerned attendance I subsumed them under one heading and condensed them into one response: What are you doing to foster students' skills for the bar exam? How are you enforcing the attendance policy? How are you taking attendance? How are you responding to nonattendance? What are you doing to develop students' cross-cultural competency? What are you doing to develop students' awareness of bias and racism? What are you doing to develop students' professional identity?

33. *Woolley v Hoffman-LaRoche* 99 N.J. 284, 298 (1985).

34. Williams College (2021, 22) (emphasis added).

35. The University of Southern California (2022, 4-A) (emphasis added).

36. Vrchota et al (2024, 17) (emphasis added).

37. Appalachian State (2023, 3.9.2) (emphasis added).

38. George Mason University (2023, 2.3.1) (emphasis added).

39. Duke University (2019, 2–2) (emphasis added).

40. Some people don't believe this, of course. William Brown, for instance, asks why universities can't rely on expert headhunters who are free from the incentive effects that Carmichael describes. Brown (1997, 447). But this kind of response just shifts the focus of analysis from justifying tenure to justifying peer hiring. Whether peer hiring is truly necessary is a question worthy of a response, but it's no flaw in Carmichael's argument that he doesn't provide one in an article dedicated to another topic.

41. Carmichael (2006, 570). See also Carmichael (1988).

42. Duffy and Shaw (2000, 119–131); Agassi (1981).

43. Kahneman et al. (1991).

44. Along with his colleagues Hermann Schwind and Terry Wagar, my father, Hari Das, was a founding co-author of *Canadian Human Resources Management*, which is published by McGraw Hill (formerly McGraw-Hill Ryerson) and is now in its thirteenth edition. Since my father's death, *CHRM* has been led by Hermann, Terry, and one or more other co-authors. My father also wrote *Performance Management* (Prentice Hall, 2002) and *Recruitment, Selection and Deployment of Human Resources: A Canadian Perspective* (Pearson, 2006).

16 "THIS IMPORTANT SERVICE"

1. Bartlett (1983, 98).
2. Rosenthal (2011, 7).
3. Tiede (2015, 18).
4. Rosenthal (2011, 4).
5. Metzger (1990, 20).
6. Quoted in Metzger (1990, 25).
7. Metzger (1990, 27) ("the uncovering of discrepancies between AAC and AAUP positions should not obscure their large area of concurrence").
8. Metzger (1990, 68).
9. Metzger (1990, 68).
10. Metzger (1990, 74).
11. Metzger (1990, 75–76).
12. Tiede (2015, 2).
13. Tiede (2015, 2).
14. Metzger (1990, 50).
15. Metzger (1990, 50).
16. Shannon (1955, 397).
17. Kirkland (1955, 421).
18. Kirkland (1955, 420).
19. Shannon (1955, 405–06).
20. Metzger (1990, 71).
21. Kirkland (1955, 421).
22. Metzger (1990, 61–64).
23. Metzger (1990, 71).
24. Metzger (1990, 72).
25. Metzger (1990, 71).
26. Rosenthal (2011, 8).
27. Rosenthal (2011, 13).
28. Rosenthal (2011, 10) (internal citations omitted).
29. Rosenthal (2011, 13–14) (internal citations omitted).
30. Metzger (1990, 14).
31. Brubacher and Rudy (1997, 100).
32. Brubacher and Rudy (1997, 84–85 and 104–05).
33. Brubacher and Rudy (1997, 23).
34. Brubacher and Rudy (1997, 102).
35. Much is often made of the fact that Hopkins was built with unprepossessing buildings integrated into the city so well that "[i]t was not unusual for a student, coming from the first time, to pass by the university without recognizing it" and that "[e]ven local Baltimoreans were apt to confuse the university buildings with a piano factory!" (Brubacher and Rudy 1997, 179).
36. Brubacher and Rudy (1997, 178).
37. Indeed, the tension that played out at Yale over the course of the nineteenth century, between educational conservatism and educational experimentation, is hard to miss. On the one hand, the university was responsible for the infamous Yale Report of 1828, which was "probably the most influential publication in the whole history of American higher education between the Revolution and the Civil War" and offered "a thoroughgoing defense of the traditional American liberal-arts college" (Brubacher and Rudy 1997, 104).

On the other hand, Yale is widely considered to have granted the very first doctorate in the United States in 1861, fifteen years *before* Hopkins was founded (Brubacher and Rudy 1997, 195).

38. Brubacher and Rudy (1997, 179).
39. Brubacher and Rudy (1997, 179).
40. Brubacher and Rudy (1997, 181).
41. Brubacher and Rudy (1997, 181).
42. Brubacher and Rudy (1997, 179).
43. Brubacher and Rudy (1997, 189).
44. Brubacher and Rudy (1997, 190).
45. Brubacher and Rudy (1997, 188–190).
46. Geiger (2014, 322); Brubacher and Rudy (1997, 190).
47. Geiger (1986, Ch. 2)
48. James (1903)
49. Brubacher and Rudy (1997, 193).
50. Quoted in Brubacher and Rudy (1997, 424).
51. Brubacher and Rudy (1997, 424).

17 PMCS UNITE?

1. American Federation of Teachers (2023).
2. All the quotations in this paragraph come from Ehrenreich and Ehrenreich (2013).
3. See, e.g., Walkowitz (2003, xi).
4. Steffen (2021), at 1:39:50 ("It's a bit shocking that in the 900 pages of *Presumed Incompetent* there is one mention of unions and that's it. There is never a moment in any of these books where a faculty member sees a union as a resource or anything.").
5. NCSCBHEP (2023); NCSCBHEP (2024).
6. Herbert et al (2020, 8).
7. Berry and Savarese (2012, vi).
8. *NLRB v. Yeshiva University* (1980).
9. *Yeshiva University* at 702.
10. Public Employee Labor Relations Board (accessed 2023).
11. Berry and Savarese (2012, x).
12. Fuchs (2020).
13. Donoghue (2008).
14. Donoghue (2008, xxv).
15. Herbert et al (2020, 15).
16. Kezar et al (2019, 122–123).
17. Kezar et al (2019, 122–123).

18 JOBS… FOR LIFE?

1. Reichman (2023).
2. Fishman (2000, 163).
3. Sitze (2022).
4. O'Meara et al. (2022).
5. O'Meara et al. (2022).
6. O'Meara et al. (2022).

7. To be sure, not all job exits will reflect career growth: professors often change universities either because they are unhappy at their current institution or because it offers them limited opportunities for promotions and other forms of career growth. The degree to which either of these is a viable option differs greatly by discipline: my law school colleagues think voluntary job exits are a significant phenomenon that demand acknowledgment because there is a lot of lateral movement in academic law. My friends in anthropology or history departments generally laugh at the idea. It's not that it *never* happens in these fields – not at all. But the options are far fewer and, unless you're a superstar, far less likely to constitute an improvement on your current situation.
8. O'Meara et al. (2022).
9. Spoon et al. (2023).
10. O'Meara et al. (2022).
11. Wolff and Regan (2022).
12. American Association of University Professors, Tenure (2024).
13. When I needed to develop denominators I usually triangulated between multiple sources including but not limited to datasets like the National Center for Education Statistics, Fast Facts: Educational Institutions (2022).
14. Ray (2016) (offering other reasons why the stigma is nonsensical).

19 THEY SAID, THEY SAID

1. The usage transformation described in this paragraph, as well as the quotation from the *Tribune*, are taken from Safire (1998).
2. Shepherd (2018).
3. Leotta (2018).
4. Leachman (2013, 26).
5. See, e.g., Macaulay (2000) (describing the relationship between contractual agreements and the relationships they pertain to from a relational contract theory perspective).
6. The codes for these three types of Sexual Misconduct are as follows: *Inappropriate Relationships*: The faculty member engaged in inappropriate intimate relationships with students. This category consists *only* of consensual relationships with students above the age of majority. *Sexual Harassment*: The faculty member engaged in nonconsensual, *but* noncriminal, acts of a sexual or intimate nature. This category consists of those actions that would not normally result in criminal charges. *Sexual Assault*: The faculty member engaged in nonconsensual, *and* criminal, acts of a sexual or intimate nature. This category consists of (1) those actions that would normally – or did – result in criminal charges; and (2) actions that would otherwise fall into the *Inappropriate Relationships* category but for the victim's underage status.
7. Cantalupo and Kidder (2018, 676).
8. Kipnis (2015).
9. Johnson (2022, 709) ("Alford pleas are frequently used to resolve cases involving violent crimes. One study estimated that, from 2003 to 2004… 50% of defendants who took an Alford plea were incarcerated for violent crimes such as murder, assault, and sexual assault").
10. Bibas (2003, 1376).
11. Bibas (2003, 1377–78); Molesworth (2008, 907–08).
12. Chi-square = 122.14; d.f. = 5; $p < 0.001$.
13. Arnow-Richman (2010, 19).

14. Flood (2012, 6) ("Traditionally deferential to academia, courts have usually sided with institutional autonomy and have been reluctant to interfere with matters of academic concern."). See also *University of Missouri v. Horowitz* (1978) (noting that academic decisions demand "expert evaluation of cumulative information and [are] not readily adapted to the procedural tools of judicial or administrative decisionmaking"); *Okruhlik v. University of Arkansas* (2005) ("The academic setting and complex nature of tenure decisions… distinguishes them from employment decisions generally."); *Mawakana v. University of D.C.* (2018) (noting that courts are "required to accord great deference to an educational institution").
15. Chi-square = 7.24; d.f. = 1; $p < 0.05$.
16. Chi-square = 36.59; d.f. = 5; $p < 0.001$.
17. Muhs et al. (2012, 1).
18. Chi-square = 12.80; d.f. = 6; $p < 0.05$.

20 PUBLIC/PRIVATE

1. National Center for Education Statistics. 1949–50 through 2020–21 (January 2021). Public four-year institutions represented 33% of all four-year nonprofit institutions in 2019–2020 and fell to 32.6% in 2020–2021. At their lowest they represented 28.6% in 2000–2001.
2. *Cleveland Board of Education v. Loudermill* (1985).
3. *Woolley v. Hoffmann-La Roche* (1985).
4. The Supreme Court has established that *formal* tenure may not be required, but this doesn't mean that "tenure" isn't what's doing the work of entitling a public university professor to a pre-termination hearing. In *Perry v. Sindermann* (1972), the Court held that even though the public college where Professor Sindermann had taught for ten years did not have a formal tenure system, it had a *de facto* system – essentially, an organizational custom – of behaving as if it did grant tenure, and that consequently Sindermann was entitled to receive a pre-termination hearing.
5. Pooley (1973).
6. This rule was based on a pair of Supreme Court cases: *Pickering v. Board of Education* (1968) and *Connick v. Myers* (1983).
7. *Garcetti v. Ceballos* (2006).
8. *Garcetti v. Ceballos* (2006).
9. Roosevelt (2012, 631).
10. *Garrity v. New Jersey* (1967).
11. Fichtner and Simpson (2015, 28). See also *Gunasekera v. Irwin* (2009) (finding, in a dispute with a public university-employer, that "an employer's custom and practice can form the basis for a protected property interest").
12. Chi-square = 18.58; d.f. = 5; $p < 0.01$.
13. See, e.g., National Center for Education Statistics, Title IX Fast Facts (2024).
14. Employers are subject to Title VII if they have "fifteen or more employees for each working day in each of twenty or more calendar weeks in the current or preceding calendar year." Even the smallest colleges – institutions like Welch, Harvey Mudd, and Sweet Briar – clearly exceed this requirement. Welch College (2024); Harvey Mudd College (accessed 2024); Sweet Briar College (2024).
15. By contrast, the same numbers for private universities were 52.3% (Doctoral), 18.6% (Bachelor's), and 29.1% (Master's). Chi-square = 27.69; d.f. = 2; $p < 0.001$.
16. Silbert and Dubé (2021, 12) (finding that "faculty and deans in traditionally male-dominated disciplines score the highest pay").

21 IF I STAY IT WILL BE DOUBLE

1. Levitt (2007).
2. Weiss, FIRE calls on Augsburg (2019).
3. Adamo (2022).
4. Weiss, Update: Augsburg professor (2019).
5. Flaherty (2019). I say *by all publicly available accounts* because Augsburg's internal explanations seem to have consisted of a reference to "an unspecified 'range of issues' raised by students" in the suspension letter it sent to Adamo. Meanwhile, Augsburg's external explanations amounted to the following statement:

   > The actions the university took were *not* solely based on the use of the n-word in the classroom. The scenario involved a wide-ranging set of issues, which are confidential… The professor was not suspended for using the n-word in context in class. There is no ban on the use of any word in the classroom. Stein (2019) (quoting Augsburg spokesperson Rebecca John).

6. Augsburg University (2016).
7. Weiss, FIRE calls on Augsburg (2019).
8. Chi-square = 15.67; d.f. = 2; $p < 0.001$. Sexual Misconduct narratives dominated all three Carnegie high-level categories, but at significantly different rates: 61.9% (Bachelor's), 62.1% (Master's), and 81.8% (Doctoral). Similarly, Unprofessional Conduct narratives occupied the second place at all three levels of Carnegie classification, but at different levels: 28.6% (Bachelor's), 19.7% (Master's), and 8.9% (Doctoral). Chi-square = 32.56; d.f. = 10; $p < 0.01$.

22 RIFFED

1. American Association of University Professors, Recommended Institutional Regulations (2023).
2. American Association of University Professors, Financial Exigency (2004).
3. American Association of University Professors, Recommended Institutional Regulations (2023).
4. American Association of University Professors, Financial Exigency (2004).
5. Young and Kaufman (1983).
6. American Association of University Professors, Financial Exigency (2004).
7. Kezar et al. (2019).
8. Merry (2016).
9. The thirteen institutions reflected in this statement are: Manhattan College, Henderson State, Dickinson State, Emporia State, Akron, West Virginia, Wright State, Canisius, Saint Rose, PASSHE (the Pennsylvania State System of Higher Education), SUNY-Potsdam, Christian Brothers, and New Jersey City. To the best of my knowledge, all the faculty terminations at these schools that are included in my calculations were of *tenured* professors – many of the schools also terminated (that is, *did not renew*) pretenure or NTT professors, who were not included in my calculations. Despite my best efforts to verify institutional practices and specific events, it's possible that one or more of these institutions should not be included in this list because they do not offer tenure to anyone or have not terminated any tenured professors since 2020. Still, the relative ease of finding *other* universities that have also terminated tenured faculty, especially since 2020, means that my broader claim about job loss due to RIFs versus job loss due to individual for-cause termination is likely unaffected.
10. Doe and Shulman (2024).

11. Ginsberg (2011); Kezar et al. (2019, 73).
12. Bousquet (2003, 135). See also Bousquet and Nelson (2008).
13. Again, stronger tenure wouldn't have directly affected Matt inasmuch as he quit voluntarily because of the overall change in his workplace environment. But stronger tenure *would* have affected that workplace environment.
14. The aftermath of the West Virginia University RIF of 2023, which is among the largest recent RIFs in a string of such events, directly impacted dozens of professors: 143 faculty were eliminated of which dozens included tenure-stream professors. But several more faculty, including many tenure-stream (and specifically *tenured*) professors, chose to leave WVU, much like Matt Dickson chose to leave his university. At WVU's College of Law, for instance, six professors announced in Spring 2024 that they were voluntarily leaving their jobs. Joshua Weishart, a tenured full professor and named-chair, was one of them. "We were not planning to leave," he said of himself and his departing colleagues, "and that's disappointing. [But] I feel like my hand was forced" (Jones 2024).

23 SO WHAT?

1. Kezar (2012, xii).
2. Kezar et al. (2019, 99).
3. Ran & Xu (2019, 1095–1098).
4. Bettinger and Long (2005, 2).
5. Ehrenberg and Zhang (2005).
6. Kezar et al. (2019, 114).
7. Parker et al. (2016, 77–78).
8. Binday (2023). Arguably, Karikó's troubled NTT relationship with Penn suggests what might be lost if we do not afford academics the job security to pursue high-risk, high-reward research.
9. National Institutes of Health (2006).
10. Jeong (2021).
11. Lemelson-MIT (accessed 2024).
12. Deubert (2023).
13. Canadian Broadcasting Corporation (2019) (describing antiracism); Taylor (2023) (describing antiracism's broad influence, as well as some of its – and Kendi's – recent struggles).
14. Graber (2012) (identifying Bork as the "original originalist"); Solum (2011) (identifying Brest as the inventor of the term); Das Acevedo (2024) (discussing Originalism's current prominence).
15. Crenshaw (1989); UCLA School of Law (2019); Colfer et al. (2018).
16. For a similar plea, with supporting (if very slightly outdated) statistics, see American Association of University Professors, Tenure and Teaching-Intensive Appointments (2024).
17. Doe and Shulman (2024, 87).
18. Doe and Shulman (2024, 88).
19. Doe and Shulman (2024, 90).
20. Readers should note that Doe and Shulman define "instructional revenue" – the inflow component of instructional surplus – to include both tuition/fees and government subsidies that "are meant to subsidize students and cover operating costs" (Doe and Shulman 2024, 90).

21. Hurlburt and McGarrah (2017a); Hurlburt and McGarrah (2017b). The Project was a collaborative venture between the American Institutes for Research, a nonprofit social science research organization, and the Teachers Insurance and Annuity Association of America Institute, which is the research wing of a nonprofit provider of retirement benefits to academics and other workers. See also the summary of the reports in Jaschik (2017).
22. National Center for Education Statistics, Price of Attending (2024).

24 TENURE 2.0

1. Boldt (2014).
2. Fishman (2000, 202).
3. Das Acevedo (2018).
4. *See e.g.*, Leachman (2013) (noting that the "primary task" of this body of scholarship "is to understand how, and the extent to which, law comes to constitute the underlying vocabulary, concepts, values, and meanings that movement actors draw on in their quest for social change").
5. American Association of University Professors, Tenure (2024).
6. Jaschik (2020) (quoting Henry Reichman).
7. Wilkins and Gulati (1998, 1659).
8. Bérubé and Ruth (2015, 142–148); Bérubé (2015); Bousquet and Nelson (2008).
9. Bessette (2015).
10. Pittman (2023) (making a similar point about diversity and awarding tenure).
11. See my comments on spousal versus partner hiring in earlier notes.
12. All the data cited in this paragraph, as well as the quotations, come from Schiebinger et al. (2008, 4–5).
13. American Association of University Professors (2022).
14. American Association of University Professors (2022).
15. Neal (2008).
16. Neal (2008).
17. Cohan (2023).

CONCLUSION

1. Boldt (2014).

APPENDIX A

1. Das Acevedo, The War on Tenure (2023).
2. One individual categorized in the dataset as "fired" has since been reinstated to his faculty position pursuant to a union grievance process. Another individual categorized as "still employed" (and therefore excluded from the tenured-terminations dataset) has since been fired. These 2022 developments are not reflected in the dataset or related analysis because the study period closed at the end of 2021. Both incidents, coincidentally, involved faculty counternarratives of Academic Freedom.
3. Cantalupo and Kidder (2018); Flood (2012).
4. The University of North Carolina at Chapel Hill (accessed 2022).
5. Libarkin (accessed 2022); Fire (accessed 2022).

6. The PA for "Event Year" (72.41%) was likely low due to a peculiarity in the data: Timing information for the event that prompted the employment dispute was not always available, was not clear, or was not easily coded. For instance, in many instances where the faculty member was accused of sexual misconduct, no single year was discoverable or no single year was relevant because the misconduct spanned several years. In these circumstances, "Event Year" was coded as the year the employment relationship ended, but this process likely produced lower overall congruence for this variable. Given its low PA score, "Event Year" has not been included in further analysis although I later recoded for this variable in 2023.
7. Graham et al. (2012) (noting that for percent agreement "values from 75% to 90% demonstrate an acceptable level of agreement").
8. The PA for "Age" (82.76%) was likely low because, during verification, I discovered age information for several entries that had previously been marked as "unknown." These were counted as disagreements for the purposes of reliability analysis, but they do not actually reflect conflicting assessments of a static source.
9. Since 1970, the Carnegie Classification® has been the most prominent categorization system for higher education institutions in the United States. The Carnegie system is periodically updated and its categories change; I have assigned Carnegie rankings based on the categories and institutional rankings used in 2021–2022.
10. *Bostock v. Clayton County* (2020).
11. 490 U.S. 228, 235 (1989)
12. No. 13-CV-82, 2013 WL 3288398, at *1 (S.D. Ohio, 2013).

Abbott, Andrew. *The System of Professions: An Essay on the Division of Expert Labor*. Chicago: University of Chicago Press, 2014.

Abrams, Roger I. and Nolan, Dennis R. Toward a Theory of 'Just Cause' in Employee Discipline Cases. *Duke Law Journal*, Vol. 1985, No. 3/4 (1985): 594–623.

Aczel, Balazs, Szaszi, Barnabas, and Holcombe, Alex O. A Billion-Dollar Donation: Estimating the Cost of Researchers' Time Spent on Peer Review. *Research Integrity & Peer Review*, Vol. 6, No. 14 (2021): 1–8. https://doi.org/10.1186/s41073-021-00118-2.

Adamo, Phillip C. *Phil Adamo.com: Curriculum Vitae* (2022). https://philadamo.com/curriculum-vitae.

Adams, Susan. The Least Stressful Jobs of 2013. *Forbes* (January 3, 2013). www.forbes.com/sites/susanadams/2013/01/03/the-least-stressful-jobs-of-2013/?sh=5c0dac406e24.

Adams, Tracey L. Sociology of Professions: International Divergences and Research Direction. *Work, Employment & Society*, Vol. 29, No. 1 (2015): 154–165.

Agassi, Joseph. Cultural Lag in Science. *Science and Society: Boston Studies in the Philosophy of Science*, Vol. 65 (1981): 119–131. https://link.springer.com/chapter/10.1007/978-94-011-6456-6_10.

American Association of University Professors. Financial Exigency, Academic Governance, and Related Matters. *aaup.org* (2004). www.aaup.org/AAUP/comm/rep/finexg.htm#b4.

American Association of University Professors. Recommended Institutional Regulations on Academic Freedom and Tenure. *AAUP Reports and Publications* (2023). www.aaup.org/report/recommended-institutional-regulations-academic-freedom-and-tenure.

American Association of University Professors. Tenure. *aaup.org* (2024). www.aaup.org/sites/default/files/AAUP_tenure_1.pdf.

American Association of University Professors. Tenure and Teaching-Intensive Appointments. *AAUP Reports and Publications* (2024). www.aaup.org/report/tenure-and-teaching-intensive-appointments.

American Association of University Professors. The 2022 AAUP Survey of Tenure Practices. *AAUP Reports and Publications* (May 2022). www.aaup.org/report/2022-aaup-survey-tenure-practices.

American Bar Association. *Schools by State*. www.americanbar.org/groups/center-pro-bono/resources/directory_of_law_school_public_interest_pro_bono_programs/schools_by_state/ (accessed July 29, 2024).

American Federation of Teachers. An Army of Temps: AFT Contingent Faculty Quality of Work/Life Report 2022, *aft.org* (2023).

ANA Enterprise. Advanced Practice Registered Nurse (APRN) (accessed 2024). www.nursingworld.org/practice-policy/workforce/what-is-nursing/aprn/.

Andalib, Maryam A., Ghaffarzadegan, Navid, and Larson, Richard C. The Postdoc Queue: A Labour Force in Waiting. *Systems Research and Behavioral*, Vol. 35, No. 6 (November/December 2018): 675–686.

Andrias, Kate and Hertel-Fernandez, Alexander. Ending At-Will Employment: A Guide. New York: *Roosevelt Institute* (2021). https://rooseveltinstitute.org/publications/ending-at-will-employment-a-guide-for-just-cause-reform/.

Anonymous. Why I'm Planning to Leave My Ph.D. Program: My family Can't Live on $17,000 a Year. *Chronicle of Higher Education* (August 22, 2022).

Appalachian State University. Appalachian State Faculty Handbook (September 27, 2023). https://facultyhandbook.appstate.edu/.

Arnow-Richman, Rachel. Just Notice: Re-reforming Employment At-Will. *UCLA Law Review*, Vol. 58 (2010): 1–72.

Arnow-Richman, Rachel. Of Power and Process: Handling Harassers in an At-Will World. *Yale Law Journal Forum*, Vol. 128 (2018–2019). www.yalelawjournal.org/forum/of-power-and-process.

Athanasiades, Christina, Stamovlasis, Dimitrios, Touloupis, Thanos, and Charalambous, Hara. University Students' Experiences of Sexual Harassment: The Role of Gender and Psychological Resilience. *Frontiers in Psychology*, Vol. 14 (July 13, 2023).

Atlanta Bar Association. 100% Firms. https://atlantabar.org/?pg=100PercentFirms (last accessed 2023).

Attorney Registration & Disciplinary Commission of the Supreme Court of Illinois. Overview of ARDC (accessed 2024). www.iardc.org/About.

Augsburg University. Star Tribune Profiles Augsburg History Professor Phil Adamo. *Augsburg University News and Media*. (March 20, 2016). www.augsburg.edu/news/2016/03/30/star-tribune-2/.

Barrow, Clyde W. Realpolitik in the American University: Charles A. Beard and the Problem of Academic Repression. *New Political Science*, Vol. 36, No. 4 (2014): 438–458.

Barry, Ellen. Moving in Childhood Contributes to Depression, Study Finds. New York Times (July 17, 2024).

Barshay, Jill. Nearly Half of Parents Don't Want Their Kids to go Straight to a Four-Year College. *The Hechinger Report* (April 7, 2021). https://hechingerreport.org/poll-nearly-half-of-parents-dont-want-their-kids-to-go-to-a-four-year-college/.

Bartlett, Paul D. James Bryant Conant: 1893–1978: A Biographical Memoir. National Academy of Sciences (1983).

Bartram, Erin. The Sublimated Grief of the Left Behind. *erinbartram.com* (February 11, 2018). http://erinbartram.com/uncategorized/the-sublimated-grief-of-the-left-behind/.

Baucher, Ellen. It's Time to Ditch Our Deadlines: Why You Should Stop Penalizing Your Students for Submitting Work Late. *Chronicle of Higher Education* (September 16, 2016).

Bauer-Wolf, Jeremy. College Presidents Are Still Overwhelmingly White Men. *Higher Ed Dive* (April 14, 2023). www.highereddive.com/news/college-presidents-are-still-overwhelmingly-white-men/647749/.

Bauerlein, Mark. Diminishing Returns in Humanities Research. *Chronicle of Higher Education*, Vol. 55, No. 42, (July 24, 2009).

Baum, Sandy and Looney, Adam. Who owes the most in student loans: New data from the Fed. Brookings (October 9, 2020). www.brookings.edu/articles/who-owes-the-most-in-student-loans-new-data-from-the-fed/.

Beam, Christopher. The case for getting rid of tenure. *Slate* (August 11, 2010). https://slate.com/news-and-politics/2010/08/the-case-for-getting-rid-of-tenure.html.

Beauboeuf-Lafontant, Tamara, Erickson, Karla A., and Thomas, Jan E. Rethinking Post-Tenure Malaise: An Interactional, Pathways Approach to Understanding the Post-Tenure Period. *The Journal of Higher Education*, Vol. 90, No. 4 (January 4, 2019): 644–664.

Beauboeuf, Tamara, Thomas, Jan E., and Erickson, Karla A. Our Fixation on Midcareer Malaise. *Chronicle of Higher Education* (March 15, 2017). www.chronicle.com/article/Our-Fixation-on-Midcareer/239476.

Bellows, Kate Hidalgo. A Tenured Professor Was Removed from the Classroom over a Pro-palestine Essay. *Chronicle of Higher Education* (April 15, 2024). www.chronicle.com/article/a-tenured-professor-was-removed-from-the-classroom-over-a-pro-palestine-essay.

Bergquist, Harold E. The Edward, W. Bemis Controversy at the University of Chicago. *AAUP Bulletin*, Vol. 58, No. 4 (1972).

Berry, Joe and Savarese, Michelle. Directory of U.S. Faculty Contracts and Bargaining Agents in Institutions of Higher Education. *National Center for the Study of Collective Bargaining in Higher Education and the Professions* (September 2012).

Bérubé, Michael and Ruth, Jennifer. *The Humanities, Higher Education, and Academic Freedom: Three Necessary Arguments*. London: Palgrave Macmillan, 2015.

Bérubé, Michael. New Model of Tenure. *InsideHigherEd* (March 9, 2015). www.InsideHigherEd.com/views/2015/03/10/essay-calling-new-teaching-oriented-model-tenure.

Bessette, Lee Skallerup. The Teaching Track. *InsideHigherEd* (June 2, 2015). www.InsideHigherEd.com/blogs/college-ready-writing/teaching-track.

Bettinger, Eric, and Long, Bridget Terry. Help or Hinder? Adjunct Professors and Student Outcomes. *National Bureau of Economic Research* (May 2005). https://archive.ilr.cornell.edu/sites/default/files/Help%20or%20Hinder%20Adjunct%20Professors%20and%20Student%20Outcomes.pdf.

Bhagyoday, Sandip. "Create high quality biodata for marriage to get faster response." *Fiverr* (accessed June 18, 2024).

Bibas, Stephanos. Harmonizing Substantive-Criminal-Law Values and Criminal Procedure: The Case of Alford and Nolo Contendere Pleas. *Cornell Law Review*, Vol. 88, No. 5 (July 2003): 1361–1411.

Binday, Ben. 'Not of faculty quality': How Penn mistreated Nobel Prize-winning researcher Katalin Karikó. *Daily Pennsylvanian* (October 26, 2023). www.thedp.com/article/2023/10/penn-katalin-kariko-university-relationship-mistreatment.

Bird, Sharon R., Litt, Jacquelyn, and Wang, Yong. Creating Status of Women Reports: Institutional Housekeeping as "Women's Work." *NWSA Journal*, Vol. 16, No. 1 (2004): 194–206.

Blackburn, Robert T. and Lawrence, Janet H. Aging and the Quality of Faculty Job Performance, *Review of Educational Research*, Vol. 56, No. 3 (Autumn 1986): 265–290.

Board of Governors of the Federal Reserve System. Economic Well-Being of U.S. Households in 2020 (May 2021).

Boldt, Josh. 99 Problems but Tenure Ain't One. *Chronicle of Higher Education* (January 21, 2014). www.chronicle.com/article/99-problems-but-tenure-aint-one.

Bondestam, Fredrik and Lundqvist, Maja. Sexual Harassment in Higher Education – A Systematic Review. *European Journal of Higher Education*, Vol. 10, No.4 (2020): 397–419.

Bousquet, Marc. The Waste Product of Graduate Education: Toward a Dictatorship of the Flexible. *Works and Days*, Vol. 21, Nos.1 & 2 (2003): 129–152.

Bousquet, Marc and Nelson, Cary. *How the University Works: Higher Education and the Low-Wage Nation*. New York: NYU Press (2008).

Brenan, Megan. Americans' Confidence in Higher Education Down Sharply. *Gallup* (July 11, 2023). https://news.gallup.com/poll/508352/americans-confidence-higher-education-down-sharply.aspx.

Brown Jr., Ralph S. and Finkin, Matthew W. The Usefulness of AAUP Policy Statements. *AAUP Bulletin*, Vol. 64, No. 1 (March 1978): 5–11.

Brown Jr., William O. University Governance and Academic Tenure: A Property Rights Explanation. *Journal of Institutional and Theoretical Economics*, Vol. 153, No. 3 (September 1997): 441–461.

Brown, H. Claire. They Quit Their Jobs. Their Ex-employers Sued Them for Training Costs. *New York Times* (September 27, 2023). www.nytimes.com/2023/09/27/business/training-repayment-agreement-debt.html

Brubacher, John S. and Willis, Rudy. *Higher Education in Transition: A History of American Colleges and Universities, Fourth Edition*. New Brunswick: Transaction Publishers, 1997.

Buck, Jane L. Why Ask If Tenure Is Necessary? *Behavioral and Brain Sciences*, Vol. 29, No. 6 (2006): 570.

Bui, Quoctrung and Miller, Claire Cain. The Typical American Lives Only 18 Miles from Mom. *New York Times* (December 23, 2015). www.nytimes.com/interactive/2015/12/24/upshot/24up-family.html?searchResultPosition=2.

Bullens, Lara. Gender-based violence in French universities: 'I decided something had to change.' *France 24* (November 11, 2023). www.france24.com/en/france/20231125-gender-based-violence-in-french-universities-i-decided-something-had-to-change.

Burgos, Russ. On Foregone Earning, or the Economics of Adjunct Life (A Guest Post). *The Professor Is In* (June 8, 2015). https://theprofessorisin.com/2015/06/08/on-foregone-earnings-or-the-economics-of-adjunct-life-a-guest-post/.

Burkhalter, Nancy. Why Your College Professor May Be on the Edge of Poverty. *Cascade PBS* (September 5, 2016). https://crosscut.com/2016/09/adjunct-professors-poverty-no-benefits-opinion-seattle-university.

Butler, Edgar W., McAllister, Ronald J., and Kaiser, Edward J. The Effects of Voluntary and Involuntary Residential Mobility on Females and Males, *Journal of Marriage and Family*, Vol. 35, No. 2 (1973): 219–227.

Butler, Judith. Further Reflections on Conversations of Our Time. *Diacritics*, Vol. 27, No. 1 (1997): 13–15.

Caballero, Cecilia. Paying the Price: The Costs of Academia for First-Gen BIPOC Scholars. *The Professor Is In* (April 8, 2022). https://theprofessorisin.com/2022/04/08/paying-the-price-the-costs-of-academia-for-first-gen-bipoc-scholars/.

California Architect Board. Becoming an Architect (accessed on July 29, 2024). www.cab.ca.gov/candidates/becoming_a_licensed_architect/.

The California State University. Salary Schedule: Fiscal Year 2023/2024 (2023)

Canadian Broadcasting Corporation. Ibram X. Kendi says we are either being racist or antiracist, there is no middle ground. *Out in the Open* (February 15, 2019). www.cbc.ca/radio/outintheopen/ibram-x-kendi-says-we-are-either-being-racist-or-antiracist-there-is-no-middle-ground-1.5350278.

Cantalupo, Nancy Chi and Kidder, William C. A Systematic Look at a Serial Problem: Sexual Harassment of Students by University Faculty. *Utah Law Review*, Vol. 2018, No. 3 (2018): 671–786.

Caplan, Lincoln. Rhetoric and Law. *Harvard Magazine* (January–February 2016). www.harvardmagazine.com/2015/12/rhetoric-and-law.

Carmichael, H. Lorne. The Economic Justification for Academic Tenure. *Behavioral and Brain Sciences*, Vol. 29, No. 6 (2006): 571–572.

Carmichael, H. Lorne. Incentives in Academics: Why Is There Tenure? *Journal of Political Economy*, Vol. 96, No. 3 (1988): 453–472.

Carroll, Aaron E. "Why Doctors Aren't Going into Pediatrics." *New York Times* (July 1, 2024). www.nytimes.com/2024/07/01/opinion/pediatrician-shortage.html.

Ceci, Stephen J., Williams, Wendy M. and Mueller-Johnson, Katrin. Is Tenure Justified? An Experimental Study of Faculty Beliefs about Tenure, Promotion, and Academic Freedom, *Behavioral and Brain Sciences*, Vol. 29, No. 6 (2006): 553–594.

Childress, Herb. *The Adjunct Underclass: How America's Colleges Betrayed Their Faculty, Their Students, and Their Mission.* United Kingdom: University of Chicago Press (2019).

Chilton, Adam, Masur, Jonathan S. and Rozema, Kyle. Rethinking Law School Tenure Standards, *Journal of Legal Studies*, Vol. 50 (2021): 1–34.

Chung, Michael B. The Mid-Career Void: Understanding the Path from Associate to Full Professor. EdD dissertation, University of Southern California (August 2018).

Cohan, Deborah J. The Tenure and Promotion Process, Reimagined. *InsideHigherEd* (March 16, 2023). www.InsideHigherEd.com/advice/2023/03/17/making-tenure-and-promotion-process-more-productive-opinion.

Colfer, Carol J. Pierce, Basnett, Bimbika Sijapati, and Ihalainen, Markus. Making sense of "intersectionality": A manual for lovers of people and forests. *Center for International Forestry Research Occasional Paper 184* (2018). www.cifor-icraf.org/publications/pdf_files/OccPapers/OP-184.pdf.

Columbia Law School Office of Financial Aid. J.D. and LL.M. Tuition and Fees. www.law.columbia.edu/about/departments/financial-aid/jd-and-llm-tuition-and-fees (accessed February 16, 2024).

Columbia University Graduate School of Arts and Sciences. Cost of Attendance. www.gsas.columbia.edu/content/cost-attendance (accessed February 16, 2024).

Conn, Patsy. Atlanta's 50 Largest Law Firms Ranked by Number of Attorneys in Atlanta. *Atlanta Business Chronicle* (Updated November 2023). www.bizjournals.com/atlanta/subscriber-only/2021/01/15/atlantas-50-largest-law-firms.html?s=print.

Cornell University Graduate School. Present Your Key Skills to an Employer (accessed 2024). https://gradschool.cornell.edu/career-and-professional-development/pathways-to-success/prepare-for-your-career/understand-yourself/present-your-key-skills-to-an-employer/.

Coulson, Garth. At-Will Employment. *Betterteam.com* (updated January 20, 2021). www.betterteam.com/at-will-employment

Crenshaw, Kimberlé. Demarginalizing the Intersection of Race and Sex: A Black Feminist Critique of Antidiscrimination Doctrine, Feminist Theory and Antiracist Politics. *University of Chicago Legal Forum*, Vol. 1989, No. 1 (1989): 139–167.

Cuff, Andrew Jacob. An Academic Lottery or a Meritocracy? *InsideHigherEd.* (May 2, 2017). www.InsideHigherEd.com/advice/2017/05/03/phds-need-real-data-how-potential-employers-make-hiring-decisions-essay

Curcic, Dimitrije. Number of Academic Papers Published Per Year, *WordsRated.com* (June 1, 2023). https://wordsrated.com/number-of-academic-papers-published-per-year/

Das Acevedo, Deepa. From Mythic Saviors to #MeToo at the Indian Supreme Court. *Asian Journal of Law and Society*, Vol. 8, No. 2 (2021): 226–254.

Das Acevedo, Deepa. Tenure as a Labor Protection. *Employee Rights and Employment Policy Journal*, Vol. 26, No. 2 (2023): 109–143.

Das Acevedo, Deepa. The Past as a Colonialist Resource, *Duke Law Journal*, Vol. 73, No. 7 (2024): 1373–1436.

Das Acevedo, Deepa. The War on Tenure. *Tennessee Law Review*, Vol. 91, No. 1 (2023): 1–52.

Das Acevedo, Deepa. Unbundling Freedom in the Sharing Economy. *Southern California Law Review*, Vol. 91, No. 5 (2018): 793–838.

Dean, Tim. How we edit science part 2: Significance testing, p-hacking and peer review. *The Conversation* (March 20, 2017). https://theconversation.com/how-we-edit-science-part-2-significance-testing-p-hacking-and-peer-review-74547.

Department of Consumer and Worker Protection. *Fair WorkWeek Law in Fast Food: Frequently Asked Questions.* (September 15, 2023).

DeSimone, Danielle. Over 200 Years of Service: The History of Women in the U.S. Military. *United Services Organization* (February 28, 2023).

Deubert, Christopher. Congress Embraces "Nudge Theory" in 401(k) Changes. *Constangy, Brooks, Smith & Prophete LLP* (January 5, 2023). www.constangy.com/employment-labor-insider/congress-embraces-nudge-theory-in-401-k-changes.

Dixon, Helen and Tervanotko, Hanna. How Do Tenure-Track Professors Really Spend Their Work Time? *Chronicle of Higher Education* (December 14, 2021).

Doe, Sue and Shulman, Steven. Contingency across Higher Education, in *Contingent Faculty and the Remaking of Higher Education: A Labor History*, edited by Eric Fure-Slocum and Claire Goldstene (Urbana: University of Illinois Press, 2024): 83–103.

Dominus, Susan. When the Revolution Came for Amy Cuddy. *New York Times* (October 18, 2017).

Donoghue, Frank. *The Last Professors: The Corporate University and the Fate of the Humanities.* New York: Fordham University Press (2008).

Dow, Neal. Terminal Associate Professors, Past and Present: Why Do Some Academics Stall at Midcareer? *Chronicle of Higher Education* (March 26, 2014).

Dreger, Alice. Alice Dreger's Letter of Resignation at Northwestern, *Academe* (August 25, 2015). https://academeblog.org/2015/08/25/alice-dregers-letter-of-resignation-at-northwestern/.

Duffy, M. K. and Shaw, J. D. The Salieri Syndrome: Consequences of Envy in Groups. *Small Group Research*, 31, No. 1 (2000): 3–23

Duke University. *The Duke University Faculty Handbook* (2019).

Dutton, Denis. Language Crimes: A Lesson in How Not to Write, Courtesy of the Professors. *Wall Street Journal* W11. Print (February 2, 1999).

Ehrenberg, Ronald G. and Zhang, Liang. Do Tenured and Tenure-Track Faculty Matter? *Journal of Human Resources*, Vol. 40, No. 3 (2005): 647–659.

Ehrenreich, Barbara and Ehrenreich, John. *Death of a Yuppie Dream.* Rosa Luxemburg Stiftung New York Office (February 2013).

Ellis, Lindsay. Behind Nikole Hannah-Jones's Tenure Case. *Chronicle of Higher Education* (May 21, 2021).

Elon University, *Using Structure for Inclusive Teaching*, Elon University Center for the Advancement of Teaching & Learning (accessed 2024).

Emanuel, Sarah. The Deflating Reality of Life on the Tenure Track – Walking Dogs Helps Me Make Rent. *Chronicle of Higher Education* (January 18, 2022). www.chronicle.com/article/the-deflating-reality-of-life-on-the-tenure-track.

Emmons, William, Kent, Ana and Ricketts, Lowell. "Is College Still Worth It? The New Calculus of Falling Returns," *Federal Reserve Bank of St. Louis Review*, Vol. 101, No. 4 (2019): 300–303.

Emory University. Emory Law Faculty Handbook (2017). https://provost.emory.edu/faculty/policies-guidelines/handbook/index.html.

Eyal, Gil. *The Crisis of Expertise.* Cambridge: Polity Press (2019).

Farley, David. In Defense of Spousal Hiring. *Chronicle of Higher Education* (April 27, 2007).

Farley, Frank. The Untouchables: Benefits, Costs, and Risks of Tenure in Real Cases. *Behavioral and Brain Sciences*, Vol. 29, No. 6 (2006): 574–575.

Ferber, Marianne A. and Loeb, Jane W. *Academic Couples: Problems and Promises.* Urbana and Chicago: University of Illinois Press (1997).

Fichtner, J. Royce and Simpson, Lou Ann. Trimming the Deadwood: Removing Tenured Faculty for Cause. *Journal of College and University Law*, Vol. 41, No. 1 (2015): 25–44.

Fire. About Us (accessed January 27, 2022). www.thefire.org/about-us.

Fishman, James J. Tenure and Its Discontents: The Worst Form of Employment Relationship Save All of the Others. *Pace Law Review*, Vol. 21 (2000): 159–202.

Flaherty, Colleen. Chatham University Expected to Adopt a Tenure System Again. *InsideHigherEd.* (February 16, 2022). www.InsideHigherEd.com/print/news/2022/02/16/chatham-u-expected-adopt-tenuresystem-Again.

Flaherty, Colleen. Dream Grant. *InsideHigherEd.* (October 11, 2021a). www.InsideHigherEd.com/news/2021/10/11/first-they-got-tenure-then-they-got-100k.

Flaherty, Colleen. Ole Miss Settles with Professor. *InsideHigherEd.* (July 29, 2021b). www.InsideHigherEd.com/news/2021/07/30/ole-miss-settles-professor.

Flaherty, Colleen. Too Taboo for Class? *InsideHigherEd.* (January 31, 2019). www.InsideHigherEd.com/news/2019/02/01/professor-suspended-using-n-word-class-discussion-language-james-baldwin-essay.

Flaherty, Colleen. A Non-Tenure-Track Profession? *InsideHigherEd.* (October 11, 2018). www.InsideHigherEd.com/news/2018/10/12/about-three-quarters-all-faculty-positions-are-tenure-track-according-new-aaup.

Flannery, Mary Ellen. "We Stepped Up and Fought Back": Behind the Explosive Growth of New Faculty Unions. *National Education Association Today* (November 29, 2020).

Flood, Julee Tate. Judicial Influence on Academic Decision-Making: A Study of Tenure Denial Litigation Cases in Which Higher Education Institutions Did Not Wholly Prevail. PhD dissertation, University of Tennessee (May 2012).

Forsythe, Eliza. Careers within Firms: Occupational Mobility over the Lifecycle. *Labour*, Vol. 33, No. 3 (2019): 241–277.

Fuchs, Sandhya. The Gift of a Bicultural Upbringing, *Sapiens* (January 10, 2020). www.sapiens.org/culture/anthropologist-parents/.

Fuller, Steve. American Ambivalence toward Academic Freedom. *Behavioral and Brain Sciences*, Vol. 29, No. 6 (2006): 577–578.

Gannon, Emma. Being a multi-hyphenate is not about hustle culture, and its not about multitasking. *Vogue India* (April 20, 2021).

Gannon, Emma. *The Multi-hyphen Life: Work Less, Create More, and Design a Life That Works for You.* Kansas City: Andrews McMeel Publishing (2020).

Geertz, Clifford. *The Interpretation of Cultures.* New York: Basic Books (1973).

Geiger, Roger L. *The History of American Higher Education: Learning and Culture from the Founding to World War II.* Princeton: Princeton University Press (2014).

Geiger, Roger L. *To Advance Knowledge: The Growth of American Research Universities, 1900–1940.* London and New York: Taylor & Francis (1986).

George Mason University. George Mason University Faculty Handbook (July 1, 2023). https://provost.gmu.edu/faculty/policies-and-guidelines.

Georgetown Law. Atlanta Legal Market (accessed 2024). www.law.georgetown.edu/your-life-career/career-exploration-professional-development/for-jd-students/explore-legal-careers/legal-markets/atlanta-legal-market/.

Georgia Secretary of State Brad Raffensperger. About the Georgia State Board of Architects and Interior Designers (accessed 2024). https://sos.ga.gov/page/about-board-architects-interior-designers.

Georgia Secretary of State Brad Raffensperger. About the Georgia State Board of Cosmetology and Barbers (accessed 2024). https://sos.ga.gov/page/about-georgia-state-board-cosmetology-and-barbers.

Gersen, Jeannie Suk. Academic Freedom and Discrimination in a Polarizing Time, *Houston Law Review*, Vol. 59, No. 4 (2022): 781–801.

Ghosh, Debaleena and Barber, Kristen. The Gender of Multiculturalism: Cultural Tokenism and the Institutional Isolation of Immigrant Women Faculty. *Sociological Perspectives*, Vol. 64, No. 6 (2021): 1063–1080.

Ginsberg, Benjamin. *The Fall of the Faculty*. Oxford and New York: Oxford University Press (2011).

Goodman, Peter. The Real Reason America Doesn't Have Enough Truck Drivers. *New York Times* (February 9, 2022). www.nytimes.com/2022/02/09/business/truck-driver-shortage.html.

Gorman, Elizabeth H. and Sandefur, Rebecca L. "Golden Age," Quiescence, and How the Sociology of Professions Became the Study of Knowledge-Based Work. *Work and Occupations*, Vol. 38, No. 3 (2011): 275–302.

Graber, Mark A. Robert Bork, the original originalist. *Baltimore Sun* (December 24, 2012). https://www.baltimoresun.com/2012/12/24/robert-bork-the-original-originalist/.

Graham, Matthew, Milanowski, Anthony, and Miller, Jackson. Measuring and Promoting Inter-Rater Agreement of Teacher and Principal Performance Ratings. *Center for Education Compensation Reform* (February 2012).

Grisard, Claudine. Time, workload model and the entrepreneurial construction of the neoliberal academic. *Critical Perspectives on Accounting*, Vol. 96 (2023): DOI: 10.1016/j.cpa.2023.102553.

Guarino, Cassandra M. and Borden, Victor M. H. Faculty Service Loads and Gender: Are Women Taking Care of the Academic Family? *Research in Higher Education*, Vol. 58, No. 6 (2017): 672–694.

Guzman, Gloria and Kollar, Melissa. Income in the United States: 2022. United States Census Bureau (September 12, 2023). www.census.gov/library/publications/2023/demo/p60-279.html.

Hallock, Kevin F. Seniority and Monopsony in the Academic Labor Market: Comment. *American Economic Review*, Vol. 85, No.3 (1995): 654–657.

Hanson, Melanie. Average Graduate Student Loan Debt. Education Data Initiative (September 1, 2024). https://educationdata.org/average-graduate-student-loan-debt.

Harvard University. Multihyphenate, *Harvard Design Magazine*, Vol. 51, Fall/Winter (2023).

Harvey Mudd College, Fast Facts: Harvey Mudd College (accessed April 30, 2024). www.hmc.edu/about/facts/.

The Haynesville Project. James A. Tinsley: Early Years (accessed 2024). www.thehaynesvilleproject.org/history.

Helfand, David J. Tenure: Thanks but No Thanks. *Chronicle of Higher Education* (December 15, 1995). www.chronicle.com/article/tenure-thanks-but-no-thanks/.

Herbert, William A., Apkarian, Jacob, and van der Naald, Joseph. Supplemental Directory of New Bargaining Agents and Contracts in Institutions of Higher Education, 2013–2019. National Center for the Study of Collective Bargaining in Higher Education and the Professions (November 2020).

Hernández, Javier C. Philharmonic Sidelines 2 Players It Tried to Fire for Misconduct. *New York Times* (April 15, 2024).

Higham, John. The Matrix of Specialization. *Bulletin of the American Academy of Arts and Sciences*, Vol. 33, No.5 (1980) 9–29.

Holley, John W. Tenure and Research Productivity. *Research in Higher Education*, Vol. 6, No. 2 (1977): 181–192.

Howard, Jacqueline. Concern grows around US health-care workforce shortage. *CNN* (May 16, 2023). www.cnn.com/2023/05/16/health/health-care-worker-shortage/index.html.

Humbert, Anne Laure, et al. Gender-based violence and institutional responses: Building a knowledge base and operational tools to make universities and research organisations safe (December 21, 2022).

Hurlburt, Steven and McGarrah, Michael. Cost Savings or Cost Shifting? The Relationship Between Part-Time Contingent Faculty and Institutional Spending. Delta Cost Project (2017a).

Hurlburt, Steven and McGarrah, Michael. The Shifting Academic Workforce: Where Are the Contingent Faculty? Delta Cost Project (2017b).

Ilies, Remus, Hauserman, Nancy, Schwochau, Susan, and Stibal, John. Reported Incidence Rates of Work-Related Sexual Harassment in the United States: Using Meta-Analysis to Explain Reported Rate Disparities. *Personnel Psychology*, Vol. 56 (2003): 607–631.

ImaginePhD, Graduate Career Consortium (2024). www.imaginephd.com.

India Today. CJI-Led Bench Holds Hearing on Sexual Harassment Charges against CJI Ranjan Gogoi. April 20, 2019. www.indiatoday.in/india/story/cji-led-supreme-court-bench-hold-unusual-hearing-on-matterof-great-public-importance-1506092–2019–04–20.

Iqbal, Saima S. and Muthukumar, Akila V. Going Hungry at Harvard. *Harvard Crimson* (April 1, 2021). www.thecrimson.com/article/2021/4/1/grad-students-food-insecurity/.

Jacobs, Jerry A. *In Defense of Disciplines: Interdisciplinarity and Specialization in the Research University*. Chicago: University of Chicago Press (2013).

Jacobson, Anne Jaap. Tenure and The Political Autonomy of Faculty Inquiry. *Behavioral and Brain Sciences*, Vol. 29, No. 6 (2006): 579–580.

James, William. The Ph.D. Octopus. *Harvard Monthly* (March 1903).

Jaschik, Scott. When Colleges Rely on Adjuncts, Where Does the Money Go? *InsideHigherEd* (January 4, 2017), www.InsideHigherEd.com/news/2017/01/05/study-looks-impact…20are, counseling%2C%20student%20organizations%20and%20athletics.

Jaschik, Scott. New Push for a Shift in Promotion and Tenure. *InsideHigherEd* (September 29, 2020). www.insidehighered.com/news/2020/09/30/proposal-add-innovation-and-entrepreneurship-tenure-and-promotion-criteria#:~:text=Academics%20from%2067%20universities%20nationally,education%20faculty%20promotion%20and%20tenure.

Jeong, Minseo. Dr. Patricia Bath: The expert who revolutionized cataract surgery. *Medical News Today* (February 26, 2021). www.medicalnewstoday.com/articles/dr-patricia-bath-the-expert-who-revolutionized-cataract-surgery.

Johns Hopkins University Press. *Critical University Studies* (series description). https://press.jhu.edu/books/series/critical-university-studies (accessed July 29, 2024).

Johnson, Kelli. How much money do you need to live comfortably in Los Angeles? *Fox 11* (March 29, 2023). www.foxla.com/news/heres-how-much-it-costs-to-live-comfortably-in-los-angeles-in-2023.

Johnson, Thea. Lying at Plea Bargaining. *Georgia State University Law Review*, Vol. 38, No. 3 (2022): 673–733.

Jones, Savannah. "My hand was forced" *Law school faculty department amid "Academic Transformation" fallout, the DA* (April 10, 2024, updated April 12, 2024). www.thedaonline.com/news/wvucuts/my-hand-was-forced/article_3acof6f8-f6b0-11ee-ae2e-23118c829cae.html.

Jotkoff, Eric. NEA Survey: Massive staff shortages in schools leading to educator burnout; alarming number of educators indicating they plan to leave profession. *National Education Association* (February 1, 2022). www.nea.org/about-nea/media-center/press-releases/nea-survey-massive-staff-shortages-schools-leading-educator-burnout-alarming-number-educators.

June, Audrey Williams. The Invisible Labor of Minority Professors. *Chronicle of Higher Education* (November 8, 2015).

Kahneman, Daniel, Knetsch, Jack L. and Thaler, Richard H. The Endowment Effect, Loss Aversion, and Status Quo Bias. *Journal of Economic Perspectives*, Vol. 5, No. 1 (1991): 193–206.

Kalmijn, Matthijs. Assortative Mating by Cultural and Economic Occupational Status. *American Journal of Sociology*, Vol. 100, No. 2 (1994): 422–452.

Kay, Joseph. Too Many Couples. *Chronicle of Higher Education* (April 9, 2007). www.chronicle.com/article/too-many-couples/.

Kelsky, Karen. Academia Is a Cult: Story of a TEDx Talk. *The Professor Is In* (March 26, 2021). https://theprofessorisin.com/2021/03/26/academia-is-a-cult-story-of-a-tedx-talk/.

Kelsky, Karen. #MeTooPhD – Sexual Harassment in the Academy Survey. *The Professor Is In* (accessed 2024). https://theprofessorisin.com/metoophd-sexual-harassment-in-the-academy-survey/.

Kenny, John, Fluck, Andrew, and Johnson, Tim. Placing a Value on Academic Work. *Australian University Review*, Vol. 54, No. 2. (2012): 50–60.

Kezar, Adrianna. Preface. In *Embracing Non-Tenure Track Faculty: Changing Campuses for the New Faculty Majority*, edited by Adrianna Kezar, x–xxiv. New York: Routledge (2012).

Kezar, Adrianna, DePaola, Tom, and Scott, Daniel. *The Gig Academy: Mapping Labor in the Neoliberal University*. Baltimore: Johns Hopkins University Press (2019).

Kim, Pauline T. Bargaining with Imperfect Information: A Study of Worker Perceptions of Legal Protection in an At-Will World. *Cornell Law Review*, Vol. 83, No. 1 (1997): 105–159.

Kipnis, Laura. Sexual Paranoia Strikes Academe. *Chronicle of Higher Education* (February 27, 2015). www.chronicle.com/article/Sexual-Paranoia-Strikes/190351.

Kirkland, Edward C. R.E.H.: As I Remember Him. *Bulletin of the American Association of University Professors*, Vol. 41, No. 3 (1955): 419–422.

Klayman, Ben. UAW says GM outlines EV investment plans, will raise wages for US workers. *Reuters*. (November 4, 2023). www.reuters.com/business/autos-transportation/uaw-says-gm-outlines-ev-investment-plans-will-raise-wages-us-workers-2023-11-04/#:~:text=Under%20the%20deal%2C%20starting%20base,from%20eight%20years%2C%20he%20said.

Krishnan, Murali. The Bizarre Order in the Sexual Harassment Allegations against CJI Ranjan Gogoi. *Bar and Bench* (April 20, 2019). www.barandbench.com/columns/bizarre-order-sexual-harassment-allegations-cjiranjan-gogoi.

Kumar, Divya. Desantis Signs Bill Limiting Tenure at Florida Public Universities. *Tampa Bay Times* (April 19, 2022). www.tampabay.com/news/education/2022/04/19/desantis-signs-bill-limiting-tenure-at-florida-public-universities/.

Kurtz, Thomas. The End of the Profession as a Sociological Category? Systems-Theoretical Remarks on the Relationship between Profession and Society. *American Sociologist*, Vol. 53 (2022): 265–282.

Kwok, Roberta. How a long-distance job move can leave early-career researchers short of cash. Nature (July 3, 2019). www.nature.com/articles/d41586-019-02047-z

Lawsky, Sarah. Lawsky Entry Level Hiring Report 2024. *PrawfsBlawg* (May 14, 2024). https://prawfsblawg.blogs.com/prawfsblawg/entry-level-hiring-report/.

Lawsky, Sarah. Law School Hiring Spreadsheet and Clearinghouse for Questions, 2023–2024. *PrawfsBlawg* (August 28, 2023). https://prawfsblawg.blogs.com/prawfsblawg/2023/08/law-school-hiring-spreadsheet-and-clearinghouse-for-questions-2023-2024.html.

Leachman, Gwendolyn. Legal Framing. *Studies in Law, Politics, and Society*, Vol. 61 (2013): 25–59.

Lee, Oliver. I have one of the best jobs in academia. Here's why I'm walking away. *Vox* (September 8, 2015). www.vox.com/2015/9/8/9261531/professor-quitting-job.

Lemelson-MIT. Raymond Damadian: Magnetic Resonance (MR) Scanning Machine. https://lemelson.mit.edu/resources/raymond-damadian (accessed July 29, 2024).

Leotta, Allison. I Was a Sex-Crimes Prosecutor. Here's Why 'He Said, She Said' Is a Myth. *Time* (October 3, 2018). https://time.com/5413814/he-said-she-said-kavanaugh-ford-mitchell/.

Levitt, Steven D. Let's Just Get Rid of Tenure (Including Mine). *Freakonomics* (March 3, 2007). https://freakonomics.com/2007/03/lets-just-get-rid-of-tenure/.

Lewis-Kraus, Gideon. They Studied Dishonesty. Was Their Work a Lie? *The New Yorker* (September 30, 2023). www.newyorker.com/magazine/2023/10/09/they-studied-dishonesty-was-their-work-a-lie

Libarkin, Julie. Academic Sexual Misconduct Database. (accessed January 27, 2022). https:// academic-sexual-misconduct-database.org.

Linton, Alaya, Shepard, Dan, and Martinez-White, Xiomara. 57% of Young Americans Live in Their Hometowns, but 47% Who Don't Would Consider Moving Back. Lendingtree .com (December 18, 2023). www.lendingtree.com/home/mortgage/hometown-survey/.

Livingston, Margit. Tenure Revisited. *Boston College Law Review Electronic Supplement*, Vol. 61, No. 9 (2020): I.-12.

Lorenz, Katherine, Kirkner, Anne, and Mazar, Laurel. Graduate Student Experiences with Sexual Harassment and Academic and Social (Dis)engagement in Higher Education. *Journal of Women and Gender in Higher Education*, Vol. 12, No. 2 (2019): 205–223.

Ludema, Jim and Johnson, Amber. Survivor's Guilt and Survivor's Envy: How Downsizing Impacts Those Who Stay – An Interview with Dr. Kim Cameron. *Forbes* (June 8, 2020). www.forbes.com/sites/amberjohnson-jimludema/2020/06/08/downsizing-with-dr-kim-cameron/.

Lufkin, Bryan. The smoke and mirrors of unlimited paid time off. *BBC.com*. (May 23, 2022). www.bbc.com/worklife/article/20220520-the-smoke-and-mirrors-of-unlimited-paid-time-off.

Macaulay, Stewart. Relational Contracts Floating on a Sea of Custom? Thoughts about the Ideas of Ian McNeil and Lisa Bernstein. *Northwestern University Law Review*, Vol. 94, No. 3 (2000): 775–804.

Macdonald, Danielle A. and Stevens, Laura M. Associate Professors and the 'Second Book Problem.' *Chronicle of Higher Education* (April 5, 2024). www.chronicle.com/article/ associate-professors-and-the-second-book-problem.

Macfarlane, Bruce and Jefferson, Alison Elizabeth. The closed academy? Guild power and academic social class. *Higher Education Quarterly*, Vol. 76, No. 1 (2022): 36–47.

Mackey, Robert. Professor's Angry Tweets on Gaza Cost Him a Job. *New York Times* (September 12, 2014). www.nytimes.com/2014/09/13/world/middleeast/professors-angry-tweets-on-gaza-cost-him-a-job.html.

MacLeod, W. Bentley. Tenure Is Justifiable. *Behavioral and Brain Sciences*, Vol. 29, No. 6 (2006): 581–583.

Magdol, Lynn. Is Moving Gendered? The Effects of Residential Mobility on the Psychological Well-Being of Men and Women. *Sex Roles*, Vol. 47 (2002): 553–560.

Main, Joyce B., Prenovitz, Sarah, and Ehrenberg, Ronald G. In Pursuit of a Tenure-Track Faculty Position: Career Progression and Satisfaction of Humanities and Social Sciences Doctorates. *Review of Higher Education*, Vol. 42, No. 4 (2019): 1309–1336.

Mano, B. MIT's policies force many graduate students to live in poverty. *The Tech* (October 31, 2019). https://thetech.com/2019/10/31/mit-grad-students-poverty.

Marsh, Jaimee, Patel, Sonya, Gelaye, Bizu, Goshu, Miruts, Worku, Alemayehu, Williams, Michelle A., and Berhane, Yemane. Prevalence of Workplace Abuse and Sexual Harassment among Female Faculty and Staff. *Journal of Occupational Health*, Vol. 51, No.4 (2009): 314–322.

mathgirl. Comment: "Solving" the Two-Body Problem. *Tenure, She Wrote* (September 18, 2013). https://tenureshewrote.wordpress.com/2013/09/18/solving-the-two-body-problem/.

Matthews, Kiernan. Perspectives on Midcareer Faculty and Advice for Supporting Them. *Collaborative on Academic Careers in Higher Education (COACHE)*. Cambridge: Harvard Graduate School of Education (2014).

McGee, Kate. Lt. Gov. Dan Patrick Proposes Ending University Tenure to Combat Critical Race Theory Teachings. *Texas Tribune* (February 18, 2022). www.texastribune .org/2022/02/18/dan-patrick-texas-tenure-critical-race-theory/.

McNeilly, Mark. Does Tenure Matter? James G. Martin Center for Academic Renewal (September 6, 2023). www.jamesgmartin.center/2023/09/does-tenure-matter/#:~:text=Tenure%20 does%20appear%20to%20enable,who%20have%20it%20from%20termination.

Merritt, Deborah J. Summer Research Grants. *Law School Café* (March 20, 2013). www
    .lawschoolcafe.org/2013/03/20/summer-research-grants/.
Merry, Sally Engle. *The Seductions of Quantification: Measuring Human Rights, Gender
    Violence, and Sex Trafficking*. Chicago: University of Chicago Press (2016).
Metzger, Walter P. Academic Tenure in America: A Historical Essay, in *Faculty Tenure: A
    Report and Recommendations by the Commission on Academic Tenure in Higher Education*
    (William R. Keast & John W. Macy, Jr. eds., 1st ed. (1973): 93-159
Metzger, Walter P. Profession and Constitution: Two Definitions of Academic Freedom in
    America. *Texas Law Review*, Vol. 66, No. 7 (1988): 1265–1322.
Metzger, Walter P. The 1940 Statement of Principles on Academic Freedom and Tenure.
    Law and Contemporary Problems, Vol. 53, No. 3 (1990): 3–77.
Molesworth, Claire L. Knowledge versus Acknowledgment: Rethinking the Alford Plea In
    Sexual Assault Cases. *Seattle Journal for Social Justice*, Vol. 6, No. 2 (2008): 907–951.
Moody, Josh. A Guide to the Changing Number of U.S. Universities. *U.S. News & World
    Report* (April 27, 2021). www.usnews.com/education/best-colleges/articles/how-many-
    universities-are-in-the-us-and-why-that-number-is-changing.
Mueller II, Alfred G. Saving Yourself during Downsizings. *InsideHigherEd* (March 26, 2024).
Muhs, Gabriella Gutiérrez y, Niemann, Yolanda Flores, González, Carmen G. and Harris,
    Angela P. *Presumed Incompetent: The Intersections of Race and Class for Women in
    Academia*. Boulder: University Press of Colorado (2012).
Narayanan, V.G. Online Financial Accounting course for Harvard Business School (accessed
    2024). https://online.hbs.edu/courses/financial-accounting/.
National Association of Colleges and Employers. NACE Salary Survey – Winter 2023 (2023).
    www.naceweb.org/mynace/salary-survey.
National Center for Education Statistics. 1949–50 through 2020–21 (January 2021). https://
    nces.ed.gov/programs/digest/d22/tables/dt22_325.65.asp.
National Center for Education Statistics. The Condition of Education: Characteristics of
    Postsecondary Students. U.S. Department of Education, Institute of Education Sciences
    (2023). https://nces.ed.gov/programs/coe/indicator/csb/postsecondary-students.
National Center for Education Statistics. The Condition of Education: Characteristics of
    Postsecondary Faculty. U.S. Department of Education, Institute of Education Sciences
    (2024). https://nces.ed.gov/programs/coe/indicator/csc/postsecondary-faculty.
National Center for Education Statistics. Fast Facts: Educational Institutions. U.S.
    Department of Education, Institute of Education Sciences (2022). https://nces.ed.gov/
    fastfacts/display.asp?id=1122.
National Center for Education Statistics. The Condition of Education: Price of Attending
    an Undergraduate Institution. U.S. Department of Education, Institute of Education
    Sciences (2024). https://nces.ed.gov/programs/coe/indicator/cua.
National Center for Education Statistics. Trend Generator (2024). https://nces.ed.gov/ipeds/
    trendgenerator/.
National Center for Education Statistics. Title IX Fast Facts (2024). https://nces.ed
    .gov/fastfacts/display.asp?id=93.
National Center for Faculty Development and Diversity. ncfdd.org (2024). www.ncfdd
    .org/home.
National Center for Science and Engineering Statistics, Doctorate Recipients from U.S.
    Universities: 2021 (2022).
NCSCBHEP (National Center for the Study of Collective Bargaining in Higher Education
    and the Professions). *April Newsletter* (2024).
NCSCBHEP (National Center for the Study of Collective Bargaining in Higher Education
    and the Professions). *May Newsletter* (2023).

National Employment Law Project. *Fired on a Whim: The Precarious Existence of NYC Fast-Food Workers*. New York: National Employment Law Project. (February 2019). https://www.nelp.org/app/uploads/2019/02/Just-Cause-February-2019.pdf.

National Institutes of Health. Advanced HIV Drug Approved for Resistant Infections. *NIH Research Matters* (September 1, 2006). www.nih.gov/news-events/nih-research-matters/advanced-hiv-drug-approved-resistant-infections.

Neal, Anne D. Reviewing Post-Tenure Review. *American Council of Trustees and Alumni*. (September 1, 2008). www.goacta.org/news-item/reviewing_post_tenure_review/#

Nerdwallet. Cost of Living Calculator. *Nerdwallet.com* (accessed October 23, 2023). www.nerdwallet.com/cost-of-living-calculator/city-life/los-angeles-long-beach-ca

New York State Unified Court System. Complaints about Attorneys (accessed July 29, 2024). https://ww2.nycourts.gov/attorneys/grievance/complaints.shtml.

Newhouse, Margaret. Transferring Your Skills to a Non-Academic Setting. *Chronicle of Higher Education* (December 4, 1998). www.chronicle.com/article/transferring-your-skills-to-a-non-academic-setting/.

Newman, Jay. Freedom and the Power of the Guild. *Improving College and University Teaching*, Vol. 30, No. 1 (1982): 8–11.

Nichols, Tom. *The Death of Expertise: The Campaign against Established Knowledge and Why It Matters*. New York: Oxford University Press (2017).

The Nobel Foundation. All prizes in economic sciences (Last updated 2023). www.nobelprize.org/prizes/lists/all-prizes-in-economic-sciences/.

Northwestern University. Student Funding Policies (Last updated August 19, 2022). www.tgs.northwestern.edu/academic-policies-procedures/policies/student-funding-policies.html.

Nussbaum, Martha C. The Professor of Parody – The Hip Defeatism of Judith Butler. *New Republic*, 22 (February 22, 1999): 37–45. https://newrepublic.com/article/150687/professor-parody.

O'Meara, KerryAnn, White-Lewis, Damani K., Mathews, Kiernan, and Harvey, Nicholas. Leaving the Institution or Leaving the Academy? Analyzing the Factors that Faculty Weigh in Actual Departure Decisions. *Research in Higher Education*, Vol. 64 (2022): 473–494.

Oishi, Shigehiro and Schimmack, Ulrich. Residential Mobility, Well-Being, and Mortality. *Journal of Personality and Social Psychology*, Vol. 98, No. 6 (2010): 980–994.

Oishi, Shigehiro, Miao, Felicity F., Koo, Minkyung, Kisling, Jason, and Ratliff, Kate A. Residential Mobility Breeds Familiarity-Seeking. *Journal of Personality and Social Psychology*, Vol. 102, No. 1 (2012): 149–162.

Orpen, Christopher. Tenure and Academic Productivity: Another Look. *Improving College and University Teaching*, Vol. 30, No. 2 (1982): 60–62.

Padilla, Amado M. Ethnic Minority Scholars, Research, and Mentoring: Current and Future Issues. *Educational Researcher*, Vol. 23, No. 4 (1994): 24–27.

Palmer, Kathryn. Indiana U Sanctions Professor Who Advised Pro-palestinian Students. InsideHigherEd (January 11, 2024).

Pannapacker, William. On Why I'm Leaving Academe, *Chronicle of Higher Education* (September 13, 2021). www.chronicle.com/article/on-why-im-leaving-academe.

Parker, Kim et al. *The State of American Jobs*. Pew Research Center (October 6, 2016).

Patton, Stacey. *The Ph.D. Now Comes with Food Stamps*. Chronicle of Higher Education, (May 6, 2012).

Pavan, Ronni. The Role of Career Choice in Understanding Job Mobility. *Labour*, Vol. 24, No. 2 (2010): 107–127.

Payscale. Cost of Living in Los Angeles, California. *Payscale.com* (accessed 2023). www.payscale.com/cost-of-living-calculator/California-Los-Angeles.

Perlmutter, David D. Avoiding PTDS: Post-Tenure Depression Syndrome. *Chronicle of Higher Education* (February 2, 2015). www.chronicle.com/article/avoiding-ptds-post-tenure-depression-syndrome/.

Petriglieri, Jennifer. How Dual-Career Couples Make it Work. Harvard Business Review, (September–October 2019). https://hbr.org/2019/09/how-dual-career-couples-make-it-work.

Phelan, Thomas J. Measures of Success in American Sociology. *Sociological Forum*, Vol. 10, No.3 (1995): 481–491.

Pinto, Maya and Tung, Irene. Email from Maya Pinto and Irene Tung to Deepa Das Acevedo, (20 September 2023) (on file with author).

Pittman, Chavella T. Achieving Racial Equity in Promotion and Tenure. *Academe*, Vol. 109, No. 1 (Winter, 2023). www.aaup.org/article/achieving-racial-equity-promotion-and-tenure.

Pollitt, Daniel H. and Kurland, Jordan E. Entering the Academic Freedom Arena Running: The AAUP's First Year. *Academe*, Vol. 84, No. 4 (July–August 1998): 50–51.

Pomeranz, Kenneth. The Next Big Thing. *Perspectives on History* (September 1, 2013). www.historians.org/research-and-publications/perspectives-on-history/september-2013/the-next-big-thing-supporting-the-second-book.

Pooley, James H. Pre-termination Hearings in Public Employment. *Administrative Law Review*, Vol. 25, No. 3 (1973): 313–328.

Posner, Adrienne. "Transferable Skills" Are A Lie. *The Professor Is In* (April 25, 2019). https://theprofessorisin.com/2019/04/25/transferable-skills-are-a-lie-realac-guest-post-by-adrienne-posner/.

Posner, Richard A. Rational Choice, Behavioral Economics, and the Law. *Stanford Law Review*, Vol. 50 (1997–1998): 1551–1575.

Preston, Elise. College students struggling with food insecurity turn to campus food pantries. *CBS Evening News* (February 19, 2024). www.cbsnews.com/news/college-students-food-insecurity-pantry-uc-davis/.

Public Employee Labor Relations Board. Public Sector Collective Bargaining by State (accessed 2023). www.pelrb.nm.gov/wp-content/uploads/2023/03/Public-Sector-Collective-Bargaining-by-State.pdf.

Quinn, Ryan. Columbia President Accused of Dishonest Testimony, Throwing Professors 'Under the Bus.' *InsideHigherEd* (April 19, 2024). www.insidehighered.com/news/faculty-issues/academic-freedom/2024/04/19/columbia-president-accused-throwing-profs-under-bus#:~:text=Columbia%20President%20Accused%20of%20Dishonest,some%20faculty%20members%20are%20alarmed.

Quinn, Ryan. Firing Tenured Faculty, with No Appeal Right. *InsideHigherEd* (January 25, 2023a). www.InsideHigherEd.com/news/2023/01/26/bill-north-dakota-presidents-could-fire-tenured-faculty#.Y9KB4yNwVUI.link.

Quinn, Ryan. Historic Faculty Pay Increase Still Beaten by Inflation. *InsideHigherEd* (April 7, 2023b). www.insidehighered.com/news/2023/04/07/historic-faculty-pay-increase-still-beaten-inflation#:~:text=%E2%80%9CTenure%2Dtrack%20faculty%20salary%20increases,year%20in%20inflation%2Dadjusted%20dollars.

Ran, Florence Xiaotao and Xu, Di. Does Contractual Form Matter? The Impact of Different Types of Non-Tenure Track Faculty on College Students' Academic Outcomes. *Journal of Human Resources*, Vol. 54, No. 4 (2019): 1081–1120.

Random Asst. Prof. Comment: 9 month salaries and summer service. *Tenure, She Wrote* (June 16, 2014). https://tenureshewrote.wordpress.com/2014/06/16/9-month-salaries-and-summer-service/.

Ransom, Michael R. Seniority and Monopsony in the Academic Labor Market. *American Economic Review*, Vol. 83, No. 1 (1993): 221–233.

Ray, Victor. The Unbearable Whiteness of Mesearch. *InsideHigherEd* (October 20, 2016). www.insidehighered.com/advice/2016/10/21/me-studies-are-not-just-conducted-people-color-essay.

raycam. The VAP Trap. *The Faculty Lounge* (October 10, 2014). www.thefacultylounge.org/2014/10/the-vap-trap.html.

Reichman, Harry. Eight Myths about Tenure. *Academe*, Vol. 109, No. 1 (Winter, 2023). www.aaup.org/article/eight-myths-about-tenure.

Rhoades, Gary. *Managed Professionals: Unionized Faculty and Restructuring Academic Labor*. Albany: State University of New York Press (1998).

Richardson, Cheryl and le Blanc, Sophie. *Diversity and Equity in Learning*. The University of Delaware Center for Teaching and Assessment of Learning (2016).

Richman, Judith A., Rospenda, Kathleen M., Nawyn, Stephanie J., Flaherty, Joseph A., Fendrich, Michael, Drum, Melinda L., and Johnson, Timothy P. Sexual Harassment and Generalized Workplace Abuse among University Employees: Prevalence and Mental Health Correlates. *American Journal of Public Health*, Vol. 89, No. 3 (1999): 358–363.

Ritter, Kelly. Want to Be a College Professor? Get Ready to Move. *Slate* (October 30, 2023). https://slate.com/human-interest/2023/10/faculty-mobility-academic-job-market.html.

Rockquemore, Kerry Ann. Advice for the Newly Tenured. *InsideHigherEd* (June 7, 2016). www.insidehighered.com/advice/2016/06/08/mistakes-newly-tenured-professors-can-make-essay.

Roosevelt, Kermit III. Not as Bad as You Think: Why Garcetti v. Ceballos Makes Sense. *University of Pennsylvania Journal of Constitutional Law*, Vol. 14, No. 3 (2012): 631–660.

Rosenthal, Caitlin. Fundamental Freedom or Fringe Benefit? Rice University and the Administrative History of Tenure 1935–1963. *AAUP Journal of Academic Freedom*, Vol. 2 (2011). www.aaup.org/sites/default/files/Rosenthal.pdf.

Ross, Jack. The University of Southern California Hires People Fired by the LAPD as Campus Police Officers. *Newsweek* (February 12, 2021).

Rothman, Stanley, Kelly-Woessner, April, and Woessner, Matthew. *The Still Divided Academy: How Competing Visions of Power, Politics, and Diversity Complicate the Mission of Higher Education*. Plymouth: Rowman & Littlefield (2011).

Rowell, Arden. Legal Knowledge, Belief, and Aspiration. *Arizona State Law Journal*, Vol. 51, No. 1 (2019): 225–291.

Rubinstein, David. Fat City: Thank You, Illinois Taxpayers, for My Cushy Life. *Weekly Standard* (May 30, 2011).

Rucks-Ahidiana, Zawadi. The Inequities of the Tenure Track System. *InsideHigherEd* (June 6, 2019). www.insidehighered.com/advice/2019/06/07/nonwhite-faculty-face-significant-disadvantages-tenure-track-opinion.

Safire, William. On Language; He-Said, She-Said. *New York Times Magazine* (April 12, 1998). www.nytimes.com/1998/04/12/magazine/on-language-he-said-she-said.html.

Salih, Sara. On Judith Butler and Performativity. In *Judith Butler: Essential Guides for Literary Studies*, 55–68. New York: Routledge (2002).

Samuels, Warren J. The Firing of E. A. Ross from Stanford University: Injustice Compounded by Deception? *Journal of Economic Education*, Vol. 22, No. 2 (1991): 183–90.

Sarcozona, Poverty in the Ivory Tower. *Tenure, She Wrote* (January 16, 2014). https://tenureshewrote.wordpress.com/2014/01/16/succeeding-in-graduate-school-despite-poverty/.

Sarkissian, Arek. University of Florida turns against Joe Ladapo. *Politico* (November 27, 2023). www.politico.com/news/2023/11/27/joe-ladapo-university-of-florida-00128541.

Saunders, Shari and Kardia, Diana. Creating Inclusive College Classrooms. University of Michigan Center for Research on Learning and Teaching (1997). https://crlt.umich.edu/gsis/p3_1.

Scheiber, Noam. The Harvard Professor and the Bloggers. *New York Times* (September 30, 2023). www.nytimes.com/2023/09/30/business/the-harvard-professor-and-the-bloggers.html.

Schermele, Zachary. Who Had a Say in Derailing Texas A&M's Hiring of Kathleen McElroy. *Chronicle of Higher Education* (August 4, 2023). www.chronicle.com/article/who-had-a-say-in-derailing-texas-a-ms-hiring-of-kathleen-mcelroy#:~:text=The%20Regents%20React%20%E2%80%94%20and%20Intervene,hoped%20it%20wasn't%20true.

Schiebinger, Londa, Henderson, Andrea Davies, and Gilmartin, Shannon K. *Dual-Career Academic Couples: What Universities Need to Know*. Stanford University: Michelle R. Clayman Institute for Gender Research (2008). https://gender.stanford.edu/sites/gender/files/dualcareerfinal_0.pdf.

Schuman, Rebecca. Thesis Hatement. *Slate* (April 5, 2013). www.slate.com/articles/life/culturebox/2013/04/there_are_no_academic_jobs_and_getting_a_ph_d_will_make_you_into_a_horrible.html.

Schwartz, Christine R., Wang, Yu, and Mare, Robert D. Opportunity and Change in Occupational Assortative Mating. *Social Science Research*, Vol. 99 (2021). https://doi.org/10.1016/j.ssresearch.2021.102600.

Shannon, George Pope., Ralph E. Himstead and the Central Office. *Bulletin of the American Association of University Professors*, Vol. 41, No. 3 (1955): 397–406.

Shapiro, Fred R. The Most-Cited Legal Scholars Revisited. *The University of Chicago Law School Review*, Vol. 88, No. 7 (2021): 1595–1618.

Shaw, George Bernard. *Man and Superman: A Comedy and a Philosophy*. New York: Brentano's, 1903.

Shepherd, Lois. The danger of the 'he said, she said' expression. *The Hill* (October 12, 2018). https://thehill.com/opinion/judiciary/411157-the-danger-of-the-he-said-she-said-expression/.

Silbert, Andrea and Dubé, Christy Mach. The Power Gap among Top Earners at America's Elite Universities 2021 Study. *Eos Foundation* (February 2021). www.womenspowergap.org/wp-content/uploads/2021/02/WPG-Power-Gap-at-Elite-Universities-2021-Study-4.pdf.

Sinche, Melanie V. To Postdoc or Not? *InsideHigherEd* (August 22, 2016). www.InsideHigherEd.com/advice/2016/08/23/should-you-pursue-postdoc-or-not-essay.

Singh, Vineeta, and Vora, Neha. Critical University Studies. *Annual Review of Anthropology*, Vol. 52 (2023): 39–54. https://doi.org/10.1146/annurev-anthro-052721-040011.

Sitze, Adam. The Strange, Secret History of Tenure. *Chronicle of Higher Education* (August 4, 2022). www.chronicle.com/article/the-strange-secret-history-of-tenure.

Slaughter, Sheila, and Rhoades, Gary. *Academic Capitalism and the New Economy: Markets, State, and Higher Education*. Baltimore: Johns Hopkins University Press (2009).

Solum, Lawrence B. What Is Originalism? The Evolution of Contemporary Originalist Theory (2011). http://dx.doi.org/10.2139/ssrn.1825543.

Spitz, Judith. The Scarcity of AI Talent: A Problem of Our Own Making Is a Problem We Can Solve. *Forbes* (March 30, 2022). www.forbes.com/sites/judithspitz/2022/03/30/the-scarcity-of-ai-talent-a-problem-of-our-own-making-is-a-problem-we-can-solve/?sh=1a805a99700f.

Spoon, Katie, LaBerge, Nicholas, Wapman, K Hunter, Zhang, Sam, Morgan, Allison C., Galesic, Mirta, Fosdick, Bailey K., Larremore, Daniel B., and Clauset, Aaron. Gender and Retention Patterns among U.S. Faculty. *Science Advance*, Vol. 9, No. 42 (2023). DOI: 10.1126/sciadv.adi2205.

Stafforini, Pablo. Estimation of probabilities to get tenure track in academia: baseline and publications during the PhD. *Effective Altruism Forum* (September 20, 2020). https://forum.effectivealtruism.org/posts/3TQTec6FKcMSRBT2T/estimation-of-probabilities-to-get-tenure-track-in-academia#.

Stanford Eugenics History Project. Edward Ross (accessed April 4, 2024). www
.stanfordeugenics.com/edward-ross.

Stanford Historical Society. How a Stanford Speech Scandal Led to the Invention of
Academic Freedom: The Case of Edward A. Ross (March 1, 2023). https://news.stanford
.edu/stories/2023/05/origin-story-academic-freedom.

Stanford University. Building an Inclusive Syllabus, Stanford Teaching Commons (2024).
https://teachingcommons.stanford.edu/teaching-guides/inclusive-teaching-guide/planning-
inclusive-course/building-inclusive-syllabus.

State Bar Court of California. *statebarcourt.ca.gov* (accessed 2024). www.statebarcourt.ca.gov.

Statista. Estimated number of universities worldwide as of July 2023, by country (accessed
2024). www.statista.com/statistics/918403/number-of-universities-worldwide-by-country/.

Steffen, Heather. Imagining Academic Labor. Chicago Center for Contemporary Theory
(May 12, 2021). www.youtube.com/watch?v=ECapHVb8cgM.

Stein, Matthew. Universities repeatedly discipline professors for referring to the n-word. *The
College Fix* (April 11, 2019). www.thecollegefix.com/universities-repeatedly-discipline-
professors-for-referring-to-the-n-word/.

Storey, Jenna Silber and Storey, Benjamin. Sometimes the Right Is Right. *InsideHigherEd*
(April 9, 2024). www.insidehighered.com/opinion/views/2024/04/09/colleges-should-work-
right-leaning-critics-opinion.

Street, Steve et al. Who is Professor "Staff" – And how can this person teach so many classes?
Center for the Future of Higher Education Policy Report No. 2 (August 23, 2012).

Sunstein, Cass R., Jolls, Christine, and Thaler, Richard H. A Behavioral Approach to Law
and Economics. *Stanford Law Review*, Vol. 50 (1998): 1471–1550.

Sweet Briar College. Sweet Briar at a Glance (2024). www.sbc.edu/about/sweet-briar-at-a-
glance/.

Taylor, Keeanga-Yamahtta. Ibram X. Kendi's Anti-racism. *The New Yorker* (October 21, 2023).
www.newyorker.com/news/our-columnists/ibram-x-kendis-anti-racism.

Taylor, Mark C. *Crisis on Campus: A Bold Plan for Reforming Our Colleges and Universities.*
New York: Alfred A. Knopf (2010).

Tiede, Hans-Joerg. "To Make Collective Action Possible": The Founding of the AAUP.
AAUP Journal of Academic Freedom, Vol. 5 (2014). www.aaup.org/JAF5/%E2%80%98-
make-collective-action-possible%E2%80%99-founding-aaup#.V6yyvfkrLRY.

Tiede, Hans-Joerg. *University Reform: The Founding of the American Association of University
Professors.* Baltimore: Johns Hopkins University Press (2015).

Tierney, William G. *Higher Education for Democracy: The Role of the University in Civil
Society.* Albany: State University of New York Press (2021).

Topel Robert H. and Ward, Michael P. Job Mobility and the Careers of Young Men.
Quarterly Journal of Economics, Vol. 107, No. 2 (1992): 439–479.

Trejo, JoAnn. The Burden of Service for Faculty of Color to Achieve Diversity and Inclusion:
The Minority Tax. *Molecular Biology of the Cell*, Vol. 31, No. 25 (2020): 2752–2754.

Tversky, Amos and Kahneman, Daniel. Availability: A Heuristic for Judging Frequency and
Probability. *Cognitive Psychology*, Vol. 5, No. 2 (1973): 207–232.

U.S. Bureau of Economic Analysis. Personal Consumption Expenditures by State 2021
(October 6, 2022). www.bea.gov/news/2022/personal-consumption-expenditures-state-2021.

U.S. Bureau of Labor Statistics. About the U.S. Bureau of Labor Statistics (accessed 2024).
www.bls.gov/bls/about-bls.htm.

U.S. Bureau of Labor Statistics. Employment Research and Program Development (accessed
2024). www.bls.gov/ers/.

U.S. Bureau of Labor Statistics. Occupational Employment and Wage Statistics (accessed
2024). www.bls.gov/oes/oes_emp.htm.

U.S. Bureau of Labor Statistics. Occupational Employment and Wage Statistics (OEWS): Frequently Asked Questions (accessed 2024). www.bls.gov/oes/oes_ques.htm#def.

U.S. Bureau of Labor Statistics. Occupational Employment and Wages (OEWS): Anthropologists and Archeologists (accessed 2024). www.bls.gov/oes/current/oes193091 .htm.

U.S. Bureau of Labor Statistics. Occupational Employment and Wages (OEWS): Anthropology and Archeology Teachers, Postsecondary (accessed 2024). www.bls.gov/oes/ current/oes251061.htm.

U.S. Bureau of Labor Statistics. Occupational Outlook Handbook (OOH): Anthropologists and Archeologists (accessed 2024). www.bls.gov/ooh/life-physical-and-social-science/ anthropologists-and-archeologists.htm#tab-3.

U.S. Bureau of Labor Statistics. Occupational Outlook Handbook (accessed 2024).

U.S. Bureau of Labor Statistics. Table A-12: Unemployed persons by duration of unemployment. (accessed 2025).

U.S. Census Bureau. 2019 SUSB Annual Data Tables by Establishment Industry: U.S. & States, 6-digit NAICS (October 30, 2023). www.census.gov/data/tables/2019/econ/susb/2019-susb-annual.html.

U.S. Equal Employment Opportunity Commission. Pre-employment Inquiries and Marital Status or Number of Children (accessed July, 29 2024). www.eeoc.gov/pre-employment-inquiries-and-marital-status-or-number-children#:~:text=Questions%20 about%20marital%20status%20and,(or%20vice%2Dversa).

U.S. Merit Systems Protection Board. What Is Due Process in Federal Civil Service Employment? (May 2015). www.mspb.gov/studies/studies/What_is_Due_Process_in_ Federal_Civil_Service_Employment_1166935.pdf.

The University of Alabama. Faculty Handbook, Ch. 2, Art. XIV, Sec. A (October 18, 2023). https://facultyhandbook.ua.edu/.

UCLA School of Law. Intersectionality at 30: Q&A with Kimberlé Crenshaw (October 29, 2019). https://law.ucla.edu/news/intersectionality-30-qa-kimberle-crenshaw.

UCLA School of Law. CRT Forward Tracking Project (accessed 2024). https://crtforward.law .ucla.edu/.

University of Massachusetts Amherst. How Do I Write an Inclusive Syllabus? *Center for Teaching & Learning* (accessed July 2024). www.umass.edu/ctl/resources/how-do-i/how-do-i-write-inclusive-syllabus.

The University of North Carolina at Chapel Hill Office of Faculty Governance. Faculty Hearings Committee (accessed January 27, 2022). https://facultygov.unc.edu/committees/ electedcommittees/faculty-hearings-committee/.

The University of Southern California. Faculty Handbook (2022). https://policy.usc.edu/ faculty-handbook/.

The University of Texas at Austin. *Lorene Lane Rogers* (accessed 2024). https://president .utexas.edu/past-presidents/lorene-lane-rogers.

The University of Tulsa. Second Book Institute (accessed 2024). https://utulsa.edu/about/ facilities/henneke-center/second-book-institute/.

The Versatile PhD (2024) https://versatilephd.com.

Viladrich, Anahi. Is there "life after tenure" after all? The Voice of Latina Scholars, *Anahi-viladrich.com* (October 27, 2018). www.anahi-viladrich.com/blog/is-there-life-after-tenure-after-all.

Vrchota, Denise, Timothy Day, Carol Faber, Steven Freeman and Robert Wallace. Iowa State Faculty Handbook. Faculty Handbook Editing Task Force 2021–2022 (January 2024). www.provost.iastate.edu/files/documents/2024-07/Faculty%20Handbook%20-%20July%20 2024%20-%20final.pdf.

Walkowitz, Daniel J. *Working with Class: Social Workers and the Politics of Middle-Class Identity*. Chapel Hill and London: University of North Carolina Press (2003).

Ware, Mark and Mabe, Michael. The STM report: An overview of scientific and scholarly journal publishing. *International Association of Scientific, Technical and Medical Publishers* (2012). www.stm-assoc.org/2018_10_04_STM_Report_2018.pdf.

Warren, John Robert. How Much Do You Have to Publish to Get a Job in a Top Sociology Department? Or to Get Tenure? Trends over a Generation. *Sociological Science*, Vol. 6 (2019): 172–196.

Way, Samuel F., Morgan, Allison C., Clauset, Aaron, and Larremore, Daniel B. The Misleading Narrative of the Canonical Faculty Productivity Trajectory, *PNAS*, Vol. 114, No. 44 (2017). https://doi.org/10.1073/pnas.1702121114.

Weber, Max. Science as a Vocation. In *From Max Weber: Essays in Sociology*, translated and edited by H.H. Gerth and C. Wright Mills, 129–156. New York: Oxford University Press, 1946 [1919].

Weiss, Ryne. FIRE calls on Augsburg University to reinstate professor suspended for in-class discussion about racial slur, *FIRE* (February 11, 2019). www.thefire.org/news/fire-calls-augsburg-university-reinstate-professor-suspended-class-discussion-about-racial.

Weiss, Ryne. Update: Augsburg professor removed from classroom for discussion of racial slur will return to teaching, *FIRE* (March 15, 2019). www.thefire.org/news/update-augsburg-professor-removed-classroom-discussion-racial-slur-will-return-teaching.

Welch College. Faculty and Staff Listing (accessed July 29, 2024). https://welch.edu/academics/faculty-staff-listing/.

Wetherbe, James C. It's Time for Tenure to Lose Tenure. *Harvard Business Review* (March 13, 2013). https://hbr.org/2013/03/its-time-for-tenure-to-lose-te.

Wettersten, John. Put Tenure in Today's Social Context. *Behavioral and Brain Sciences*, Vol. 29, No. 6 (2006): 585–586.

White, Gillian B. Staying Close to Home, No Matter What. *The Atlantic* (March 18, 2015). www.theatlantic.com/business/archive/2015/03/staying-close-to-home-no-matter-what/387736/

Whitehead, Alfred North. *Process and Reality: An Essay in Cosmology*. New York: Free Press (1985).

Wilder, Esther Isabelle and Walters, William H. Publishing Productivity of Sociologists at American Colleges and Universities: Institution Type, Gender, and Other Correlates of Book and Article Counts. *Sociological Perspectives*, Vol. 63, No. 2 (2020): 249–275.

Wilkins, David B. and Gulati, Mitu G. Reconceiving the Tournament of Lawyers: Tracking, Seeing, and Information Control in the Internal Labor Markets of Elite Law Firms. *Virginia Law Review*, Vol. 84, No. 8 (1998): 1581–1681.

Williams College. Williams College Faculty Handbook, 2021–2022 (2021). https://faculty.williams.edu/faculty-governance/faculty-handbook/

Wilson, John K. The AAUP's 1915 Declaration of Principles: Conservative and Radical, Visionary and Myopic. AAUP *Journal of Academic Freedom*, Vol. 7 (2016). www.aaup.org/JAF7/aaups-1915-declaration-principles-conservative-and-radical-visionary-and-myopic.

Wilson, Robin. The backlash against hiring couples. *Chronicle of Higher Education* (April 13, 2001). www.chronicle.com/article/the-backlash-against-hiring-couples/.

Wise, Jacqui. Boldt: The Great Pretender. *BMJ*, Vol. 346 (March 23, 2013). www.bmj.com/bmj/section-pdf/187846?path=/bmj/346/7900/Feature.full.pdf

Wolf-Wendel, Lisa, Twombly, Susan and Rice, Suzanne. *The Two-Body Problem: Dual-Career-Couple Hiring Practices in Higher Education*. Baltimore: Johns Hopkins University Press (2004).

Wolff, Abbie and Regan, Emma Mae. Nine faculty resign from Hamilton; resignees disproportionately women and people of color. *The Spectator* (April 28, 2022). https://spec .hamilton.edu/nine-faculty-resign-from-hamilton-resignees-disproportionately-women-and-people-of-color-7f8672a7c77.

Wood, L. Maren. Odds Are, Your Doctorate Will Not Prepare You for a Profession Outside Academe. *Chronicle of Higher Education* (July 9, 2019). www.chronicle.com/article/odds-are-your-doctorate-will-not-prepare-you-for-a-profession-outside-academe/.

The White House, The Executive Branch (2023). www.whitehouse.gov/about-the-white-house/our-government/the-executive-branch/.

Yale University Office of Career Strategy. PhD Transferable Skills (accessed 2020). https://ocs.yale.edu/blog/2020/08/03/phd-transferable-skills/.

Yankow, Jeffrey J. The Effect of Cumulative Job Mobility on Early-Career Wage Development: Does Job Mobility Actually Pay? *Social Science Quarterly*, Vol. 103 (2022): 709–723.

Young, Stanley J. and Kaufman, Marjorie R. Academic Freedom and Tenure: American International College (Massachusetts). *Academe*, Vol. 69, No. 3. (May–June 1983): 42–46.

CASE LAW

Board of Curators of University of Missouri v. Horowitz, 435 U.S. 78 (1978).

Bostock v. Clayton County, 590 U.S. 644 (2020).

Cleveland Board of Education v. Loudermill, 470 U.S. 532 (1985).

Connick v. Myers, 461 U.S. 138 (1983)

Garcetti v. Ceballos, 547 U.S. 410 (2006).

Garrity v. New Jersey, 385 U.S. 493 (1967).

Gunasekera v. Irwin, 551 F.3d 461 (6th Cir. 2009).

Integrity Staffing Solutions v. Busk, 574 U.S. 27 (2014).

Kunkle v. Q-Mark, Inc., No. 13-CV-82, 2013 WL 3288398, at *1 (S.D. Ohio, 2013).

Mawakana v. Board of Trustees of University of D.C., 315 F. Supp. 3d 189 (D.D.C. 2018)

NLRB v. Yeshiva University, 444 U.S. 672 (1980).

Northern Securities Co. v. United States, 193 U.S. 197 (1904).

Okruhlik v. University of Arkansas, 395 F.3d 872 (8th Cir. 2005).

Perry v. Sindermann, 408 U.S. 593 (1972).

Pickering v. Board of Education, 391 U.S. 563 (1968)

Price Waterhouse v. Hopkins, 490 U.S. 228 (1989).

Sandifer v. U.S. Steel, 571 U.S. 220 (2014).

Woolley v. Hoffmann-La Roche, 99 N.J. 284 (1985).

<h1 style="text-align:center">Index</h1>

For EU product safety concerns, contact us at Calle de José Abascal, 56–1°,
28003 Madrid, Spain or eugpsr@cambridge.org.